TORMENTED LOYALTY

By the same author
FOUR STUDIES IN LOYALTY
ANSWER TO QUESTION 33
CHARACTER AND SITUATION
TWO STUDIES IN VIRTUE
A SONG OF A SHIRT
DATES AND PARTIES
ORDE WINGATE
CROSS ROADS TO ISRAEL

TORMENTED LOYALTY

The Story of a German Aristocrat
Who Defied Hitler

CHRISTOPHER SYKES

1817

HARPER & ROW, PUBLISHERS
New York and Evanston

FIRST U.S. EDITION

LIBRARY OF CONGRESS CATALOG CARD NUMBER: 69-15266

CONTENTS

ILLUSTRATIONS

The following are grouped in a separate section after page 158

The following are grouped in a separate section after page 318

All these illustrations with the exception of the portrait *As a young man* are reproduced by courtesy of Frau Doktor Clarita von Trott. The portrait is reproduced by courtesy of Mrs. David Hopkinson.

PUBLISHER'S NOTE

Some of the important personalities in this book may be unfamiliar to American readers:

Lord Lothian, journalist and politician, with whom Trott conferred at Cliveden, was at the time Secretary of the Rhodes Trust, which administers the Rhodes Scholarships. He was appointed British Ambassador to the United States in 1939. He died in Washington in December 1940.

Lord Halifax, another participant in the Cliveden meetings, had succeeded Anthony Eden in February 1938 as Foreign Secretary. As Lord Irwin he had been a successful and conciliatory Viceroy of India from 1926 to 1931. He was British Ambassador to the United States from 1941 to 1946, being succeeded as Foreign Secretary by Anthony Eden.

Lady Astor, who helped Trott make contact with supporters of Neville Chamberlain's appeasement policies and arranged the Cliveden gathering, was of American origin. She was the first woman to be seated in the House of Commons (1919) and was for nearly twenty-six years a colorful figure in English politics. Her political influence was small, however, outside of matters affecting women's rights and child welfare.

Of Trott's academic friends at Oxford, A. L. Rowse, then a Fellow of All Souls, is now a prominent English historian; Sir Isaiah Berlin, later Chichele Professor of Social and Political Theory, a Fellow of All Souls, and Master of Wolfson College, was at the time a Fellow of New College; and Sir C. M. Bowra, tutor of Wadham College during Trott's Oxford years, is a noted classicist, critic of modern European literature, and currently Warden of Wadham.

The following explanations pertaining to British university life may be helpful to the reader of *Tormented Loyalty:*

All Souls College, Oxford. Founded by Henry Chichele, Archbishop of Canterbury, in 1437. There are at present sixty-four Fellows or members. A proportion of the Fellows are always drawn from outside academic life and usually from the political world. All Souls has the unique distinction of being a University college containing graduates only. In the years before World War II, All Souls enjoyed a much exaggerated reputation as an influence on Neville Chamberlain's appeasement policy. This was probably due to the fact that two prominent members of his Government, Foreign Secretary Lord Halifax and Sir John (later Lord) Simon, and Chamberlain's friend Geoffrey Dawson, editor of the *Times*, were prominent Fellows of the college.

"Modern Greats." This term of Oxford slang derives from an older one, "Greats," still used to designate the Literae Humaniores curriculum, which is concentrated on ancient Greek and Latin history, and ancient and modern philosophy. When in the 1920's the Philosophy, Politics, and Economics (P.P.E.) curriculum was introduced, the wits of Oxford dubbed the innovation "Modern Greats." In time the ridicule became a title of honour. In British as opposed to American universities, it is usual for the student to devote his whole learning time to one broad-based course, and exceptions to this are rare.

The terms in the English universities share their names with those of the Law Courts, and derive from medieval Church custom. They are as follows:

The Hilary term, which lasts from mid-January to mid-March. (The name is from St. Hilarius, whose festival falls on January 14th. The term is sometimes referred to as the Lent Term.)

The Trinity term, which lasts from mid-April to mid-June. (The name is from the summer Church festival, Trinity Sunday.)

The Michaelmas term, which lasts from early October to early December. (The name is from the festival of Saint Michael, maintained as "quarter day," on September 29th.)

ACKNOWLEDGEMENTS

The writer is under obligation to many people who have furnished him with information and appraisal in the preparation of this book. Their names will be found in the course of the footnotes. Certain of them, however, should be the subject of special mention.

Pre-eminent among these are the family of Adam von Trott zu Solz: his sister Frau Vera von Trott, his brother Herr Heinrich von Trott, and in particular his widow Frau Doktor Clarita von Trott zu Solz who helped with discussion and criticism and gave full access to papers. The writer also remembers with gratitude and affection his discussions with the late Herr Werner von Trott and his family.

The writer would like to express his gratitude to Frau Irma von Buch who, in collaboration with Professor Hans Rothfels, made a valuable collection of papers relative to Adam von Trott's biography; to Mr and Mrs Peter Bielenberg who collected further material in Germany and Britain and helped greatly with discussion and criticism; to Mr David Astor whose munificence enabled the writer to visit America in 1965; to Mrs Elke Jessett who produced an English text of Doctor Clarita von Trott's memoir, and to Mr Harold Kurtz who helped the writer in the translation and interpretation of many of the German documents.

As before, the writer is under obligation to Mrs Dorothy Baker for valuable literary advice, and to Mrs Marjorie Girgis for producing typescripts.

It must be strongly emphasised that the opinions and conclusions expressed in this book are the writer's, and should nowhere be assumed to be in agreement with those of Frau Doktor von Trott, or of Mr and Mrs Bielenberg.

Chapter 1

THE BACKGROUND

There is no more pleasing landscape in Germany than that of Hesse-Kassel. Others, such as those of the Rhine valley and of the Alpine foothills and the great mountains, are more dramatic, spectacular and famous, but there are none more amiable than this one. Here is a classic countryside, entirely characteristic of the western stretches of central Europe, an undulating land of light soil and wide fields but far more thickly wooded than similar country in France. In the British Isles the country closest to this in contour is probably found on the east coast of Scotland, for example in Fife. As often in such wold country of Europe, a constant colour is a delicate silver.

It needs no effort of the imagination to enter into the feelings of a man born in these surroundings who drew from them an intense love of home, and with it an ardent and ever sensitive love of his native country.

Of such a kind was the patriotism of Adam von Trott zu Solz, the subject of this book. His life was one of unusual versatility and he was at home in many very different worlds, or rather he seemed to be so, for in fact the affection he had for his homeland was so passionate, so bound up with the inmost core of his being, that it excluded from first place all other impersonal attachments, strong as some of these were. At all times in his life, his thoughts would go back to the landscape of Hesse which he had first learned to love as that of his home.

He came of a family which had been known in Hesse since the Middle Ages. They are first mentioned, so far as is known to-day, in documents of the 13th century: a man of this name appears as a Burgmann, a man-at-arms, in the service of the Imperial castle of Boineburg.[1] The family are

[1]*Gothaisches Genealogisches Taschenbuch der Adeligen Hauser Deutscher Uradel.* 1938.

found in subsequent records as feudal tenants, holding such posts as hereditary cupbearer in noble houses. The name Adam is common in Hesse. It seems to have been first used in the Trott family by a knight who fought against the Turks in the 16th century and later earned some historical fame as the Consilius Intimus of the Elector Joachim II of Brandenburg.

During the succeeding ages the Trotts maintained a tradition of state service in the Landgravate of Hesse-Kassel, their home remaining in the southern part of the principality by the little town of Solz, situated about forty miles south-east of Kassel and about ninety miles north-east of Frankfurt. From this home territory the full family name became von Trott zu Solz.

The father of the 20th-century Adam von Trott was born in 1855 and he grew up, as his own sons were to do, in a political environment. His own father, Werner von Trott, was a diplomat in the service of the last Elector of Hesse-Kassel. He was Hessian envoy to Württemberg for some years. He died at the age of thirty-nine, and so his son, August von Trott zu Solz,[2] came into his inheritance early, but not before the Electorate had ceased to exist. In 1866, as part of Bismarck's policy of German unification by means of Prussian aggrandisement, and largely through the folly of the last Elector, Hesse-Kassel was forcibly incorporated into Prussia. When August von Trott reached manhood he entered the service of the Prussian state.

His first experience of public life was in local government, and before long he was made Landrat or provincial adviser in Hesse. He became a Vortragender Rat in the Prussian Home Ministry. The title means literally Lecturing Counsellor and indicated an official of senior status with right of access to the Minister, and on occasion to the Sovereign.

At the age of forty-four in 1899 he was promoted chief of Administration (Regierungspräsident) first in Coblenz and then in Kassel. The post was similar to that of an English High Sheriff, but, in those times, of far more active authority. In 1905 he was promoted Oberpräsident of Brandenburg. Four years later in 1909 this successful career in the Civil Service became political. August von Trott was appointed Kultusminister in the Prussian Government. The office, originally that of a Minister of Public

[2]His full name was August Bodo Wilhelm Klemens Paul von Trott zu Solz.

Worship, combined educational and cultural administration. He remained in this post, which he is recorded as filling with distinction, imagination and marked conservatism, until 1917.[3] He resigned in protest against the contemplated enlargement of the Prussian franchise. He was then obliged to accept a post beneath ministerial level, that of Oberpräsident of Hesse-Kassel. Here he remained till 1920 when, at the age of sixty-four, he retired from the service.

After leaving Potsdam he lived with his wife and children in the official state residence at Kassel. The changed life of the family had one enjoyable new feature: they now saw more of the family home which Herr von Trott had inherited from his father. Not till his retirement in 1920, however, did they live there permanently. The place is called Imshausen. It is a country house of moderate size which had been built on the site of an ancient Trott castle in the late 18th century, and in the engaging style of that period. Imshausen is about two miles from Solz.

His second son Adam was born in 1909 when August von Trott was in his first year of ministerial office and at the height of his career, so Adam's first young memories were of the life of Potsdam as it was led in the days of the Hohenzollern Empire. Later and more vivid and more effective memories were of wartime Germany, and of wretched childhood experiences at school in Kassel in 1917 where he found himself the object of sudden and utterly incomprehensible scorn as the son of a fallen minister. He was ridiculed on account of the family disaster and resented by his Hessian classmates as a person who supposedly embodied the extravagantly elegant manners of Berlin, Potsdam, and the Court. When he was nine he had to try to understand the meaning of nation-wide disaster. The age-groups within his immediate family were such that he knew no very close loss through death in the First World War, but all the evidence of his adult life forcibly suggests that the wound of defeat entered deep into his being, little understood as it must have been at the time.

His mother, Eleonore von Trott zu Solz, came of an aristocratic Silesian family. Her father was called Lothar von Schweinitz and he was a man of considerable talent. He had but the barest fortune and began his career

---

[3]*Adam von Trott zu Solz* by Clarita von Trott, *for his friends*. Unpublished. Referred to later as C. T. Also *Das Tagebuch der Baronin Spitzemberg*.

as an impoverished officer in the Prussian Army. He was favourably
noticed, found quick promotion, and in early middle age was appointed
military attaché to the Prussian Legation in Vienna. He returned to Vienna
as Prussian Envoy after the Austro-Prussian war in 1866 and remained
there for ten years. He made a success of his mission and ended his career
as German ambassador to St Petersburg from 1876 to 1892. In the meantime his private life had taken a dramatic turn. While he was Prussian
representative in Vienna, he became close friends with his American colleague. The latter was called Mr William Jay and was the grandson of
John Jay, the friend of Washington and the first Chief Justice of the
United States. Von Schweinitz found himself attracted to his American
colleague's daughter, Miss Anna Jay. At this time von Schweinitz was
fifty years old and Anna Jay twenty-three. They fell in love and married.
Eleonore was the second of their eight children.

This daughter of the Prussian virtues and the American Revolution
was a very formidable being. Of alert mind and unbending principle,
she had in full measure the stern Puritanism of her American ancestors.
As usually happens with deep-grounded severity of character, its gravity
was sometimes taken to excess with unhappy results, but, as appears later
in the story, this fact must not be given excessive importance. They
married in February of 1901 when August von Trott was Regierungspräsident in Kassel. As in the case of her parents, the husband was much
older than his wife. He was forty-five; she was twenty-six.

They were well suited to each other and throughout their married life
they enjoyed that most high felicity, love with mutual respect. August
von Trott, from all the accounts of people who knew them both, was
the less decisive character of the two, but it is important to avoid any
idea that the wife ruled the home while the nominal master was of
small account. People who knew the family while August von Trott
was still alive had an opposite impression. The husband was the subtler
character, and in a sense, though not the usual sense, he was more
forceful.

Eleonore von Trott usually impressed her German acquaintance as
being more American than Prussian. She remained throughout life intensely conscious that she was the descendant of a man who bore a famous
name in the history of liberty, and this family pride she handed on to her
children. It was to prove a precious moral heritage. Even though this

meant suffering for her son, she would not have had it otherwise. From their earliest days her children were taught to think of themselves as owing loyalties to libertarian traditions and ideas.

Prussian and American Puritanism are very dissimilar but not essentially divided, and in Eleonore von Trott they were found together as different facets of the dominant feature of her being. She was as fully Prussian as any of her father's ancestors, and she had a rare, ardent and discerning devotion to the Prussian way of life whose faults are better known than its merits to the outside world. It so happened that nearly forty years after the birth of Adam she gave clear expression to her devotion in a letter written to an Englishman who had been a friend of her son. By this time her son was dead and the Second World War was over. The occasion was the decision of the United Nations in 1947 to bring the existence of Prussia as a state to an end, and on 15th March she wrote from Imshausen to David Astor as follows:

'I cannot miss the opportunity of sending you a letter which might perhaps not pass the Censor. But these things *must* be said and I am one of the few surviving people who both know something of our politics during the last century and at the same time realise how it is being judged and often misjudged by the younger generation including our own. Much of what I say will seem to you ancient history.

'I have been deeply moved by the dissolution of the Prussian state and the words of contumely with which it was made public.

'I grew up in the Prussian tradition and my husband, though born a Hessian, chose to become a Prussian official and finally was Prussian Minister of Education from 1909 to 1917. The older I grow, the more whole-heartedly do I appreciate the values of *real* Prussianism—the high sense of honour, the selfless devotion to King and Country, the absolute probity. That which has figured as Prussianism during the past decades is a distortion, a caricature . . .

'The dissolution of the Prussian state is perhaps unavoidable and the fate a deserved one. But it was deserved not because we were "Prussian" but because we had turned our backs upon the *real* Prussian ideals, and that which took their place was a horrible travesty.

'Almost all our Kings were sincere Christians, certainly the five who reigned during the 19th century. They felt a deep and humble responsibility before God. According to modern standards they took too much responsibility upon themselves instead of sharing it. But that was a mistake, not a sin. Hitler's irresponsible rule of force was a sin—and our disgraceful downfall is the consequence of and the punishment for our not having the spiritual strength to cast off a government of men who were possessed by devils. But I sometimes feel inclined to say "England and America, beware, lest Satan turn his legions loose upon you. May you then have strength to resist them." Of course there is wickedness everywhere, in all countries. But the difference is, that in Germany the absolute wickedness was in authority.

'The object of this letter is to ask you to consider my claim thàt Prussia had an important contribution to make to the history of the world and that it did realise and fulfil its mission to a very high degree. Its army used to be a training ground for manliness, self-reliance and trustworthiness.

'I feel sure that the time will come when England at least will recognise this. Perhaps it is too much to expect as yet. But it is a curious fact that two of our greatest men, Frederick the Great and the Baron vom Stein, have in my opinion been better understood by English (or Scotch) men than by any of their compatriots.'[4]

A historian may not accept this without qualifications as a valid picture of Prussia and Prussianism, but there can be no doubt that the letter conveys a valid self-portrait of the person who wrote it.

August and Eleonore von Trott had eight children, of whom Adam was the fourth. The eldest son, Werner August, was born in Kassel in March 1902. The eldest daughter, Vera, was born in Potsdam in June 1906. Another daughter, Irene, followed the next year. (She died in early childhood.) A third daughter, Ursula, was born in February 1908. As mentioned already Adam was born in Potsdam in 1909. His birthday was on the 9th of August. He was christened Friedrich Adam, but his first name was ignored from the beginning and seems only to have been prominently used on one occasion, as appears much later. A fourth daughter was born

[4]*Astor Papers*, referred to later as A.P. The closing references are to Carlyle's Life of *Frederick the Great*, and to *The Life and Times of Stein* by Robert Seeley.

in Berlin in April 1911, Monika Eleonore. The youngest son was born in Kassel in May 1918 after Herr von Trott had left ministerial office. He was christened Hans Heinrich Siegfried and always known as Heinrich or 'Heini.' The last child, a daughter, Eleonore Augusta, was born at Imshausen in February of 1920.

There were two circumstances of life at Imshausen which ought to be mentioned. There was another family of Trott living nearby at a house as large as Imshausen and situated in Solz. They were the same family as that of Imshausen but the two branches had not intermarried for many generations so that the relationship was by now distant. Nevertheless they were always known to the family at Imshausen as 'the Solz cousins' and the relationship was maintained as intimately as if it had been a close one. In England such a situation is so rare as to be almost unknown, but in Germany the existence of two or more branches of a prominent family in the same district, maintaining cousinship even when this has become remote, is quite commonly found. One reason for the persistence of such family feeling can be found in the German system of land tenure. These two families, like many others of the kind, held lands and funds in jointure, and shared the profits.

The Trotts of Imshausen, with their international and political associations, were considered extremely sophisticated people by the country society of Hesse; but 'the Solz cousins' were typical of their kind, occupied with their lands and local interests to the exclusion of others, rarely leaving their corner of Hesse, and finding their relaxation in sport, horses, dogs and all that goes with them. The two families seem to have enjoyed agreeable relations though they had not a great deal in common. When he was older the most popular visitor from Imshausen to Solz was the second son Adam. From his earliest days he had an extraordinary ability to make friends with many different kinds of people, and it started here when he was a boy of ten.[5]

The second circumstance probably passed unnoticed in Adam's childhood and youth but had an inevitable influence on his later life in worse days. It involves a point of history. In the era of reactionary rule which came over Germany after the fall of Napoleon, it seemed only logical to revive the penal codes against the Jews, which had been abolished under

[5]Dr Clarita von Trott, discussion, and C.T.

the French Empire. This was done throughout the German kingdoms and principalities, with an exception. It occurred in the Grand Duchy of Hesse-Darmstadt, next door to Hesse-Kassel. On the formation of the Duchy in 1820 Ludwig I repealed the anti-Jewish laws, and it followed that Hesse-Darmstadt became something of a Promised Land for Central European Jews. It can be said to the honour of the Germany of those days that the anti-Jewish movement ended in complete failure, but by the time this fact was clear, and Jewish fears were allayed, the Jewish population in Hesse-Darmstadt had grown appreciably. As the reaction weakened, this Jewish population overspilled into neighbouring lands, including Hesse-Kassel where a fairly large Jewish population had existed for a relatively long period. The penal code was abolished in 1833. The point to notice is that by the time that the family of August von Trott came to Imshausen in 1917 there were more Jews in this part of Germany than was usual in such a predominantly rural area. From childhood Adam von Trott met Jews and made friends with them, and the effect on him was that he came to have a special feeling of attraction towards Jewish people.

An early experience probably influenced him. At a period when he was living at home, he used to have lessons in Latin from the Vicar of Solz. On his walk home to Imshausen, and especially in the cold of winter, he used to stop at the home of an old Jewish villager called Seelig, who was, for some reason, nicknamed 'Binnes.' He was acknowledged as the sage of Solz and from him the little boy learned the country lore and tales of the Trottenwald, as the woods around Solz are called. In Binnes's cottage he probably had his first close sight of working-class life, an experience which could sometimes startle him, coming as he did from a household of scrupulous delicacy, as when on one occasion at a birthday party Frau Seelig cut the cake with the same knife with which she had beheaded a mouse a moment before, only wiping the blade on her apron. But such shocks to sensibility were rare; the old Jew appealed to the romantic streak in Adam which was already strong in his childish character and was to remain with him. From Binnes he grew familiar with the ancient Hebrew religious observances and used to take some part in them: it was a special treat to help in the lighting of the Sabbath lamp on Friday evenings, and he never forgot the mystery and excitement of helping

Binnes to make a booth in his little garden fit for the solemnities to be held on the Feast of Tabernacles.[6]

The record of Adam's schooldays need not be long as most of them formed a dreary part of his life to which he rarely looked back, and which seem, on the whole, to have influenced his character rather less than is the usual case. He did not grow up to be a wearer of old school ties.

His very first education, however, when he was a child in Potsdam, was extremely happy and came from his nurse, an Englishwoman called Louisa Barret. She was by all accounts a first-rate specimen of her once famous kind, and she gave the Trott children abundant affection.

Adam loved his nurse in return, loved her passionately. In manhood years he often spoke of her with emotion and of how much she had meant to his early life. The truth was that Eleonore von Trott was so austere a character that her children could hardly feel the natural unrestrained love of children for a mother without some inhibiting sense of fear; and so it followed that much of the love due to the mother was given to the nurse instead. In later years, looking at his childhood at a distance, Adam even went so far as to say that without this passionate outlet towards his nurse he might have grown up into a perverse or emotionally deprived being and that such was the extent of his debt to Louisa Barret.

None of this need be doubted or qualified. What must be guarded against is exaggeration. It must be remembered that in these years Eleonore von Trott, as the wife of a Minister, had less time to give to her children than she would have had in normal circumstances. But more importantly it should be remembered that, though his first allegiance was to his father, and his first filial love to his nurse, Adam's love for his mother was profound and remained so throughout life. All that should be stressed is that the love of the son for his mother was delayed, and that it is perhaps unnatural if there is ever any delay in the matter.

Louisa Barret had to leave the family in the summer of 1914, when they were living in Berlin. The parting was not agonising. The children supposed that Louisa Barret would soon be back in Berlin and all would be again as it had been. At this time Adam was five years old.

[6]C.T. and a discussion with Trott's sister, Frau Vera von Trott zu Solz.

A year later he began to attend the Französisches Gymnasium in Berlin as a day-pupil. This continued for two years till the removal of the family from Berlin when, as mentioned already, he attended a school in Kassel where he was miserable. That ordeal lasted a year. Then from 1919 to 1922 he studied at home, at Imshausen, under the care of the family governess. It was during this time that he used to learn Latin from the Vicar of Solz. In 1921 he was condemned to return to school in Kassel.

His health had caused great concern in the last two years, and there were fears that he might be suffering from some chronic weakness. His heart seemed unsteady and he was often afflicted by sore throat, stomach-ache and sudden high temperatures. In fact his poor health at this time seems to have been chiefly due to the disorders which often attend the course of growth. In his later years he enjoyed good health which was, however, liable to breakdowns; he only suffered from one chronic physical weakness which is common among people who are above the average height: a tendency to be overcome by sudden fatigue. At this time, however, he was seen as a person in need of the utmost care, and this added to the miseries of his Kassel schooldays.

He was from infancy a lover of outdoor life and strenuous exercise, but now he was forbidden to join in any of the school sports or games, and to make sure that he would be under proper supervision, he was lodged with an elderly clergyman in the old part of the town. The clergyman himself doubted the wisdom of this gloomy arrangement. The good man's fears were justified. The twelve-year-old Adam soon began to suffer from depression. Of more lasting seriousness, life with his mentor caused his religious orthodoxy to weaken. This weakening process continued throughout his adolescent years and his young manhood, and the first recorded evidence is of 1921, soon after he had returned to the scene of his first wretchedness. He wrote to his mother as follows:

'I should like to ask you something, and for you to think about it and tell me. I cannot understand the Herr Pfarrer's kind of Christianity, this sort of trembling and shaking. We should be brave and not always pray and pray—it sounds like whining!—we should try to resolve things by what we do. It says in the Bible: "To us is not given a servile spirit so that we should be for ever fearful." Luther and Arndt are the kind that never show a "servile spirit" in this way. Now please do not misunder-

stand me, but try to see what I am thinking. Such thoughts as these come
to me very often when the Herr Pfarrer says his prayers.'

He complained of being lonely and that his motto 'See it through'
(expressed as *Durch*) was of no help to him. Some sympathy should be
extended to the unfortunate Herr Pfarrer. His charge was a boy who was
going through a difficult phase of irritable moodiness. He could be rebellious and priggish by turns, as often happens with growing talents. But
if this was a period of early sorrow, it should not be overlooked that, as
with most childhoods, it was not wanting in light relief.

He was on one occasion the centre of a grotesque comedy which was
never forgotten in the family. His Latin master seems to have been a person wholly lacking in sense of humour, and one day he was thrown into
a state of hysterical rage on finding a piece of paper with the message
Magister asinus est in young Trott's handwriting. His indignation was
such that he saw this as a matter too grave for summary punishment, and,
the culprit's father being in Kassel at the time, he went to him to lay his
grievance before 'His Excellency the Minister.' The latter stifled his
amusement and played the diplomat. Deploring his son's lapse of taste
he felt obliged, he said, to point out that his brief composition showed
nevertheless a mastery which was beyond criticism, and that Tacitus
himself could hardly have expressed himself with greater brevity or in
purer idiom. He concluded by saying that though Adam's action was
indefensible, he had undeniably proved by it that he had a classical tutor
of no mean order. The poor schoolmaster could not resist these blandish-
ments and returned soothed and exalted.

The real stuff of Adam's life at this time were the holidays at Imshausen,
and highlights of these were when he stayed with the Solz cousins and
took full part in their hearty outdoor life. Anxiety about Adam's health
was diminishing and the visits were not discouraged. He grew especially
attached to his Solz cousin Bobby von Trott and the two boys used to go
on wild excursions in the Trottenwald, sometimes in search of game,
sometimes merely for the fun of the thing, and often so exhausting themselves that they could scarcely make their way home. This was the life
he loved and was always to love best.

In 1923 the dismal chapter of school in Kassel came to an end, and in
the spring, when he was between thirteen and fourteen, Adam became
a schoolboy in the full sense of the term; he became a pupil at the large

boarding establishment known as the Alumnat des Klosters Loccum, a
former monastic foundation situated at Hannoversch-Münden which lies
about twenty miles north-east of Kassel, half-way between it and Göttingen. Here he spent his next four years, most of them gloomy except for
the holidays.

The school at Hannoversch-Münden was considered second-rate in
those days, and that he was sent there and not to a better school was one
of the few things with which Adam occasionally reproached his parents
in later years. But there is no reason to suppose that the school was bad.
Clearly it was not. It gave Adam an academic equipment which was to
take him far. What the school did not and could not do was to minister
to the deeper needs of an ardent temperament, and of a young vigorous
mind growing with sudden acceleration, filled with youthful dreams,
some impossible, some wise. There is no more hateful situation than to
be conscious of talent, and yet to have no way of showing it; to have to
submit helplessly to people in authority whom one knows to be mediocre.
This was young Adam's predicament during the four years he spent as a
schoolboy from 1923 to 1927.

Through most of his days at Hannoversch-Münden, however, he was
on affectionate terms with the master in charge of German studies, and
this man not only gave him the support he needed, but may have been
among the first to awaken his mind. When he had left school he described
something of what he owed to this master. 'I always found the German
classes particularly rewarding,' he wrote. 'I soon learned to overcome a
tendency whereby I forgot the content in favour of the surface beauty
of words. I began to make serious efforts to explore poetic works. My
first experience of this kind of endeavour was with Goethe's *Iphigenie*. I
also found something quite new in the world of Hebbel and his tragedies,
and this new world so fascinated me that I was led on to read his diaries
and those of his works which we did not study at school, and so I tried
to explore him more and more deeply. I am still engaged in this task, one
of the most delightful of my schooldays.'

Unfortunately his happy relations with his German master came to
grief at the end of his time at Hannoversch-Münden. Adam, with the absurd touchiness of adolescence, took great offence at the master's criticism
of his 'youthful immaturity.' Worse followed. This same once-loved
master was the moving spirit in a humiliating episode when Adam gave,

or rather attempted to give, a lecture which he had prepared with the help of his elder brother Werner. The lecture seems to have been a disastrous failure and the speaker was sent off the dais. 'Nobody could understand.me', he reported in a letter, 'and I did not seem to understand it myself.'

Hurt in his pride, he added haughtily, 'They remain as they are—and I change.'

Life at Hannoversch-Münden was most enlivened for him by a very interesting and illuminating episode which belongs to the first part of this melancholy school story. There grew up in the Germany of the nineteen twenties the curious Wandervögel (literally Wanderbird) movement. It had been founded some years before the First World War. Influenced partly by the Boy Scouts, partly by German country tradition, and partly by the lingering mental habits of the Gothic revival, the Wandervögel became a widespread cult throughout the country, and after the First World War it became a movement of some social importance. The Wanderbirds' main occupation was hiking, usually along the forest paths, and in return for a very small subscription to various loosely co-ordinated clubs, the boys and girls of Germany could wander from rough hostelry to hostelry, living on plain fare, delighting in nature, amusing themselves at the end of the day's march with singing. They could live the simple life on terms which even the poorest could afford. Clever people sneered at the Wandervögel for their sentimentality, and moralists deplored the opening that this anti-bourgeois movement gave to free love. Both accusations were true. For all that, it was a very valuable movement at a time when unemployment and extreme poverty were everywhere, and when the alternative for German youth was idleness on the streets.

The movement, being without much central organisation, gave rise to many different kinds of youth group endeavour. One of these had its origin in Kassel and had been taken over by a former cavalry officer named Gustav Ecke. He called his group the Nibelungenbund, though it seems to have had nothing to do with the Nibelung legends of Germany, or Wagner's operas. He chose a white rose as its badge. Ecke was the son of a Divinity Professor of Bonn. He had fought in the Great War from 1914 to 1918. He had graduated from Bonn University after post-war studies in philosophy and history, and, like many men who had endured the horrors of the trenches, he wanted to find some means of making the military comradeship of war a natural part of ordinary peaceful life. He turned to the Wandervögel movement.

Most of the Youth Groups of the Wandervögel type were unpolitical, but many of them had something of a socialist tinge. The Nibelungenbund was likewise unpolitical, but had an odd Right Wing tendency. Like others of these clubs, it went in for a belief in the ancient virtues of a mythical Middle Age, sustained by folk-dancing and folk-music and folk-poetry, but in the case of the Nibelungenbund this 'folksiness' was somehow vaguely envisaged as leading to a New Society in close touch with nature, and through a noble élite mysteriously formed out of hiking, leading ultimately to the salvation of defeated Germany. There was much talk of armoured Knights and Nibelungentreue and undying Bruderschaft.

Adam at the age of fourteen eagerly embraced the hazy but pleasing ideas of the Nibelungenbund, as befitted his years. He had a practical reason for doing so too. The family anxiety about his health was still there, and he was still forbidden to take part in school games, but as with his holiday excursions at Solz, his parents made a somewhat illogical distinction between the exertions involved in games and those involved in field sports and long walks. Forbidden to play football, Adam was allowed to walk for miles, sometimes over exacting hilly country, on the excursions of the Nibelungenbund. His health rapidly improved. He loved the open-air life, the romance of this knightly band, the camp-fire jollities, but most of all he loved the man who had founded the group, Gustav Ecke. The personality of this idealist made an immense impression on the boys he had assembled in his organisation, so much so that after it came to an end he remained something of an inspiration and a legend for many of them. Adam was his faithful follower during his first year at Hannoversch-Münden in 1923. In that year, after a festival held at a place called Tannenburg in South Hesse, Ecke left Germany for China. But Adam remained a faithful Niebelung till 1925.

Then something happened which was strange though expectable. Quite suddenly Adam became bored with the Nibelungenbund. The knightly hiking suddenly appeared silly; the exalted talk about Nibelungentreue and the New Society was suddenly seen as a set of grotesque fairy tales.

Adam's brief adventure as a member of the Nibelungenbund is of more than passing interest. His devotion to Gustav Ecke remained with him for life and was to have a considerable influence on him at a crucial moment. The rather woolly romantic notions of the group, which Adam put away with 'the things of a child,' did not completely vanish from his mind, as he probably supposed they did at the time. He was too much of a romantic, too open to the romantic appeal, to be able to discard entirely a romantic conception of any worth. Occasionally in his later years, an echo of these Nibelung ideas can be faintly but distinctly heard.[7]

In the spring of 1927, when he was approaching eighteen, he passed his Abitur examination with good marks and so qualified for the University. School was at an end and he left it joyfully and eagerly. It has been said already that he rarely looked back to those days. They had been unhappy. Nevertheless he was capable of remembering them with sentimental nostalgia, on rare occasions. One of these occurred a little over sixteen years later, after an Allied air raid on Berlin. He wrote to his wife: 'Yesterday as I was salvaging things in the Kurfürstenstrasse, I found as I flashed my torch over the walls of a dark room, a very pretty old-fashioned painting of Hannoversch-Münden, done in the manner of Merian but bigger and more naïve. In that strange moment it brought back to me the memory of the lovely, half-obscure, half-threatening, half-simple minded years of my boyhood in that town, embedded in huge forests and valleys which I will show you one day. There too I loved life in a way and was sometimes very happy.'

But more typical of his reaction to these memories was a letter to his mother, also written during the war. He had been to church and had heard a sermon preached by one of the Kloster Loccum clergy.

'The touch of middle-class smugness and self-satisfaction in the church atmosphere of Münden and the school came back to my memory with irresistible force, and it erected round me that wall of irritation from which I find it extremely hard to escape, even to-day.'

[7]The Nibelungenbund episode is outlined in C.T. Detailed information was given to the writer by Dr Helmut Boehncke of Hamburg who was a fellow member with Trott, and by Gustav Ecke. The latter stressed that the degree of seriousness in its romantic programme was and remains hard to assess.

Chapter 2

FOUR UNIVERSITIES

The schoolboy who occupies most of the preceding chapter bore only occasional resemblance to the man who was to follow. On the other hand, Adam von Trott as an undergraduate, soon shows the distinct outline of his essential character. It is true that he still retained the moody bitterness of his unhappy years at school; like many young men before they have found themselves he would purposely distress those about him by destructive cynicism, by indulging his melancholy and suspicion, and he would still on occasion show exasperating touchiness.[1] Something of this side of his mind and feeling remained with him till the last period of his life, but at the same time there developed and came more and more prominently to maturity in him that quality which from his childhood had caused him to be surrounded by love: an infectious gladness of character, a delight in the sheer act of living. 'When he came into a room', said Gustav Ecke, 'one's heart laughed!'[2] This was the memory he was to leave with hundreds of friends. But the shadows never quite disappeared. At the end of his life, when he was living in a nightmare world, some of his friends found that the gladness and the overflowing humour had left him altogether. This is not surprising, but the impression is, in fact, misleading. Those who were closest to him in that frightful time found that his humour was never more resilient and that his occasional moods of pathological depression had vanished entirely; astonishing proof of the depth of his joy in life.

Following his father's wishes he decided to take law as his University subject and he envisaged for himself a career similar to that of August von

[1]Frau Vera von Trott. Discussion. [2]Helmut Boehncke. Discussion.

Trott; after qualifying as a lawyer he would enter the Civil Service and from there enter politics. At the beginning of the summer term of 1927 he took the first step in this progress. He became a student in the University of Munich, and a new phase of his life began.

It was a time when the world could seem wonderfully good to a young European, and paradoxically this illusion was nowhere stronger than in Germany. The hideous years of defeat, revolution, counter-revolution, inflation and utter failure seemed at an end. The social and political resilience of the Stresemann years, and the vigorous (if largely meretricious) intellectual revival which accompanied it, made Germany the marvel of the West. In the heady atmosphere of Weimar Germany Adam threw himself with exemplary abandon into the intoxicating experience of furnishing his mind and looking with new intelligence at the world around him.

In Munich he found lodgings with a family called Jank who lived in the Georgenstrasse. He was rather lonely as most young men are in their first days at the University, and he spent most of his time reading with the furious appetite of the young awakened mind. He read the novels of Dostoyevski and for lighter fare, Gogol's *Dead Souls*. His favourite German author at this time was Hölderlin. He also began serious study of the English language. Although, like his brothers and sisters, he had spoken English fluently from his first years, and was soon to be almost bilingual, he was as yet unable to write English with any semblance of correctness. He found an incentive to improve in two attractive American girls who were also lodging in the Jank household. He joined them once in a fashionable outing and reported to his mother in English: 'I saw the so-called great life, but I don't think very high of it. Of course it was very interesting to be a week one of those rich people.' Of the American girls he says that they gave him 'a very good connections to America. The father of one is a very famous Pork-Swift.'

Some time during this Munich summer he went on a short holiday excursion and for the first time saw the world outside Germany. He went to Vienna and then to Budapest. It is not known whom he went with or what happened on the journey, but his letters afterwards have a gayer air.[3] It was the first of many foreign travels he was to take in the course of his

[3] C.T.

life, and this experience seems to have first shown him that he had a taste in that direction.

During this early spring-time of his life, spent in the most engaging of all German cities, and while he was first tasting the delights of freedom and manhood, he also first became conscious of some sinister threads running through the German life of those days. He was made aware at close quarters of German anti-Semitism. It was stronger in Bavaria than in any other part of the country, so strong, for example, that in the Munich of 1927 the murderer of Kurt Eisner was still something of a social lion.[4] Adam does not seem to have witnessed any gross atrocity, but his experience was of the kind to make a painful impression on a young sensitive mind. He had gone to Munich University with two schoolfellows from Hannoversch-Münden. One of them was a Jew and his Munich landlord considered him fair game. He swindled him in all his dealings and boasted of his success.[5] Such things were happening in many European countries in those days, and Adam must often have heard stories about them. As sometimes happens, confrontation came as a great shock, as much as though he had been completely ignorant of this evil.

He does not seem to have had any defined political interest at this time. Occasionally, however, he went to political meetings, just for the fun of it in all likelihood. One evening he and a party of students attended a rally of one of the lunatic fringe Rightist parties which were still fairly numerous in Bavaria. This one, unlike most others of the kind, had the rare distinction of having achieved a small, and, as people thought, quite irrelevant representation in the Reichstag. The meeting was to be addressed by an orator who was well known in Munich, so much so that jokes about his Austrian accent and his ludicrous Charlie Chaplin appearance were becoming commonplace in the town, though outside political circles he was as yet little known in Berlin and the North. His name, as the reader may have guessed, was Adolf Hitler, sometimes misspelt as Hittler by foreign newspapermen even so late as this. His speech on this summer evening of 1927 was presumably his usual torrent of ranting rubbish

---

[4]Kurt Eisner, a Jewish socialist journalist, set up an extreme Left government in Bavaria immediately after the war. He was murdered by Count Anton Arco-Valley in February 1919.

[5]C.T. and Frau Vera von Trott.

delivered with the agitator technique of which he was a perfect master. Young Adam was not unimpressed by the performance. 'Er ist schon ein ganzer Kerl,' he wrote home, 'aber die Leute, die ihm zuhören, ungebildet und unfähig bis dorthinaus.' One can translate this as: 'He is quite a chap, but the people who listen to him are uneducated and inferior in the extreme.'[6]

Adam's Munich career came to an end after this single summer term. Once again his health caused family concern. The water of Munich is apt to disagree with some people, and when he began to suffer from sore throat it was decided that he must continue his studies elsewhere. He obtained a matriculation transfer from Munich to the famous University of Göttingen. This change delighted his father who was himself a graduate of Göttingen, and he took pains to see that Adam set about his new career on the right lines. One of his first cares was to make sure that his son became a member of the best student corps. Göttingen had the most famous of all these, the Hannoverana, which owed its celebrity to the membership of Bismarck, but Herr von Trott insisted that his own corps, the Göttingen Saxons, was superior, and in his first term Adam was elected a member.

At first he was shy at Göttingen, as he had been at Munich, but he was growing up rapidly, and before his first term was out he was in love with the new life, stimulated by his work, by new companionship, and entering with zest into the activities of the Göttingen Sachsen. He seems to have had no inhibitions about the somewhat brutal customs which have given these clubs a bad name outside Germany, and a letter home tells all we need to know about this. It also shows early evidence of that preoccupation with philosophy applied to day-to-day life which was always to be strong in him.

'I am on good terms,' he wrote, 'with nearly all the members of my Corps. On Saturday we had Landwehr,[7] that is, the first day of real fencing, and blood flowed in streams. Although a complete novice, I did not faint in spite of taking part in all the bouts of my Corps. I regard fencing as the main and most positive thing about being in a Corps, be-

---

[6]C.T.
[7]Literally 'land-defence.' Here employed as a euphemism for duelling which was illegal under the Weimar Republic.

cause then it becomes clear whether or not one is capable of self-discipline.
I have almost got used to the drinking by now. It looks worse than it is.
My fencing is coming on too, though slowly because it is rather strenuous
at the beginning.' He adds that he has some friends outside the Corps to
whom he can go if he wants to spend a quiet evening. He was still, and
was to remain, a voracious reader.

At one party in Göttingen he met a young girl of his own age and they
fell in love with each other. This, so far as is known, was his first experience of amorous passion, and, unlike most first loves, it endured for as
long as two years at least. The relationship seems to have developed into
an exquisite boy-and-girl romance, heavy with deep adolescent thoughts
about the nature of love and that kind of infatuation which in German is
described as schwärmerei. They wrote poetic letters to each other. One
of hers has survived. In it she refers to the fact that she knows some men
who rob her of her time, others who take as much as they give, 'and then'
she goes on, 'came you, Adam, and with us there is no question of a
stronger or a weaker, nor even really of giving and taking. You are just
there, and you are a human being. I cannot define it better. When I think
of you, I feel neither pain nor need nor excitement—sondern nur immer
Freude—always joy only. The joy I feel has its spring and source not so
much in your personal life and what you do, but solely in the fact that
you are a living man. You are there, Adam, and our friendship is there.'

This letter must not be taken with solemn seriousness, but neither should
it be dismissed as nothing but a girlish foolery. There is no more perfect
evidence than this candid young effusion to convey the magic of Adam's
personality, the way that he could compel surrender to a quality which
has, unfortunately, no description except that of 'charm,' a description
which provokes suspicion, for the good reason that charm unsupported
by graver qualities provides the hall-mark of the charlatan. No anxiety
on that score need be entertained in the case of Adam, but it must be
insisted that he had charm in a quite exceptional degree, and that, weak and
ephemeral as the quality is usually held to be, his possession of it was one
of the important facts of his life. It brought him many friends, as noted
already, but as well distress and complication, sometimes through his own
fault. In his public life it brought him a large measure of what success he
enjoyed, a success which at one illusive moment seemed to carry him to
the consummation of his highest ambitions.

In a novel, a great artist can sometimes convey the quality of charm. We would like to meet Lily Dale in real life, and, in spite of the obvious dangers, Mr Micawber, because thanks to the literary skill of Trollope and Dickens, we have felt the charm of these imaginary beings as strongly as that of any real person. In biography the feat of representing charm faithfully is only possible if the subject of the book has left written material in which the quality undeniably appears, or a mass of wholly reliable and precisely illustrative anecdote. Without both these Doctor Johnson, for all Boswell's exquisite art, would be remembered as an intolerable human being. In the case of Adam, the fact of his charm can rarely be proved by such precise evidence as Boswell had to hand. His infectious attractiveness is only very occasionally reflected in what he wrote, and rarely convincingly recorded in detailed anecdote. It must be taken on trust from the evidence of great numbers of very different kinds of people who remember that, as Doctor Margaret Boveri has told the writer, when Adam came into the room everything seemed to be changed, to be gayer, more stimulating, or as Gustav Ecke said, one's heart laughed. Such testimony may only faintly echo an elusive reality, but it must be stressed because the mysterious quality of charm was so essential a part of this man. The pretty phrase of this girl should be remembered as typical of what many felt about him: 'Du bist eben da und Du bist ein Mensch.'

He wanted to travel, to adventure beyond the German-speaking world and meet other people, notably his American relations about whom he had much curiosity. His mother came to his help at this point. She was a leading member of various Protestant religious bodies, some of them international in character, and she now used this acquaintance to arrange that her son's eagerness to travel should be satisfied in a way that safeguarded his morals. So through colleagues and fellow members of religious societies she obtained an invitation for Adam to go to Switzerland in the late summer of 1928. Here he was to attend a meeting of the YMCA presided over by a senior American official of the organisation, Mr Tracy Strong. Adam spent three weeks of September in Geneva.

It might be supposed that for a fiery young man who found some of his pleasure in duelling and wild nights of heavy drinking with other young University blades, and who had fallen in love, these three weeks

spent in attending a largely clerical meeting might have been irksome.
They were not so in the event. His curiosity was extreme, and any reluctance to engage in the affairs of the YMCA was quite swallowed up in
the excitement of seeing a new country, and making new friends.

The organisation to which Tracy Strong was secretary-general was the
World Alliance of the YMCA, a body whose purpose was to give co-
herence to the national branches of this originally British movement.
Among the executives was a Dutch Protestant clergyman who had not
then been ordained because YMCA work was not accepted as 'pastoral'
by the Church to which he belonged. He was Doctor Willem Adolf
Visser't Hooft.[8] In those days his name was little known. Adam was
immediately attracted to this man who, in his turn, perceived rare quality
in the young undergraduate with his unsettled enthusiasms and unformed
convictions and engaging manner. A friendship grew between them and
Adam felt constrained to treat Visser't Hooft as a father-confessor. He
told him that he was going through a crisis of faith. He said he could no
longer read the Bible and that through the novels of Dostoyevski he felt
in closer touch with the religion in which he had been brought up than
he did through any orthodox spiritual reading. Visser't Hooft listened
sympathetically to these youthful confidences. Adam was still very young
and very naïve. He seems to have been rather shocked that in their debates
these champions of Christian endeavour spent so much of their time discussing political questions.

At this conference Adam first met British people who were to influence
his future. It may be that these were the first British people, apart from his
nurse, whom he met in the course of his life. One of them was a contemporary, Geoffrey Wilson, whose parents lived in Switzerland and were
friends of Tracy Strong. Another British guest at the conference was a
remarkable Scotsman, Charles Frederick Andrews. Adam met him and
found himself talking to a close friend of Mahatma Ghandi and of Rabin-
dranath Tagore; he found himself being shown a new world, and the
experience made an irresistible appeal to the constant romanticism in his
character. Andrews was an attractive, unconventional and passionately
sincere man, impractical as idealists often are, and wise too. Adam said
at the time that the experience of meeting this man excited his imagination

[8]This name is pronounced 'Fisser Toaft.'

so much as almost to obliterate the impression that he had gone out purposely to receive: that of America through Mr Strong and his colleagues, and through some Schieffelin relations of his mother who were then in Geneva. His meeting with Andrews seems to have been the beginning of his interest in the East.

Among the movements associated with this YMCA conference was the World Student Christian Federation, whose general secretary was Conrad Hoffmann. He also took a liking to the young German visitor and wrote about him to his British colleague, Mr Tatlow, of the Students Christian Movement of Great Britain and Ireland. This introduction shaped Adam's future very soon after. The trip to Switzerland, which his mother seems to have arranged as a design for keeping a restless youth out of mischief, turned out in the end to be a cross-roads in his life.

There were to be several in the course of the next few years.

His next term at Göttingen was uneventful as he once more fell ill, this time with inflammation of the kidneys and with tonsillitis for which he had to undergo an operation. From November till the end of the year he spent his time on a sick bed, or convalescing at Imshausen, but his mind was active with new plans. In due course he received an invitation from Mr Tatlow to attend a conference organised by the Students Christian Movement, to be held in Liverpool from the 1st to the 8th January 1929. He was very anxious to accept and he asked his parents to let him go.[9] They agreed. The decision, however, led to some stress at home.

This is a convenient point to consider his relations with his elder brother.

Werner von Trott was the most complicated member of the family. His character was restive and moody, like that of his younger brother, but far more and even oppressively so. His tendency to melancholy and bitter reflection was not lightened by the other's easy charm of manner. His relations with his parents, especially with his mother, were far more painfully tense than was at any time the case with Adam. Of these two extremely German brothers Werner was then the more characteristic of his time. The Germany of the late nineteen twenties was given to exaggerated optimism. As with most ages the opposite of the dominant characteristic was not hard to find. This was especially true of the Weimar years

[9] C.T.

in Germany because this was a time of hectic unsettlement, and also because, or so it seems, there is something in German tradition and culture
which makes for total contrast. Werner was typical of the gnawing sense
of dissatisfaction which haunted Germans since the disaster of 1918 and
was to be found (in the same person sometimes) under the optimism and
too ostentatious gaiety and show of self-confidence. Unlike Adam, Werner had witnessed as a grown man the disaster of the war years and those
which followed, and the result was that he, like many of his contemporaries, took to political extremism. He wanted to have done with the
Germany into which he had been born, and which had been but partially
overthrown by the only partially accomplished revolution. The economic
structure was, with little modification, that of the Hohenzollern regime;
the class distinctions of those days were still in operation under a shallow
pretence of class equality;[10] in Hindenburg the country was ruled under
what amounted to an elective monarchy. Werner saw no prospect under
the Weimar republic of that radical change which he believed that the
Fatherland needed, and to the deep distress of his parents he went along
with the Communist party.

He did not do so in the spirit, which was fashionable then, of a 'parlour
pink.' He became a factory hand and tried, though without any success,
to become a working-class man. He had an astonishingly strong personality. In appearance he was not unlike Adam, with the handsome looks
and high forehead of all his family, but with a gruff directness which, in
conjunction with a disturbed temperament, proved intimidating and even
repellent to many who knew him. But to those who loved him his roughness could prove strangely persuasive. On Adam who loved and respected
him his influence was very strong, and from about this time, when
Werner became a Communist by conviction, he was to some extent responsible for forming his younger brother's ideas. From now on Adam was
increasingly preoccupied with Socialism. He became a Leftist.

But there was another matter in which Werner exercised influence over
Adam, though not directly, but through controversy and even fierce disagreement. The family, as mentioned in the first chapter, were acutely

[10]It is reliably reported that Stresemann himself set a bad example. The former
Crown Prince's family used to call him 'Uncle Gustav' and this was said to be
the source of excessive pleasure to the Republican statesman.

conscious of a double inheritance from Germany and America. This affected Adam in the expected way: he wished to use the accident of his birth to enlarge his sphere of activity; to belong in a real sense to the country and traditions of his Jay ancestors, to be a citizen not only of Germany but of the whole Western world, of Europe and its huge transatlantic extension.

Werner was of a wholly different mind and he looked with dismay at his younger brother's evident and increasing tendency towards a cult of internationalism. He felt anxiety at the ease with which Adam made friends with people of every kind, and he disapproved of what he held to be the too facile identification with widely differing interests and cultures which he had shown in his brief excursion to Geneva. He disapproved more when Adam went to Liverpool and again succeeded in winning the approbation of foreigners, and to such an extent that he was invited to pass the Hilary term, from January to March, as a student-guest in Mansfield College, Oxford. Adam's place, he felt, was not at Oxford but at Göttingen. There were heated arguments between the brothers, such as were to be pursued for years ahead.

Friends of the family who heard the debate raging at Imshausen sometimes said that Werner was jealous of Adam's social success which, even at this early age, was much more than Werner had ever enjoyed or was likely to enjoy. There may have been something in this. Jealousy is a universal weakness. But it would be a most unjust denigration of Werner to say that this was the essence of the difference.

Werner was undoubtedly something of a crank, and one may be bewildered by the spectacle of a man who, at great cost to himself in esteem, identified himself with the most international of all political movements, and at the same time raised these objections to his younger brother making friends with foreigners! But if Werner's ideas were eccentric, they were not shallow. There was no xenophobia in him, and no chauvinism. He was patriotic like Adam, and with a highly rational patriotism. His objection to these young excursions to Switzerland and Liverpool, and now to Oxford, was this: that a family such as his generation of the Trotts, with their American connections, had to make for themselves a decision which is usually made for one, namely to what people they were to belong. There was nothing to prevent any of them emigrating to America and taking up citizenship of the United States; there was nothing to prevent them remaining in Germany as citizens of the Reich. But what they could not do, and what they were tempted to do, more than people of more usual background, was to become citizens of nowhere in particular: to lose their character in an aimless breadth of sympathy, necessarily spread thin, and to end up as unauthentic, as sham English or Americans, or as Germans who had lost their essential Deutschtum. He was not a nationalist in the ordinary meaning of the term, but he passionately believed that in the age of nationalism one must be a national in the fullest sense.[11]

It is possible that Werner may have formed these ideas under the influence of Stefan George, whose reputation was then at its height, and conceivably from the writings of G. K. Chesterton who was widely read in Weimar Germany.[12] Adam never accepted Werner's notions and followed the more common-sense path, but there is plentiful indication that his brother's beliefs, conveyed with the stimulus of his personality, made a deep impression on Adam nevertheless. The two brothers were very different but both were under the spell of a subtle mutual attraction.

To return to Adam's adventures, some of which have been already indicated. Not much can be deduced from his letters home about his first visit to England. It is perhaps true to say that Liverpool at the turn of the year is less conducive to self-expression than Switzerland in the glow of the last days of summer. The conference had as its subject 'The Purpose of God in the Life of this World.' It does not seem that Adam made any contribution to the debate. He told his parents that he met the leading personalities but that there was no time for any interchange of ideas, 'da sie alle very busy waren.' However he made friends with one of the secretaries to the conference, a certain Miss Denham, and she introduced him to the principal of an Oxford College.

He was the Reverend Doctor William Boothby Selbie who had been principal of Mansfield College since the year of Adam's birth. He was a diminutive, spectacled, bearded old gentleman, who through age-long tenure of his post, and forceful character, had become something of a

[11]The late Herr Werner von Trott zu Solz explained these ideas to the writer in a long conversation in October 1964. Herr von Trott indicated that since his younger days he had modified though not abandoned them. They are reflected in his posthumously published *Der Untergang des Vaterlandes*. Walter-Verlag, Olten und Freiburg im Breisgau. 1965.
[12]See his *Tales of the Long Bow*.

legend in the University. He was known there as 'the inspired mouse.' He spoke German fluently, as befitted a leading scholar of German thought and the author of the best English book on the theologian and philosopher Schleiermacher, and he was disposed to like the handsome young German visitor. This inclination was effectively strengthened when he found that Adam shared interest, supported by commendable study, of the period of German history in which Doctor Selbie had specialised. Adam had already been seized with a violent passion—the description is not exaggerated—for the writings of Schleiermacher's most famous contemporary, Georg Wilhelm Friedrich Hegel. His preoccupation seems to have begun some appreciable time before this, perhaps in his first University years at Munich, and was growing apace. Even so early as this Adam had resolved to write a work of enduring value on the most complex and baffling of modern philosophers.

Doctor Selbie invited the ardent young scholar to spend a term as his guest in Mansfield College which, as a Congregational foundation outside the Church of England, is not strictly a component of Oxford University. He said that he would require his guest to follow the College studies. Adam accepted and for the purpose was granted a term's leave of absence from Göttingen. He went to Oxford in mid-January of 1929.

England, and Oxford especially, was to be one of the great things in Adam's life. He was immediately and emotionally attracted to English life, as though irresistibly drawn into a love affair, and as is usually the case in Anglo-German relationships, both in public and private life, the love affair was frequently and sometimes agonisingly disturbed by a sense of injury on both sides. In one of his first letters home to his mother, written on the 2nd February, 1929, he describes his first impression of his new life, and what he says already implies a certain tension, or at least the possibility of uneasy relations in the future, together with the instinctive attraction.

'Every time,' he wrote, 'that I walk through the town and the colleges, it is really to experience a special kind of adventure, but when you ask me if I have formed any close friendship with anyone, then I cannot say Yes. It may be that at first one is somewhat bewildered in this really very alien and strongly imprinted (ausgeprägten) atmosphere, or it may be that, being impressed by the differences in our national outlooks, one appears isolated, wretched, and not very attractive. I don't know the answer but

I have full confidence in that receptivity which enables me to absorb new experiences. In my present state, in which I worry about other matters, I lack one thing and that thing is one of the great Oxford characteristics— distance! Not only towards all people but towards all experience! This distance makes life much easier and may well be the secret of the English art of living. But you may easily imagine how this characteristic could drive me into an attitude of opposition and resentment. And from all this there comes again a great lack of self-assurance and self-confidence.'[13]

It was a curious interlude in his life, this period of study in a college primarily devoted to the training of dissenting ministers. Though there was never any question of Adam becoming any sort of clergyman, he was obliged in conformity with the character of Mansfield College to de-vote most of his time to theological study. This could not be wholly con-genial to him, but it must be remembered that his loss of allegiance to the Church in which he was brought up never meant that he lost a religi-ous sense. He was a dissenter in the strict and original meaning of the word, so he did not fit too awkwardly into Mansfield College.

He met a number of the leading men of the Oxford of the late nineteen twenties, but he made acquaintances rather than friends. There was how-ever one important and striking exception. This was with a rising lumin-ary of the University, who had shortly before been elected a Fellow of All Souls: Alfred Leslie Rowse. He had entered Christ Church as a scholar of English Literature and had then turned to history in which he had gained a first class degree. He was six years older than Adam. They met through the Chichele Professor of Military History, Sir Ernest Swinton, and were immediately attracted to each other. One of the great joys of earlier life is that of friendship between young men who are not equals in experience, so that while they can delight in shared youth, they can at the same time enjoy the unique happiness which comes from an affec-tionate relationship between master and pupil. This idyllic experience was realised in the friendship of Adam and A. L. Rowse, a mutual affection which began, instantly ripening, in the later part of Adam's single term at Mansfield College. The friendship was destined to break down.

In this early period of their association, however, in the early spring of

[13]Letters collected by Dr Clarita von Trott referred to later as Letters C.T. The keyword in the original German is 'Distanz.'

1929, all was joy and the excitement of mental adventure, and Adam told his friends that Rowse's sympathy and affection meant more to him than that of anyone else. He said, 'I felt that I was being taken seriously for the first time in my life.'[14]

Rowse was a Socialist and was shortly to stand for Parliament as a Labour Party candidate. At this time Adam was a 'Leftist,' as remarked already, and no close definition of his political attitude is possible. The notions which he had absorbed from his brother Werner were exercises in the faculty of the imagination, rather than part of a coherent political theory. They had about them some of the glamorous want of meaning which had briefly excited his mind in the Nibelungenbund, and which had soon left him dissatisfied. Here at length, and in the course of the most stirring friendship of his experience hitherto, the ideas to which he was groping were given a coherent, systematic shape. His whole life was given a new significance and he saw a new purpose in his political ambitions.[15] The term was soon over. Adam was resolved that this was not to be the end of his association with Oxford.

He spent some days in London with one of his American cousins, Mrs de Candole, a somewhat eccentric lady with a gift for watercolour painting who, with her diminutive husband, lived permanently in hotels. She was a social person and she introduced Adam to many members of her large London acquaintance.[16] He returned home by way of Holland, where he attended a further meeting of the World Student Movement, all the time making friends with people of many different nationalities, departing thus all the time from Werner's counsel which he nevertheless always remembered.

---

[14]C.T.

[15]The friendship of Trott and Dr A. L. Rowse is described in the latter's *All Souls and Appeasement*. The book has been criticised as ungenerous to Trott's memory. Except for one brief paragraph, this part of the book, while not commanding his complete agreement with all the opinions expressed, seems to the writer a remarkable and wholly reliable document.

[16]Beatrix de Candole was descended from a sister of Trott's maternal grandmother, Anne Jay. She was regarded with affection but as a comical person by the Trott family. Adam's sister Vera accused her brother of seeking her society because she kept a good table. Adam retorted that 'so verrückt ist die garnicht' (She's not so crazy as you think). A letter from Dr Clarita von Trott.

He returned to Göttingen for the next term which forms something of a blank in his life. No interesting letters survive, and this is probably due to the undoubted fact that after Oxford he found Göttingen much less enjoyable than before. Student acquaintance in a German university tends to be restricted to the Student Corps and Adam had grown used to a life where the different 'sets' into which young men congregate had no rigid basis, and where you could belong to as few or as many 'sets' as you wanted. He found the Göttingen world small and petty, and Werner did not hesitate to point out that Switzerland and Oxford and Holland were spoiling Adam. If he was not careful he would rapidly turn into Shakespeare's 'every man in no man.'[17] The dialogue between the two brothers became ever more heated. Its subject, Adam's impatience with the University life of Göttingen, must not however be exaggerated. To the very end Adam retained affectionate comradeship with his fellow Göttingen Sachsen and kept their annual festivals in later years as religiously as any of them. He never turned against Göttingen, so to speak, but the early rapture was lost for good, and he sought escape.

Some escape he found in a literary undertaking, and spent much of his time in this spring term writing an essay in English which he called *Impressions of a German student in England*. When finished, it was around 4,500 words in length.

He was not yet twenty when he wrote this piece which, so far as any one knows, was his first serious attempt at composition. With his sensitive ear he could now speak English fluently and with hardly a mistake in idiom or a trace of a German accent; but he was still a long way from writing the English language correctly or clearly. His first essay, not written for publication, must not be harshly judged.

The 'impressions' are surprising from the very first page. The title leads the reader to suppose that he is being presented with a nice, simple, probably gently humorous travel piece, written under the influence of the numerous literary entertainers then operating in France, Germany and England. He might expect, and forgive, a youthful essay in the lighter

[17]In the conversation aforementioned the writer suggested this quotation from *The Merchant of Venice* as summarising Werner von Trott's fears. He agreed that this exactly described them and he seemed to regret that he had not used the quotation, so far as he remembered, at the time.

style of André Maurois or Paul Morand. He finds himself confronted with
something very different. The author, having introduced himself in a
long first sentence stating that this is written from the point of view of a
German student with experience of Liverpool and Oxford, continues in
his second sentence as follows: 'Of course every meeting of this kind
has its individual conditions and casualties in getting certain experiences
and missing others (in a comparatively short time) which on the one hand
makes generalisation doubtful, but on the other hand makes it advisable
to leave out the description of some special contrasts which could be mentioned, and rather to describe this experience as a whole.' This is not the
charm-school.

The most interesting characteristic of the essay is that it throws light
on Adam's inner life. Here, for example, he brings clearly before the
reader, for all the opaqueness of his prose, a general state of mind in Germany which must have been discernible in the scenes of his childhood and
youth and in the happy atmosphere of beloved Imshausen: 'Every definition [of the state of mind of a German in England] leaves out those
features of nervous discomfort and hardly concealed unhappiness which
are so significant about us people in Germany, and which only a sympathetic imagination can realise. My country in all respects stands under
the impression of a lost war and an inner political collapse, the consequences of which are to be found in the material as well as in the intellectual and spiritual sphere.'

His feelings towards England were those of an instinctive attraction
which, also instinctively, provoked distrust.

'One always hears that England is an older country than Germany and
that being older makes for disillusionment. But the wish to understand
and to learn from each other should, like between brothers of different
age—a parabole which is not yet enough used—impel the younger one
to consider the elder without resentment, and the elder one to put away
that smile of superiority which really ought not to make him happier
and makes it impossible for the younger to speak to him and learn from
him without giving up his particular values.'

There is one curious passage towards the end where, through the con-
fusions of his imperfect English, it is easy to detect a preoccupation and
an influence.

'If thought doesn't find any real possibility of living projection,' (of

being projected into life), 'it will happen that everything becomes prob-
lematic, that perspective and direction are missed, and we find ourselves
in that state of entire perplexity which must renounce those numerous
securities and guarantees which do connect the man of action with the
outer world, a state where you can't any more accept answers of a sym-
bolic nature and where life gives an answer—in a peculiar and often hard
way—to which a doctrinal response is mere phrase.'

Not too much importance must be given to youthful flourishes of style
written in a language in which the writer was still not at home, especially
as it is not possible to be certain now to what sort of political development
'where life gives an answer' he was referring. Nevertheless it is not extravagant to see from this passage the hold which Hegel's ideas already
had on his mind, and how they were informing the growth of his intellect.
Hegel's influence is even more apparent in a passage in which he is dealing
with nothing more abstruse than a plea for mutual understanding between
German and English students despite their differing traditions. The young
Trott succeeded in making this plain subject magnificently obscure.

'And another thing has to be said, which also in this connection ought
not to be forgotten, that however differently these two spiritual positions
may have impressed me, there always remains the feeling that there can
never be found a quantitatively measurable different distance to the absolute or the Eternal—however it may be emphasized—but that this means
always the same qualitatively comprehensible jump, even if the immediate
action has to bear a different character.'

As with some of the Master's pronouncements, this can be held to
mean more or less whatever the reader chooses. Again not too much
must be made of an absurd piece of undergraduate extravagance—else
who shall stand? But the undoubted presence of Hegel in this unexpected
appeal to the Absolute has to be noted. In the opinion of some of Adam's
friends, especially his English friends and notably Rowse, Hegel was an
evil genius in his life.

Dissatisfaction with Göttingen led to another change. While remaining
a member of the University Adam obtained permission to leave Göttingen again for two terms in order to continue his studies at the University
of Berlin. (The English reader, unfamiliar with the freedom of German

University ways, may be surprised at how little time this Göttingen graduate spent at that illustrious seat of learning.) This was the first time that he had lived in Berlin for more than a day or two together since his Potsdam childhood. He lived now in a couple of cheap rooms in the Olivaerplatz, a small square on the Wilmersdorf side of the Kurfürstendamm.

Berlin is one of the strangest of European capitals: exquisitely beautiful in its Frederician centre; in many other quarters, notably Wilmersdorf, ugly as only a German town can be; homely at one moment, drab at another, bombastic the next; magnificently planned and liberally supplied with handsome buildings and eyesores. It was in those days, and perhaps has always been, a stimulating city. But for a normal taste it can never have been one in which to be happy, although, thanks largely to the presence of an extraordinarily good-humoured population (similar in many characteristics to the London cockney crowd), it has always been a place where enjoyment is easy to come by. Only a dolt could have missed having fun in 1929 Berlin, but any person of sensibility was likely to experience moments of revulsion in a city so remarkably lacking in peace and calm. This is reflected in the letters home which Adam wrote at this time. The very style, sometimes contorted, sometimes lucid and gay, reflects changes of mood, often to be found in the same document.

We have a few descriptions from outside the family circle of how Adam lived in Berlin, and how he impressed others. Oxford had given him a taste for the society of Englishmen and about this time he made friends with one of the secretaries of the British Embassy, Hugh Montgomery.[18] This large and benevolent man, about ten years older than Adam, took a great liking to him. Writing more than thirty years later he described their relationship thus:

'I remember his very fine appearance so well, his beautiful sensitive face and his young eager voice. I remember a few things about our conversation. For instance I remember him being much distressed at one time by "the pangs of despised love" (I can't remember who the young Fräulein concerned was nor did I meet her) and I have an idea that I was not as

[18]Now Monsignor Montgomery. He left the diplomatic service in order to take Holy Orders shortly after the Second World War. The writer is indebted to him for much information. The quotation is from a letter to the writer.

sympathetic as I ought to have been. I remember too our arguing about
student-duelling (Die Mensur) and he defended the custom though I myself denounced it as barbarous—probably without much tact! I have an
idea that he brought fox-hunting, or some other barbarous English custom, into the argument.'

Through Montgomery Adam met one who became a life-long friend,
Albrecht von Kessel. At that time he was a junior in the German Ministry
of Foreign Affairs, the Auswärtige Amt which was ten years after to
become a central part of Adam's short and tragic life. Herr von Kessel
recalled him in these first Berlin days as follows.

'I met him (in 1929) in Berlin, where he attracted attention with his
doctor's thesis on Hegel. He was then still very young, and spent his
days in a dark, cheap, rented room containing one shaky table on which
was a copy of *Das Kapital*, a hairbrush, Hölderlin's poems and a sandwich,
arranged in a picturesque still life. He did not like it when I came to visit
him, for he was ashamed of his acquaintance with me before the Socialist
and Communist workers with whom I found him engaged in endless
discussions. *Weltschmerz*, Russian literature and extremely Left political
ideas were the fare on which he lived. But he was young enough to forget
these ideals for hours when, beautiful as a young god, he amazed the
Berlin salons in the evening. He was a young genius, sensitive and irritable, and no one found it easy to get along with him. Nevertheless we
were for years attached to each other in a tense, often endangered, but
always steadfast friendship.'[19]

Few of Adam's friendships were not tense and 'endangered,' but very
few broke down. Herr von Kessel's memory is at fault on one point,
namely that Adam attracted attention in Berlin by his thesis on Hegel.
In 1929 it was not yet written, but the mistake is interesting because it
indicates so clearly that 1929 memories of Adam were sure to be memories
of Hegel too, and that one or other of his works, and perhaps the whole
lot, shared the table with *Das Kapital* and Hölderlin. Inwardly and outwardly, as Adam might have expressed it, his life in Berlin, as with all
other phases of his life, was one of extreme variety. The main current in

[19]*Ein Leben für die Freiheit.* Edited by Dr August Franke. Bärenreiter Verlag,
Kassel. 1960. This gives biographies of several of the 1944 conspirators, the chief
essay being on Adam von Trott, in whose honour the book was compiled.

a mass of different preoccupations was socialism, and the most frequent meeting place was the office of a Left-Wing weekly paper *Neue Blätter für den Sozialismus* to which Adam occasionally contributed. As a Göttingen Saxon his attendance at socialist discussion groups and suchlike occasioned suspicion of his sincerity, but he seems to have quickly overcome this inevitable obstacle. After describing a debate at which he had caused surprise by supporting the more Left-Wing side he confided to his mother, 'However that may be, I believe that I am at last on the right path, and I am grateful to my worker friends for having helped me to it.'

Berlin proved too exciting for the purpose which had led Adam to go there. Plain evidence comes from his letters to show he found study of the law thoroughly uncongenial, and, as the reader will learn without surprise, he had spent so much time in socialist discussion, in cultivating new rewarding friendships, in tasting the meretricious joys of fashionable society, in indulging in such irresistible pleasures as an ecstatic visit to Dresden (his first sight of that once lovely city) with his friend A. L. Rowse, that he had done relatively little work on his University subject. He began to fear that he was ill-equipped for his finals which he had to take in 1930. He stayed on in Berlin to the end of 1929. In 1930 he returned to Göttingen. There he spent a year in what has been described as the "Hochburg des Hegelianismus.' Least of all in Göttingen was he likely to forget his major intellectual passion.

Chapter 3

FROM GÖTTINGEN TO OXFORD

The return to Göttingen was a difficult journey into time which he had made once before, and his weariness in 1928 with the young, frolicsome life of the Göttingen Saxons was with him again in 1930. His father came to his help and advised him how to remain a faithful member of his corps without involving himself in more than he wanted of the Mensur, Landwehr, drinking bouts, parties and so on, and with his never-failing charm Adam kept on good terms with his fellows. He was helped by the fact that since this was a necessary period of intense work in his law studies, and in the writings and criticism of Hegel, he had less inclination towards social life than usual. Among some enigmatical entries in his diary, most of which show the influence of his intellectual hero, there is one, for some time at the end of his first 1930 term, which throws a clear light on this phase:

'It is indeed true,' he wrote, 'that my day-to-day plans and my thoughts lie in such different fields that they involve a leap over a chasm which divides two worlds.'

His teacher was Professor Herbert Kraus, one of the outstanding personalities of Göttingen, especially congenial to Adam as he was not only a master of law but also a considerable authority on Hegel. It was now that he began systematic as opposed to what might be called dilettante studies of the great thinker, choosing as his special subject the *Rechts-Philosophie*—or *Philosophy of the Law*. His fellow-student at the feet of Kraus was called Alexander Werth. They were good companions in those days. At a much later date their friendship grew deep, and Alexander Werth was to play a significant part in Adam's story.

The 'second Göttingen period' was very important to Adam for another more personal reason. He became involved in a profoundly emotional relationship which was to influence him for years, indeed till the end.

He had many natural advantages; an active mind, good looks and charm, as already mentioned. Everyone who met him, almost without exception, found him extraordinarily attractive. The boy-and-girl romance of his early Göttingen days has been noted, and an unhappy love-entanglement in Berlin. Neither of these adventures (and there may have been others of the kind) appear to have been of lasting significance. But as Adam grew and became more mature in character and appearance, as his boyish good looks turned to classical beauty, as his charm developed into a wonderful power of communication, the emotional involvements to which this indefinable quality made him liable became serious. He had always enjoyed, and always was to enjoy, the society of women, and he soon found that he was quite unusually attractive to them, far more so than is ordinarily the case with a handsome young man. Like most men who find themselves in this often-desired and usually unenviable situation, he surrendered to its temptations. It had better be said candidly that in this matter he showed weakness of character—though such a statement must not be interpreted as a stone-throwing act of the kind rebuked by the Saviour. Nevertheless the fact must be faced that he was not often able to resist the opportunity of exerting the emotional power which his natural endowment gave him, and this often involved him in unworthy intrigues and the endangering of his honour. It must be said in his defence that the Germany in which he grew to manhood was one in which moral values, especially the more conventional ones, had become immensely enfeebled under the shock of defeat and the demoralisation accompanying the economic obliteration of whole classes in the inflation of 1922 and 1923. Free love was the order of the day, and Adam was no saint. His Lutheran conscience, for all his rejection of formal religion, tortured him often enough with feelings of guilt and remorse, but nevertheless he could not obey this conscience and so was led to other temptations, towards what might be called 'inner casuistry.' Perhaps the most unhappy moral effect of philandering on Adam was that it increased his tendency towards the complicated and extravagant reasoning which he learned from his philosophic interests, and his need, especially in the difficult years ahead, was for clarification and standards whose very simplicity made them compelling.

This is to look into the future. The story must return to Göttingen in the first half of 1930.

Among the students was one whose presence was a matter for very great surprise. She was a handsome, strong and independent-minded American woman. She was about forty years old, recently divorced, and she had come to Göttingen in order to study German philosophy so as to equip herself to meet an examination in one of the leading American universities. Accompanied by her five young children she was living in Göttingen, and as an enthusiastic student of the German philosophers, including Hegel, she soon met Adam. They made friends immediately. Any very young man is liable to be attracted towards a woman of beauty and personality who is markedly his senior in age and experience; and, without adopting the fashionable rôle of the amateur psychiatrist, one can say that it is fairly plain that in the case of Adam, who had felt his son-mother relationship to be in some sense deficient, this commonly-felt attraction was especially strong.[1] His new friend held decided views on the emergence of a new world, and a new morality, and a new conception of things, from the wreck of old societies. For Germany she had a generous admiration, as the defeated land which had bravely abandoned its past and sought salvation in democratic progress. With her dauntless American spirit she embodied the idea of a new world, an idea to which, in his days in Berlin, young Adam had been aspiring. Somewhat as had happened to him at Oxford, he suddenly and utterly unexpectedly found a friend who could confirm and make more understandable to himself his own ideas; a friend, this time, who was also an irresistibly attractive woman who shared his deepest interests, sympathised with his ambitions, and understood them. On her side she found a magnificent young man who fairly personified all her hopes for a regenerate new age. Inevitably and swiftly they fell deeply in love.

In the summer vacation he brought her and her children to Imshausen and shared with them his never-ending exploration of the Trottenwald and of the beauties of this lovely corner of rural Germany. With her too he pursued his adventures of the mind, and she could enlarge them. Through her he struck up another ardent admiring friendship with a

[1]This opinion is given by a close friend of the Trott family.

Viennese student of literature, Franz Golfing. Of him Adam said: 'He is the most remarkable man of intellect I know, and the most tolerant and human.'[2] It is a deep and illogical delight of intellectual youth that, despite a sceptical attitude to all established reputations, the same people can be dazzled by mutual admiration of each other's genius.

Through Golfing he first met members of the Heidegger School and his intellectual acquaintance began to broaden in other directions too. He also came, through Golfing, to enjoy easier relations with his brother Werner. In Berlin, judging from a letter written by Adam after a meeting of the two brothers, the antagonism had become extremely painful. Adam now showed some of Werner's writings to Golfing who was greatly interested. He met him and tried (though without success) to find him a publisher in Vienna. 1930 was a time of spreading poverty, increasing unemployment, and fear of the future in Germany, but youth has defences against 'general woe.' Although he had a keen social conscience, this time remained one of joy for Adam, living under the influence of a passionate love. Only one small cloud cast a shadow.

There was towards the end of this year a distressing disagreement between Adam and his father concerning politics.

In August of 1930 Adam attained his majority and this meant among other things that he was now entitled to vote. His chance to do so came immediately. In September there was held one of the most fateful general elections in modern European history, though very few people, and certainly not the Trott family, saw at the time what the results could mean for Germany. Chancellor Brüning's judgment seems to have completely deserted him at this moment, and without having attempted an alliance with the Social Democratic party he called a general election, his purpose being, as he stated himself, 'to secure a Reichstag with a democratic majority.'[3] This the election achieved only in the most dubious technical sense. The Social Democrats remained, after some losses, the strongest party in the Reichstag, and the Catholic Centre slightly increased its representation. But all this meant little compared to the success enjoyed by the parties of extremism. With an enormous increase in their vote and numbers in the Reichstag, the Communists could now challenge the

[2]Quoted in C.T.
[3]Erich Eyck. *A History of the Weimar Republic*, Oxford University Press. 1964.

Social Democrat claim to be the workers' representatives. At the same
time the Communists themselves were being challenged by the National
Socialist party which gained almost the whole vote of Germany's three
million and more unemployed.[4] By Parliamentary means Hitler had
reached the opening of the last phase of what he called Mein Kampf.
After the 1930 elections the Reichstag contained a' hundred and seven
National Socialists. Freedom, peace, honour, civilisation itself were now
endangered as never before. It was not easy then to know this.

At Imshausen the concern was not so much over the shift in the parties
as over one single vote: that of Adam. He voted for the Social Democrats.

He told his father by letter of what he had done. The old gentleman felt
the blow keenly and he wrote back to his son, who had returned to
Göttingen for the autumn term, a letter of troubled affection: 'Your letter
confirms me in a consoling expectation that what unites us is, to the great
joy of my old age, stronger than what is at the moment between us. Certainly, from our former talks together, I had come to understand your
leanings towards the Social Democrat Party, but on these same occasions
I have heard you express views which are completely opposed to the
principles and aims of this party. A young man in your position who cannot reconcile his conscience with the demands of paternal authority, of
his origins, family and tradition, will in the last resort act more honourably if he keeps away from voting than if he takes part.'

He went on to insist that in the twelve years since 1918 the Social
Democrats had not shown themselves to be a party with any constructive
ability, and yet these same people were proposing to refashion the State.
A far more promising development, he went on, would be a clarification
by revision of the vague programme being put forward by the National
Socialists . . .

Adam had told his father that he was concentrating hard on his forthcoming exams, and the old gentleman concluded his admonition by expressing his approval, and urging him to forget politics for the time being.
Adam replied in a conciliatory tone. His letter contains the following:
'Now that I have a sense of purpose in my activities and in their context,

[4]Eyck. Op. cit. The unemployed vote accounted for about half the Nazi total of
votes.

I feel very close to you and I am conscious of the potent help which comes to me from your understanding and will. Hegel calls that which enables the individual to take an active part in the life of the State "the Spirit of the Penates." In this your sons are at one, although their ways differ, and the service of the State will remain for them the unifying and permanent principle.'

So ended this episode. It is not necessary to emphasise its tragic irony.

At the end of 1930 he took the law examination known in German as the Referendarexamen. It was held on this occasion at the Superior Provincial Court, the Oberlandesgericht, at Celle in Hanover, on the 20th December. Adam came through the ordeal successfully. His papers were marked Vollbefriedigend—'Fully satisfactory.' In English examination terms this is equal to a 'good second.' The Referendarexamen was not the end of his University days at Göttingen, for he needed to study further in order to pass an oral examination set for the summer of 1931. If he passed this, he would then be qualified to practise as a junior barrister without fee. His next step would then be to sit for a second examination for the post of 'Assessor' which allows the successful candidate the full privilege of legal practice in the Courts including that of assistant judge. Such was the path ahead, to appearances. Adam was in no hurry to follow it. He had already made other plans. To follow them it is necessary to go back a few months.

Oxford haunted Adam's memory, and he saw a way of returning there. In his Berlin days he had met and made friends with a German diplomat who was some twenty years his senior, and a man of singular and lovable character. He was Albrecht von Bernstorff, the grandson of the Count von Bernstorff who was Prussian representative in London at the time of the war of 1870, and a nephew of the Bernstorff in the succeeding generation who was German ambassador in Washington up to 1917. At this time Albrecht von Bernstorff held the post of Counsellor in the German Embassy in London. He was a good-humoured, fat, blond man whose appearance suggested a humorous, easy-going and luxury-loving attitude to life, and it was not easy to guess on first acquaintance that he was in fact a man of firm principle, and that of the very noblest kind.

Before the First World War Bernstorff had gone to Oxford as a Rhodes scholar, among the last to be appointed, according to the terms of Cecil

Rhodes's will, by the German Emperor.[5] Like many other Rhodes scholars he fell in love with Oxford, and the refusal of the University to accept German scholars after the war was for him a matter of deep personal distress. Just at this time, however, the Rhodes Trust were successfully bringing pressure on the University authorities and heads of Colleges for a revival of the original system whereby German scholars were admitted. This meant much to Bernstorff who looked eagerly among his acquaintance for worthy candidates, and he saw one in Adam.

There seems to have followed something like an 'Oxford conspiracy.' Circumstances forced this, as Adam's father fell seriously ill during this summer, and was unable to attend to any business. It thus came about that, if he was not to lose time, Adam had to assure his position before the great new venture could come up for family discussion. After his successful Referendarexamen he did not need any further academic qualification for the scholarship, but he had to obtain the recommendation of six persons holding professorships. He also needed support within the citadel, and this he obtained from A. L. Rowse.[6] By the end of the year, with Bernstorff's help, he had succeeded in his undertaking. On 9th January, 1931, the Warden of Rhodes House Oxford officially informed him that he had been elected to a scholarship. The next move was to find a vacancy in a college and the Warden asked him for a list of eight in order of preference. In submitting the list Adam wrote 'I have named Balliol first not only because it was my uncle's (Schweinitz) College but because from all I know it would meet my tendencies most.' On the 3rd February the Warden wrote to tell Adam that he was accepted by Balliol College 'to come into residence next October.'[7] The first stage in the conquest of Oxford was achieved.

When these arrangements were nearly complete Adam was able at last to confront his father with a request for his approval of them. The old man would have preferred his son to stick to his law studies, to graduate

[5]By the terms of his will Cecil Rhodes endowed 160 scholarships at Oxford to be held by two students from every State of the U.S.A., three from each of 18 British Colonies (in those days the term covered British Dominions) and 15 from Germany to be appointed by the German Emperor. William II behaved constitutionally in the matter and was guided by a German Selection Committee.
[6]*All Souls and Appeasement.*   [7]Rhodes House archives.

to the post of Regierungsreferendar, to have passed his examination for Assessorship and then to enter State service unless he wished to remain a lawyer. But he loved Adam too much to stand in the way of what he knew to be the desire of his heart. 'Du bist ein aufregender Sohn' he wrote to him. One may translate this as 'You are an exciting son,' but the word aufregender has no precise equivalent in English. It can also mean 'disturbing,' and the overtone is there in what his father wrote. He loved Adam, not any the less because he so often caused him anxiety.

The feelings of Werner at this latest adventure into cosmopolitanism may be imagined, but his reaction was milder than might have been expected. Possibly this was a result of the better relations they enjoyed through Franz Golfing; at all events the bitter and despairing antagonism of a year before is not to be detected in the events of early 1931. Though Werner never disguised his disapproval of Adam's 'Anglomania,' he was moved through affection to travel to England and to Oxford in order to satisfy himself that his younger brother would have tolerable lodgings in Balliol. He approved of the rooms which were on the first floor of the building attached to the College Hall on the west side. This journey abroad was one of only two (the other being to Italy) voluntarily made by Werner in the course of his life. He heartily disliked both.[8]

To return now to Adam's last term at Göttingen. Always under the influence of his requited love for his American friend and fellow student, he settled into a routine of work to complete his law studies, and at the same time, and with passionate ardour, he set forth on his first major adventure of the mind: to write a thesis on the subject of Hegel. He had already completed his research into *The Philosophy of the Law* and into the enormous modern European literature on Hegelian philosophy in general.[9] He now set to work to translate his studies into a short, and he hoped definitive, treatise.

There is no more wonderful intellectual experience than that of expressing, with a sense of confidence, the accumulated thoughts and reflections which come to a man after intense study of a subject which means everything in the world to him. It is not surprising to learn that when Adam at last came to give shape to ideas with which he had lived for a

---

[8]Werner von Trott. Discussion.
[9]His bibliography contains 53 titles apart from the whole of Hegel's works.

long time (or what seemed a long time to a young man), he found the mental stimulus almost too much for his strength, and that the interest grew obsessive. What had begun as a toy and a delight (to remember a saying of Sir Winston Churchill about the pains of authorship) had become a tyrant. We hear of Adam[10] being pursued by his preoccupation with Hegel, not only into the little leisure time that he allowed himself, but even into his dreams, and that he would wake up with his mind all astir with some new solution of one of the thousand difficulties which face every Hegelian student, or some new turn of phrase that would make his meaning more exact, and that he would find himself often enough 'in the deep vast and middle of the night' forced by the thoughts that would not let him alone to toil at his desk till dawn.

By March he began to show signs of strain and overwork, and the family doctor declared that he must take a holiday as soon as the vacation began. At the end of the month he left Göttingen as a student for the last time; he took the prescribed holiday in Northern Italy, and then, with his mind refreshed, he worked with more moderation at the text of his thesis. By the autumn of 1931 he had completed the first part.

In the meantime he had to fill up the spring and summer months before he 'commenced scholar' at Balliol. He used this period to obtain some legal experience, and he worked as a Referendar at Nentershausen, a little town very close to Imshausen and Solz, in the Trottenwald. Nothing of great interest seems to have happened to him there but the experience was useful and in July he passed his oral examination, being judged 'Very good.'

He often went back to Göttingen to consult with Professor Kraus, and, a yet more compelling reason one may suppose, to see his American friend who was finishing her studies. In May 1931 he wrote a letter to Frau von Trott, very expressive of the delicate and tender relationship that had now grown up between son and mother. He wrote: 'For your two letters I thank you from my heart. The first one especially gave me joy because what you wrote taught me how much you have begun to understand my inclinations and desires.' The letter ends with a touching reference to his American friend: 'About the end of June she had to go back with

[10]C.T.

her children to America . . . Noch kann ich diesen Abschnitt selbst nicht glauben—Not yet can I myself believe that this happened.'

The summer of 1931 was enlivened by a visit from A. L. Rowse. As before they did some travelling together and for a while they stayed with Adam's Balliol uncle, Wilhelm von Schweinitz, who, as a member of the Trustee staff of the Hohenzollern estate, lived in the vast black stone palace of the Kings of Prussia which, as the only truly ugly building of the 18th century, used to cast a gloom over the Friedrichstadt, as the old centre of Berlin is known.[11] 'In the evenings', recorded A. L. Rowse later, 'Adam and I used to roam around the palace. I well recall the Kaiser's study: the telephone cords looking as if they had just been cut, the big desk made of timbers from Nelson's *Victory*, the books half German and half English, half Lutheran theology, half contemporary history and biography.'

On the 10th October, 1931, Adam wrote from Balliol to his parents as follows: 'By and large I do not think it will be difficult for me to find my feet in Oxford again. It is not so much a question of reliving old impressions as of changing oneself . . . When I first saw Magdalen Tower again from a bus coming from London my feelings were almost overwhelming. The "tender" (zärtliche) emotion that one has towards this architecture is not mere sentimentality.'

The Oxford to which he now came was one well suited to his tastes and hopes in life. British universities have a way of changing their character from year to year, dominated at one moment by teachers who fire the minds of the undergraduates, at another by leaders who arise among the men themselves; and since a normal life-span of an undergraduate generation is three years, these different phases, when they are in the hands of the men themselves, as they usually are, succeed one another rapidly, sometimes with effects of total contrast. The extravagant, hedonist, foppish

[11]In a Vansittartist mood the victorious Russians pulled the palace down, on orders from Stalin. More unfortunately they confiscated as unsuitable for the eyes of common men the superb equestrian statue of Frederick the Great which used to stand at the east end of Unter den Linden. At the same time the Potsdam residences were all conscientiously restored.

and poseur Oxford of 'the aesthetes,' immortalised in the novels of Evelyn Waugh, had wholly passed away some four or five years before, and in its place there had arisen a very different one which remains without a chronicler. Two undergraduate generations of a more earnest and sincere mind than that of their predecessors had, while never for an instant renouncing the gaiety of young life at Oxford, turned away from the frivolities of the nineteen twenties to the stern interests of politics and economics. By the time Adam arrived by bus from London the second of these generations was in its stride, and he was just the sort of person that its members liked to welcome. His preoccupations were theirs; he inclined to the Left, and 'Leftist thinking' was growing increasingly fashionable in neo-political Oxford, and this circumstance formed a further bond of sympathy between Adam, as one of the first German Rhodes scholars since the war, and his hosts. The aesthetes had taken their cue from Paris; they had prided themselves on speaking fluent French, on enormous acquaintance with French literature, and affected to eat, drink, smoke, and even to dress in the French fashion. Their successors looked with disdain on Paris and France as strongholds of reaction and injustice. This resulted in a massive swing of opinion towards a love of Germany.

It is true to say that, among the youthful elements, Oxford was in a more Germanophil mood than at any time since the late 19th century. Disgust at the incapacity of successive British Governments led to a reaction not only against the Conservative party, but against anything which seemed the result of their predominant rôle in British policy. The Treaty of Versailles seemed just such a worthy object of disgust, and there was a growing sympathy, growing nowhere more than among the undergraduates and many of their teachers in Oxford, with the German indignation against its harsher clauses. In his new university Adam found not only sympathy but active admiration for his native country.

Oxford is fickle and flirtatious, however, and the welcome might easily have turned into reaction. But for Adam then this danger hardly existed. He had, for one thing, what he described as his 'dauernd rezeptive Tätigkeit,' translated above,[12] for the sake of simplicity, as his 'receptivity,' and his authenticity, like that of his elder brother, was undeniable. He was to suffer great distress in the years ahead from what he took to

[12]See Chapter 2, page 36 above.

be Oxford's hard-hearted misunderstanding of his purpose. In that place that he loved so deeply he was to be falsely accused, and many of his admirers have said bitter things about fair-weather friends. These are matters which belong to a future chapter. What needs to be stressed here is that most of the abundant affection which surrounds Adam's name in England to-day stems from Oxford where he is officially honoured in Rhodes House and his college, and privately in many memories.

A fellow undergraduate, C. E. Collins, who began his Oxford career at Balliol in the same term as Adam, wrote a memoir fifteen years later. 'The impression which he made on meeting one was immediate;' he relates, 'it was produced by his very tall figure, striking features, and a sense of power in his manner. But one came to like him for more important things than these: for his quick sympathy and understanding, his good humour, his great kindliness, his intelligence, and his complete integrity of purpose. He was always good company.'

Adam always maintained old acquaintance and he took up again with his first Oxford patron, the inspired mouse, Doctor Selbie. He found a fellow-student of Mansfield days still in Oxford, an Indian called Hom-ayun Kabir.[13] The latter was a devoted follower of Kant, and the two young men, the Kantian and the Hegelian, had used to engage in long philosophical conversations when they were at Mansfield together. They resumed the habit now. But of all his first Oxford friendships the one which had meant most to Adam, and still did so, was that with A. L. Rowse. Through him he met many of the personalities of All Souls, and he thus became known to several influential people in the world of public affairs who believed that the most important task facing British policy was a lasting Anglo-German accord. He met Lionel Curtis early on in these Rhodes scholarship days, and at some uncertain date, but still early on, Lord Lothian. He enjoyed instant and wide social success.

He also encountered its reverse in that same first intense friendship, that with A. L. Rowse. It remained fruitful and persisted but (to remember Albrecht von Kessel's phrase) it grew manifestly 'endangered.' As Doctor Rowse says in his brief and remarkable book, there was an emotional tension in their relationship, and against this affection could not

[13]Later he became Minister of Culture in the Government of Jawaharlal Nehru. He wrote a brief account of his friendship with Trott.

make headway. Other people remembering Adam as an undergraduate refer to his high spirits, his sense of fun and his popularity. Doctor Rowse refers to his sinister capacity to create unhappiness around him, a remark which immediately recalls the evidence of his elder sister and people who knew him in more adolescent years.

Gradually, by hardly perceptible stages, a certain unease began to creep into Adam's relationship with A. L. Rowse, a sense of disaccord of a particularly Anglo-German kind in the place of the close understanding that there had been. Doctor Rowse has told the writer that in all his acquaintance he never met a man with so perfect a gift of sympathy as Adam: he could anticipate the other's thoughts when they were together with a precision that he can only describe as uncanny; it was as though Adam had some power of establishing telepathic communication at will, and the friendship that included such almost supernatural accord was rare and precious indeed. All the more painful was the threat of break-down when it came, and it came for the reason most easy to expect.

Adam, from the moment he arrived in Oxford, devoted a great deal of his thought and time to working on the second part of his doctorial thesis on Hegel, and Hegel's thoughts and beliefs more and more took possession of his intellect and imagination. To Rowse, whose ideas were informed by a devotion to English empiricism and Latin logic, this growing influence was not intellectually antipathetic so much as morally repulsive. He himself has eloquently expressed his reaction.

'We diverged deeply. He gave himself up to Hegelianism; it profoundly affected his mind, though his mind must have been inherently disposed to it: for all external appearances, Adam was deeply German. With him black was never black, and white white; black was always in process of becoming white, white of becoming black. Nothing was clearly defined from anything else; nothing ultimately was different from anything else; the boundaries of everything were unclear, nor was there any certainty anywhere in the universe.

'This was the constant burden of his letters,[14] and I could not bear it. No doubt it represented the bottomless uncertainty of an upheaved epoch in Germany, a universal Verschmelzung. But I had no sympathy whatever

[14]Doctor Rowse is here referring to a slightly later period than Trott's first term at Balliol.

with Adam making that the principle of his intellectual life. I loathed Hegelianism—as I still do.'

Elsewhere in his book Doctor Rowse says of the threatened relationship that 'It was like England and Germany.' The remark is very penetrating, for in the intellectual sphere, no more totally effective agent of Anglo-German discord than Hegel can be imagined. Two things, however, should be mentioned now, though they anticipate a future which at that moment was distant. The friendship with Rowse was the most 'endangered' of all Adam's relationships but, as Doctor Rowse himself makes clear, this one, though it grew cold, never wholly dissolved, and never met the fate of many broken friendships, transformation into hate. The second thing to be remembered is that when Doctor Rowse wrote his book *All Souls and Appeasement*, he did not know the final chapter in the story, (which was in truth, a love story) of Hegel and this latter-day disciple. It came late in Adam's life, tragically so, but it completely disposes of the idea (which has never been stated though often hinted at) that the cult of Hegel corrupted his mind.

To turn to the day-to-day life of Adam once more. Following the advice of his college he decided to sit for the Philosophy, Politics and Economics school, known as 'P.P.E.,' and to an older slang as 'Modern Greats.' His regular tutor was Humphrey Sumner, later to be Warden of All Souls, and he was also taught philosophy by the Master of Balliol, Professor A. D. Lindsay. Another don of his college with whom he studied was John Scott Fulton.

He was older than his fellow 'freshmen' at Balliol, and so it was natural for him to seek a good deal of his companionship among the Fellows of Colleges. Through A. L. Rowse, as mentioned already, he became known to many of the Fellows of All Souls. He met Richard Crossman and through him personalities of New College, Lord David Cecil and Isaiah Berlin among others. With Berlin there developed another close friendship which was also to be endangered, though never catastrophically as in the case of A. L. Rowse.

Among undergraduates he found one whom he had met before, outside Oxford. This was Geoffrey Wilson, last mentioned in connection with Geneva and Tracy Strong. He belonged to many of the same clubs as

Adam and, as with his Indian friend, they indulged together that predilection and delight of young days, long, rambling, infinitely explorative
conversations, accompanied by liberal drinking, and for subject politics,
the still new discovery and passion of young Oxford. When, with a mind
more mature than in Mansfield days, and widely experienced for his
years, Adam met the politically conscious Oxford generation which was
younger than himself, he seems at first to have been somewhat shocked
at their incapacity, perhaps giving too much importance to the hardly
avoidable element of insularity. He wrote to his parents early in his first
Balliol term: 'There is a lack here of leading politicians. There are some
exceptions, but the political conceptions of the undergraduates are only
expressions of ignorant emotional attitudes.' His own political ideas were
as impractical and unformed as their own but very different, and drawn
from a wider range of sources. This may have given them an appearance
of greater depth and reality.

Geoffrey Wilson remembers their talks together. 'The first thing that
struck anyone about Adam', so he has told the writer,[15] 'was the really
extraordinary charm of the man. He had attractiveness in the highest
degree. It came in part from his wonderful physical presence and good
looks, and in yet greater part from his enjoyable liveliness of mind—
there was no turn in the talk to which he did not instantly add something,
and he could often anticipate the drift of a discussion. Everyone who knew
him loved him; they had, so to speak, no option. We had a great deal of
talk together about the political affairs of the time, and also about the
great subjects which undergraduates find so irresistible, such as the future
of Europe, indeed of the whole world. I cannot remember any of the
ideas he put forward in precise detail, but I remember the impression they
left on me: one that he was a person of intensely German mind and
that the kind of ideas he had could only have come from a German, and
secondly that there was an extraordinary vein of sentimental romanticism
in him which somehow took me aback, for it was something I had not
met before.

'He had a passionate love of his country, yet, as I remember those
Balliol talks, I do not have the impression of a nationalistically-minded

[15]This account is reconstructed from a conversation between the writer and Mr
Wilson early in 1966, of which a note was taken within a few hours.

man, but rather of a very international-minded man who was at the same time intensely "German-centred." This came out in the sort of ideas he liked to discuss and of which I have only a very general memory now. He used to encourage me to share his enthusiasm for a dream of united Europe, modelled on the Holy Roman Empire in its first phase in the age of Charlemagne. Somehow or other this revived Imperium was to accomplish all that the League of Nations was supposed to, while avoiding all the League's faults. I do not remember whether he planned that we would elect an Emperor or not, but the whole thing was to be very glamorous, and furiously Left-Wing. It was to embody the past, present and future in the most wonderful way!

'These ideas were not more fantastic than a good deal of the current political chatter, and when Adam launched into his Holy Roman Empire schemes we used to take them quite seriously.'

Another undergraduate who first came up to the University in this same term, and who was to become one of Adam's greatest friends, was David Astor, a younger son of the second Lord Astor and the famous and eccentric American lady who has a permanent place in history as the first woman to take her seat as an elected member of the House of Commons. David Astor and the Astor family were to play a large rôle in the fortunes of Adam. For the moment it should be stressed that (with great differences) the friendship of Adam and David Astor was comparable to that of A. L. Rowse and Adam as it had been two years before: a devoted master and pupil relationship, in this case the scholar Adam on one side, rich in the experience of Munich, Göttingen, Berlin, practice in the law, familiarity with the Left intelligentsia of Germany; on the other side the pupil, a youth of fine intellectual promise, fresh from Eton and experienced in the world and its ways only in the sense that he came from a home that literally buzzed with political discussion.

In his first term Adam was involved in one very odd incident.

In early November, when he had been at Balliol for less than a month he became the centre of another family dispute, and on the same subject as that in September 1930, his political ideas. With the alarming example of Werner before them, there was evidently a recurrent family fear that his Left-Wing ideas would carry Adam, along with so many other trusting young men, into the Communist camp.

A debate was held in the German Club. The subject was whether

National Socialism was a desirable thing or not, and Adam wrote to his
mother that he had spoken on the opposition side. This caused a great
flurry at Imshausen and Frau von Trott was moved to write him a letter
of some severity. 'You write to tell me', she said, 'that you have spoken
against National Socialism at Oxford. I do not think that you have done
right. You know that, so far as I understand the movement, I reject it.
Nevertheless this is a national movement which you should not denigrate
or belittle outside your own country.'

Adam replied in the course of a letter to his father. After describing
his joy in the life of Oxford and in 'the whole atmosphere which I find
peaceful and above all things stimulating' he turned to a defence of his
action. 'In a letter which I received to-day Mother writes very disapprov-
ingly of my remark that I made a speech here which was not favourable
to National Socialism. There is no need for such a letter, as my speech
was part of a debate in which a sober attempt was made to discuss National
Socialist possibilities with regard to home and foreign policy. No one
spoke "for" or "against" National Socialism, and for that reason you
may be sure that my own letter was misunderstood.'

The apologia does not seem to have quietened the anxieties of his
mother who may possibly have felt some fear for her son's safety. The
Nazis were showing increasing boldness and ferocity as their confidence
grew, and the movement was plentifully stained already with vendetta
blood. Whatever the reason the disapproval persisted and Adam felt
obliged to return to the subject in a long letter to his father written on the
2nd December, 1931. 'When I spoke, I did so in a non-partisan and objective manner. *Now* however there is the danger that certain National
Socialist Germans and above all certain Englishmen (!) are trying to get
the club into N.S. hands, which would certainly be a great mistake.'

Here the dispute seems to have ended.

In this first term he had won golden opinions. Rhodes House reported
to the Selection Committee in Berlin, 'His College speaks very highly of
him both with regard to his work, which shows admirable and promising
quality, and his general standing as an individual. A scholar who is as
charming as he is able, and one who ought to do notable credit to the
German Rhodes Scholarship.'[16]

[16]Rhodes House archives.

The term ended with a touching episode. In December Adam was struck down with a severe attack of influenza, at the end of which he needed to spend a week in convalescence. He spent this week in the country cottage of his old nurse Louisa Barret. It seems likely that he had visited her on one or perhaps both of his previous visits to England. On all subsequent ones he saw her. It has been said already that throughout life he was a faithful friend.

Chapter 4

A CRUCIAL YEAR

The year 1932 was a very important one in Adam's life. He finished his treatise on Hegel and it was published later in the year. Such a work as this, on a subject round which an enormous literature in several languages has assembled, inevitably took him a long time, rather longer than he probably expected when he began the work with such frenzied enthusiasm. Letters to his parents show that his English experience forced him into many second thoughts, and later he said that this had left some blemish on the work: the second part was written from a point of view different from his original one, and he believed that this gave a certain indeterminacy and illogicality to the whole.[1] This was perhaps needlessly severe self-criticism.

Hegel, as said already, is a major figure in this story. Conscious of acting temerariously, Adam's biographer must nevertheless give some notion of this most influential philosopher of the modern world. Otherwise the story might make no sense to many readers. Only a scholar thoroughly familiar with the immense volume of Western thought is capable of giving an objective and wholly trustworthy account of Hegel, and the present writer is not such a being. He cannot do more than offer borrowed opinions, and personal impressions with no claim to be considered learned. He should also, in honesty, make it quite clear at the beginning that he is not able to share Adam von Trott's intense admiration, though this does not mean that he is puzzled or estranged by his enthusiasm.

Hegel lived from 1770 to 1831. He is probably the most difficult to understand of all philosophers ancient or modern. His very vocabulary

[1] C.T.

confronts the student with matter for perplexity. To take one example, in the *Rechtsphilosophie*, which was Adam's particular study, the terms Sittlich and Sittlichkeit occur on many pages. The terms derive from the substantive Sitte whose primary meaning is 'Custom.' By an obvious process this meaning has been extended to cover an equivalent of 'propriety,' 'manners' (chiefly in the sense of correct manners), and 'morals.' The range of meaning and association of 'Sitte' and its derivations is thus wide. The student might pardonably suppose that a philosopher who attached such importance to the terms Sittlich and Sittlichkeit would be at the utmost pains to indicate quite precisely the sense in which he uses them. This Hegel rarely if ever does. What he does do by way of compensation (if such compensation is indeed his intention) is to qualify his every statement with elaborations of an intellectual subtlety and refinement such as can hardly be paralleled in any other writer.

If Hegel had been a great master of classic prose, the initial difficulty of his meaning and the complexity of his qualifications might have been combined in such a way as to give a compelling vision of the world, immediate and irresistible, to whomever has the strength to scale the heights under his leadership. To Hegelians, but to them alone, this is the rewarding experience of studying his works. The general reader can find no pleasure in the adventure. In the highly individual and somewhat eccentric language of the original, Hegel presents an agonising task to the non-German reader, but this task is only a little lightened by the translators, of whom Hegel has had some of the best in the world. Nothing can make him lucid. 'The truth is', wrote Logan Pearsall Smith, 'that the world's great writers are apt to become the world's great bores.' There can be little doubt that Hegel qualifies as one whom this generalisation covers, and when the unconverted reader calls to mind the bloodthirsty systems of government which have found inspiration in Hegel's ideas, he is to be pardoned if he is tempted to cast the whole of this imposing body of work out of the window, and to join A. L. Rowse in declaring it to be no more than a vast imposture.

It must never be forgotten, however, that Hegel was a man of genius if ever there was one, and that he remains a supreme figure of the world we live in. Nonsensical as that world may be, its founders deserve more than peevish disgust. A. L. Rowse is privileged by study. Other people must approach Hegel with respect.

It seems incontestable that Hegel's writings on history and its philosophical interpretation are his most influential work,[2] and this is contained
in the small area of his *Philosophy of History* and *Philosophy of Law*, the
latter entitled *Naturrecht und Staatswissenschaft im Grundrisse oder Grund-
linien der Philosophie des Rechts* (A Ground plan of Natural Law and Political Science, or Outlines of the Philosophy of Law), known usually as
Die Rechtsphilosophie. The last-named book reads as an elaboration of
certain principles enunciated in the first-named, but in fact the *Philosophy
of Law* was composed before the *Philosophy of History*. It was published
under Hegel's careful supervision in 1821, whereas the *Philosophy of
History* was compiled from notes for lectures given in Berlin between
1823 and 1827, and published by his disciples six years after the master's
death in 1831. Its full title is *Vorlesungen über die Philosophie der Geschichte*.
From the circumstances of its publication the text remains and perhaps
must for ever remain a matter of learned and sometimes embittered dispute. Adam was wise to concentrate on the less stimulating though equally
portentous *Philosophy of Law*. The ideas in it remain a matter for vigorous
debate, but at least it has a settled text. Adam could concentrate on the
ideas.

What were the ideas?

Would that one could indicate their character in a single clear paragraph! When put crudely, as by the present writer, Hegel's ideas sound
as though they never rose above wondrously gifted lunacy. It is possible
that they did not. It is more than likely, however, that what Gibbon called
'the unerring sentence of time' will show that there resides a precious
kernel of truth, such as is not to be found elsewhere, in Hegel's philosophy
of history and law. The two subjects overlap in his treatment, and one
book cannot be discussed without reference to the other.

The whole interpretation of history by Hegel depended on his notion
of reaching logical truth by a triadic operation involving thesis, followed
by antithesis, concluded by synthesis. The synthesis might provide an
answer for this or that question raised by the thesis, but usually led to a
further thesis and a new venture with the triadic operation. The system is
known as the 'dialectic' or debate, the Greek philosophic term revived in

[2]Bertrand Russell, in common with most modern critics, regards Hegel's *Logic*
as his most important work.

the generation preceding Hegel, by Kant. This logical movement was used by Hegel to prove his basic conception, that truth resides in 'the whole' and never in 'the part,' and that the part is only true in so far as it reflects some aspect of the whole. The more it reflects of the whole the more true it is, or, as Hegel expressed it, the more it was 'rational' and partook of 'reality.' The rational and the real were with him interchangeable terms. This may seem strange at first. Since all Hegel's ideas have a strong flavour of mysticism, the student of his works might expect that he would regard the rational as essential but, in the final analysis, not of primary importance. The *Philosophy of History* explains why this could never be Hegel's position.

The main subject of this daunting book is the World Spirit, Der Weltgeist. Hegel's notions of the rational and the real are expressed in terms of the history of the world. History, it is explained, is only to be understood if regard is paid to the working of the human soul, and the soul and the intellect are not differentiated. It was Hegel who first produced the notion that human history ought to be regarded as the gradual unfolding of a vast and consistent process. He himself saw the process as one by which earthly activity ascended by definite stages to a state of perfection described as 'the Absolute Idea,' the quintessence of reason. If Hegel had lived and written after Darwin he might have been the first exponent of some such theory as that of 'creative evolution.' As it was, he took his ideas more from religion than science and he is concerned, not with man's place in nature as a whole, but with explaining the character, meaning and destiny of man's supernatural faculty of mind, his power to reason, and what must be his relation to a higher mind and higher reason: 'the Absolute.' This preoccupation is closely akin to that of much orthodox mysticism, both Christian and otherwise, and it is true that most of Hegel's ideas were not only derived from religion but could only have been conceived by the mind of a deeply religious man. Here is another great irony in Hegelianism. An eminent authority, Robert S. Hartman, has said: 'The most rational and religious philosopher, Hegel, unchained the most irrational and irreligious movements.'

The reasons for this paradox are not far to seek. Mystical writers as a whole treat mystical experience, and the revelation to which it is a means, as something reserved to a few, as a favour of God, a call to sainthood to be answered only after self-question and in fear. Hegel on the other hand saw the whole historical experience as mystical, and regarded historical consequences as objects of religious veneration. The greatest and most divine historical consequence was the emergence of the State, and men realised themselves in proportion as they partook of the 'whole' character of the State. His most famous saying is that 'What ought to be, is.' The basic convictions on which he built his philosophy reflected Christian dogma inversely. Like Rousseau he believed as strenuously in Original Virtue as more conventional people believe in Original Sin. World History became the story of Original Virtue in practice, its adventures and character. While accepting a great deal of Hegel's view of history his followers reached more matter-of-fact conclusions.

Hegel's vision of World History is certainly very peculiar. Bertrand Russell (who can rarely resist a dig at the master) comments on it in his *History of Western Philosophy*: 'It was an interesting thesis, giving unity and meaning to the revolutions of human affairs. Like other historical theories it required, if it was to be made plausible, some distortion of facts and considerable ignorance. Hegel, like Marx and Spengler after him, possessed both these qualifications.'

The great human purpose, according to Hegel, is to achieve freedom, because only through freedom can the World Spirit of Man attain to the Absolute. Three main phases are discerned in the historical course of the process: that of the ancient Oriental civilisations, who, we are told, 'knew only that One is free'; the Hellenistic World which knew 'that *Some* are free'; and then the Germans, of whom we are assured: 'the German world knows that *All* are free.' This great German manifestation is in turn subdivided into three phases to indicate its movement and flowering: the first, from the time of the rude German clans described by Tacitus up to the age of Charlemagne, forms a period which Hegel calls the Kingdom of the Father; the second, from Charlemagne to the time of Luther, is the Kingdom of the Son; and the third, from the Reformation to the present time, is identified as the Kingdom of the Holy Ghost. This strange conception moves Bertrand Russell to give Hegel another highly enjoyable dig. 'It seems a little odd that the Kingdom of the Holy Ghost should have begun with the bloody and utterly abominable atrocities committed in suppressing the Peasants' War, but Hegel, naturally, does not mention so trivial an incident. Instead, he goes off, as might be expected, into praises of Machiavelli.'

The freedom which Hegel preaches is nothing to do with individual rights or the freedom of assembly, speech, the Press and suchlike everyday things. It is a more mystical, more deeply stirring, and what many people would consider a far more mischievous kind of freedom: the right to build a state, the right to support it, the right to obey its laws, to serve in its armies, to join in war for its sake, or, if one is in the higher ranks of state service, to work for war or even declare it in the State's interest. War is regarded by Hegel as a noble activity, and apart from concern over the interest of the State, he seems to make no distinction between wars of aggression or defence, of honourable or dishonourable cause. Recusants and non-jurors, and their claims to freedom have no place in Hegel's conception of the developing world and its Weltgeist, as one would expect, but neither has loyal opposition, nor indeed any manifestation by citizens of any spirit of criticism of the State. Yet a primary agent of history, according to Hegel, is the hero who, in all but a few rare cases must open his career in opposition to the established order. Caesar and Napoleon, rebellious generals who abjured their first loyalties to their states, are held up to admiration. From the mass of innuendo and qualification with which Hegel surrounds the subject, it would seem that we are asked to believe that the hero is endowed with a lofty genius which enables him to discern the point of time when the old order must change, yielding place to new, and this gives him immense privileges. For a while, so long as he serves the World Spirit, he can disregard the moral order, and the obedient servants of the State who, following the Hegelian ethic, oppose him, automatically become 'lackeys and parasites.' The hero himself has a great time. 'So mighty a figure', we are told, 'must trample down many an innocent flower, crush to pieces many things in its path.' What ought to be, is. One may legitimately add a gloss: according to the terms of Hegel's dialectic, the hero who succeeds ought to have undertaken his great career, and therefore is; the hero who fails ought not to have tried to be a hero and deserves his chastisement because he does not exist in the highest sense: he does not partake of the Weltgeist, the Whole, the Absolute.

Such, in the coarsest outline, are Hegel's political ideas. Many people have found them immoral and ridiculous; others have found in them the most fascinating of studies. At the moment, thanks to an absurdly exaggerated idea of the genuine relationship of Hegel to Nazi ideas, the great philosopher has more enemies than admirers, and the defence, at the moment, is not very strong. Two lines of defence are usually manned by the admirers. Both seem to the writer very doubtful, though worth manning.

Hegel has been represented as an idolator of the Prussian State, and this accusation is certainly a gross over-simplification. That he admired Prussia with a fiery enthusiasm is undoubtedly true, but it is quite untrue that, as is often alleged, he saw in the Monarchical Prussia of his day the culmination and perfect realisation of the World Spirit, a proposition which would automatically make nonsense of his philosophy. In fact, in so far as Hegel committed himself to an identification of the ideal state, his choice did not fall on Prussia but on America, and not the America of his time but one that he prophesied would come into being in the not distant future.

As a defence this point appears hopelessly vulnerable to the present writer because Hegel's ignorance of America seems to have been extraordinary. He revered the achievement of the United States for more or less the opposite reasons that have moved men to admiration since the age of George Washington. He contrived to see in America an enormous realisation of the morals and ideas of Prussian despotism. He took no note of the libertarian and egalitarian spirit of the American Revolution or the American way of life. He saluted an imaginary country which was shorn of American liberalism, and which, he believed, was likely to reach its final and highest manifestation through the ordeal of a stupendous war between the North and South Continents. As mentioned already, he always spoke of war as a beneficial activity. He devoted his life to historical study but he never seems to have noticed the historical importance of one of the most remarkable events of his time, namely the Industrial Revolution. It never occurred to him that this must radically alter the very nature of war and rule out any hope or belief that war could be anything but a plague to be avoided by any honourable means. The same oversight is to be found in nearly all the European statesmen and thinkers of Hegel's own time and of the generations succeeding him, almost up to the present time. In the case of a philosopher, however, who made the vast claims that Hegel did the fault cannot be ignored easily.

The other line of defence concerns Hegel's essential doctrine. His thought is held to have been a major contribution to that worship of the State which was growing in his time, and has grown with increased acceleration since. Such an opinion is clearly true. What is not true is that such worship was the object of Hegel's teaching. The latter has been compared to the teaching of St Augustine of Hippo. Both St Augustine and Hegel saw the liberation of the spirit in freedom to obey—one the Church, one the State. If, from reading St Augustine, a sect were to arise which renounced belief in God in favour of belief in the Church, and saw in the Church, and no more in God, the object of adoration, then it would be a clear case of damnable heresy proceeding from a culpable misreading! Yet substitute State for Church and this is exactly what has happened to Hegel's teaching through misreading of his works, especially his philosophies of history and law.

Is the misreading by later generations culpable? Possibly not. Given faith, the notion of a Church which is itself the object of exclusive adoration is completely farcical, because the essential claim of a Church is to some form of Divine foundation or inspiration which the Church serves, and which is anterior to itself. A man who cannot accept the claim does not, in circumstances of religious toleration, belong to the Church. But the idea of the State as something of sacred foundation serving the Divine Absolute does not come naturally to men, and in the present age-long condition of society men cannot help belonging to states, whether they want to or not, nor does citizenship compel belief in a power beyond that of the State. From Hegel's teaching, the descent to State-worship, a barbaric form of religion from which Christianity rescued the Roman world, may be considered as more or less inevitable. One must never condemn a man for not foreseeing the future, however, even if the man in question is as didactic and opinionated as Hegel.

Before considering Adam's contribution to Hegel studies, one point should be made. The impression of Hegel as no more than an unpleasant curiosity of thought is difficult to avoid when his ideas are described in outline, but this is not the impression which remains after reading Hegel himself. As said already, he is not a clear, elegant or (except to a disciple) a pleasing writer, but though very wearying he is an extraordinarily impressive writer. The reader knows that he is in the presence of a mind of stupendous energy and force. Hegel demands complete surrender to his ideas. The only alternative is complete revolt from them. It is impossible to 'quite like' Hegel. His place in thought and literature may be compared to that of Wagner in music. A bare recital of the notions and stories put forward in *The Ring of the Nibelung* may strike someone who has not heard that work as a mass of nonsense to which no sane man would give his attention. Surrounded by Wagner's music the same ideas and legends can take on immense depth of meaning, and even the atrocities of the style, and the long, elaborate and wearying repetitions begin to appear essential to their expression. Few people 'quite like' Wagner. As with Hegel, the normal reaction is either surrender or disgust. This is a fact which is not appreciable without some reading of Hegel, but it ought to be borne in mind.

And now, briefly, Adam's book.

His title was *Hegels Staatsphilosophie und das Internationale Recht*. The treatise was originally in the form of a paper prepared for a seminar which had for its subject international law and diplomacy, and was organised at Göttingen by Adam's teacher Herbert Kraus. At the discussion Adam expressed his purpose, and from what he said on that occasion (a record of which has survived) he evidently intended to write a critique of the *Rechtsphilosophie*. In fact he wrote something different, what might be described as an exposé with commentary, and it should be added that to write an exposé of Hegel without commentary is virtually impossible, and that he was taking on a great task.

The treatise is around 42,500 words in length, the first part, *International Law in the System of the Philosophy of Law*, being nearly a third longer than the second part which is entitled *Moral decisions of Conscience and the Will of the Sovereign State*.

Some of Adam's friends have seen in this work a wonderful clarification of Hegel's ideas as expressed in the *Philosophy of Law*. The present writer cannot agree with this. Clarification, though at one time intended, according to Adam's letters, is not the book's salient merit. This need not be said in disparagement. The book must be taken as definitely not addressed to the general reader; it was addressed to a scholarly readership. Adam wrote in the hope of getting the approval of acknowledged academic authorities, and this he obtained in the highest degree.

The extent to which he wrote the book within the confines of academic thought and language, within, as one might say, the thick and hardly penetrable walls of the Hochburg des Hegelianismus, can be illustrated by a passage from the introduction in which the hero makes his first dramatic entry on the stage.

'Already from this outline of the principles referred to in the Kantian treatment of our problem, the opposing critical attitude of Hegel emerges clearly. The main point of confrontation in his disagreement is already to be found in his essay, *On the Scientific Method of treating Natural Law*, containing an exposition which discusses Kant's teaching on Law.

'First of all he opposes the above-mentioned radical separation of Legality and Morality, which separation not only involves infidelity to the basic principle already postulated concerning the moral freedom of the individual, but expressly destroys the principle, because thus the system of Freedom is rendered impotent through the introduction of coercion in unreconciled opposition to it. The desirable reconciliation of Freedom and Necessity, of moral self-determination and the power of the Law must needs remain impracticable in this context, since, as a result of beginning with the individualistic starting point, what is missing from this teaching is, quite apart from any firm definition of morality, a view of the moral sphere as a whole. This "Whole" appears to Hegel at this point as "Moral Totality," shaping the concrete life of a People. From such Totality Law and Morality find their function which is limited by, and can be comprehended only from the Whole.'

There is a passage of much interest in the fourth chapter of the first part, that dealing with Hegel's teaching on Society with reference to international law. It is aimed at current Nazi teaching. In 1932 the Nazis claimed Hegel as their prophet. They had not yet recognised that his insistence on reason made him inconsistent with essential Nazi belief. Adam says as follows about Hegel's conception of the individual:

'It is only when an individual, by participating in, and reflecting on the social "substance," has become a "civilised" being, that there arises the need for making the Law regulate his exterior sphere of life and permeate it in every conceivable sort of detail.

'This teaching on the applicability of Law gains an emphatic significance in our context from the following: there is no national limitation to the observance of the principle of the individual. Hegel says: "The individual is regarded as such because he is an individual, and not because he is a Jew, a Roman Catholic, a Protestant, a German, an Italian, etc." '

In a footnote three pages later he again tilts at the Nazis. 'In my opinion, the modern conception of the power of the State can only be blamed on

a misunderstood Hegel.' A few years later the Nazis gave up the cult of
Hegel. Reading of him was not encouraged, though Doctor Goebbels's
agents tactfully did not burn his books as they did those of Einstein. But
this does not mean that Hegel was quite innocent of encouraging the sort
of nationalism which found an expression in Nazism.

As said already, the book is essentially an exposé. Its theme may be
stated as follows: that Hegel's conception of the State as the Whole to
which men are in duty bound to give themselves, with little if any
reserve, can only be understood in the light of his idealism which refers to a
national state far in advance of any he knew or we know to-day. The individual, according to Hegel, must himself achieve the most perfect moral
development of which he is capable before he can fully identify himself
with that most wonderful historical realisation so far of the Weltgeist,
namely the State; thereafter the State must perfect itself in accordance with
the perfection of its members and its aspirations towards the Absolute.

Quotations give the sense of Adam's thought here.

'That the individual citizen and his will belong absolutely to, and
coalesce with the general substance of the State, becomes manifest in
the conduct of the State as a whole. Hegel, for this reason, sees the test
of this all-embracing membership in "the shape of some event or in
an involvement in accidental occurrences which arrive from without."'

And to this he adds a revealing footnote, with his eye again on the
Nazis:

'It is interesting that Hegel, in spite of a fairly obvious relationship
between these things, does not mention national consciousness or patriotic
states of mind, but merely "the nature of the totality and the pride which
a people feels in its independence." The determining factor here is not
natural instinct, but awareness of the direct unity between the individual
and the spirit of morality representing the general substance. Terms like
"fatherland" and "nation" are not used.'

According to Adam, Hegel believed that not until the multitude of
civilised states have achieved the tremendous moral feat of integration
between polity and individual, can international tranquillity be obtained.
To attempt this prematurely is to deny the needs of the Weltgeist and
to invite catastrophe.

'Hegel's concept of the Law includes a possible reconciliation of the principle which declares *lex suprema salus populi* with an ordered system of inter-state relations, limited by the organised morality in each individual state, and based on dependable foundations.

'These international relations are not to be pursued through an all-exclusive (*monistisch*) system, that is to say according to a principle set over the idiosyncrasies of the various states, but should come into being dialectically from relations between ultimately self-responsible states. This results, speaking empirically and historically, in a more realistic view of international relations.'

When Hegel wrote with disapproval about international bodies endeavouring to regulate the foreign policies of various states, he had the Holy Alliance in mind, a fact which can explain and a little justify his point of view. It seems allowable to believe that when Adam wrote about Hegel's ideas on this subject he had in mind the League of Nations which a German patriot most easily thought of, and with some justice, as an instrument of oppression against Germany. Hence a discernible sympathy with these very questionable Hegelian ideas. This sympathy led him into the most involved and least successful part of his book in which he endeavours to explain away as innocuous Hegel's approval of war. The text of the master, which Adam quotes, is perhaps more complex here than in any other part of his writing, and Adam's exposition, it must be said, only adds darkness to darkness. At this point Adam has recourse to arguments whose over-subtlety defeat their own object, as he tries to explain away the utterly damning evidence of Hegel's pronouncements. Towards the end of the book, however, there is a refreshing footnote which redeems much of what has gone before. Here again is one of the rare personal touches and one feels that this at last is the real Adam speaking.

'One can argue,' the footnote reads, 'and in detail as to whether a development towards international relationship is increasing or not. One thing the strongest opponent of a world economy and international co-operation is forced to admit: that as things are at the moment the question concerns facts and forces which mean so much to the basis of social existence that no theory of national sovereignty can ignore them, without endangering to the utmost the life of the national state concerned.'

At a more mature age Adam was to show in the most striking way that, however deeply and passionately he may have been influenced by

Hegel, he was never for one moment deceived by him into love of war
or contempt of peace.[3]

The essay was submitted to the judgment of the faculty at Göttingen
and received the fullest official approval, 'summa cum laude.' Henceforth
Adam could style himself Herr Doktor, a privilege highly esteemed in
Germany. He rarely used the title however. In the autumn the essay was
published in book form by the Göttingen firm of Vandenhoeck and
Ruprecht. He dedicated it to his father.

As noted by Albrecht von Kessell, the book gave Adam some reputation not only in learned circles in Göttingen but beyond—he was 'somebody' now. Yet it seems probable that he himself, after the first flush of
success and the nervous delight that accompanies first publication, was
dissatisfied with what he had done. In part this may have been because he
had not written the book he originally intended, and in part a natural
reaction from intense study of a particular subject. But there seems to
have been more in it than that. He never quite recaptured his earlier
passion. To the end of his life he toyed with the idea of writing a full
critique of Hegel, but he never did more than toy with it, and he was
easily diverted into other fields of study. He did not abandon his interest
or his enthusiasm until the last phase of his life, but very slowly and yet
perceptibly Hegel became a less dominant influence on his mind. This
was soon to be dramatically illustrated.

Adam's adventure with Hegel has taken the story of his life to the last
months of 1932. In the meantime his Oxford life had continued and ex-
panded, and to know something about that it is necessary to take another
step back in time.

One of the differences, a wholly beneficial one, between the more traditional Oxford which had come to an end in the late twenties, and the

[3]The interested reader may consult Trott's text which has been republished with
an introduction by Professor Hans Rothfels. Vandenhoeck and Ruprecht. Göttingen. 1967. For help in studying Trott's text, the writer is indebted to Mrs
James Stern and Mr Harold Kurtz.

new Oxford to which Adam belonged, was the far greater rôle that women now played in the University. This was more noticeable in under-graduate society than among Fellows of Colleges, in whose way of life segregation persisted. Till shortly before Adam's time women under-graduates had kept to themselves and were not much encouraged to make friends with the men. A new generation made light of prudish regulations; the girls and the men mixed far more freely than they had done in Oxford at any time before.

With two women undergraduates Adam made friends who remained important in his life till the end. One was with Miss Diana Hubback whom he met in his first term. Her mother was Eva Hubback who in 1927 had become principal of Morley College in South London, a post which she held till her death in 1949. The other friendship was with Diana Hubback's close friend, Miss Shiela Grant-Duff, a grand-daughter through her mother of the naturalist and philanthropist Sir John Lubbock. Adam met her early in 1932. Diana Hubback (now Mrs David Hopkin-son) has left a vivid picture of Adam as a young man. She begins by telling of the letters which they exchanged in the course of years.

'Very occasionally Adam wrote to me in German, but [most of his letters were] in English. He was very conscious of his limitations and con-stantly accused himself of writing in a heavy or obscure manner. He made no claim to be a good linguist and he never mastered French. His English accent, however, was excellent and he had a most beautifully modulated and expressive speaking voice. He put great colour and emphasis into his voice, making it a rich instrument for the English language. I cannot for-get his voice. As he spoke he made lavish and gentle gestures with his long hands which were most expressive.

'His habitual expression was one of great candour and serenity, but in laughing his whole face was convulsed, his large mouth stretched wide and sometimes tears fell from his eyes. When unhappy or depressed his face had a heavy almost desperate expression. But perhaps for his friends his smile remains most clearly in their memory, with the particular lift of his eyebrows, his head slightly on one side, and his forehead wrinkled.'[4]

The friendship remained superficial for most of a year and became close

[4]Diana Hopkinson. An account of Trott's life compiled chiefly from their letters. Unpublished. Referred to later as D.H.

when Adam joined a reading party with the Hubback family at Trey-
arnon Bay in Cornwall. This was the summer of 1932.

It was during this visit to the Hubback family that Adam met one of
his intellectual heroes, Bertrand Russell. The meeting was agreeable but
not entirely successful. Writing thirty years after Lord Russell recalled
the occasion as follows: ' . . . I liked and admired him. The only thing I
remember at all vividly about him is a walk to a very stormy Cornish
coast during which he expressed admiration for Hegel as to which I disagreed.'[5]

Ambition was growing ever stronger in Adam and he made it his business to meet distinguished men in furtherance of the great career he still
saw for himself. Let this not be taken to mean that he was prone to soulless
careerism—such an idea is at variance with the very essence of the man,
but he made practical use of his social advantages. At Oxford he knew
and made an impression on most of the leading figures. He knew Professor Adams, the Warden of All Souls; he knew the eminent Warden
of New College, the historian H. A. L. Fisher, and he knew the philosopher and logician H. W. B. Joseph, also of New College, stories about
whose hair-splitting exactitude in conversations held at his weekly Wednesday 'philosophical teas' were numerous in Oxford. Among his contemporaries there grew, with many others, a friendship with John Cripps
the son of the leader of the extreme Left Wing of the Labour Party, Sir
Stafford Cripps. Adam met John Cripps's father, in those days an object
either of worship or furious revulsion. Sir Stafford Cripps was immediately impressed by Adam and proved a valuable friend.

But Adam's first great Oxford friendship, that with A. L. Rowse, was
running into more and more trouble. In a letter to his father written in
February of 1932 Adam said as follows: 'I only see Rowse very rarely as
he is teaching in London, but when we meet we understand each other
fairly well in spite of obstacles caused by earlier misunderstandings. He
has just published a book (*Politics and the Younger Generation*) which has
made a stir but it has not made the impact which he hoped it would.
Of course he is very disappointed that he lost his election.' The great
misunderstanding between them was Hegel, and greater ones were to
follow.

[5]A letter written in 1962 by Lord Russell to Mrs Bielenberg.

The news which reached Adam from home was very disturbing. The world economic crisis which began in 1929 was nowhere of more devastating effect than in Germany. The unemployment figures were now well over the six million mark, and these official statistics could be multiplied by three at least if the real figures of the German destitute were to be known. Desperation gave extremism its chance, and with fear of Communism and fear of a repetition of the horrors which accompanied the 1922 inflation, there was no question now of the Nazi party being a passing phase in German political life. Early in the year Adam's mother wrote to him from Imshausen: 'This man Hitler—nothing but Hitler's name in the train, in the shops, in the streets (I have been in Kassel for two days)—and although I have the feeling that there may be some merit in his movement, I also feel more and more revolted by the deification of the racial idea which is supposed to be the criterion for everything.' When Brüning's resignation was enforced by Hindenburg at the end of May 1932, his father wrote a grave letter to Adam in which he urged his son to fight against feelings of depression which he felt might be overtaking him. He said, 'Anyone who deeply cares for Germany and its people is likely to be deeply depressed by the present state of things.' In an earlier letter he had already warned Adam that civil war might break out in Germany and that he might have to earn his living in England, at least for some time.[6]

He had a dream of becoming a Fellow of All Souls College. It seemed to offer a temporary and perhaps even an ultimate solution of the troubles which now crowded on him as on many of his fellow-Germans. But to obtain a fellowship a promising (though not essential) first move would be to pass with first-class honours in the schools, and his chances of doing this were small. The Master of Balliol took a close and affectionate interest in his work but came to believe that he had not the kind of mind which achieves first-rate academic success. His reports to Rhodes House show how his opinion formed. 'We are very much pleased with him,' he wrote at the end of the Hilary term in the spring of 1932, 'He is an admirable scholar and is working well and is also an excellent member of the college.' At the end of the Trinity term in the summer he wrote: 'Very able, intelligent, charming fellow. Doing excellent work.' But at the end of the

[6]C.T.

Michaelmas term in December 1932 he wrote: 'Is enormously good up to a point then rather sticky. A very fine fellow.' And at the end of the Hilary term of the next year Lindsay wrote: 'A charming man. He won't do very well in Schools. His work is a bit vague but he is very interesting.'[7] His hope of being able to enter All Souls was an illusion.

From this year 1932, from what might almost be called his last year of complete mental freedom, three incidents, one slight, two important, may be recalled from Adam's life. At the beginning of this year he made one of his rare appearances at the Union and spoke for five minutes. He told his father that although he had been well received the report of the speech in one of the Oxford undergraduate papers amounted to no more than the following: 'Mr Adam von Trott zu Solz's name is so long that we have nothing else to say.' He seems to have taken this crude comical attack in good part.

In August, after attending the reading party in Cornwall, he went to Germany in order to meet the American friend who had meant so much to him in his early years of manhood, and was to continue to mean much in his life. It was a year now since they had met, and it would seem that the reunion was ecstatic but unhappy. Deep emotions such as they mutually felt could not exclude jealousies and suspicions. The circumstances of the relationship into which these two had so boldly entered made unhappiness inevitable, but the most important thing about the relationship is that Adam and his American friend remained passionately in love after this long delayed and distressing reunion. Compared to that the rest is trivial.

The importance of the third episode which may be now remembered of that year most certainly escaped notice at the time. From the end of December 1932 until the second week of January 1933 an Anglo-German Conference was held in Oxford, and Adam attended as one of the team of translators. Among the speakers at this meeting was Otto Gessler, the former Minister of Defence, an honoured figure among old-guard German Socialists, though somewhat suspect among others for his apparent subservience to the veiled authority of the German High Command in the days of von Seeckt. Gessler was the star turn, but from the point of view of Adam's life the most interesting thing about the conference was

[7]Rhodes House Papers.

his first meeting with a man of about his own age called Hans-Bernd von Haeften.

On a late afternoon, shortly after the beginning of the 1933 Hilary term, Adam was having tea in the Junior Common Room of his College, according to the Oxford custom. The date was the 30th of January. C. E. Collins recalls the occasion.

'When Adam read in an evening paper in the Junior Common Room at Balliol that Hitler had become Chancellor, he knew at once that a terrible disaster had befallen his country; that the prospects for his own future had undergone a fundamental change; that it was a future in which a bitter struggle would be needed to achieve even the smallest results; that many of his friends and acquaintances were at once in personal danger. A number of things he was sure of immediately: that overt opposition to the new regime would be useless for a long time to come; that nevertheless he must oppose it by all the means in his power; that a common ground must be found for as many opponents of the regime as possible, and that he himself would try to find that ground in a struggle for "liberal" rights; that, although it would certainly be at the cost of handicap to his own career, he would not join the Nazi party unless it became his clear duty to do so in furtherance of his anti-Nazi activity. All these things he expressed to me on the same night as he learned of Hitler's coming to power.

'The new turn of events made still stronger his sense of the unreality of Oxford and its pleasures. But he remained the same good company as before.'

Chapter 5

A NEW WORLD
AND RECEDING HOPE

From Balliol, soon after Hitler had become Chancellor, Adam wrote in pain to his father. The date was the 13th February, 1933.

'I must say that the news of the German situation (though scanty) disturbs me greatly: constant dismissals of political officials (often arbitrarily and suddenly), encouragement of provocative demonstrations, and worst of all the arming of the Storm Troops as election police!! Are we really at the beginning of German fascism, of the domination of the State by this party which, both by its programme and its ideas about class, excludes large sections of the population, a party which will have to resort to brutal suppression in order to hold on to power? I feel heavy at heart when I think of the way devoted loyalty to the State is being daily caricatured,[1] and that this is being done by people like the Nazis who owe their power only to abnormalities such as the economic crisis and the consequences of war, neither of which the previous regime can be blamed for. As for my own personal affairs, I only see ahead dimly, because I realise that for a long time to come I shall be forced into the rôle of the anvil. Although I believe that I am in agreement with you about most questions of responsible Government, I think nevertheless that I have different ideas about the positive rights of the individual and of men in the mass. Responsible Government is not even open to discussion unless it is first agreed that these rights are maintained as sacred, and for this neither Hitler nor Papen seem to offer the smallest guarantee.[2] The neglect

---

[1] The German runs literally: . . 'when I think of the daily wrong which is being done to the most serious and responsible attitude to the State.' The meaning may be more personal than in the translation above.
[2] In the first Nazi Administration the former Chancellor Franz von Papen was Vice-Chancellor.

of these rights must provoke a harsh reaction, and constructive forces will
be needed to canalise such justifiable outbreaks into ways which make for
lasting order. It is for this task that I will prepare myself, and in the meantime I shall not enter into any sort of alliance with this authoritarian
nationalism. To see how I can best serve the task, as a judge, or a civil
servant, or a University teacher, or a writer—for that we must wait until
my return, and, I am afraid, until even later, indeed until my education
is finished. To serve the rights of individuals, or of "human beings" as
students of natural law say: to do this, both in association and in conflict
with the outer order and with what is in opposition, is to me infinitely
more important than to give service to "The State" which has now surrendered itself to tyranny.'[3]

This is one of the most significant letters that Adam wrote at any time.
His purpose is set out here with a clarity and simplicity which did not
come easily to him, and with which he was not able to follow his purpose
in the tangle of events and differing attractions and inclinations which
lay ahead. The letter has one feature of remarkable interest, anticipated in
the preceding chapter. It dramatically shows how at this most fateful
moment, when he had to look into his heart and mind to search out his
honourable course, he did not find his guide in the philosopher of the
State. A year or two before he must have been at least tempted to seek
his answer in Hegel, but not now, and the clear answer which he gave
was such as could have come from no true Hegelian.

This is not the end of the story of Adam and Hegel by any means. The
fascination and influence were to persist and were to cause Adam to
suffer grievous misunderstanding through his Hegel-influenced intellectual attitudes towards what he first and instinctively recognised as
wickedness personified. Sometimes the influence of Hegel (to look further
into the future) was to lead him seriously astray, but never for long: whenever it led him anywhere near Nazism he turned away in horror, all the
more so because Nazism tried to establish a kinship with people of his
sort, and could in fact only falsify the traditions that were inalienably his
own. There was undoubtedly something of nationalism in Adam, but
it is vital to an understanding of his character to grasp and remember that
the nationalism to which he could be drawn was of that pre-Bismarckian

[3]Letters. C.T.

kind which, under Prussian leadership, had made German language, literature and culture a great and often beneficient influence in all Eastern Europe, the Baltic lands, and the Russian Empire. If it was assertive, this does not mean that the warlike traditions of Prussia (which could pervert it) had made it aggressive or bellicose in essence, or inimical to international concord. Like the French nationalism which was its first stimulus, it gave to its land of origin a valuable and enduring prestige. That was the heightened patriotic force which influenced Adam's mind, and when an element of nationalism in him is mentioned in this book, it is to such a kind, belonging to a former age, that reference is made. It survived vigorously in the North German aristocracy to which, for all his socialism, Adam firmly belonged. The state of mind to which he perennially returned, as to a centre of gravity, found expression in this letter written in the first days of Hitler's rule to the father whom he respected and loved.

His immediate concern, and that of the whole family, was for the safety of Werner. The latter was in Berlin at this time and he had till the last done nothing to appease the rising power, and much to aggravate it. He remained as indiscreet as ever. For doing far less than Werner had done, men and women had lost their lives or been rounded up and held in improvised prisons (the dread camps came later). But Werner, though he bated not a jot of his natural arrogance, was to lead a charmed life throughout the days of Hitler's rule. At the present juncture he was saved by the fact that he did not hold a Communist party membership card, and it is very probable that he also owed his safety to the loyalty of Communist friends. He needed this loyalty and all the help he could get when the Nazi Government for the first time went into full action against the Communists and other opponents. This occurred after the 27th February.

As soon as the Hilary term was over, in mid-March 1933, Adam went to Berlin to see his brother. He arrived ten days or so after the Reichstag elections which had been held on the 5th. These were the last elections in the Reich to be conducted with any freedom, and they were marked not only by unprecedented violence but an atmosphere of sudden and hysterical panic. Probably by a coincidence most fortunate for the Nazis, and possibly as the result of an ingenious Nazi plot, the Reichstag building had been destroyed by fire on the night of the 27th February, and a lunatic incendiary, Marinus van der Lubbe, a former Communist, had been found on the scene of the crime. This gave Hitler and his party their cue. On the 28th February Hindenburg was persuaded to sign a decree 'for the Protection of the People and the State' by which the most important civil rights were suspended, and the Government was empowered to carry out wholesale arrests. In the confusion of a panic-stricken moment Hitler was given personal power which might otherwise have taken him months of intrigue to amass. He was now dictator. But hope was not yet dead among those who rejected the new course. The Nazi party, in spite of their bullying and in spite of the Communist scare, did not do so very well in the election. They obtained 288 seats out of the total of 647 in the Reichstag, and could only form a majority by going into coalition with the National German People's Party led by the Minister of Economic and Financial Affairs, Alfred Hugenberg. The Social Democrats had lost only one seat. For eighteen days hope centred on this weakly but unexpectedly liberal Reichstag. On the 23rd March Hitler, thanks largely to his new powers, was able to sweep these hopes away. The pusillanimity of the non-Nazi parties, with the magnificent exception of the Social Democrats, allowed Hitler to push an enabling Act through the Reichstag. This had the effect of removing legislative power and the conduct of foreign affairs from the Reichstag to a Reich executive council which meant himself. After this the dictator did not have to bother any more about Parliamentary opposition.

Not long after Adam arrived in Berlin he wrote a letter in English to Shiela Grant-Duff. It is undated but it was evidently written before April, and appears to refer to the events of the 23rd of March.

'You are now in Cornwall I expect, enjoying sun, winds and spring colours, while I am moving in gloomy grey streets, libraries, and at best the somewhat barren surroundings of Berlin. However I have not really regretted to have come here to experience at close sight a first rate political crisis—or rather a transformation of human and social fates on the biggest scale. One will have to rub one's eyes before one will really see what has come about—and not only its being yet too early is a good reason for not writing too much about that . . . We are a simple and sometimes (it seems to me) almost imbecile race—all our talents are unsocial, and there are all our sins too, the worst of which being that, unable to run our public affairs properly, we leave them to most extraordinary forces and figures. This I agree is bad enough, but the mix-up that is the consequence of this fouling is no more due to the German "national character" but to a mixture of normality with those abnormal delegates [meaning the men in power]. It is like wanting to play marionettes and real theatre on the same stage.'[4]

There is here the suggestion of second thoughts which become clearer in another letter, also in English, written to Shiela on the 2nd April, 1933.

'No, it is not only abnormal delegacy, but a dangerous crowd that has got hold of things. Individual happenings are *not* the character of the whole thing—but the whole thing has put business on a move. The western capitalist states will make a lot more of the disorder here than is legitimate in view of the veiled brutality of any capitalist state. I am sure that fear of the setting in of a revolutionary transformation of even the economic side—is one of the sources of indignation and hostility. It is here that the friends of European and world development must be careful with their criticism. I wish I could put this across to G. R. [Goronwy Rees]—but I cannot do it in a "Conspiratorial" enough manner. I hope to Heaven (in spite of all the worlds of pure thought) that the right thing is on the move as well!'[5]

The second thoughts, which were now more lucid, were to remain with him. They followed a familiar pattern: no greater injustice could be committed than to equate the abominations of the Nazis with essential German character; revolutions must not be thoughtlessly condemned for their early excesses, for only by revolution can 'the right thing' come to be 'on the move as well'; the old regime (in this case capitalist democracy) against whose corruption the revolution was an inevitable protest, had thus only a limited right to judge. Adam was to press this argument on his English and later his American friends, but not on his own countrymen. With them he felt no patriotic inhibitions against siding with the opposition.

In the course of this stay in Berlin during the spring of 1933 he sought out his old friends of *Die Neuen Blätter für den Sozialismus*, and, as he must have expected, he found them in a melancholy state after the defeat of March. Many of them had friends among the victims of the recent arrests and atrocities, and many had suffered personal tragedies. Their professional prospects were bleak. A considerable part of the Left Wing

---

[4]Correspondence collected by Shiela Grant-Duff. Referred to later as G.D.
[5]G.D.

press, on which they counted to earn a living, had been banned as long ago as Von Papen's emergency decree of July 1932, and further suppressions had followed since January 1933. *Die Neuen Blätter* was one of very few survivors, and its chances of further survival under the cultural supervision of Josef Goebbels were slender indeed.

The chief people of the group which the paper represented were Alfred Loewen, the eminent political economist, Theodor Haubach, who at that time was a prominent Left-Wing journalist and also held the post of press officer to the Prussian police, the theologian Paul Tillich (shortly to leave Germany for the United States) and Carlo Mirendorff, one of the last representatives in the Reichstag of the Social Democrat Party. The moving spirit in *Die Neuen Blätter* was Peter Mayer, best known to-day as the leading authority on De Tocqueville, and in those days an object of special distrust to the Nazis as the editor and publisher, a short time before, of the early writings of Karl Marx. The ideal which united these men could be described as religious socialism, somewhat similar in character to modern humanist Marxism. They were in reaction against what they held to be the excessive materialism of the Social Democrats, and were thus in the most bitter conflict with the fraudulent spirituality of the Nazis.

Adam in his Berlin days before Oxford had known the juniors of this group and now met some of the leaders. He became friends with Peter Mayer and for several years they remained on terms of affection until this friendship, like some others, came to grief. They had a great interest in common, for at this time *Die Neuen Blätter* was translating A. L. Rowse's book *Politics and the Younger Generation* and bringing it out in instalments.[6]

Adam and Peter Mayer had many long discussions together, sometimes alone and sometimes with other members of the group. Most of these took place in Mayer's flat which was situated in one of the working-class districts of North Berlin where model housing estates had grown up in the post-war years. There Adam learned something about the group's political belief and programme regarding the new situation facing Germany. The belief was simple and valid: that a Nazi-controlled Germany could have no final result other than a second world war, for which reason

[6] *All Souls and Appeasement.*

their immediate object must be to bring about the downfall of the Nazi
Government. In contrast to this clear objective, their programme did
not as yet show the same grasp of what was facing them.

Hitler's ignoble appearance and the nonsensical incoherence of many
of his public statements still hid from the unconverted his astounding
ability. This fact allowed these liberal and socialist enemies of the Nazi
regime to continue to think in terms of opposition by political manoeuvre
long after Hitler's complete political triumph of the 23rd March. They
knew that opposition by parliamentary means was now impossible, but
with their underestimate of Hitler, they inevitably underestimated the
remarkable skill with which he could turn to his advantage the senility
of President Hindenburg, 'that feeble-minded old bull' as Hitler aptly
described him about this time. Adam's friends still believed that the broken
old Field Marshal was capable of presiding over a beneficial palace revolution and they hoped for one that would displace Hitler and his Nazi colleagues in favour of the former chancellor General Kurt von Schleicher.
They gave their energies to devising elaborate combinations through
sympathisers in other political parties, in the army, and in the Trades
Unions, with this will-o'-the-wisp purpose of a Schleicher restoration.
The whole proposition has a strange air of unreality to-day, but it must
never be forgotten that while these men appreciated from the very beginning the danger of Hitler, his greatness in evil was hard to recognise
in any fullness. He seemed rather the outward symbol and instrument, or
in Adam's revealing phrase, the 'delegate' of a vast terrifying impersonal
force, rather than an architect of that force, as in reality he was. As intellectuals, some of them Marxist, Peter Mayer and the rest of this group
tended to underestimate the rôle of individuals in history. Many people
then, both inside and outside Germany, looked on Hitler as no more than
a fatuous imitation of Mussolini.

The men of *Die Neuen Blätter* were agreed that an international understanding about Nazism must be sought among European socialists. They
looked to Adam to help them with his wide acquaintance outside Germany. He had an immediate proposal and he urged that Mayer should
come over to England in the summer to meet the English socialist G. D.
H. Cole who was at that moment organising a small-scale international
conference. Mayer agreed and did travel to England later to attend the
meeting.

He and his new friend spent much time comparing their political ideas. Mayer found that Adam's were much more conservative than his own, as was to be expected, but he found also that though they erred, in his opinion, on the side of romanticism, they were refreshingly free from the prejudices of rigid political theory, the bane of Left-Wing thinking. Rather to his surprise he found that the influence of Hegel was not at this moment strongly noticeable, and he had the impression that his interest in the subject was cooling in favour of a new intellectual preoccupation, with Hegel's far more attractive contemporary Heinrich von Kleist. The friendship between the two young men flourished.

From the foregoing it will be seen that, not without serious personal risk, Adam was with the opposition from the very beginning. But he was such an unorthodox member of a Left-Wing Society that from the very beginning he caused anxiety and, among people who knew him little, incurred some degree of suspicion. He was ill-suited then to the life of secrecy and subterfuge. He was too extrovert, too social, too prone genuinely to make friends with many different sorts of people, including Nazis. He was free by nature and could not be otherwise. He ignored warnings that he was being watched, treating the dangers surrounding him with arrogant contempt, as though to say 'let them dare touch a von Trott!' In vain Mayer urged him to be discreet. He was incapable of that dull virtue. Among some Leftist associates, (and class-feeling may have played a part), he got something of a bad name.[7] News of this reached him in May as appears from a letter which he wrote to Diana Hubback.

'I have had a severe warning as to gossip about me in Socialist circles in—Zurich! Isn't it awful? But I am edified of what I hear of people's pluck and readiness to sacrifice. There will be a long, long way.'[8]

An editorial note may be put in here without pedantry. The first two sentences in the above quotation are obviously ironic. Socialist circles in Berlin or Munich were one thing, but German socialist circles in— Zurich! These were something very different, and they could mind their own business. With this understood, the rest of the letter becomes meaningful. Adam, following his principles and his temperament, sometimes

---

[7] This account of the *Neuen Blätter* group and Trott's relations with it follows one given by Mr J. P. Mayer to the writer.
[8] D.H.

tended to judge German refugees too harshly. He had a continual belief that it was better for a German to remain in his own country, even under the Third Reich, and temperamentally he was aggrieved at the way expatriates led the anti-German propaganda abroad. He was not narrow in this matter. He knew that many Germans had no alternative, and he would never have criticised the flight of a German Jew. But his general disposition was against flight, in which, however, he was soon to show himself most pardonably inconsistent.

Before he went back to Oxford for his last term his American friend left Europe and was not to return in Adam's lifetime. Not long before this, in October 1932, Adam had described his relationship to this friend as one 'on which, since I have known her, my emotional life has almost entirely been centred.'[9] She had been in Berlin on the fatal 30th of January and after, and had seen the atrocities of the opening Nazi phase. With exemplary courage, and fortified by her American passport, she had stood up for her liberal faith. When the one-day boycott was declared throughout Germany on Jewish stores, she boldly pushed her way past the loutish Storm Trooper guards outside one shop, made a purchase within, and, on returning to the street addressed the sheepish crowd and asked them why they obeyed such orders and what they had against the proprietors, to which sheepish silence was the answer.[10] She and Adam had always enjoyed agreement on political principles, and events such as this, and there were several, drew her yet closer to him. All the more agonising was their parting. It was as deeply painful as could be imagined, and not in any way less because there was the memory of differences. They both knew that it was unlikely that either would see the other again.[11]

He returned to England. Before the beginning of the term he went to Cornwall for a few days to stay with the Hubback family. Diana was somewhat shocked at his appearance which gave signs of his having been through a bitter ordeal. He had parted from this friend who had become a great part of his life, and he had seen for himself the degradation of his country.

He returned to Oxford and his last term, and there, throughout those two months, he found himself tempted again towards that very expatriation which he sometimes unfairly condemned in others. He was still taken

[9]D.H. [10]A personal account. [11]D.H.

with the idea of trying for an All Souls fellowship, although his college and some friends among the dons must have made it clear to him that his chances of success were slight. Lindsay's opinion that 'he won't do very well in Schools' would not have been kept from him, but he persisted in his hope. It is fairly clear that, as men do in times of dire stress, he was indulging in wishful thinking; for, quite apart from the fact that he was unlikely to gain an All Souls fellowship, the notion of this intensely German man living permanently outside Germany was unreal. He belonged to Germany and could not be otherwise. (At no point must one forget the influence of Werner.) Nevertheless, for all his sarcasms about Zurich, the temptation towards emigration was there. However Adam did not lose his sense of the practical. Aware that his bid for All Souls might fail, he proposed as well a less ambitious and more temporary return to Oxford. On the 22nd May, 1933, he wrote as follows to the Warden of Rhodes House:

'I shall have finished at the end of this year a two-year course of Philosophy, Politics and Economics. After taking this degree and in continuation of my legal career at home, I have to undergo three years preparatory practice at the courts. I should then very much like to return to Oxford for a year to write a thesis . . . preferably on some aspect of the *Political Doctrines of Modern Europe*.

'I took a doctorate on Hegel's philosophy of State before leaving Germany and during my time here naturally interested myself mostly in the traditions and doctrines which underlie English politics.'[12]

This proposal was referred to the Secretary of the Rhodes Trust, Lord Lothian, and agreed. The decision was to have an interesting and important effect on Adam's life four years later.

He occupied the summer term as all men do who face the Schools at its end, with hard work, although as usual he continued to lead a full social life with his wide circle of friends. As before he delighted in Oxford and in English life, but more often than in the previous terms, this delight would be interrupted by moods of impatience and irritation. Some of his undergraduate contemporaries, Philip Hope-Wallace among others,

[12]Rhodes House Archives. The letter may suggest that Trott obtained his doctorate before first coming to Oxford, but 'before leaving Germany' evidently refers to the summer vacation of 1932.

noticed how apt he became at this time to imagine slights, and to see an
'international incident' where none conceivably existed. The reason was
not far to seek.

In a letter to Diana Hubback, written shortly before his return from
Germany, he said as follows: 'What personally I fear most in the world is
that the development of things here—painful enough in itself—will es-
trange my few friends in your country to an extent harmful to relations
which are still very dear to me. I know this will not be the case with you
but there are very very few that I can likewise be sure of.'[13]

If his fears were often exaggerated, as such fears on the part of sensitive
people usually are, they were not wholly unjustified. In England there
was at first a good deal of sympathy with the Nazis arising out of an uncritical sense that the Germans had been hardly used in the post-war years
and were now setting about their difficulties in manly fashion. This goodwill was rapidly dissipated by disgust at Nazi atrocity, especially the persecution of the Jews, and there was a reaction, as uncritical and uninformed
as the earlier sympathy, which gave rise to a furious British hatred of all
things German. As usual fanaticism had begotten its like. Adam could
not but be aware of this latent hostility, and he remained determined,
as he had told his father he would, never to forget 'our special position.'

The new climate of feeling and opinion inevitably came to wreak further havoc on his already much endangered friendship with A. L. Rowse.
All the latter's feeling against Germany was aroused by the Nazi triumph,
and when Adam defended his country in such terms, it may be supposed,
as he had used in his letters to Shiela, Rowse was apt to suspect sympathy
with Hitler and the new tyranny. The friendship took on more and more
the character of Anglo-German conflict and misunderstanding. On one
occasion Rowse angrily asked Adam why the Germans were so prone to
strident self-assertion, to aggressive emotionalism; why they could never
be content to live in peace like other civilised people; why they preferred
to live in the poisonous atmosphere of *Sturm und Drang*. And Adam, with
perfect honesty and rare insight, replied as follows: 'Because unless we
live in that way, we feel that we are nothing.' Rowse was immensely
shocked. He had been angered by Adam's defence of the German charac-

[13]D.H.

ter; he was now equally exasperated by this candid self-criticism. The friendship was close to dissolution.[14]

One of Adam's passing moods of exasperation led to an absurd scandal which should be remembered, though not too solemnly. Among undergraduates whom he knew was Anthony Rumbold, the son of the British Ambassador in Berlin, Sir Horace Rumbold. On 29th June, 1933, the Prince of Wales came on an official visit to Oxford. One of the functions was to be held in Worcester College, and it was arranged that the Prince should leave the college in procession by way of Beaumont Street. Here Anthony Rumbold had 'digs' on the first floor of a house, thus giving him an admirable view of the occasion. He gathered a number of friends, including Adam, to share it with him. Great was the astonishment of the party when, at the moment of climax as the Prince passed the house, Adam saluted him with a wolf-whistle. His action caused much offence in the room in Beaumont Street, and not any less when Adam defended his behaviour by saying that since he was not a royalist he refused to join in acts of homage which he disapproved. The friendship with Rumbold ceased. It was a silly episode, a prank such as many men live to regret (and forgive in others) in after years, but it is worth recalling as an illustration of the occasional extremity of those angry moods which afflicted him at this time.[15]

It would be very much of a mistake, however, to regard moods of aggressive impatience as typical of Adam's Oxford life in these days. His last term was not a 'Dark Period,' indeed very much the reverse according to his friend Richard Crossman who recalls it as more of a last fling of heedless youthful enjoyment before he needed to face in all their grimness the decisions of his manhood.

Another friend, Moira Lynd, a daughter of the essayist Robert Lynd, has memories which tell the same story: 'I would often be on the roof of the little tower of the Warden's Lodgings New College (where I lived) pretending to work, and Adam would sometimes be on the roof of the Barn, the immense mediaeval building at the end of which Dick Crossman lived. Adam would wave and call "Shall we go on the river"? and we would walk across New College playing fields to where I had a little green canoe. On those pleasant afternoons on the river we would seldom

[14]A. L. Rowse. Discussion.   [15]Sir Anthony Rumbold. Discussion.

talk about philosophy (I found his ideas impossible to understand) or politics, although we were both interested in politics, but would talk frivo-
lously or not at all and just enjoy the buttercups and the sunlight. There
was one particularly good day when the canoe moved away from the
shore as we were embarking. We both fell in the water and laughed all
the way home.'

The term drew to an end. Lindsay sent a last report on Adam to Rhodes
House. 'Charming and able fellow,' he wrote. 'His range is rather narrow.
I doubt his getting a first but he ought to go far.'

A day or two later Adam went to the Schools wearing his cap and
gown, a dark suit and a white tie, according to the ancient laws. (He sat
immediately in front of Anthony Rumbold.) The ordeal lasted five days.
He left Oxford when it was over but was back on the 7th July when he
was moved to write a letter to his father. 'I returned here yesterday. Most
of the undergraduates have gone down, and Oxford is of an almost
miraculous beauty in its summer stillness. It has given me more than perhaps I shall ever be able to tell. Europe's noblest traditions live on here,
hardly noticeably, unconsciously, kept alive by a race which is simple and
genuinely political But about that let us speak more later.'[16]

That year a ball was held at Balliol after the end of the term in a mar-
quee set up in the main quadrangle: a Commem. Adam went to it with
Diana Hubback and they danced together till morning. He was to make
one more appearance as an undergraduate Rhodes scholar in Oxford, being
due to appear at the schools on the 25th July for a *viva voce* examination.

Before this there occurred an interlude which can remind one of the
adventures of Disraeli and the Young England party. After leaving Oxford
he spent a few days in London with the Hubback family, and then he and
his friend David Astor started on a tour of the Midlands to see working-
class life for themselves in the great industrial centres. They went to
Rugby, Birmingham and Manchester, intending to go on to Newcastle
and then Glasgow, but Adam fell ill in Manchester and the rest of this
research trip into the life of the two nations of Britain was called off, but
not the holiday jaunt with which it was to end. When Adam was well
enough to travel again, the two friends went to the Astor property on
the island of Jura in the Inner Hebrides for a few days' sport. On the 22nd

[16]Letters. C.T.

July Adam was back in Glasgow where he wrote an account of his adventures to Shiela Grant-Duff. He was about to leave England for good,
and Oxford the enchantress beckoned to him. The style of the letter is
occasionally confused, but the conflicting impulses of his mind are clear:

'I have been walking through the crowded streets of this place in search
of somewhere quiet to write to you as I long intended to do. People's
expression is so different here from London—and much pleasanter on the
whole. They look much more shabby, more worn, and harder—but at
the same time human, friendly and very much alive.

'I have come back just an hour ago from Jura which is a lovely island
where I staid four days—two at the East and two on the Atlantic coast. I
like your Scotland though at first its woodlessness and uninhabitedness
made me feel a little lost. I walked hours and hours seeing nothing but
bare hills, stags, and seagulls of most varied types.

'I was so sorry, Shiela, to see so little of you in London—though the
one time I saw you was as good a success as might have been expected
from a charity dance. Will I perhaps see you in Germany—Don't waste
your opportunity of going there on a casual week-end! I think a great deal
about the implication of my returning home this time—the balance of
possibilities lies with its being a final return. Lord Lothian, who is or
was a Fellow of All Souls, and especially concerned with Rhodes Scholars,
has told somebody I know that my chances of getting in are nil and
Lionel Curtis (do you know the man?) has said something to the same
effect. I don't take this as ultimate, but I think I must acknowledge it as
the prevailing bias. I don't want the argument of pity to be used in my
favour. I would take the f'ship mainly because of then not having to be
humiliated by the Hitlerites—but I would not exchange this exemption
for another humiliation. It is humiliating to be an emigrant—and this I
think I least want to be. I think you know and understand.

'I passed the statue of the Duke of Wellington just now—you know he
had a very strong and impressive head, but he was hard to brutality; it
is that one must be, I felt, to be a politician.

'In contrast to that I have a sensation of not belonging to that world of
happenings which rules and upsets my chances—and almost cynical realisation of homelessness which is most unnerving and which I must get
out of. To read on the brick walls of a Glasgow slum "Fight or Starve!"—
or reading of the split amongst the French Socialists—or a pamphlet on

Fascist activities in Germany, seem nothing but confirmation of something.
—And together with all that fragments of personal relations and endeavours conveying a clear feeling of my unimportance—like a glass con-
tainer which hinders no insight into the crude and mixed facts. Some
people think a great deal of reducing themselves to this state—I think
Keats must have meant something very similar when talking of "negative
capability"—and maybe when no selfish ambition hinders your assimi-
lation of experience one may really put forward truth.

'I hope a great deal from a period of rest and it looks as if I will have it in
August.'[17]

The penultimate paragraph quoted from this letter is obscure even by
Adam's standards, but it is probably the key passage to the whole, and the
involutions of the style seem to indicate that at this point in writing the
letter he felt that he must search his heart anew and make the resolution
of his life, and that he found this extremely difficult. His meaning appears
to be that in contrast to his recognition (excited by looking at a statue of
the Iron Duke!) that one must be 'hard to brutality' in the career he wished
for himself, he had a feeling of total (and culpable) alienation from Germany, and with this an unreal detachment from all the important issues
of the day, not only in Germany but everywhere. His friendships serve
only to expose himself cruelly to himself. He is oppressed by a feeling
of his own unimportance, and takes comfort, though not readily, in
the fact that such self-disillusion leads to the recognition of truth. Such
seems to have been his governing thought. It was clearly related to his
ceaseless inward debate on whether or not he must return to a Germany
desecrated and corrupted by the Third Reich. This debate persisted for
years, and in fact was not finally resolved till as late as 1940. Yet in view
of his strong conviction against emigration (except when absolutely unavoidable), it is no rash guess to say that he knew his answer from the
first, nor is it irreverent presumption to say that like all men who must
face, however perfectly or imperfectly, a heroic decision, he prayed that
the cup might pass from him.

On the 25th July he faced his *viva voce* at Oxford, once again clad in a
dark suit and a white tie with cap and gown. In the meantime he had
written to the leader of the Labour Party, George Lansbury, asking him

[17]G.D.

his opinion as to whether he should return to Nazi Germany or not. He had met Lansbury some time before, probably at the conference arranged by Cole, and had had a long and friendly conversation with him. Lansbury's reply was typical of this lovable and woolly-minded pacifist statesman: Adam's question, he wrote, was one which every generation had to resolve for itself, for every generation must face a moral struggle as to its duties regarding the demands of law and conscience.[18]

Soon after the 25th he heard the results of his final examination. He was awarded a second class degree in Modern Greats. When the news came he was stunned with disappointment. Why that should have been so is a matter for puzzlement, because an Oxford second, especially when gained by a man to whom English is a foreign language, can be rated as a very honourable and indeed remarkable academic achievement. If he had obtained a third or a pass degree then he might with reason have felt some humiliation, but a second was a matter for pride. Nevertheless his distress was great, and he spoke with such bitterness about this failure, as he regarded it, that he was to cause some completely false impressions. Some of his German friends got the idea that he considered he had been unfairly treated. Other friends were left with an equally fallacious impression that he had been promised an opportunity to try for All Souls if he got a first, and thus great hopes were cruelly dashed.[19] For long after he referred to the episode with bitterness. What is the explanation?

It is to be noted that he had not obtained a first class degree (a doctorate is a different matter) in his own country, and it is therefore not surprising that he did not do so in England. Lindsay's shrewd and affectionate reports left no doubt that he was not the kind of student to do so. He was not a 'natural examinee.'

Apart from the inevitable blow to his pride—and he was not wanting in pride—some of the explanation of his bitterness may be found in self-misunderstanding. Though Adam was very much an intellectual, he was not an academic intellectual, as the term is commonly understood. But

[18]C.T. The original has been lost. Dr Clarita von Trott thus recollects the contents: 'In seinem Brief sagt (Lansbury), Adams Fragen seien die, die jede Generation wieder lösen muss, wie jede darum zu kämpfen habe, dass sie der Stimme des Rechtes und Gewissens folge.'
[19]J. P. Mayer. Discussion.

his intellectual agility, and his strong bias towards intellectual pursuits may have misled him here and deceived him into believing that his vocation could lie, if he chose, in the academic world. But, as his letters show, he lacked the exactness of mind which is essential for success in an academic career. The failure to get a first class degree may have brought this home to him with painful force.

Humphrey Sumner wrote him a letter of tactful condolence. 'I always felt', he said, 'that you were really too mature to do these hour-written papers up to your real standard. What would have suited you would have been a thesis and a very long oral examination.'[20]

He went to London for a few days. His American cousin Mrs de Candole and her husband were staying in one of the numerous hotels which they patronised. He spent much time with Diana Hubback who had been with him when the news of his degree came to him, after which they had gone for a melancholy evening walk in Hyde Park while she tried to raise his spirits. 'I spoke to him', she recalls in her memoir, 'of all he had gained at Oxford and the love and respect of his friends there, which I considered would be more important than any examination result in his future life.'

He returned to Oxford to pack up for the last time, and before setting out for Germany he sent a letter to Diana in which he said: 'I am viewing this return as perhaps the greatest venture in my whole life, and though I know it will be half as externally dramatic as people suggest, I am diffident as to the ultimate success.'[21]

He went first to Hamburg where he stayed with the well-known Jewish banking family, the Warburgs. He knew them through their daughter Ingrid Warburg with whom also he had made friends at Oxford. From there he went to Berlin where he found another Oxford friend, Goronwy Rees. He was the same age as Adam and had become a Fellow of All Souls in 1931. This meeting was a fortunate chance as Rees was exactly the sort of companion he needed at that moment when he was going through a period of anxiety and unhappiness. They understood each other well and enjoyed a special relationship together. With most others of his acquaintance, men and women, Adam had essentially serious friendships, but that with Goronwy Rees was essentially frivolous. They loved to

[20]C.T.   [21]D.H.

make fun of each other, to ridicule each other's ideas and even appearance, and Adam, sometimes prone to be over-sensitive, never took the smallest offence but on the contrary a great deal of pleasure at the sometimes merciless teasing of this friend. With him Adam could now enjoy one of the great anodynes, shared laughter.[22]

At length he returned home to rest and, as Diana Hubback wrote many years later, 'to draw upon the physical and spiritual resources of Imshausen which were always to mean much to him.'[23] He needed them now as never before.

[22]Goronwy Rees. Discussion. [23]D.H.

Chapter 6

A YEAR OF TRIAL AND DISTRUST

In the summer of 1933 Adam returned to the life which he had left for Oxford two years before. He would now continue as a Referendar, completing the three years' apprenticeship required to enable him to take the law examination for assessorship, after which he could enter State service with assessorial rank. In Adam's case this final examination would fall due in the summer of 1936. Before taking up his work anew he was owed a month's vacation, and this he spent at Imshausen with his family and the Solz cousins, and among the woods he loved, now in their last summery splendour. He had two visits from Oxford friends, from Humphrey Sumner on his way to a conference in Warsaw, and the first of many visits to Imshausen by Diana Hubback.[1] It was a happy time. Immediately after it Adam had his first close experience of Nazi life.

This was not as a lawyer but as an inmate of one of the new Nazi institutions known as Wehrsportslager, or 'defence sports camps,' places where training for sports and athletics was combined with military education, and of course instruction in the new national philosophy. On the whole these places, superficially at all events, were among the reputable features of Nazi rule. They varied. Some of them were hateful but most of them were not unlike Boy Scout rallies anywhere in the world, though adapted to people of more mature years. In September Adam went to the camp at Marburg in his native Hesse. He went voluntarily for two reasons: for the sake of his career he wished to make some honourable concession to the party in power, and secondly he still persisted in a vain hope, which he could not bear to relinquish, that for all the crudity of

[1]C.T. and D.H.

the surface, the national revival in Germany under the Nazis was basically beneficent and patriotic, worthy to compel German loyalty.[2] He persisted in that hope for many years, sometimes to the point of self-delusion. Yet, in keeping with the many-sidedness of his character, this hope, stemming clearly from his deep-seated patriotism, never prevented him working courageously, and sometimes recklessly, for the liberal belief which was also deep in him and whose values he treasured instinctively. Though there was plenty of complication in the way events fell out, the story of the next three years in Adam's life has an essentially simple theme: he wanted and tried to compound honourably with Nazism, and he found that he could not.

The great majority of his fellow campers at Marburg were much younger than he, far less educated, simple folk who swallowed eagerly the mess of half truths and bogus science with which Alfred Rosenberg ministered to the intellectual needs of young Nazi Germany. Adam seems to have found the experience of Marburg less atrocious than grotesque. There is a photograph of him standing in a large group. He alone is hatless and carries no Nazi badge. He towers over his young companions. He looks intensely embarrassed. His main grief in 'this barbarous camp,' as he described the Wehrsportslager in a letter to Diana, seems to have been extreme boredom. In one letter to Diana he wrote: 'I am certainly not joining the children [their codeword for the Nazis]. I shall never be considered one of them by the children. Nothing could be more clear and distinct. I am very alone, but not desperately so. It has been important for me to discover that children and grown-ups belong to different worlds.'[3]

The ordeal was over in October 1933 and he went to his first postOxford 'Referendarstation'. This was at the district court of Rotenburg, a little Hessian town on the River Fulda, about nine miles or so from Imshausen. Here he stayed for a short time, till the end of January of the new year, and bent his energy to getting back into the routine of his profession. He was allotted a task which, in English terms, was similar to that of clerk of the court. He and the judge were the only court members who were not also members of the Nazi party, and as a result his advice was often sought unofficially by people in trouble with the new regime.

[2]C.T. and D.H.   [3]D.H.

One case, of which he left some record in a letter to Diana, is probably typical of many others:

'I am advising peasants or their wives, and struggle with their obstinate ignorance of the legal implications of what they have done, do, or will do. The other day a certain tradesman from Bebra described his extreme difficulties, and started to cry—he was a big man with a big moustache, had been in the war etc., but now suffers a lot—I had to try to work with him on behalf of his creditors. It is already four weeks that I am following his fortunes through the papers we accumulate on his affairs—I had tried to put things off, but probably his ruin can't be helped. I felt very much ashamed of being asked for advice and protection by someone so very much my superior in the actual struggle of making a living, and in age and suffering. I think he saw that, and it comforted him—moreover he saw that I wasn't one of his childish [Nazi] enemies—a fact which is very much appreciated by the other members of his community already. All this makes me sick and fed up with the utter ineffectiveness and negligibility of one's reactions. I wonder if I shall ever live in a friendly world and with friends again.'[4]

In this small-town life, whose monotony was often relieved by visits to Imshausen in a rickety little car, by writing letters, and by reading a trio of books, *War and Peace*, *Anna Karenina* and *Jane Eyre*,[5] he sometimes heard siren voices from Oxford. For example in late October he had a letter from All Souls, prompted by the tragic news of one of Adam's Oxford friends, Charles Henderson, who had died soon after his marriage at which Adam had been an usher. It was from Isaiah Berlin.

'As I write the usual All Souls scene is going on. By the fire X and Y are discussing the prospects of politics in Germany. I am unable to listen. X is again saying the same things. This conversation rotates in ever-re-current cycles, 3 or 4 are over, the 5th is beginning.' He went on to say that the examiners for election to the college had not regarded the 1933 field as exceptionally strong, and that if Adam had been a candidate he would have stood a reasonable chance of success. He ended the letter: 'Do write to me. I require every sort of support from spiritually vigorous people.'[6]

[4]D.H.   [5]D.H. and C.T.
[6]Letters collected by Mrs Christabel Bielenberg. Referred to later as Letters C.B.

The thought that he might have got an All Souls fellowship after all, may have awakened regrets for Oxford again. But if so he did not listen to the siren voice for more than a moment. As he had done when he volunteered for the Wehrsportslager, he once more sought for something more in Nazism than its tyranny and chauvinism. In a wishful-thinking spirit he studied the life of his country as it was reflected in the affairs of this little town and its countryside. When he referred to Oxford in his letters to Diana and Shiela Grant-Duff he usually did so as to a remote experience. On the other hand his references to Germany often constitute an apologia prompted by optimism struggling against anxiety. As early as August 1933, before he went to Rotenburg, he wrote to Shiela as follows:

'I have not found my feet yet, quite. While the general look of things was more depressing in the big towns (Hamburg, Berlin), there are the most encouraging features in the countryside. I think you would even find your sinister Thuringians woken up to a better form of life and awareness.'

In November he wrote this in a letter to her from Rotenburg.

'You see the great change appears in a somewhat gratifying if theatrical cloak in this old residence of some petty prince of Hesse . . . There is a large core of the most loyal, decent, and idealistic following, and they are by far the majority in the rural districts. Naturally, 20th century conditions cannot be loyally handled with the peasants' world of concept without hypocrisy, and hypocrisy will eat a sinister and satanic rift into the moral unity of the whole. The situation then arising will be the life and death of this country. The alternatives are too tremendous to sustain a cynical judgment on the present changes. They will initiate quite clearly the last great European decision. The western countries may find that in taking a positive or negative attitude they will involve their own existence.

'Did you really get a taste of what this country is really like when you were here those few times? Of this quite extraordinary potential power if only it finds its way to ordered creativeness? This extraordinary simplicity behind a screen of big words, and the hard wide beauty of its most typical landscape? Nature is hard and somewhat ungenerous here, and it has made men poor and fierce at places, but extremely open to friendliness and persuasion . . . They are the only people in Europe I know which

cannot yet be simply identified with their social and political pattern—
however much doing so feeds the pens of unkind observers . . .'[7]

He was to write other letters with the salient characteristics of this one:
recognition of a fateful situation, longing optimism nevertheless and a
determination to see the best, flashes of prophetic insight, resentment of
foreign criticism of Germany, especially from England.

Had he written to Shiela a month later the optimism might have been
less in evidence. In December 1933 he was given a further insight into
what living under Nazi rule meant in day-to-day terms. As the only
junior member of the district court of Rotenburg who was not a Nazi,
his situation was seen to be anomalous, and pressure was brought to bear
on him, evidently in a very unpleasant way, to apply for party membership or at least to join some Nazi organisation considered suitable for
members of the legal profession. 'I am in a terrible impasse', he wrote to
Diana, 'and I hope things will be clarified in the next few weeks.' They
were. On leaving Oxford he had been elected to membership of the
Rhodes Scholarship Selection Committee in Berlin and he was able to
argue plausibly that party membership would diminish his usefulness in
this post with reference to the Oxford authorities. He won his point, and
then his optimism, so inherent a part of his life-loving character, immediately reasserted itself. 'I have indicated in my last letters,' he wrote to
Diana, 'that pressure has set in from a certain direction. It is inevitable
and it was foolish of me to lose my nerve about it even for a moment. It
neither frightened nor even worries me really . . .'[8] His optimism remained with him.

At the end of the year he received notice that he was to be moved from
his Rotenburg station, and he went at the end of January 1934 to his new
assignment. This was at Hanau. Adam wanted naturally enough to increase his opportunities and his sphere of activity in a large city, and he
considered that he had earned the right to do so, with his doctorate and
two University degrees. He consulted with his father who was impressed
by a recent pronouncement of Hitler to the effect that he preferred the
co-operation of candid critics, of those honestly outside the Nazi movement, to the servile ministrations of opportunists. With these generous
words in mind the old gentleman urged Adam to apply for a transfer to

[7]G.D.   [8]D.H.

Kassel. He did so, but his evasion of Nazi party membership told decisively against him. While others of his colleagues with less qualification were given promotion to larger and more interesting courts, Adam was condemned to remain in Hanau, mostly dealing with divorce litigation, till August 1934.[9] The next few months after January were to tax his optimism about the regime sorely, but not till that optimism had led him into making one of the worst mistakes of his whole life.

To judge great events it is sometimes misleading to be too near them. To witness catastrophe while living in a country going through an appalling crisis, or even in a capital in a state of turmoil, one usually has to go out and look hard for it, sometimes being rewarded with seeing nothing unusual at all. The Nazi revolution was, in its first stages, a striking example of how consoling everydayness can persist throughout days which were leading inexorably to what Adam had called 'the last great European decision.' Its real character was in fact easier to grasp by reading the sensational press outside Germany, or Jewish propaganda, than by visiting Germany. There it was easy to be deceived into complacency by noticing several things which were now going better: the sense of utter despair had often given place, especially among young people, to one of buoyant hope; the new regime (unlike other European Governments) gave every sign of fully redeeming its promise to solve the problem of unemployment. There was no blatantly obvious lack of reason for acquiescence. Who would wish to go back to the chaotic economy and the hideous poverty and the weak misrule which was all the country had obtained immediately before Hitler from a quarrelsome parliament incapable of efficiency through its fatuous disunity? And everydayness could make a man think twice even about those aspects of the regime which were most easily condemned. For those who feared war, the new Chancellor, in speech after ferocious speech, asserted his inalienable will for peace. On a humbler level, not everyone in a brown shirt was an incarnate fiend. One met Jews in Germany who seemed to be living a normal life. Since April 1933 there had been no further anti-Semitic legislation, and in the summer of the same year the Führer himself had allowed assurances on his behalf that the Jews would not be called upon to suffer further economic discrimination. So what was all the fuss about? But more important

[9]C.T.

than argument as an anodyne was the simple fact of everyday ordinariness itself.

Adam shared one weakness with the Nazis. He was sensitive to foreign newspaper criticism of Germany. Perspicacious in so many ways, he tended now and later to assume that the national press always formed the majority opinion of a country, and seemed unaware that most of the time it merely reflected it. Given this prejudice it is not surprising that he was roused to anger by two articles which appeared in the *Manchester Guardian* on the 22nd and 23rd of January, 1934. They were by a special correspondent and were entitled *A Survey of Ten Months Anti-Semitic Persecution by the Nazis*.

The two articles made special reference to Hesse, and the plight of its large Jewish population. They were written with ability and there is no reason to suppose that what they reported was in any way untrue or even exaggerated. But reading them, Adam remembered again now what he had described as 'unsere besondere lage'—our special position. One way in which he interpreted his duty towards that position is indicated by a revealing phrase in a letter to his father written in March 1931 when Hitler and the threat of Nazism were not in his thoughts. Referring to the weak state of the country he wrote: 'I feel horror at going abroad this year, and having to act the German "representative" there.' This was a role which he took on throughout life, especially when Germany was under attack, rightly or wrongly, and it was the high-intentioned cause of many of his difficulties.

The articles in the *Manchester Guardian* appeared at a time when Adam was in deep perplexity as to what was his honourable course. The question was the original and persistent one: how far one could honourably go as a patriot in collaboration with a regime of which one disapproved. At this moment he seems to have had a typically impetuous idea that one should go very far indeed, and, just about the time the two articles appeared, he had written to his brother Werner saying that he was thinking of joining the Storm Troops in order to obtain some humble task in Göring's Ministry. Werner emphatically disapproved. 'There is nothing I would consider more dangerous', he replied, in a letter of the 6th of February, adding that it would be morally indefensible to avoid the unwelcome pressure of the Nazis by seeking the advantage of a privileged position within the

Nazi party.[10] As Adam's chimerical plan was never referred to again in any surviving correspondence, it can be assumed that it was thereupon dismissed wholly. It was unfortunate, however, that the two articles, with their references to Hesse, should have appeared at this moment of flirtation. He was roused to such indignation that his judgment left him. Here was the eternally mischief-making British press up to its old tricks! He worked off some of his wrath in a letter to Diana in which he swiftly reviewed his own unhappy situation, implied that of Germany, and challenged the right of England to criticise.

'I shall end all claims', he wrote, 'to a practical political existence (for which I think I was made) . . . or I am ending an existence of uncompromising aloofness which is spiritually important to me, but which I am ready to sacrifice if the real chance of a political life is given to me. You cannot as an Englishwoman understand this, especially not the issue on the moral side, for it is based on something (so it seems to me) essentially different from the kind of indignation that is so lavishly displayed in England over anything that happens in this country.

'And I fundamentally disclaim the categories on which that English capacity of moral judgment is based. It is based on the untold and never fully articulated cruelty of social relationships, on the very inhumanity of a system that is at least being contested, though as yet not articulately, over here. This may sound all very social and vague to you. I will not try to force on you a way of thinking which I believe is naturally alien to you. But sometimes when you want to check my feelings on matters like these, one of these many words might furnish an explanation.'[11]

Since the latest outbreak of British criticism against Germany had been

---

[10]C.T.

[11]D.H. Though the letter is in English the second paragraph of this extract is obscure enough to warrant a 'free translation'. The meaning seems to be 'I am in essential disagreement with the ethical attitude which leads English people to suppose they have a right to pass judgment. I disagree with a moral argument which takes no note of the cruelty and inhumanity (possibly unintentional) of the social system which gives English people the powerful material position from which they speak. This social system is being challenged here though not as yet with clarity. I do not force an unwelcome opinion on you, but in it you will find an explanation of my own attitude and sentiments.'

on the subject of Nazi persecution of the Jews, Adam should have remembered that his correspondent was herself half-Jewish. But, a complete stranger to anti-Semitism himself, he took no thought of this, or of anything except the insult to Germany and Hesse, and in his indignation (spurred on perhaps by frustration) he unhappily did not stop at private letters, but wrote to the *Manchester Guardian*:

'Sir,

I have read the articles by your special correspondent in your issues of January 22nd and 23rd on the persecution of the Jews in Germany and other similar articles in earlier issues. Will you allow me to rectify this in some respects that may be within reach of my immediate personal experience?

'First, and foremost, the charge that partiality of German courts forms an instrument of anti-Semitic persecution. I served for several months on a small country court (Amtsgericht) in Hessen, one of the very parts of Germany mentioned by your correspondent's article as being notorious for persecution. This work at the law brought me in close contact with the business and social life of a small semi-rural district. There was a pretty strong element of Jewish tradesmen in the small Hessian towns, small shopkeepers, traders in cattle and corn and artisans. Although the general economic situation makes things difficult for everybody, it was also evident that some of them were not thriving owing to political reasons. A great number of them however, notably of the cattle and grain merchants, were doing the same business as before because of customary connections with the Hessian peasants. I have not once during four months heard, as I certainly would have done, working at the court, if it had happened at this time, of any case of active persecution of the kind overheard or of anything corresponding to it.

'In court there was most emphatically no distinction against Jews. I have been present at a great many cases which were brought up by or against Jews, and I can therefore assert this fact from personal observation. Attempts to influence the court by suggestions that the claimant was a Jew were checked with unhesitating firmness.

'There is a recent regulation by which the prosecution of a debtor by his creditors can be temporarily suspended if the debtor "owing to a general deterioration of economic circumstances, and without personal guilt" proves incapable of paying. Now, this regulation was equally applied to such Jewish businesses as had suffered general deterioration, and I have witnessed its being applied with extreme liberality to sustain the very shaky business of a Jewish shopkeeper. As to discrimination on the Bench itself—after leaving the first place I continued to work at a district court, and there found that my supervising judge was a Jew and in the first meeting of the Court that several of the pleading lawyers were of Jewish extraction.

'Hanau, being a bigger town, business life is naturally different. Formerly it was a famous centre of the manufacture and trade of jewellery, a large proportion of which again was being carried out by the Jews. Now it is quite clear that a deterioration of their economic position cannot possibly be attributed to local or national, but only foreign boycotting. Cases of the most appalling come-downs inflicted by the compulsory sale of stocks on a closed market to meet their obligations might easily be related as a striking example for this assumed "aid" of German Jewry from abroad.

'Again and again I have spoken to active Storm Troopers who feel themselves pledged to the race doctrine of their leaders, but would never consider themselves justified to execute it with methods of violence, and who turn with indignation from the suggestion of atrocities being committed in their presence. It is to this effect definitely that the content of their superior orders is directed. And the very observation of your correspondent that national socialists are to be found in concentration camps proves that those who do not obey these orders are finding punishments.'

As often happens when a man writes a letter to the press in a rage, so soon as the envelope was in the post-box and on its way, he had misgivings. He wrote to his mother: 'I have written a rather silly letter to the *Manchester Guardian* which I hope will not be published.'

It was published on the 21st of February, 1934, as from Baron Adam von Trott.[12] In a footnote the author of the two articles struck back at

[12]*Manchester Guardian* 21.2.34. By a curious convention originated by Kaiser Wilhelm II, families entitled to the prefix 'von' could legitimately describe themselves as Baron *outside* their home state.

Adam's defence mercilessly. 'The persecution of the Jews has been more ferocious in Hessen, particularly Oberhessen, than anywhere else in Germany. It has also been the most obvious there, in the sense that innumerable Jews were so beaten that they could only limp home or were picked up bleeding and unconscious, in the sense that whole families had to seek refuge in the forests or in other districts, in the sense that they had to be taken to Frankfurt for hospital treatment. These things are known to everyone in Hessen who has eyes to see and ears to hear. If Mr Adam von Trott is blind and deaf to them he will be at least equally blind and deaf to the less obvious legal victimisation of the Jews. As for the Nazis in concentration camps they are much more likely to have been sent there for persecuting the Jews too little than for persecuting them too much.'

On the 27th of February Adam wrote to his mother: 'Try to get the weekly edition of the *Manchester Guardian*. They have played me a nasty trick.' This did not refer to the crushing rejoinder of the special correspondent, nor to an unfortunate misprint in the first sentence of the fourth paragraph by which the word 'prosecution' was transformed into 'persecution'! He meant that a paragraph had been omitted, and without it his letter (so he told Diana) 'could be taken as a defence against an entirely untrue charge, which I never intended.' However, he was to have the chance to put the omission straight. After a rather long interval Adam's letter inevitably aroused a correspondence in which he had the right to join.

It would be tedious and is unnecessary to give all the details of this newspaper episode. Only significant ones need be recalled. The first is touching. The ensuing correspondence opened on the 5th of March with a letter from Adam's first Oxford friend. He wrote that his 'attention had been called' to the letter and the rejoinder. 'I hope', he continued, 'that it is not too late to assure you and your readers that Mr von Trott is by no means the blind and prejudiced reporter he [the special correspondent] imagines him to be. I knew Mr von Trott well when he was recently a Rhodes scholar at Balliol, and admired his sound judgment and scrupulous fairness and truthfulness. He is devoted to the task of bringing about a better understanding between his country and our own, and it is most unfortunate that his efforts should be discounted beforehand by the suggestion that he is an untrustworthy witness. Yours etc. W. B. Selbie.'

On the 7th March the *Manchester Guardian* published a letter from Mr Harrison Brown. Relying on German press reports alone, he effectively demolished Adam's contention that many Jewish tradesmen 'notably of the cattle and grain merchants, were doing the same business as before because of customary connections with the Hessian peasants.' On the 8th of March came Adam's second letter whose purpose was to make good the missing paragraph.

'Sir,

In his rejoinder to my letter on the charge of anti-Semitism at German courts, your correspondent might have denounced my facts as "untypical" or "unimportant." But since I claimed immediate personal experience as the only basis of my communication, it seems at least odd to insinuate that they are false.

'Surely he cannot make his case dependent on denying the very possibility of any honest, empirical judgment within this country, more than which I did not try to give.

'I cannot therefore consider myself refuted on the points presented by my letter, more especially concerning the complete impartiality of the courts at which I have been working. Yours etc. Adam von Trott. Hanau, Landgericht.'

Some of the subsequent items in the correspondence are interesting to-day as showing early appearances of the *genus* Appeaser. 'We do not like National Socialism,' wrote a citizen of Halifax, 'but we shall have to live with it. Why make it appear worse than it is by publishing only adverse reports, and by giving publicity to those who have every reason to be afraid of it?'

There was also an intervention by that beaming type of enormously unruffled reader who is a distinguishing feature of British journalism. There was a great deal, this specimen assured the readership, in everything that everyone had said. The last letter appeared on the 19th of March and was again from Mr Harrison Brown. It was polite and made acknowledgement of Adam's sincerity. 'So long, however,' the letter concluded, 'as the Minister of Propaganda uses every channel of publicity to foment feeling against racial and other minorities, and so long as official measures and general policy sanction this persecution, letters which show that there are still civilised Germans in Germany can scarcely pass as representative of the situation.' And there the correspondence in the *Manchester Guardian* ended, with a bad defeat for Adam.

This was not the end of the affair: it persisted in Oxford. The Universities have always been great places for rows and the 'Trott-row' which opened on the appearance of the letter continued into the summer. This is not surprising, for whereas many University rows are about nothing very much, this was about something important. Casualties were not wanting. From this time the friendship with A. L. Rowse ceased for several years,[13] and there was a breach with Isaiah Berlin. To go forward for a moment to the later part of the year, a vivid idea of what happened in Oxford emerges from a letter written by Isaiah Berlin to Adam just after the Trinity term, in July 1934. It was sent in answer to a letter (now lost) in which Adam had made peace overtures. Here are some extracts from the reply.

'Dear Adam, Forgive me for my very long silence. I was extremely moved by your letter, both by its contents and by the fact that you wrote it. I never intended to raise an issue between you and me—the M.G. incident led to a very small explosion on my part, I admit, both because I thought it in itself harmful, not in keeping with your character and beliefs, and more particularly because of the idiotic defences of you put up in a spirit of uncritical loyalty by all your other friends. This last must please you—had the rôles been reversed it would have pleased me enormously—but I, who felt that for once I was arguing with an almost disinterested passion, and had got away from personalities, felt irritation that all my arguments were taken only as evidences of personal treachery and not estimated *an sich*. You yourself are so much better aware of the pros and cons of such actions than your allies—if I were you I really should declare *non tali auxilo nec defensoribus istis*. I should very much like to see you ... [here follow details of summer plans] ... I should very very much like to—on every sort of ground, because I am attached to you, because I want to learn your views on a variety of subjects, because one ought to meet at regular intervals and give an account of the past and the future, because the thought of seeing you would excite me for some time to come. If there is the remotest possibility will you let me know? ... [Further details of summer plans] ... As for Oxford I should give almost

---

[13]*All Souls and Appeasement.*

anything to have you back there this coming term. The place is going to be a Mausoleum next year, the constants all there, the variables all gone.'

The letter is long and touches on many subjects. It ends as follows: 'I have not really adequately conveyed what I wished to convey: how unpleasant it was to prevent oneself from writing, with what relief your letter was received (I am sentimental and was very greatly moved), how much I want to see you, how unshaken and unchanged everything to the last tittle is at Oxford, how you ought to come and spend a week during a vacation, just at the beginning of one, in All Souls. Must go, but write, write.'[14]

The episode of the *Manchester Guardian* letter would never have happened if Adam's optimism about Germany had been less resilient, and it could not have been as resilient as it was if he had been informed about what was really happening in the highest councils of Germany. The dates of this *Manchester Guardian* correspondence could not be more ironical. On the 28th of February, 1934, exactly one week after the appearance of Adam's letter, the Führer called a meeting which was attended by Ernst Röhm with other Storm Troop and party leaders, the Minister of War, and leading senior officers of the German army. The occasion was among the most crucial in the early history of the Third Reich. Among the army leaders who attended was Major-General (later Field-Marshal) Maximilian von Weichs who kept a record (the only one surviving) of what was said. The purpose of the meeting was to define the areas of activity in which the Reichswehr and the Storm Troops should operate, and thus bring to an end the acrimonious dispute between them; but as was usually the case when Hitler took part in a debate, the original theme was not strictly adhered to. Here follows the account given in Weichs' memoir of Hitler's main speech.

'He began. "The German people is going to face frightful destitution." This opinion had been noisily contradicted by Hitler himself, for indeed we had always heard from him and from Goebbels that everything in the Third Reich would be so wonderful. This prophecy was not related to circumstances as they actually stood, but he based it on the following reasoning: the N.S.D.A.P. had overcome unemployment. These blossoms would only last for about eight years, however, as then an economic re-

[14]Letters C.B.

cession must ensue. This evil could be remedied only by creating living space for the surplus population. However the Western powers would not let us do this. Therefore, short decisive blows to the West and then to the East would be necessary. A militia, as Röhm suggested, would not be the least bit suitable for national defence. He sought to establish this by examples from military history. In the course of the exposition he came to his own experience. The hastily and superficially trained division, to which he belonged in 1914 as a private, had come to grief at Lange-marck with very heavy losses. Therefore he was resolved to raise a people's army, built upon the Reichswehr, rigorously trained and equip-ped with the most modern weapons. He also rejected a Fascist Militia on the Italian pattern. This new army would have to be ready for any defence purposes after five years, and after eight years must be suitable for attacking. The S.A. must confine itself to internal political tasks. One must be loyal in an internal political sense, while externally one could break one's word. In this connection he referred to Bismarck who once said that treaties only apply so long as they are of use to both partners. He would therefore demand of the S.A. that it submit to his instructions. For the transitional period until the establishment of the planned armed forces, he would consent to the suggestion of the War Minister to employ the S.A. for the task of frontier protection and pre-military training. Otherwise the Wehrmacht must be the only bearer of the arms of the nation.

'On reflection, one can say that Hitler had set forth his complete foreign policy programme and had already intimated the probability of aggressive war. Considering the great numbers of listeners, it is almost miraculous that this prophecy of 1934 has never become known. The only detail which did not correspond to later developments was the actual timing of the predicted entanglements of war.'[15]

---

[15]Quoted in Robert J. O'Neill's *The German Army and the Nazi Party 1933-1939* Cassell—London, 1966. The memoir of F. M. von Weichs was not known to his-torians before the publication of this remarkable book. The fact that such a declar-ation of policy remained unknown throughout Hitler's years of rule and for long after remains puzzling. It may be that his listeners, aware of Hitler's pathological insincerity, did not take the declaration as seriously as it deserved, and regarded it as no more than a forensic device to strengthen the case against the S.A. becom-ing the main military force of the Reich.

This was what was really going on in the Germany which Adam so typically and so generously, if thoughtlessly, defended. So much evil was not readily believed in or guessed at.

Adam's life in Germany during the first part of 1934 provided a remarkable contrast in character to his public appearance in the British press, and (by the very nature of things) none of his Oxford friends were in a position to appreciate this. If they had, the 'Trott-row' would have been rapidly stilled.

The conflict in his mind continued unabated; how could he reconcile his enmity towards the Nazi regime with his present circumstances in which he entertained ambitions of a successful career which would lead to high employment in the service of the State? In other words, where was the point of honour beyond which collaboration became indefensible? He had already jeopardised his career to some extent by his refusal to join the Nazi party, and on that account had been denied the sort of posting to which he rightly considered himself entitled. But now, in early March (while the *Manchester Guardian* correspondence was running its course) his problem seemed open to solution. He was given an opportunity to obtain a post much superior to that of Hanau without the necessity of any surrender of principle. The offer could not have been other than tempting, and his behaviour at this moment is very instructive.

The offer came from a certain Professor Binder of Göttingen University. Adam had known this man in his student days, and it seems that there was mutual attraction and antipathy between them. Evidence of the antipathy appears in 1931, when Adam was still a student of Göttingen, and wrote a mocking letter about the professor to his father. He said: 'Behind his somewhat robust political activities there is the totally resigned patriot, a species that always leaves a painful impression on me. He says "he serves this State (although it is a bad one), because that State notwithstanding is the embodiment of Reason in this world (Hegel!), and he works with all his energy for its transformation, which task he believes to be quite hopeless, however, and only wishes that he should not be considered an accessory to it "and so on and so on".'[16] Nevertheless Binder had

[16]Quoted in C.T.

acted as one of Adam's sponsors when he applied for his Rhodes scholarship.

In late February or early March of 1934 Binder came to know of Adam's professional difficulties and disappointments, and he made a move to help him. But Adam refused his help because it meant association with a fervent Nazi. He described his feelings in a letter to his father of the 8th of March.

'What do you say to this: the "famous" Professor Binder who to begin with most provokingly kept me at a distance from his throne, and afterwards ill-used me at his court, and when I sent him my dissertation [on Hegel] did not thank me for a year and a half, now invites me, through a former assistant, to take up a position as his private assistant in which I may help him and his circle to master "the great academic task on which they are engaged" and for which I have made myself proficient through my own former work. After that "nothing would then stand in my way" regarding a transfer to the district court of Göttingen. Binder is now known to be a court-philosopher, an enthusiastic party member etc. I shall very politely refuse. Although acceptance would mean that I would enjoy the protection of a professional dynasty which is now powerful, I do not esteem these gentlemen.'[17]

A letter to his father of the 22nd March shows him in a less buoyant, less decided mood. He wonders whether, in face of all his mounting difficulties, he would not be best advised to abandon an active and practical career altogether in favour of theoretical work, or whether 'without harming that which one would serve' it would be better 'simply to resign.' This reflection in turn brings him to put down his thoughts on his ceaseless inner debate as to whether one should accept the present regime at all, and if so, how far. He tells his father that his main concern at the moment is with German foreign policy where he finds himself in opposition to the Government state of mind (herrschende Staatsgesinnung) though at the same time he sees in the existing situation 'the possibility of vital importance to us, that there will be a reform of international law as at present accepted in Europe (the Treaty of Versailles, the discrimination against Germany etc.). Certainly we are, under various given assumptions, setting in motion the only right and safe foreign policy, but these "given assumptions", which depend partly on the legal, econo-

[17]Letters C.T.

mic and cultural bases of our national purpose, and partly on the unhappy history of our country in the last ten years, these things, so it seems to me, must be adapted to the co-operation of national states.'

If there was still much perplexity in his thoughts—not surprising during such a time—the bias of his mind was against the essence of Nazism, however much he might approve certain details of Nazi administration or policy. But the strength of the bias does not often appear in fullness in what he wrote in his letters. This may be because he found that he must now take note of the increasing censorship, and thus expressed himself with a moderation which he did not feel. Certainly the bias appears far more clearly in what he did.

Around this time, in the spring of 1934, he became involved in a most curious episode which was to continue as part of his life for the next two years. It came about as follows. The routine of a Referendar who aspired to Assessorship meant spending a certain specified time in an office of the Public Prosecutor's department. There he was assigned two main duties. One was to study prison conditions at first hand; the other was to examine a certain number of cases on which he was required to give a recommendation for further action or otherwise. Examination of cases included interviews with the convicts.

Sometime in April (it would seem) Adam received instructions to go on attachment to the Public Prosecutor's office in Kassel, and here he worked on and off (for he continued his duties in Hanau) for over three months. Following the usual arrangements he was one of several young lawyers of the same seniority engaged together on the same business, and the cases were divided among them.

In the prison of Kassel there was a man called Hans Siebert who had been condemned to a term of imprisonment in September 1933 for activity on behalf of the Communist party to which he belonged. In fact he was one of the leading Communists of Hesse, but the authorities do not seem to have discovered this. His was one of the cases which Adam had to investigate. It may have been deliberately chosen by himself, but more probably it came his way by chance.

The prisoner was duly informed that he was to be examined in private by Herr Doktor von Trott zu Solz, Referendar of Hanau, and he was immediately and naturally on his guard, not least because the examining Referendar bore a name of, to him, such repulsive aristocracy. He was expecting some loud-voiced junkerish bully, and he was greatly surprised when a handsome, friendly and somewhat sprightly young man walked into his cell and shook hands with him. But his suspicions remained, indeed they increased. This, he thought, is one of the crafty ones who knows how to charm secrets out of a man.

Adam had brought a sandwich lunch with him. He put the packet on the table and invited Siebert to help himself. This seemed to the prisoner a typical and clever manoeuvre, and he felt the more convinced that here was the most dangerous adversary he had met. 'Why do you offer me sandwiches?' He asked. 'Because I don't like to talk to a man who may be hungry,' laughed Adam. 'Go on, they're all for you. I've had something to eat outside.' The sandwiches were of the most excellent kind and the prisoner could not resist them, but they only strengthened him in his determination to tell this man nothing. His suspicion was not lessened when Adam drew out of his overcoat pocket a number of banned newspapers which had been published by the Confessional Churches and contained anti-Nazi articles. 'You'll want something to read here', said Adam, 'so I've brought you these. If anyone asks questions, refer them to me.' Siebert wondered if he was in the presence of Mephistopheles in person. The ensuing conversation between the Referendar and his 'victim' was not fruitful.

Adam was back again the next day, with another packet of sandwiches and more reading matter, and again there was no diminution of distrust on the prisoner's side. He thought it highly suspicious that Adam seemed far more anxious to discuss political matters than the details of the case. Siebert maintained a glum and obstinate opposition. At one point Adam told him he was sympathetic to his ideas, and that though he might not be in complete agreement with them, he wanted Siebert to understand that he was not a dedicated enemy of Communism. Siebert was thereupon moved to say something of this kind: 'How is it possible for a man such as you, bearing a name such as yours, to have any sympathy with my ideas?' Adam replied: 'It is not difficult for me at all,' and he then told him about his brother Werner, and how his affection for Werner (who might well have been in Siebert's place now) gave him a special and personal interest in this case. He told him that through Werner he had what might be called a Left-Wing family allegiance, and through him also had many Left-Wing friends and acquaintances. And what was all this

nonsense about his name? Had Siebert forgotten that Lenin was of aristocratic birth?

The ice was not yet broken but it was giving. Though Siebert's distrust
was still with him after this second interview, yet he could not help
wondering, after Adam's family confidence, whether the Referendar's
kindly manner, his sandwiches, the illegal newspapers, the way he seemed
to bring an air of gaiety even into the gloom of prison, might not in
reality be what it appeared to be: the expression of a good-hearted and
generous nature, and not the tricks-of-the-trade of an *agent provocateur*
after all! Improbable, but——

At the next meeting Adam not only brought sandwiches but a friendly
message from Siebert's former tutor in theology, Professor Schafft of the
Paedagogische Akadamie of Kassel, a training school for teachers where
Siebert had studied. The prisoner's distrust began finally to disappear
when Adam gave him another message, from Siebert's fiancée who was
not a member of the Communist party but used to work for them. 'But
how do you come to know her?' asked Siebert in amazement. 'What
is surprising about that?' replied Adam. 'She's anti-Nazi, and so am I.'

It had become evident to Siebert that Adam had close relations with
the anti-Nazi interest within the Confessional Churches, and now on
personal grounds as well he became sure that his former distrust was unworthy. At long last they began to discuss politics, and their subject was
one which was coming into fashion in Left-Wing circles, namely how to
form a coalition, a popular front as it was called, of all the Left-Wing
parties, including the Communist, in opposition to the totalitarian menace.
They were in agreement on principle here, but hardly at all when it came
to comparing their individual political beliefs. Though Adam gave evidence that his preoccupation with Hegel was weakening in favour of an
increasing interest in Karl Marx, Siebert found that his ideas were still
tinged with a traditionalism and conservatism quite unacceptable to a
Communist.

Their discussion came to include history and literature, and Siebert
learned about Adam's preferences. He found that he admired the Prussian
heroes of the wars of liberation, especially Yorck von Wartenburg,
Scharnhorst and Stein. Among the writers and poets of that great German age he loved especially Kleist and Arndt, but for Schiller he had not
only affection but veneration. Siebert was surprised at Adam's intense

dislike of the most famous of all German writers, and the dismal pettiness
of prison life was enlivened by the young Referendar's denunciation of
Goethe as a shallow opportunist, an unpatriotic German whose pose as a
great internationalist could not disguise his essentially provincial mind and
outlook. Between this 'perfect man' and the authentically great Schiller,
with his love of Germany and breadth of understanding, there was no
possible comparison! At one moment, realising that he was overstating
his case, Adam with a typical change of mood laughed at himself. 'You
know,' he told Siebert, 'one of the reasons why I belong to the Left-Wing
is because I like Engels because he hated Goethe.'

They talked about modern literature too, and among books which
seemed to have influenced Adam, Siebert noted a once very famous and
now justly forgotten work *Das Dritte Reich* by Moeller van den Bruck. It
had appeared long before Hitler came to power, was not Nazi in character, but seems to have provided the Nazis with the idea of calling their
regime the Third Empire of the Germans, the predecessors being the
Empires of Charlemagne and Bismarck. This Third Empire idea was
not Adam's interest in the book (or if it had been, Nazi adoption made it
distasteful now) but the author's conception of the ideal patriot as 'the
conservative revolutionary.' This ideal, somewhat English in character,
was long to remain with Adam.[18]

In due course Adam sent in his report. It was long and tendentious. It
laid relatively little stress on Siebert's political activity and hostility to
Nazism, and much on his character which was represented as idealist.
Adam reported that he was a man who had been led to extreme radicalism
through experience of poverty and unemployment, and through seeking
an answer to life in Christianity. The justice of his sentence was dubious;
he needed new acquaintance and free discussion if he was to change his
views and become a valuable citizen. Later events make it clear that Adam's
report was not well received by the authorities.[19]

[18]This account of the meeting of Trott and Hans Siebert was given by the latter
to the writer in 1966. Herr Siebert (now living in East Germany) was uncertain
of the precise date in the spring of 1934 when the encounter took place, and he
could not remember how many meetings occurred at this time. They were fairly
numerous.
[19]A copy of the report is among documents collected by Dr Clarita von Trott.

This is not surprising. The year 1934 was a cross-roads moment in the German courts of justice. The Reichstag Fire trial, which was not held till the end of 1933, had proved that the judiciary of Germany was not prepared to act as the unthinking instrument of the party in power. The exasperation of the party leaders was as great as their surprise, for Franz Gürtner, the Minister of Justice, was a convinced Nazi from the early days of the movement who had proved his devotion to the Führer.[20] The Nazi leaders resolved to bring the independence and integrity of the judiciary to an end. It proved one of Hitler's most difficult tasks, largely because Gürtner, although devoted to the Nazi cause, was at the same time a conscientious lawyer who stood up for the independence of the courts. What must be remembered here is that in this first half of 1934 Nazis outside the legal profession, helped by those within it, were making their first strenuous efforts to set aright the anomaly startlingly revealed by the Reichstag Fire trial, and this fact explains the continuing efforts (one of which has been noted already) to force men in Adam's position into some form of party-membership. Against that background one must estimate his courage in acting as he did in his very 'incorrect' conduct of the Siebert case. His aim was to help to freedom a man who might be useful in the struggle against the Nazis.

Before this time Adam's courage had not had to stand up to any extraordinary test, but now, when the moment came, he found that he had this virtue in abundance. Everyone who knew him testifies to it, even those who are most critical. He always wore his virtue modestly, as becomes a truly brave man.

What made Adam's conduct in the Kassel prison dangerous to himself was that concurrently he was engaging in activity where he enjoyed no semblance of official protection, and which was of a kind to bring down on him the full wrath of a vengeful state.

[20]In 1923 Gürtner was Minister of Justice in the Government of Bavaria. He became converted to Nazism early in the year and rendered Hitler invaluable service by defeating the anti-Nazi endeavours of his colleagues, the Bavarian Minister of the Interior, Franz Schweyer.

Gürtner was first appointed Reich Minister of Justice in the cabinet of von Papen where again he was of help to the Nazi cause. Hitler maintained him as Minister till Gürtner's death in 1941, except for a brief period in 1933 when the Ministry was given to Hans Frank. Immediately on the Nazi assumption of power Schweyer was sent to a concentration camp.

The dates of the Siebert case are uncertain, but it seems that the first phase probably came to an end, with Adam sending in his report, in the later part of May. The story needs to go back again to the end of March.

As before he still kept up his connection with the *Neue Blätter* group. Few of his other friends realised how active and how perilous that connection was.

The group persisted in their belief that with sufficient backing from a sufficient number of parties and interests General von Schleicher could be reappointed Chancellor, and Hitler at the same time thrust back into the shadows whence he came. It was a curious belief which indicated little appreciation of Schleicher's character and the political situation in which he would need to play a saviour's rôle. Schleicher had excessive confidence in his cleverness, and as a result he had the reputation of having betrayed every party and most of the men with whom he had worked in the course of his tortuous career. He left office utterly discredited in political and administrative circles, and with few friends in the army leadership.

During the first half of 1934 Schleicher was living in retirement in the fashionable Berlin suburb of Neu-Babelsberg. Since the Nazi seizure of power he had been inactive and had behaved as discreetly as his nature allowed. For all his prodigious vanity, he seems to have realised that his moment had passed and was unlikely to return. There is no reason to suppose that he gave encouragement to or was even aware of conspiracies on his behalf,[21] but there can be no doubt whatever that there were such conspiracies, though the evidence tends to show that they never passed beyond a rudimentary stage.

The socialist pro-Schleicher conspiracies seem to have been based on a fallacious interpretation of the army's hostility to the Nazi party. It is true that from the beginning of the Third Reich there were many officers of the German army who looked with moral revulsion on the new masters of their country. Their views were much the same as those which Adam had expressed to his father in February 1933. But if such an attitude of mind remained very common throughout the army it was far from that of the army leadership in the spring and summer of 1934. Between the military and the Nazi leadership the accord was closer now than perhaps at any other time. Ernst Röhm had not relinquished his ambitions of

[21]O'Neill p. 48-49.

making his troops into the new army of Germany with himself as Commander-in-Chief; the meeting of February the 28th had only enraged him anew against Hitler whom he now openly described as 'that ignorant war-time corporal,'[22] and the split between the Sturm-Abteilungen and the Reichswehr grew daily. When it was found that Hitler consistently sided with the army throughout the dispute, the army leaders inevitably had new ideas about this wild demagogue, and began to revise unfavourable judgments. This was not a moment when they were likely to undertake a revolutionary rôle in favour of Schleicher, especially as Schleicher was supposed to be a secret supporter of the gangsterish Röhm.

There is a dramatic story, first given anonymously in a book published in France in 1935, that on the 11th of April, 1934 Hitler, concluded an agreement with General Blomberg, General Fritsch and Admiral Raeder while sailing from Kiel to Königsberg on board the pocket-battleship *Deutschland*. Hitler had information that Hindenburg was slowly failing and would die in the near future, and his purpose in making the agreement, supposedly known as the 'Pact of the *Deutschland*,' was to obtain the support of the armed services for his candidature as Hindenburg's successor. In return for their support Hitler assured the service leaders that he would entirely eliminate the threat to the army still presented by the Storm Troops under Röhm. The support is said to have been given, and the pact later enthusiastically accepted by the senior officers of the army when they learned of its terms from Blomberg on 16th May. The story may be true, or may be a confusion with the events of 28th February,[23] but it indicates correctly enough that Hitler and most of the Nazi leadership were in active and increasingly practical alliance with the army against the Storm Troops at this time. Blomberg intensified the Nazification process, and those who put their trust in the military tradition of Germany were shocked at the May Day parades of 1934 to see swastikas among the regimental badges on the uniforms. But the army flattered itself that it had read the signs of the times correctly.

In a totalitarian state the function of a free and sensational press is taken over by free and sensational rumour; there occurs an inevitable and enor-

[22]O'Neill p. 42.
[23]The story is accepted by Sir J. Wheeler Bennett in *The Nemesis of Power* and doubted though not dismissed by R. T. O'Neill. Op. Cit. Appendix F.

mous extension of inaccurate information. Schleicher was a natural subject for rumour at all times, as can be said of any public figure who is
devoted to crooked ways. From the day that Hitler assumed power
Schleicher made no secret of his hatred and contempt of the Nazi regime,
and when it became known that the army and the Storm Troops were in
conflict, he became loud in his criticism.[24] His behaviour immediately
attracted the attention of the Nazi hierarchy, and equally of the anti-
Nazis, including the group assembled round *Die Neue Blätter*. Stories of
his active conspiring, furnished with convincing detail, and sometimes
emanating from those close to him, were believed by both sides.[25] The
Neue Blätter group, in the storm-laden atmosphere of that spring and
summer decided that they must be ready for action at short notice, and
they brought Adam into their plans. Mayer came to Hanau, bringing with
him a friend of Adam's earlier Berlin days, Hasso von Seebach.[26]

As before, the group wanted Adam to help them to establish contact
with socialists abroad. Convinced that they were indirectly in communication with Schleicher, they wanted to be sure that when the moment of
triumph over Hitler came, the new regime, which they believed would
be predominantly Social Democrat in character, would have parliamentary backing in England and France. (One of the most persistent of the
rumours was to the effect that Schleicher's friendship with the French
Ambassador, Monsieur André François-Poncet, had resulted in a guarantee of French governmental support.) The three of them talked long, and
it was decided that as Adam could not accompany them he would give
Peter Mayer an introduction to Sir Stafford Cripps with a request that
he would introduce them to the rising luminary of the Labour Party,
Major Clement Attlee.

As things turned out Mayer and Seebach did not go to England till
May. The visit disappointed them. They met Cripps and Major Attlee
and other socialist Members of Parliament. They found that the Labour
Party did not relish the idea of any forward policy regarding Germany,
and they were averse to involvement in ideological struggles abroad. They
said that struggles for power in Germany 'were a matter for the Germans.'
The two young men felt painfully disappointed.[27] The moment was ill-

[24]Wheeler-Bennett Op. cit. [25] Wheeler-Bennett Op. cit. [26]C.T.
[27]J. P. Mayer. Discussion.

chosen for the mission. In April Hitler had made an offer, conveyed to France and England by Joachin von Ribbentrop who still retained at that time some of the smooth charm of a salesman, to reduce the numbers of the Storm Troops drastically. This had cooled anti-Nazi feeling. Here, people said, was a first and very welcome sign that the Nazi revolution, after an opening phase of excess, was settling down and adopting the outlook of a reasonable regime. One cannot but be amazed at Hitler's political skill at this point. He used a split in his own party to lure the army into his power and lull his potential enemies almost into complacence.

The two secret emissaries returned downcast, but after talking with Adam whom they met in Berlin, and becoming infected by his optimism, Peter Mayer decided to return to England at the end of June in order to follow up some of the acquaintance they had made through his introductions, always with the same purpose in view. But before he did so, they discussed a new plan in which Adam would use his pen on behalf of the cause.

The plan was to revive an ancient practice of political pamphleteering, namely to publish a series of papers which would appear to be concerned with a distant subject and would in fact be equally concerned with an immediate one. They would have a two-level, a 'doppelte Boden' character, the clandestine theme being anti-Nazi. Mayer's plan was to publish a historical series. He himself had chosen Napoleon III and the plebiscite state as his subject. It was not long before Adam found his own theme, the poet and dramatist Heinrich von Kleist. It was essential to limit the subject so that it could be dealt with in a brief essay, and Adam finally decided to concentrate on Kleist's lesser known work, his political and journalistic writings. As soon as he had returned to Hanau, he threw himself into a study of Kleist which, after much delay, was to result in the most satisfying of his writings.[28]

He was helped in this new work by a young man who shared his enthusiasm for Kleist, and who in 1934 was writing a doctoral thesis on this subject. They had first met in Göttingen in 1931. His name was Clemens Lugowski, and Adam thus described him in a letter to Diana written at the beginning of 1934 when the friendship was enjoying a second spring: 'He really leads the most monk-like existence I know of.

[28]J. P. Mayer. Discussion.

He has the dignity of a Jesuit and the sensitiveness of St Francis. He is Catholic, in fact, and partly Polish in blood. I love him better every time.' Something of the character of their affectionate relationship appears from a letter written by Lugowski to Adam in late June. 'The nicest thing would be a little journey together. I believe we have much to tell each other. Besides I make a prophecy that on the completion of my book I shall have a tremendous desire to symphilosophise (symphilosophieren), a delight for which a partner is only found with difficulty just now.'[29]

The Kleist venture was to be beset with difficulties and exasperating delays. The first obstacle, a very large one which momentarily scared the promoters of the scheme into caution and second thoughts, was the sudden crisis in Germany on the last day of June and the first days of July: the Night of the Long Knives, otherwise known as the Röhm purge or the June bloodbath. The Nazis do not seem to have hit on a pleasant euphemism for this particular atrocity.

So far as this account is concerned, a few facts need to be recalled. The main purpose of the massacre which opened in the early hours of the 30th June, was to settle matters once for all with Röhm and his following in the Storm Troops. It was extended to cover some other Nazi dissidents, some private feuds and people whose lack of sympathy with the regime was held to be a political risk. Von Papen had given a speech two weeks before, and in a trenchant and dignified manner he had warned of the dangers of a 'second revolution' and made a thinly disguised attack on Goebbels. As Vice Chancellor he was thought an inappropriate subject for murder, but while he was kept under arrest his two principal secretaries and Edgar Jung who had drafted the offending speech, were shot. Gregor Strasser, though not in league with Röhm, met his fate and was shot as a dangerous radical within the party, while two eminent reactionaries outside it, the royalist political agent Freiherr von Guttenberg and Gustav von Kahr, were murdered with the effect of restoring the balance. Kahr who, as Bavarian Prime Minister, had successfully obstructed Hitler in 1923 was now an old man in retirement. He appears to have been murdered in circumstances of incredible and obscene barbarism as an act of personal spite on the part of the Führer. The number of those murdered is not known because all records of the affair were destroyed on the orders

[29]C.T.

of Göring. The highest total given is four hundred.[30] This is probably excessive, but the figure may well have been over three hundred. No party was immune and distinction and former service gave no protection, for which reason Hitler's decision not to visit his murderous rage on ministerial colleagues, notably von Papen, is surprising and out of keeping with the spirit of the enterprise, which was that of an African Kraal. It is generally agreed that if Brüning had not left Germany in response to warnings he would have fallen. The most famous of the victims was Brüning's successor Kurt von Schleicher who was murdered with his wife in their house. The corpses were discovered shortly after by Schleicher's daughter when she returned home to luncheon.[31]

During the three days of this week-end Adam was in Kassel. There can be no doubt that if the Nazi authorities had known the true character of his recent conversations with Hans Siebert, and of his close involvement in the approaches which had been attempted towards Schleicher, and of his plans to help in further anti-Nazi movements abroad, then he most certainly would have been one of the victims. He was in great danger if only a part of his activities was known, and he could not fail to be aware of this. Then, in the middle of these three days of terrified rumour which was often outstripped by the officially conveyed news, a time when some of the bravest found themselves overcome with fear, Adam was rung up by Peter Mayer. The latter had just arrived in Hamburg from England where he had been continuing his efforts to rally Socialist support for a post-Nazi Germany of which Schleicher would be the Chancellor. He had been warned that Berlin was unsafe for him, and he was now ringing up for advice as to what he should do.

If Adam had urged him to keep at a distance from him and all his acquaintance of *Die Neue Blätter*, indeed if he had protested at Mayer's ringing him up at all, his conduct would not only have been defensible but prudent. But it would have been utterly out of character. He did what anyone who knew him well would have expected. He invited Peter Mayer to come and stay in his lodgings in Kassel. He would have nothing to fear

---

[30]In Weissbuch über die Erschiessungen des 30 Juni 1934. Paris 1935.
[31]This brief reference to 30th June-2nd July 1934 follows Alan Bullock's *Hitler, a Study in Tyranny* (Revised version 1963). Wheeler-Bennett Op. cit. and O'Neill Op. cit.

with him, he laughed down the telephone (somewhat to the other's dismay), as the authorities would hardly arrest the friend of a Referendar working in the Public Prosecutor's office! Telephone conversations were not widely tapped or reported on by operators in the first years of the Nazi regime. If this one was, it passed as innocuous, as others did in later and even more dangerous days. Adam's gaiety of manner, which was never assumed, may have seemed to preclude conspiracy.

Peter Mayer accepted the invitation and came down to Kassel where the two of them spent some days together. In spite of the horror of the time they were gay happy days. The truth was that Adam was always at his best in times of crisis; in fact he sometimes rather enjoyed them.[32] When Adam had finished his work for the day, he and Mayer would motor out to the woods. It was the time of the rutting season, the Hirschbrunst, and they would walk round the darkening forest listening for the belling of stags. In later years Peter Mayer also remembered how on some of their walks they would sing old German songs.

When the hunt died down and the state of emergency was clearly at an end, and when his friends assured him that the worst was now over, Mayer returned to Berlin. The intrigue with Schleicher's friends in which he and Adam had taken part, was never discovered during the Nazi years.[33]

Adam's political activities at this time when he was in Kassel and Hanau, and which show clearly what sort of man he was, are entirely undocumented. In his many surviving letters there appears to be only one reference to the events of the 30th of June when he wrote in the course of a letter to his father 'a chill wind is blowing just now.' Though discretion always came to him with difficulty, he had to be discreet to the point of absolute secrecy about the hopes and plans and actions of that part of the opposition to which he belonged, and it was rash to put anything on paper, or keep any paper which could be used as evidence. This was a condition of survival and he owed it to his friends to maintain it. So it came about that while he tried at the risk of his life to show real patriotism by opposing the diseased tyranny which had fastened on his country, most of his English friends and acquaintance only knew him,

[32]Doctor Margaret Boveri strongly suggests this in her sketch of Trott in her *Treason in the Twentieth Century*. Putnam. New York. 1963.
[33]J. P. Mayer. Discussion.

and could only know him, as the author of a letter to the *Manchester Guardian* in which he appeared to declare his sympathy with the Nazi regime.

This was part of the crushing penalty which he, in common with other men of good will, had to endure in living under that tyranny. It is not surprising that he sought to find a breach in the wall of misunderstanding which surrounded him, for which reason, one may guess, he sent a 'peace-overture' to his friend Isaiah Berlin. One must be grateful that, without any knowledge of the facts, the other answered with such instinctive generosity.

Chapter 7

FRUSTRATIONS AND A SUCCESS

In our age of diminishing leisure and increasing use of the telephone, it is often said that the custom and art of letter-writing have ceased. If that is the rule, Adam von Trott provides a striking exception. After he reached manhood there were few periods in his life when he did not give a large part of every day to writing letters which he usually composed with much literary care. Those which have survived, a small part of the whole, contain with their answers, some three quarters of a million words: as with most people with whom the habit is strong, he was the cause of much letter-writing in others. Even in the days before the invention of the telephone, even in the eighteenth century, he would have been remarked as a prolific correspondent with his family and friends.

In the period from his return to Germany in 1933 to the end of 1936, he seems to have pursued three main lines of private correspondence; with his parents, with Diana Hubback and with Shiela Grant-Duff. As already suggested he had to be increasingly on his guard against the censorship though this never meant that he deliberately falsified his opinions. The camouflage is thin, but as has appeared already in the case of the 30th June, 1934, there is often remarkably little mention of public events compared to what there must have been if he had been writing in a time of freedom.

The correspondence with his parents never changed in character except for evidence of growing warmth of feeling for his mother. Towards Herr von Trott he maintained throughout life the same deeply affectionate veneration. Impatient as he was of conservatism both at home and abroad (especially in England), he was never impatient of the views or predilections of this very conservative old gentleman and retired servant of the State. Herr von Trott remained for him, and rightly so, the embodiment of a German ideal.

A common characteristic of his three main correspondences is much lyrical description of nature, especially when telling of the night-walks which he used to make, sometimes with a companion such as his cousin Bobby, and often alone, during the summer months. He delighted to set out at the hour when 'the West yet glimmers with some streaks of day' and then he would walk through the forests of the Trottenwald or the woods near Kassel, sometimes not coming home till sunrise. His descriptions show exact and informed observation of trees, flowers, the changing seasons, and (especially when he does not try too hard for it) often rise to beautiful expression both in English and German. Such things are found throughout his letters, but most often in those written to Diana.

His third main correspondence in these years appears less in the present chapter, but for convenience may be considered here with the others. It was with Shiela Grant-Duff. It is very interesting and shows much contrast to the other two. At some periods they wrote to each other as often as four times in a week, and almost the whole of this collection of letters has survived on both sides. It reflects an intense and stormy relationship, often sailing towards total shipwreck and saved—usually at the very last minute—by the abundant affection and sense of humour on both sides. The disagreement between them, which was as much an essential of their relationship as their mutual sympathy, was largely concerned with Adam's private life and Shiela's disapproval of certain aspects of it involving people whom she knew. About this there is no need to say more, but the fact should be stated. Quite unconnected with this private disagreement was the vigorous, usually amicable though sometimes wrathful debate between these two high-spirited, very intelligent and politically inexperienced friends, on the subject of Germany's worsening relations with England and the rest of what it is not presumptuous to call, and Adam hesitated to call, the free world. The debate gives the correspondence its chief significance.

The quality of this remarkable exchange of letters is best conveyed by quotation. Here are two passages from a letter from Adam written in mid-November of 1934 at a time when Shiela was in Paris about to take up a journalistic career, a move which Adam, needless to say, regretted.

'Regarding my country, provincial life of course makes me see things "from too harmless an angle," but I wonder whether journalists do not often commit the opposite mistake. You will never become like them, if I know you— and for your final purposes you certainly seem to be in a centre now from which to understand things and people and the development of the last ten years. But do not remain "eccentric" in your views of Germany, you know more of it than me, B, M and H[1] already, and yours will not be an outlook of the "safe world of democracy" which seems to me as unsafe spiritually as any other human world I know with the possible exception of certain parts of Russia.

'It is moving and in no way an anachronistic vision to see Christian Germany re-emerge powerfully beneath the already crumbling artifices of newer experiments.'

Shiela was apt to be on her guard against Adam's persuasion and often found herself in the rôle of 'the spokeswoman of democracy.' This comes out in her reply from Paris dated a week later.

'Do you attack the "safe world of democracy"? Who calls it "safe" anyway? It is a curious description of it, but all the same it is still the most admirable form of government possible. Natural aristocracies are perhaps better—or at least have been realised more often, but the ruling aristocracies of to-day, if you can call any governments that, are pretty disagreeable . . .

'What you say in your letter of "Christian Germany" re-emerging is very hopeful and encouraging, and I'm terribly glad if it's true—but I wonder what you mean by Christian Germany. I'm told Rosenberg describes God as being the nation. He is certainly a genius of great originality. From the things I read in your papers, I believe your hair must be falling out because of the rivers of peroxide. How is your hair now? I hope it is growing more firmly attached.'

In his next letter of the 7th December he said nothing of the re-emergence of Christian Germany. He had probably been referring to the opposition to Nazism in the Confessional Churches, and to the courageous stand of Cardinal-Archbishop Faulhaber of Munich, copies of whose sermons used to reach Adam from Ingrid Warburg.[2] He discreetly did not pursue this subject, but he counter-attacked on that of democracy, at the end of his long and affectionate reply.

[1]B is doubtful, but M is Mayer and H Hasso von Seebach.   [2]D.H.

'As to the political arguments, I think, Shiela, we agree about essence and appearance of democracy much more than you seem prepared to take for granted. I wrote a long thesis about this to you in that letter from the Café—but I shall leave it at that.[3] I was aiming at the inanity of making "the world safe for democracy" by a fratricidal war, and afterwards making the world or rather the beaten equally safe for dictatorship by a fratricidal peace.'

This was the year 1934 when the Nazis were still something of an enigma to many people. The debate was later to grow more heated and with good cause. Adam was not often to score off Shiela so well. It was usually the other way round.

They were both influenced by the ideas of the Left Wing of that time, by its genuine idealism and some of its delusions (instanced above by the tribute to 'certain parts' of Stalin's Russia) but neither of them found an intellectual home in any defined Left-Wing party. Against the background of his parents' conservatism Adam's 'Leftism' stood out with an effect of contrast which did not appear in the case of Shiela whose family background was of the Liberal party. Adam's traditionalism was in fact stronger than Shiela's.

To return to the progress of Adam's life from the time of the June massacre. This was a period of much difficulty. Once more pressure was brought on him to conform. Some time before this he had been sent the official form needed for application to join the Nazi party or an affiliated organisation. He had returned the form uncompleted. Six days before the 30th June the form was sent to him again, this time by the president of the Supreme Court of his district, with a request, which was more or less an order, that he should join an appropriate Nazi organisation. He wrote to his father, not for advice but to tell him of this latest development and that he planned to refuse the request and again to return the form uncompleted. He would give as his reasons that he was shortly to leave Hanau and, as before, giving a sop to authority by declaring that he proposed to volunteer for two months' duty in the Labour service.[4]

[3]Earlier in the letter he referred to a letter which he wrote but did not send because 'I found its English intolerable bad.'
[4]Letters C.T.

In the event he did not send his reply till after the June atrocities, and it is entirely typical of him that the reply he did send in that moment of danger was even less conciliatory than the one he had first intended. He wrote to his father on the 6th of July: 'I based my argument for not having finally joined these doubtful organisations, not on evasive reasoning but on a matter of principle.' It was at the end of this letter that he wrote his one comment on those days 'Es geht scharfe Luft.'

Inevitably Adam had to pay for this defiance. His term of service in Hanau was due to expire in August and he hoped for promotion to Regierungsreferendar status. This was refused, nor did he receive a transfer to Berlin. Yet he was not condemned to a further term in the same place, but obtained a transfer to Kassel. The disappointment though mitigated was nonetheless serious. He was ambitious, and now he had to endure further the wretchedness, which he had foreseen on the 30th of January, 1933, of seeing his career deferred and perhaps reduced to irremediable mediocrity, if he was to remain true to his principles. All the time it was perfectly evident that some act of appeasement (no disgraceful surrender), towards the Nazi authority, would make his path tolerable and promising, while in the eyes of many good people his honour would be safe.

There were compensations in the life of Kassel. He lived on the outskirts, in Kassel-Mulang in the pleasant home of a family of friends called Noll, and from the window of his room he would look on the sort of Hessian view he loved, parkland, fields and distant wooded hills. He was near Imshausen, and he had many visits from friends. But his professional life had little reward, and he was on bad terms with a new kind of superior who had been invented by the Nazis on the model of the Soviet commissar. In Kassel this took the form of a certain Doktor Kessler, a groupleader or Gemeinschaftsleiter whose duty put him in charge of the ideological and political education of the young lawyers of Adam's seniority.[5]

Such were the outward circumstances of Adam's life in the later part of 1934. Considering his declared hostility to the regime, they might have been worse. The inner circumstances were possibly yet more disturbing, and it is not quite fanciful to suppose that they were the cause of as much distress and unhappiness.

[5]C.T.

The death of Schleicher was the occasion for some thorough reappraisal among the *Neue Blätter* group. It seemed to them that the time had gone by, if it ever existed, when the overthrow of the Nazis could be accomplished by political manoeuvring: what was needed now, they concluded, was a policy of conspiracy which did not stop short of violence, and if this proved to be beyond their reach, then they must not scruple to encourage intervention from outside. They believed that to accomplish the fall of Hitler it was even worth while suffering another defeat of Germany in war.

Adam was a long way from approving any intrigue which involved the fall of his country and the triumph over her of foreign powers. That his friends, the people in whom, so he believed, lay the hope of Germany's future, should be driven by despair to belief in such courses utterly horrified him. He found himself in a new phase of spiritual isolation.

Mutual relations between him and them became strained, and that element of distrust which had grown, owing to what seemed to Adam's friends his too open behaviour, deepened and was to lead to distressing incidents later. This unpleasant situation however must not be exaggerated. If there was disagreement and disapproval on both sides, there remained esteem and affection in sufficient force not only to maintain relations, but to maintain them to good effect. Indeed, after Adam's valiant loyalty to Peter Mayer during the days of the June massacre, it would have been strange if it had been otherwise. But something of the former intimacy had been irrecoverably lost. The Kleist venture went forward, though in the new circumstances this also had a troublesome passage before the craft made harbour.[6]

The point cannot be proved, naturally enough, but the main reason that publication of Adam's remarkable essay became so difficult is probably to be found in the facts of life as led in opposition. It is one thing to live in an opposition with hopes of achieving power, quite another to live among men whose hopes dwindle day by day and for whom there is no foreseeable future except an endless prolongation of their dismal state.

On the 1st of August, 1934, a month after the Röhm purge, Hindenburg died and Hitler was immediately proclaimed President. He was now

[6]This account of Trott's relations with the *Neue Blätter* group follows the account given to the writer by J. P. Mayer.

absolute in theory and fact. The restraints upon him had always been less than optimists had imagined, and now they were removed: the German armed services took a new oath to the Führer pledging loyalty to him personally, not, as was the normal custom, to an unnamed Head of State. This was the official seal on Nazi autocracy, and those who still looked for rescue from the service chiefs deluded themselves. Opposition had been outmanoeuvred in the most masterly fashion. Inevitably many members of that thwarted opposition began to fall into the quarrelsomeness of despair. Italian anti-Fascists had suffered in this way for years, and the German anti-Nazis now began to go the same way.

Adam had made his selection from Kleist's political journalism and had completed the introduction (the main purpose of this work of *double entente*) by the late summer of 1934. The publishers, the Protteverlag of Potsdam, appeared satisfied, and by late September 1934 Adam had the galley proofs. Then Herr Protte began to have doubts and self-questionings. In mid-October he declared that the proposed book was irrelevant to the present situation, and he went on to suggest that Adam should start again, writing in collaboration with a certain Michael Freund. Adam turned down this 'joint solution of the task,' as he called it, with some indignation. He suspected that Herr Protte's real anxiety was that the book, far from being irrelevant, was too much the other way, and might rouse the Nazi authorities against his publishing firm. There was a quarrel and Adam offered the book to another firm, the Sozietätsverlag, who refused it. This was in November 1934. In the end Herr Protte repented his unworthy fears. The quarrel was made up, and Adam's book was published by the Protteverlag without any serious alteration, but not till June 1935. He had had to wait nearly a year.[7]

It is most convenient to consider the book here, though this advances the story to a new phase of Adam's life.

The essay on Kleist is undoubtedly the best evidence available that Adam had in him the makings of a writer. He showed, and this is essential proof of literary skill, that he could rise so far above his early imperfections that a reader who did not know his other work could not guess what those imperfections were. On this occasion he never forgot his reader. The whole purpose of the book was to make his fellow-men think and see in

[7]C.T., G.D., D.H.

the predicament of Kleist and his response to it a lesson for themselves.

This concern with his readership gives the book another interesting literary feature. Though Adam was a man of buoyant temperament who liked to lose himself sometimes in laughter and high spirits, little of this appears in his writing—not even in his letters. When he put pen to paper he was easily tempted towards undue solemnity. But in his essay on Kleist his sense of humour could not be excluded. It would be completely to misrepresent him and it to say that he wrote the essay with his tongue in his cheek. His love and admiration for Kleist were serious and deeply felt. But it would be to miss an essential value of what he wrote about that great poet, if one were to ignore the fact that Adam, in writing his essay, was thinking of an audience which would relish with amusement the disguised references to Napoleon's base imitator.

Here is the opening:

'The decisive years of Kleist's creative work lay under the sign of the French Revolution, of the final disintegration of the old German Reich, and the rise of Napoleon whose fall he did not live to see. The bourgeois revolution in France was followed by the dissolution of such remnants of the medieval systems everywhere as had preserved influence and fol-lowers. The army which Kleist had joined at fifteen as a cadet in the Potsdam Guard, suffered the worst defeat of its history at Jena. The Prus-sian Monarchy to which he remained loyal in traditional reverence, even though military service had oppressed him, had to bow before the alien upstart. Enemy forces were marching through the German countryside while in the towns all public life languished captive in dismal or dis-honourable subjugation to foreign overlords. At the same time peaceful family life had been destroyed in Germany. Young men could either serve under foreign flags, or living between hope and despair, endure the fate of political adventurers.

'Because the old system in Germany which Napoleon had swept away had been false and in some respects intolerable, the Germans showed but little political clarity of judgment and only rarely civic firmness in the midst of these unprecedented events.'

It is probably just to say that Adam was well placed to write fluently on this occasion because his 'cover-plan' was one which he could follow with feeling and sincerity. The cover-plan in this case was to insist on Kleist's German patriotism in the face of foreign domination, and the allusion for 1935 might seem to a superficial reader to be concerned with recent and exasperating memories (whose bitterness Adam shared to the full) of the Allied Occupation of the Rhineland. This was to be the answer to a suspicious Nazi whose reading habits were likely to be very superficial indeed. (People who burn books do not make perceptive critics.) But of course a true Berliner (and this Potsdam-produced book was addressed to Berlin), with wits sharpened by the guile of the cabaret comedians, had no hesitation in referring the subject-matter to the native tyranny afflicting Germany, and seeing in the 'alien upstart,' *der fremder Emporkömmling* as Adam phrased it, not the Emperor of the French so readily as 'the Bohemian corporal' who had acquired German citizenship only three years before.[8]

Here are two comments on Kleist's private letters.

'The genuine virility of Kleist's political conduct may well become clearer to us than it did to his contemporaries, most of whom stood helplessly aside from that grave and crucial struggle. Such letters of his as have survived make us feel immediately and vividly the spirit of that time, the personal and political disappointments which swept over him, and how no blow could lay him low for ever. The acute sensitiveness of his political character was revealed in his early protest against being hedged in by convention, and in his later struggle against the corroding and undermining of inherited values for which the cynical military rulers of Europe were responsible.

'The political aspect of his work, which it is here proposed to recall, cannot be understood from reading his letters or considering the anxiety which gives them a sombre tone. Admittedly these letters give us much insight into the struggle against despair in a period of history which shattered and often threatened to obliterate the man and his work. But it is in truth his work, accomplished in a hostile age, that is the essence of his political achievement; that work in which the inadequate is conquered by satire, the nonsensical by laughter, the vulgar by a proud refusal of recognition, and in which none of the things he strove against was allowed to gain a torturing upper hand.'

[8]Hitler resigned his Austrian citizenship in April 1927 and was then stateless till granted German citizenship by the Nazi-controlled State of Brunswick in February 1932.

Early in the essay (about a quarter way from the beginning) we meet one of those passages where the reader may have the sensation of exchanging a wink with the author. Adam briefly refers to Kleist's historical novel *Michael Kohlhaas*, one of the best of his prose works. Somewhat unnecessarily, it would seem, since the essay is addressed to an educated audience, he gives a résumé of Kleist's variation on the theme of Luther's contemporary, the historical Hans Kohlhase.

'This honest horse-dealer has suffered grave wrong at the hands of some robber-knights, but the magistrates of his country refuse him protection until his sense of justice forces him into rebellion against arbitrary tyranny. Then, with all the primitive strength of an elemental force, he masters the powers which are opposed to him. The castles of the Knights are destroyed; whole cities are given over to fire and slaughter, and the lives of men wantonly sacrificed. The public authorities who had hitherto ruled in well protected complacence, now abase themselves, one after the other, before the rallying cry of insulted justice. At length the Elector of Brandenburg punishes the injustice which has been committed, and he includes therein the outrageous despotism (die ausschreitende Eigenmacht) of Kohlhaas himself.'

Adam's readers could hardly take this résumé other than as a parable on the subject of Hitler's seizure of power from the Weimar Republic. It immediately provoked a question: who was to play the part of that most necessary *deus ex machina*, the good Elector?

The answer to the question is implied, and it is simple. 'You and I,' he seems to say, 'Germans who believe in Germany's past and future, we are the people who have to step in.' It is subtly implied two paragraphs after the last quoted section, when he considers Kleist's philosophical position.

'The secret of Kleist's prose work is that each sentence and each thought is the outcome of close experience, immediate and not theoretical, of the struggle with reality. "Whoever does not grasp life like a wrestler in his embrace, and who in the thousand turns and twists of the struggle, has not felt and known its resistance, its pressure, its evasions—such a man will never gain the upper hand in debate, and never conceivably in battle".'

In his penultimate paragraph Adam gives effective expression to his feelings about Kleist as a writer and as a political phenomenon.

'[Kleist aimed to reach] the straightforward mind of the individual citizen. There he sensed the real source of power through which his compatriots could liberate themselves from a gruesome and demoralising despotism. Those with ears to hear will realise that in his least striking as well as in his most tremendous utterance Kleist always appeals to the individual's sense of his rights, to his bold defiance of anything alien, unnatural, cowardly, or dishonest which men may try to force on him from without. This struggle for free and individual responsibility and his inner conviction that here was the ultimate authority for all human order, penetrated down into every detail of his daily life, for which reason Kleist's journalism is not basically different from his poetry. The nature of "the common people," which is only too often merely dimly imagined, was to him something known and clear. No matter at what he aims in his polemics, whether it is an act of the sovereign state, the educational obtuseness of academic and pedantic luminaries, the contemporary theatre—whatever it may be—the reader will be hypnotised by that magic eye . . . His spontaneous defensiveness against inferior people in daily life, his heart-felt recognition of chivalrous independence, his capacity for arousing men from political apathy, his observation and his imagination; through Kleist these things become, as perhaps they have never since become, the means of saving our language and our freedom of thought from molestation.'[9]

The disguise is thin at this point, and one must admire the spirit of a man who could write thus at a moment when his contempt for the Nazi regime was becoming dangerous to himself. One must also remember that the original plan was that Adam's preface to Kleist's political writings should come out only some four months after the June massacre.

Here are the concluding words of the essay:

'In small things as in great, Kleist's political conduct had one aim: a bold vindication of the right of men to live candid lives for the sake of the individual's own greatness, and thereby the greatness of his country. That right had been fought for, with medieval cruelty, by Michael Kohl-

[9]The fear that the German language would virtually disappear and be superseded by French in educated society became a national obsession, with some reason, in the 18th century. Napoleon's victorious career kept the obsession alive in the golden age of German letters and it lingered on till within living memory. In the eighteen sixties Wagner gave expression to it in Die Meistersinger; it was an element in Bismarck's *Kulturkampf*, and a defensive attitude regarding the German language was prominent in Nazi education.

haas. Until his voluntary death the same purpose determined the life of Kleist, a life which for all its misfortune was glorious.'[10]

The book aroused interest but was not the subject of political scandal. It sold to the public which had supported the *Neue Blätter* in times of freedom and still supported the Protteverlag. Like most of these enterprises, it was a case of preaching to the converted, and (a point usually forgotten in times of stress) much to be commended for that reason. In their concern for their enemies, propagandists of a good cause too easily forget their friends. Adam enjoyed his well-earned literary success, but he was very disappointed at the lack of political response, and he regretted that he had not made the purpose of his essay quite plain for a large public to understand.[11] But he had written a good book, and that has its consolation.

To return to his life in Kassel during the second half of 1934.

After the Siebert case his professional career, for the rest of that year, produced nothing of biographical interest, in contrast to his private life. As before he sought satisfaction for his restless spirit in many excursions with friends, often undertaken in a light-hearted spirit and with many odd adventures.[12]

As before he often went wandering through the woods, and in a letter to Diana, vividly describing a ramble undertaken with a chance companion who had a weakness for the bottle, he tells of his solitary return through the woods before dawn. In this fine letter one can recapture the delight of an escape that was often open to him through his keen understanding of the natural scene of his homeland. 'It grew very dark indeed and I lost my way, trying to fix my direction vaguely by the stars. I encountered strange sounds and touches in the wood—a branch of beech stroking past me, or a trunk of peeled wood across the path, or deep mud under my feet suddenly. The sounds of the wood at night—the stampede of frightened deer when you feel every nerve of their limbs in the dark,

---

[10]Heinrich von Kleist. Politische und Journalistische Schriften. Ausgewählt und eingeleitet von Adam von Trott. 1935. Alfred Protte Verlag. Potsdam.
The translations of the text are by Mr Harold Kurtz and the writer.
[11]Julie Braun-Vogelstein. Autobiography *Was Niemals Stirbt* Deutsche Verlags-Anstalt. Stuttgart 1966. Referred to later as J.B.V.
[12]C.T.; Letters C.T.

and the owls or birds frightened out of their sleep; very occasionally a
dog barking in the distance.'

In August 1934, a friend, whom Adam had not seen for two years,
came into his life once more. He was called Helmut Conrad.

They had been fellow students at Berlin University in the last months
of 1929, and had again met there some time in 1932. Conrad was a man
of working-class origin. He had been born in Berlin where he got his
first schooling, till his parents moved to Waldersee near Dessau in Anhalt.
From secondary school he obtained a scholarship in 1929 and entered
Berlin University. Like Adam he was a law student. While he was still
a schoolboy in Dessau, in 1927, Conrad had become a member of the
Social Democratic party and among University students he was a
prominent member of socialist clubs.

While Adam completed his education at Oxford, Helmut Conrad continued student at Heidelberg and Halle where he was about to take his
University law finals, making him eligible for referendarship, when the
arrival of Hitler to power forced him to leave the University. The local
Nazis knew all about his Social Democrat interests. Before long he was
warned that he was in danger, and in May of 1933 he emigrated to the
South of France where he made a living as a workman, finally obtaining
employment in a book-selling business in Lyons. In the autumn of the
same year he appealed, with success, for the annulment of legal proceedings which were pending against him and he was able to return to
Germany. At this time, in 1935, he wanted to resume his University
career and take the examination for which he had not been able to sit in
1933. During his days of exile Adam had applied for help for Conrad
through the International Student Service, and Conrad now asked Adam
to help him to regain University status. This Adam was able to do. He
obtained his admission to Bonn through Professor Count Dohna.

In August Helmut Conrad came to Imshausen as Adam's guest, and
the earlier acquaintance deepened. He came to occupy a position in
Adam's life for which there were parallels. Although he was Adam's
junior by half a year, he became in some sort an elder brother to him, as
A. L. Rowse had once been. For his actual elder brother Adam was never
wanting in affection, but Werner was so strange, so authoritative, so
egocentric for all his generosity of mind, that relations with him could
never be easy; hence this search, occasionally apparent in Adam's life,

for a substitute brother. On this occasion the search was successful. With his rougher experience of the world, Conrad's political ideas were more firmly rooted in fact. He could act as a political mentor and at times as a severe critic to Adam, and in his turn Adam was grateful because he knew well that his impulsiveness often needed a check and that his delight in complex ideas could be self-defeating. The relationship which sprang up between them was a very happy one.[13]

Another visitor in that August was Shiela Grant-Duff. She came to Kassel and in the course of her stay was driven out by Adam to spend a day at Imshausen. The first meeting of Shiela and Adam's mother was not auspicious. The conversation unhappily turned to the subject of the Polish Corridor, which no German of any party could contemplate except with indignation against the peace-makers of 1919 who had devised it. Frau von Trott voiced this indignation. Shiela, dutifully liberal, insisted that since the frontier was ethnographically precise it was just and should not be revised. The tension in the room rose. No one seems to have made the point that since the victory of Nazism no frontiers could be rectified in Germany's favour anywhere without inflicting appalling injustice on the inhabitants of disputed areas. The debate seems to have remained strictly national in character. Though there was no rudeness Shiela did not mince her words. Nor did Frau von Trott. They both felt very strongly on the subject and while the argument persisted, Adam suffered quietly in the background.[14]

The episode had a happy ending however. When the visit was over Shiela was beset by feelings of regret for her inconsiderate behaviour. A few days later, after she had left for Salzburg, Adam was able to reassure her. 'You must not be sorry for a single more second to have "quarrelled" with my mother; she told me that your talk afterwards had brought you nearer than if you hadn't previously misunderstood each other—that she liked you a great deal and was extremely sorry for her impatience, very apologetic indeed for she felt she had spoilt something with it for us. It was entirely due to her extremely bad nervous depression at the present, and there's truly no cause for the slightest depression—you are very

[13]C.T. An interview with Conrad in C.B. An autobiographical note by Helmut Conrad dated 20.12.54.
[14]Shiela Grant-Duff. Discussion.

affectionately remembered at I.' Shiela remained, and at the moment of
writing remains 'affectionately remembered at I.'

In December Adam's professional luck turned at last. He obtained the
coveted transfer to Berlin, being appointed to a firm of lawyers there who
specialised in his favourite legal subject (in so far as he had one), namely
international law. His chief was Paul Leverkühn whom Adam described
to his father as 'a generally respected, rather obstinate, but friendly and
intelligent Hanseatic man who invariably gives me ten minutes of his
time, never more, every day.' This was written early in their association, and at a later date Adam might have expressed himself about Herr
Leverkühn in more encouraging terms. In fact his chief took a great
liking to his new associate and admired his ability. When he came to
know Adam better in the course of this Berlin period, which lasted a little
less than six months, Leverkühn went so far as to offer him a partnership
in his firm which was one of the most distinguished in Germany. Adam
refused this flattering offer, though it is not difficult to imagine how tempting it must have been.

The reasons for his refusal are well expressed in what he wrote himself
some time before this in a letter to Diana. 'Time reckoning must be essentially different for you than for me. You can afford to plan for a lifetime
ahead, while I can reckon for a few months only, but I am determined as
ever not to let my little boat smash in these preparatory stages of the great
tide.' He was still holding on to his ever more desperate belief that the
upheaval in Germany might turn out to be a beneficial revolution, and
Hitler no more than another Robespierre, doomed, like the original, to
fall after a short reign.

Adam's new appointment to Berlin was by no means the everyday
transaction which it appeared to be. It had a clandestine political character,
and had been made possible in large part by the efforts of one of his first
patrons, Albrecht Bernstorff.[15] Since long before the Nazi regime Bernstorff had been a declared and uncompromising enemy of Hitler and
everything he stood for. As Counsellor in the German Embassy in London
till 1933, he was loud in his denunciation of the rising power, and, aware
of the growth of some soft-hearted and soft-minded acceptance of the
Nazi case in England, he was never louder than in places where he was

[15]C.T.

likely to be overheard, notably the Savoy Grill which he frequented with a devotion to good living worthy of the novelist whom the Savoy Hotel inspired.[16] Soon after January 1933 he was obliged to resign from the Foreign Service. He then entered the employment of a noted Jewish firm, the Wassermann Bank. He often returned to England where he kept up his loud and almost public condemnation of the Nazis. His German and English friends advised caution in vain. In Bernstorff's view Hitler incarnated evil and no considerations of personal safety or German national advantage must inhibit opposition.

Bernstorff was in touch with the *Neue Blätter* group which now, since the cessation of the paper, had a centre in Peter Mayer's book-shop in Berlin. (The shop survived a natural Nazi wish to suppress it because it ministered to the dubious literary tastes of certain prominent party members who for that reason gave it precarious protection.)[17] There were opposition elements in the Leverkühn firm and Adam's association was facilitated by Bernstorff in secret consultation with the *Neue Blätter* group. A socialist acquaintance of Adam, Arnold von Borsig, lent him his flat in the Meiningenallee. Borsig was also in clandestine relations with Peter Mayer and his friends, and Adam was given these quarters in a large block overlooking a new working-class settlement area of Northern Berlin because this opposition group wanted the flat occupied by a reliable non-Nazi in Borsig's absence. They found it useful for storing purposes and as a meeting-place.[18] Adam's transfer was surrounded by conspiracy.

The gloom of 'living between hope and despair, enduring the fate of political adventurers'—to quote from Adam's essay on Kleist—was not often visible in Adam's conduct or way of life. After his long experience of provincial tedium he threw himself enthusiastically into the life of Berlin, and as before what he most enjoyed was Berlin's immense variety. As in his student days he loved to take part in long political arguments with Left-Wing enthusiasts including Communist party members in the working-class district near which he lived, or, relishing the contrast, to go out in fashionable society, or to go to wild parties with fellow-mem-

---

[16]The writer had some acquaintance with Bernstorff in London at this time. The Savoy Grill instituted the *Omelette Arnold Bennett* (incorporating haddock and cheese) in memory of the novelist shortly after his death in 1931.
[17]Goronwy Rees. Discussion. [18]J. P. Mayer. Discussion.

bers of his student corps, and, as always in his life, to make a large number of new friends.[19] Here in the capital he again met many foreigners and sometimes found opportunity for reviving Oxford friendships. 'The day before yesterday', he wrote soon after his arrival, 'Maurice Bowra suddenly turned up . . . Strange how almost two years' absence had done hardly anything to this contact.'[20] The main difference between this Berlin period and the first was that whereas in his younger days he had neglected his studies in the pursuit of pleasure, he was now extremely hardworking, both in his profession and in his serious interests outside it.

During this time he was involved in the frustrating arguments with the Protteverlag mentioned already. They were probably all the more exasperating because Kleist had become such an absorbing interest with him. Living in Prussia he found his imagination kindled by a sense of being near to the life which Kleist had known. One member of this family belonged to Adam's student corps, the Göttingen Saxons, and he invited him to a Kleist estate, Gross-Tychow, for the Christmas holiday.

Among those whom he met was Ewald von Kleist-Schmenzin, one of the finest German men of his time. He had boldly opposed Nazism from the beginning and continued to do so until the end of his life, undeterred by frequent threat and even arrest. He was marked down for death in the June massacre of 1934 and had escaped by a combination of great skill and luck. He took to Adam immediately and letters show that they became friends and often met after this in Berlin. But the friendship did not mature, by accidental circumstances in all likelihood, so that Adam's endeavours were pursued independently of those of the older man with whom he shared a main objective in life.[21]

A very good letter to Shiela conveys the delight and admiration with which Adam discovered for himself the superficially forbidding world of Pomerania.

'I had one of the most interesting experiences of my life—my first time in East Elbian squirearchy. I have met with human greatness in struggle that made my heart jump with joy and pride. And I have met with life "solid and ordered" as one does rarely nowadays. Think of infinite planes

[19]Mrs Hopkinson. Discussion and D.H., C.T. [20]D.H.
[21]The best account available in English of Ewald von Kleist-Schmenzin is to be found in Fabian von Schlabrendorff's *The Secret War Against Hitler*. London 1965.

of acres with hard (no longer sinister) lines of pine-trees along which horses are galloping with the light carriage, my friend explaining to me the cultivation and history of their administering it. Though I was a little ill, I was extremely happy there.

'Yesterday I came all the way (very near our Eastern frontier) with a little open car I borrowed, with a thick fox-fur coat, taking 8½ hours driving in all, because most roads were iced and snowed.'

During this winter of 1934 to 1935 Adam, among his many new friend-ships, made another of those lasting ones which influenced him. This was with a Jewish lady of remarkable intelligence, the widow of the Social Democrat thinker and politician Heinrich Braun. She retained her maiden name and was thus known in Berlin society as Frau Braun-Vogelstein. In her Adam found an irresistible combination of qualities: a woman of strong personality and mind, which was agreeably lightened by a ready sense of humour. She was almost a generation older than he was, and in the ardent friendship that grew up between them one may again discern that search for a mother-figure which has inevitably become something of a characteristic of Adam's biography.

According to Julie Braun-Vogelstein's own account Adam first visited her some time in January 1935. He came to her house on the Erlenweg in the suburb of Klein-Machnow, which lies about twelve miles from the centre of Berlin and six from Potsdam. He met her through two friends, Hasso von Seebach and Peter Mayer, and his reason for seeking her acquaintance was that he wished to know more about the political ideas and career of her husband, Heinrich Braun. She had written a biography of him which had come out three weeks before Hitler was appointed Chancellor. The critics pusillanimously neglected it in the press and the booksellers followed suit. They calculated the prevailing mood correctly. But the book had had three weeks of freedom in which to find readers, and one of them had been Adam for which reason he wanted to meet the author. Julie Braun-Vogelstein remembered this first meeting many years after.

'So far I had hardly heard of him, but the very fact of his visiting Jews gave him away as hostile to the Nazi regime. When entering my study in the attic, he seemed too tall for the low ceiling; but far more striking was the inner stature revealed in his expression and in the intensity of his eyes. None of the crimes perpetrated by the Nazi regime were mentioned; the moment I saw him I knew—here is a European and a Christian, and here the two are one. As he concentrated on the topics discussed, his whole being made itself felt in all its complexity. A casual remark about his ancestral estate which dates back to the Middle Ages suggested how highly he valued tradition; yet he was on fire to find new forms to rectify social iniquities. His was a keen and delicate sense of justice which we had many an opportunity later on to test; although expressed in Hegelian terms, it evidently sprang from his own heart, from his feeling for the dignity of man and the sacredness of the human soul.'[22]

The friendship ripened quickly. At one of their early meetings Adam's romanticism came out in a characteristic and somewhat comical manner. He asked Julie Braun-Vogelstein about her family history and she told him that she knew little of her remote paternal ancestors beyond the fact that they lived in Hersfeld in Hesse and migrated to Westphalia at the time of the Thirty Years War. Adam was thrilled by this. 'Then my ancestors protected you', he cried, 'during the Jewish persecutions of the Middle Ages and even after!' His new friend shook her head and told him that there was neither documentation nor oral tradition to the effect that the Vogelstein family had been Schutzjuden[23] of the Trotts zu Solz. But Adam would not have this. 'Oh please let me believe it was so,' he said, 'because Hersfeld belonged to our estate in those days.' She noted with amusement that this unhistorical assumption did him credit nonetheless, and she was soon to find that in these horrible days when the Jews again needed influential protection he was ready to act with resolution in the spirit of his chivalrous fancy.[24]

One day he asked her if he might come to stay for a week in Klein-Machnow. She was delighted but warned him that to take up quarters in a Jewish household, even for a short visit, might be unwise from his professional point of view. Adam scorned such fears and came to stay

---

[22]A memorandum written in English by Mrs Braun-Vogelstein before the publication of J.B.V. Referred to subsequently as Memo B.V.

[23]In penal times there were two classes of exempted Jews: Schutzjuden, or 'Jews under protection' of an influential Gentile, and Hofjuden, 'Court Jews' who were protected by the reigning prince.

[24]J.B.V.

with her and her niece. She had the impression that apart from affection, and from a wish to escape the loneliness of his flat, he wanted to stay because he thought that his presence might afford the family some protection. In all he paid three visits, the last one in April when he went there to recover from a boil-infection. During the second visit there occurred a curious and painful episode which throws light on Adam's character and his difficult relations with his fellow oppositionists.[25]

As before, the latter were worried by his lack of discretion which arose from his delight in varied acquaintance. Julie Braun-Vogelstein says in her autobiography, 'When Adam went to a dinner of the Saxo-Borussen [as his student corps was also known], he found the contrast with the Braun household thoroughly exhilarating; he took a childish delight in the fact that he could move in such diverse circles.' It seems that he overlooked the fact that what is allowable and desirable in a civilised society can be the cause of mischief in one as barbaric as the Third Reich. He could not and would not hold himself aloof from any section of society.

All the same, he would probably have been far more cautious if he had known more about the intentions and plans of Peter Mayer and his friends at this moment. As mentioned already, they had adopted extremist ideas after June 1934 and certain of them, including Mayer, were now in secret consultation with members of the Communist party for the accomplishment of the single, simple blow which they believed would deliver Germany. Hitler in those days was by no means so minutely guarded as in later years, and they believed, probably with truth, that by means of Communist workmen in charge of the scaffolding on a public occasion to be graced by the Führer, they could assassinate him. During the winter of 1934-35 they laid their plans, but, being in alliance with Communists, without whose help, it seems, the conspiracy had no hope of success, they had to obtain the approval of authorities in Moscow. For so serious an undertaking this presumably meant the approval of Stalin himself. A decision was delayed till the beginning of spring. The plan was disapproved.[26] It is interesting to learn that in all probability Stalin person-

[25]J.B.V. and an interview which Mrs Braun-Vogelstein gave the writer in New York 1965, referred to subsequently as Interview B.V. Also a letter from Trott to his mother of April 1935.
[26]J. P. Mayer. Discussion.

ally saved the life of his greatest rival in massacre. The mountain tops
saluted each other, or perhaps one should say that dog decided not to eat
dog.

Knowing how Adam differed from them over their new extremism,
the men conducting this conspiracy did not take him into their confidence,
and this did not make relations more agreeable. Worsening relations came
to a crisis over a piece of gossip. It originated with a young man who, says
Julie Braun-Vogelstein, 'was in more danger than most as a Jew; he had
as a result of his experiences grown over-sensitive or at least thoroughly
distrustful.'[27] He took a dislike to Adam and gave out his opinion that
he was a vain and haughty person like all his class, and not so whole-
heartedly opposed to Nazism as he pretended.

When this was repeated to him, Adam was beside himself with rage.
He demanded that the young man should explain himself, not only to
himself personally but in the presence of others who had heard the libel.
The meeting was held in the house on the Erlenweg, and Julie Braun-
Vogelstein was present. 'Adam refuted this accusation so brilliantly,' she
remembered long after, 'turning defence into attack, that he disarmed and
defeated the other.'[28] He angrily insisted that the spreading of gossip
likely to cast doubt on good faith was a 'breach of solidarity.' He said that
it was not only wicked from a political but from a human point of view,
and although he was a practised speaker, the unfortunate young man who
had spread the gossip found himself reduced to shame and silence. The
apology was given, the incident declared closed, and the meeting dispersed. But now that he had won his point Adam was dejected in turn.
He looked uneasy and troubled, and said to his hostess: 'kein Mensch
sollte von einem anderen Menschen so niedergedrückt werden—No man
should be crushed like that by another'[29]—in itself a telling answer to a
charge of arrogance.

A short time after, Adam had an opportunity to show the reality of
what his new friend called his 'keen and delicate sense of justice.' He often
used to motor out to the house in Klein-Machnow to spend an evening
with Frau Braun-Vogelstein and her niece Hertha Vogelstein, and Adam's
friend Hasso von Seebach who lived permanently in a room in their
house. Sometimes he would spend the night. He was drawn to this house-

[27]J.B.V.   [28]Memo B.V.   [29]J.B.V.

hold not only by his affection but because of his continuing and increasing interest in Heinrich Braun, and in his son Otto Braun who was killed in France during the First World War. His interest lay in the fact that Braun's main political purpose had been to convert the Social Democratic Party to a positive rôle, and to shake it out of its tendency to become merely a party of criticism, without ambition for responsibility and the exercise of power. He wanted it to cease to be oppositionist in character and to become a party of Government, and Adam, living much of his life among an opposition which was losing hope, saw the lesson for his time. In Klein-Machnow he could enjoy the rare felicity of intense affection conjoined to a stimulating intellectual pursuit.[30]

The presence of Seebach and the frequent visits of Adam had the desirable effect of making the local Nazis cautious about molesting this Jewish home, and for a while they left them alone except for occasional raids on the garden in the middle of the night when paladins of the new chivalry would trample the flower beds and hack the rose bushes.[31] But later there occurred more serious and official efforts at persecution. They appeared to be stimulated by the treachery of a servant who had become a Storm Trooper and been corrupted by his fellow-troopers out of his former respect for the family into believing that Braun had been an enemy of the people, and that his widow was only a semi-human being. This miserable creature had already informed on Peter Mayer in 1934 after he had lent Julie Braun-Vogelstein some forbidden books. As a result Mayer had been held for ten horrible hours by the Gestapo.[32]

One morning Adam drove his hostess into Berlin where she had business. She did not return till late in the afternoon when it was growing dark. She had a presentiment of something untoward when she caught sight of the silhouette of Adam walking up and down in her garden as though in a state of distress. He ran up to her as soon as he heard her arrive and exclaimed: 'It certainly looks like a sentence of death—but perhaps you'll survive it—Es steht zwar Todesstrafe darauf, aber vielleicht kommen Sie doch lebend davon!' She laughed at this odd greeting, and then he told her that on the spur of the moment he had blurted out bad news which he

[30]Interview B.V. In a letter to the writer Mrs Braun-Vogelstein has said: 'Hasso V. Seebach had saved my life and remained with us from then on to protect us.'
[31]Memo B.V.   [32]J. P. Mayer. Discussion.

had planned to break gently. An information had been laid against her
that on her little property there was a secret horde of weapons. Although
Adam could not know just how appallingly dangerous such an accusation
against a friend of Peter Mayer was at this time, he knew enough to
recognise that this might indeed be a sentence of death or one of those
technically milder sentences through which the Nazis loved to degrade
human nature to their purposes.

He had found out (exactly how is not remembered) that a search for
the reported weapons was about to take place. He had telephoned to
numerous friends in the Embassies and Legations requesting support. He
now drove Julie Braun-Vogelstein back to Berlin to the Leverkühn office
where it was agreed that one of Adam's senior colleagues, a fully professed
lawyer who could exert some official authority, would come out in the
morning to act as her legal adviser. Then they drove back. Adam decided
to stay with his friends till the crisis was over. Fortified by his presence
and that of Seebach the family waited. Shortly after the arrival next
morning of the lawyer, a sinister looking group of men in the black
uniform of the secret police arrived. They were accompanied by the local
constable who had known the family for more than ten years. With
fine presence of mind this good man spoilt the dramatic effect of the entry
by addressing the lady of the house in friendly fashion. 'Everything here
is just as it was in dear Herr Doktor Braun's lifetime,' he said.'That does
me good to see. And how nice that you yourself are still here.' As regards
the impending search he said, 'How do you know but that someone has
hidden things here while you were out walking in the woods ?' This was
not the correct official approach towards Jews under suspicion.

The search was then conducted for an hour. It yielded an ancient, rusty
gun which had once belonged to a long deceased relative of Heinrich
Braun. They also found a gas mask of the war. The raid proved a distinct
flop to which the guile of the Wachtmeister and the contemptuous presence of Adam and Seebach added much. A few nights later the garden
was wrecked again. The police were afraid to take action.[33] The thwarted
knights of the New Order had thus some consolation.

To appreciate Adam's valour one must again remember how much

[33]The incident is drawn from J.B.V., Memo B.V., and Interview B.V.

this spring-time of 1935 was a time for special prudence. We now take the story up again at the point where literary criticism left it: his Kleist essay was about to appear and the worldly-wise move was not to give authority any further reason for irritation. But personal loyalty and adherence to principle came first.

During Adam's last few weeks in Berlin, the Siebert case entered a second, characteristic and horrible phase. In April Siebert reached the end of his term of imprisonment. He was liberated and immediately taken into custody again. He was sent to a concentration camp.[34]

Adam took up his cause, but precisely how he worked remains undocumented. At this time Adam made another new friend, Wilfred Israel, the head of the famous Jewish Berlin store, bearing his family's name and founded by them. Wilfred Israel had the advantage of holding a British passport, and he used his anomalous position to fight a long, valiant and often successful battle for the numerous Jewish members of his staff. In this he was helped by Adam, but again only very little is known of his necessarily secret activity. The evidence is scanty but impressive and belongs to a later chapter.

In May 1935 Adam's period as a Referendar in the office of Herr Leverkühn drew to an end. They had been some of the most hectic days of his life; racked by anxiety, frustration, the spectacle of the Nazi power establishing itself impregnably as it seemed; lightened by diverse friendships, a full social life, love affairs, explorations into Marxist thinking, and, as always with Adam, relish in the excitement of danger. Yet at the end of this half year his state of mind was chiefly one of depression. He knew now from a wealth of personal experience how almost impossible it was to organise any effective resistance to the rule of the Nazis. He wrote to Diana, 'I am not sorry I am leaving Berlin, but I am sorry to have failed here.'

He was due to return to Kassel but before resuming practice he was owed a short vacation and he took the opportunity to revisit England and Oxford. This was not a sentimental pilgrimage but a duty necessitated by a tedious intrigue which had afflicted the Rhodes Selection Committee in Berlin, involving Bernstorff and himself in allegations of favouritism.

[34]Siebert. Discussion. In a letter to his mother Trott mentions his correspondence with Siebert's mother who feared that this was about to happen.

He believed that he ought to go to Oxford to explain matters in Rhodes House.

This was his first visit for nearly two years, and he expected it to be unpleasant. As before, nothing was known in Oxford of his life of continual risk on behalf of the victims of Nazism. He was still known, so far as any political activity was concerned, as the author of an extraordinarily foolish letter to the *Manchester Guardian*. He wrote a letter to Diana in which he mentioned the 'nervous malice' which he expected to meet.

In the event he found many friends in Oxford who were glad to see him. Being a city of youth it needs to be a city of forgiveness and the rows that shake the University rarely persist as long as such rows would elsewhere. Bitter feelings about the *Manchester Guardian* seemed to have dissipated. On the 17th of May he wrote to his mother, 'They have received me everywhere in the most friendly way possible, and I have many real friends here whose warm-heartedness is genuine.' He met Isaiah Berlin again. He stayed in All Souls part of the time and there was some healing of the breach between him and his first Oxford friend, A. L. Rowse. He stayed with the Cripps family for a while and then spent some time in London before returning home.[35]

The visit had been more agreeable than he had expected but it was not a success. It is difficult to know why. The fault may have partly been with Adam's temperament, and partly with circumstances. As regards the latter—knowledge of his differences with the *Neue Blätter* group were likely to have reached his English friends. Peter Mayer had paid a visit to Oxford shortly before this visit of Adam, and there he had told a meeting of socialists something of the facts of German rearmament from reliable information which he had from an opposition-sympathiser in the Reichsbank. Through Adam he had already met Stafford Cripps, and through Cripps he now met Adam's friend David Astor who put up money to cover the expense of further research and further contact.[36] It was obvious that Peter Mayer could not be the sole contact, or his frequent journeying would have excited interest, and so it came about that just at this time, in the early summer of 1935, there was rather more exchange of views by rather more personalities than usual between the *Neue Blätter* men and British socialists. Somehow this adversely affected

[35]C.T. and D.H.   [36]J. P. Mayer. Discussion.

Adam's reputation. It is not possible to know precisely how this happened but it is easy to guess. Perhaps inevitably the British people concerned would often want news of Adam who was their original go-between; perhaps inevitably they were often met by head-shakings and other expressions of regret. Whatever happened the result was that vague rumours were around that Adam, like many other estimable Germans, had abandoned opposition and become a Nazi.[37] When people heard this distressing news, they could hardly do other than remember the *Manchester Guardian* business again. Some of this may have come through to Adam and increased his aptitude to irritation.

For a fault of Adam's temperament was his curious liability to be unreasonably irritated by whatever he found to be the prevailing state of affairs in England. He loved England, expected miracles of the place, and was therefore easily exasperated by subsequent disappointment.

He returned to Kassel with relief. 'Hesse is beautiful,' he wrote to Diana, 'so warmly welcoming and reassuring that I wonder how I could ever have admired the English garden.' More reflectively he wrote on his experiences. 'My main political impression seems after all England's indecision in international affairs, fear of war, ultimate readiness to gratify the French and a change of attitude towards Russia.[38] I shall find a few subtle reasons before I describe the internal position as a satirical contrast to ours—I mean "Jubilee" and Conservative authoritarianism. It is very difficult to be inspired by English politics at the moment.'

This short passage shows how very much Adam shared at this time English Left-Wing ideas of which he must have heard much during the visit.[39] When he writes of 'fear of War' he is to be taken as repeating, with sympathy, the persistent disapproval by the Left of Baldwin's efforts to rearm. The Left clung with religious devotion to the simple notion that armament was the major cause of war, and that though opposition to Fascism and Nazism must be whole-hearted and should go to the utmost length of collective security, it must involve a minimum of armament or even no armament at all, as otherwise the danger of war was increased.

[37]Patricia, Countess Russell. A letter.
[38]Presumably this refers to the conclusion of the Franco-Soviet Treaty in May 1935.
[39]During the visit he met R. H. Tawney for the first time. C.T., D.H.

Baldwin's pitifully inadequate response to the open Nazi threat, like that of his successor Neville Chamberlain, was held to be expansionist, aggressive and a psychologically diseased product of unwholesome fear.

Adam remained in Kassel for three months only. At long last his book came out in June. He sent a copy to Shiela on the 26th: 'And this is the Kleist for you,' he wrote. 'You may like to look at the mask even if you cannot like my veiled and indirect introduction.[40] I am happy to put it in your hands now—you are the first English person who gets it. You would have loved and admired Kleist, his chivalrous, hard and noble life ... I remember telling you about him in the Reinhardswald when we were sitting under the beeches waiting a rain to pass.'

He had some visitors, English and German, during this summer in Kassel. One of the most refreshing of these was Dick Crossman with whom he took up again the discussion which was almost the basis of their friendship, and in which they furiously disagreed. It concerned Hegel again. Crossman tried to convince his friend that the great philosopher was not worth a moment's study. He would say such things as this: 'If you're interested in statist philosophy you ought to read Plato and then you can skip through to Marx and forget Hegel—yes, yes, I know what you're going to say—that Hegel is the basis of Marx—but the point is that Marx has a meaning which can only mean one thing, whereas with Hegel the meaning can be almost anything you want—you can take him as a fascist or a humanitarian or a revolutionary or a conservative or a warmonger depending on which qualification of what proposition you are going to see as his ultimate thought—and the result is that the whole thing is so much rot,' though by his own report he used a more forcible term.

With him Adam not only enjoyed the delight of strenuous intellectual combat, but as with Goronwy Rees, he also enjoyed frivolous companionship. If they had much on which to disagree, they had yet more on which to agree, and Mr Crossman has described to the writer how sometimes when they discussed together the tragedy which had engulfed the

[40]This refers to Shiela's imperfect understanding of German, not to the opinion implied in the essay which must have been very much to her taste.

country, and when the subject grew agonising, Adam would suddenly cry out, 'Oh Hell! what's the use of it—let's go out and get tight and have fun.' And they would do so.[41]

In September his life took a new turn. He moved to Hamburg, but before that he met an unpleasant check in his professional career. It came from Doctor Kessler who has been mentioned already as the 'group-leader' in charge of Adam's ideological and political education. The incident is rather odd. Doctor Kessler was required to turn in a yearly report on the young lawyers in his charge. It is evident that he had come to the conclusion that Referendar von Trott was not fully in tune with the new course under Adolf Hitler, but since he was not an acute observer, he saw very little else. He thus misdiagnosed the case in truly absurd fashion. He asserted (correctly enough) that Adam's whole attitude to the new course was one of scepticism, but from there he went on to say that this was because Adam was a man of rigid ideas who could not adopt a new outlook. Doctor Kessler went on to say that Adam was a scholar and intellectual and not a man of fighting spirit. (Fighting spirit, according to Doctor Kessler's ideas may be taken to mean acquiescence in the Nazi belief that it was a patriotic duty to do everything in one's power to provoke war and persecution.) The report concluded with the remark that though Adam was a man of many gifts, he was lacking in integration of character. In Nazi parlance integration of character meant blind devotion to whatever one was told to be devoted to by Hitler, Goebbels or Rosenberg.[42]

Considering the defiance of the Nazis which he had shown openly since his return to Germany, and considering all the oppositional activity he had undertaken and about which his mentor happily knew nothing, this report, though adverse, could be accounted very mild. Adam protested vigorously against it and at a later date did in fact succeed in getting it toned down, though not withdrawn as he demanded. Kessler was the mouthpiece and instrument of the Nazi Party, Adam of the still lingering integrity of the German legal profession, and in this struggle for principle there could be no compromise. Though there was no doubt that the Nazi was in the stronger position, Adam showed good sense in protesting: to

[41]Mr R. H. Crossman. Discussion.
[42]The gist of the report is given in a letter in D.H.

acquiesce might not decrease suspicion against him and would weaken the
cause he stood for. What is odd is that in his private letters and talk with
his friends he expressed himself bitterly about Kessler's report and described it as a gross act of injustice.[43] He seemed pained and surprised. It
would surely have been a matter for far greater surprise if Kessler had
given him a favourable report and written in glowing terms of his adherence to Nazi ideology.

His move to Hamburg in September 1935 represented another step in
the German lawyer's evolution and was known as a Verwaltungsstation—
an administrative station. There was an alternative, to serve as a 'Government Referendar,' acting in the service of the State. Adam had wished to
do this and had duly applied. After long delay he was told that he was
refused, and there was little doubt that the decision was political. By now
time was running short, and so through the good offices of Doctor Harald
Mandt, another former Rhodes scholar and a well-known Hamburg
business man and personality, Adam obtained an attachment, for three
months, to a shipping company, the Levant Line.[44]

[43]C.T., D.H.
[44]C.T.

Chapter 8

PERSISTENCE AND ESCAPE

Adam's Hamburg period was a happier time than Berlin. He had friends there, the Warburgs, Helmuth Boehncke whom he had not seen since the days of the Nibelungenbund, and not far off, at Stintenburg in Mecklenburg, was the family home of Albrecht Bernstorff.

He was at first somewhat dissatisfied with his work for as usually happens with short-term attachments to large organisations, no one was particularly anxious to entrust him with tasks which he might not be able to finish. Added to this he could only give part of his working day to his office as he needed to spend much time on his legal studies. His father gave him sage advice. 'In your office try above all to give the impression of a *diligent* young man. Business men tend to scepticism when they judge the industry of other people.'

Two events outside the world of Hamburg occupied Adam in his early days in his new post. The 15th September, 1935 was one of the blackest days of the new Germany. The annual party rally was being held in Nuremberg, and in the course of it, on the 15th, the Führer summoned the Reichstag to meet in a concert hall. There the deputies were called upon to pass an act ratifying three new measures known afterwards as the Nuremberg Laws. These defined the inferior civil status of non-Aryan people within the Reich and were aimed primarily at the Jews. Here was the beginning of the 'Final Solution.' It may seem strange that there is no comment, open or veiled, about this fatal event to be found anywhere in Adam's surviving letters, but the explanation is simple.

Since he had left Berlin in May the situation of his friends in Klein-Machnow had become more dreadful. Twice Adam had had to go back to Berlin to help them, and had done so valiantly.[1] But during the Septem-

[1]C.T.

ber of the Nuremberg Laws, suspicion and the crowd of informers thick-
ened, and in Nazi councils the idea began to take hold that Julie Braun-
Vogelstein, whose recently deceased brother Ludwig had been chairman
of the American Metal Company, was secretly the 'President of the American Copper Trust' (a non-existent body), and was engaged in a gigantic
Jewish plot to deny copper supplies to the Reich. She was seen (in all
seriousness) as a kind of female Elder of Zion. In October she and her
niece Hertha left the home where they had spent many happy years. They
left for France, their purpose being to resettle in America. Hasso von
Seebach went with them.[2]

The second event occurred very soon after.

In September 1935 Hans Siebert was liberated. He had been in a concentration camp, near Torgau on the Prussian-Saxon border. For six
months he had witnessed all the horrors associated with those places and
suffered many of them. His liberation came as a surprise to himself for
he had been given to understand that he was to serve a long term of
punishment. His Communist friends had opened intrigues of fantastic ingenuity to obtain his freedom, and he himself never knew precisely how
they succeeded. All that is important to know for the purpose of this
biography is the following: that according to what his friends told him,
it would have been impossible to manoeuvre the authorities into giving
Siebert his freedom without the help of Adam. Beyond that fact nothing is
known about what Adam did, and probably never can be known.

Adam obtained clerical employment for Siebert in Hamburg and stood
surety for him with the authorities. In keeping with the report which he
had made in 1934 he declared that he would undertake his political education. This was not entirely a camouflage plan: for all his Left-Wing enthusiasm and his increasing study of Marx, he sincerely wished to convert
Siebert to his own liberal ideas. Of course the authorities understood
by 'political education' something quite different, and so in that sense
there was deception in a good cause. In the event Adam struggled valiantly
for Siebert's soul, but not with success.

The two men grew very attached. They addressed each other as 'Du'
(a familiarity which Adam only allowed to a few of his closest friends)
and they would go down to Imshausen together for week-end visits.

[2]J.B.V. p. 370.

*General view
of Imshausen*

*Adam's grandfather:
General and
Ambassador
von Schweinitz*

Adam's mother

Adam and one of his sisters with their English nurse

Imshausen

Adam with his father

Adam's father in old age

A general view of Solz

Above. Adam (left) in the uniform of his student corps at Göttingen University. Below. With Professor Gustav Ecke in China

Adam as a young man

Husband and wife

Frau von Trott liked Adam's new friend. Once she said to Siebert something of this kind: 'As you must know by now, my son has a great deal
of Don Quixote about him and he likes to rush into battle, often without
thinking of the consequences, or making his preparations. He wants a
good Sancho Panza to look after him, and I hope you will do that for
him. Keep him out of trouble. You will find it difficult because Adam
rather likes trouble.'

On the occasion of one visit there was something of a crisis at Imshausen, as the local Nazis had complained that on a day of festival the
swastika-decorated red flag had not been flown on the house.[3] The local
Storm Troopers had threatened to hoist it forcibly. When the news was
brought to Frau von Trott she said 'They will do nothing of the kind. If
they want to try, send them to *me*.' That was the last heard of the matter.
As she grew older Frau von Trott retained her imperious strength of
character and personality, on which account even friends of the family
passing near Imshausen had sometimes found themselves afraid to call.
Yet with the hardening that often accompanies age, she lost nothing of
the warmth of heart which her stern appearance and manner could conceal. As always she had wonderful breadth of sympathy. It was not to
be expected that this stern-minded and aristocratic lady would welcome
as a frequent visitor a young man convicted of Communist activity, but
she treated Hans Siebert as one of the family.

In Hamburg Adam introduced Siebert to the Warburgs. It seems that,
warned by the fate of his friends in Klein-Machnow, Adam's purpose was
to get Siebert to make the family aware of their danger and persuade
them to leave. The two daughters, Ingrid and Eva Warburg, were both
busily occupied in the work of arranging for the transport of Jews from
the port of Hamburg to Palestine, and they were in no need of persuasion
that they were living in a dangerous country, but their father persisted,
even after the institution of the Nuremberg Laws, in regarding the future
with complacency. He did not want to seem to run away, he said, and
he reminded Siebert that his family had largely financed the building
of the Imperial navy in the days of Kaiser Wilhelm II, for which reason
the ultra-nationalists now in charge would not turn on him, for that would

[3]The first of the Nuremberg laws declared that the Nazi flag was now the national
emblem.

be grossly illogical. Adam and Siebert insisted that there was only the logic of hysteria in Nazism, that Nazi hatred of the Jews was a form of madness and brought with it a thirst for revenge that was insatiable. Herr Warburg smiled at the impetuous anxieties, as they seemed to him, of his two young friends. Hamburg is very untypical of Germany as a whole, especially in what Germans call 'stimmung'—'atmosphere'—and it is easy to feel somewhat detached from the affairs of Berlin, Munich and elsewhere in that ancient and lovely city. Nazism never obtained a full hold on Hamburg.[4] Herr Warburg's complacency is understandable.

But it was during the winter of 1935 and 1936 that the Nazis did in fact turn on the Warburg family and interests. Herr Warburg was told that he would be at liberty to leave, but on condition that he left his wealth behind. In the end (at a later date than this) the family did leave for America, with much difficulty and loss.

Siebert's political education at the hands of Adam persisted so long as they were together during that winter. The pupil was obstinate as only a Marxist can be, and Adam preached liberalism in vain. From what Hans Siebert has told the writer of their long dialogue during three months, one can see the direction of Adam's political ideas at this time. Being remembered by a dedicated Marxist they may be presented in a somewhat more Right-Wing version than is absolutely just, though the account is consistent in general with what Adam declared to be his beliefs at other times both before and after.

He still looked on himself as a 'conservative revolutionary' and it was to such a position that he hoped ultimately to lead Siebert. He insisted that he stood for a Germany that would be far more democratic in character than the Weimar Republic; in which there would be no vast estates, the land being in the possession of peasant smallholders; a Germany in which class-barriers would come to be non-existent; in which taxation would be primarily concerned with a juster distribution of wealth at the expense of those who had built great fortunes through commercial investment or possession of land—the classic socialist liberal programme, in

---

[4]To the city's lasting honour, Hitler had a great aversion to Hamburg and avoided visiting it. He is said to have insulted the inhabitants by describing them as 'no better than Englishmen.'

fact. What was novel in Adam's conservative-revolutionary programme was an element of class-preference rarely found on the Left. If this new Germany was to emerge successfully, Adam argued, it must have the advantage of being guided by the traditional leaders of the country. 'We have centuries of experience in leadership,' said Adam, 'and it would be folly not to use it.'

Siebert's answer to the latter argument was that the Prussian aristocracy and its associates were, as a matter of historical observation, lacking in the gift of leadership. When the Government was entrusted to such people, he said, their leadership of the Empire after Bismarck's time had merely carried the country into the aimless war of 1914-1918, and their latest contribution had been to facilitate the rise to power of the Nazi party. He himself was working, as a Communist, for a popular front. He had no class prejudice and would welcome members of the nobility as political colleagues—but decidedly not as leaders. He considered that the Communist Party had a far firmer grasp of the needs and technique of leadership than had been shown at any time by Prussian Junkerdom.

This would rouse Adam to renew that theme which they had already explored in the prison in Kassel. The men who had brought Communism from obscurity to a place in the world, and from there to power, Marx, Engels, Lenin, had all come from what might be described as privileged families, and Adam held that this fact alone almost proved his point, that popular movements would fail if left to proletarian leadership. (They do not seem to have discussed any possible claims by Stalin to gentle birth.)

Discussion of Siebert's hopes for a Communist-led popular front would then recall Adam to his mission, and he would try to impress on his friend that the danger of Communist rule in Germany was that the country would immediately find itself in a position of weakness, at the mercy of Russia. The aim of German foreign policy, he said, was to make the nation once more 'Das Volk in der Mitte,' (to remember Bismarck's phrase), between Russia and Western Europe. This required tact and skill and a sense of German tradition, and these qualities were to be found in the kind of families who had produced his hero Heinrich von Kleist. 'People of that kind (and I belong to them) understand how to raise Germany to this exacting and honourable position,' he would say. 'And those are the sort of people who know how to get rid of Hitler.' And Siebert would answer, 'Well, all they've done so far is to let him in.' Conversion remained out of sight.[5]

The correspondence between Adam and Shiela had persisted at the same rate and volume as before. A gap of a few days, and they were liable to accuse each other of neglect. Almost all their letters of 1934 and 1935 are so much concerned with private matters that their political debate becomes thrust into second place. Their most interesting political difference in 1934 occupied only a little more than a hundred words. It concerned the Saar. Shiela had been asked to report as a journalist on the plebiscite, organised by the League of Nations, which was to decide whether the Saar basin, which was a part of Prussia before the First World War, was to be a part of France or Germany or retain its treaty status. This coal-mining area had been detached from Germany by articles 45-50 of the Treaty of Versailles. It was then placed under the government of a League Commission and the exploitation and rights were ceded to France for fifteen years as compensation for the industrial damage inflicted on the country by the German army in its final retreat. At the end of the fifteen years the status of the Saar was to be resolved by a plebiscite which fell due in January 1935.

Most Germans believed that in justice there could only be a decision in favour of German nationality in this German-speaking province. Fair-minded Frenchmen admitted the force of the German claim, but hoped that there would be a majority for French nationality as a protest against the barbarism of Nazi Germany. In the event the German claim triumphed. Adam's attitude was not likely to be in doubt, and he expressed his feelings in the course of the same letter to Shiela in which he told of his visit to the Kleist estates.

'Why should your life, both "spiritual and material," be so upset? You are obviously too much of a Teuton for slim Paris and your wish to change it for Berlin is so much the call of your better nature.[6] Do come, Shiela—but I should if I were you under no circumstances leave out the Saar. What an opportunity of a most promising experience. Not that

[5]Hans Siebert. A discussion covering the whole period of his stay in Hamburg.
[6]Shiela had suggested a visit to Berlin in a recent letter.

there will be much going on—but a most curious incident of the Teuton combating the Latin Spirit.' Shiela replied three days later in a long letter which is again mainly concerned with private affairs, but which ends thus:

'You long as much as any of your 60 million countrymen for the victory of the Teutonic over the Latin race—but it would be a terrible thing. There is no struggle between them, not even in the Saar—and if there was, it would be worse than the end of the Roman Empire. Oh Adam—don't be taken in.'

Soon after Adam's arrival, at the end of September 1935, Shiela came on a visit to Hamburg from Paris. She stayed about five days and on one of them they drove out to spend the night at Schloss Stintenburg with Albrecht von Bernstorff. The visit was marked by a comedy which they remembered long after.

A fellow guest was the Minister in the British Embassy, a certain Mr Basil Newton. At this time Newton (at any rate in private conversation) was in the habit of assuring his friends and acquaintances that Hitler's Government was not a subject for alarm, and he was apt to dismiss any disturbing incident such as the passage of the Nuremberg Laws or some other hideous act of persecution, as 'of purely local interest.' The regularity of his assurances was such that his critics both inside and outside the diplomatic service came to use the phrase 'purely local' as his nickname. A consistent career lay ahead of him. From Berlin he was moved in 1937 to head the British Legation in Prague where he gave his familiar advice about the purely local nature of the Sudeten-Deutsch dispute until, on Czechoslovakia ceasing to exist as an independent country in mid-March 1939, his Legation was automatically withdrawn. His last and most spectacular performance was in Baghdad to which crucial post he was appointed as ambassador after his enforced return from Prague. He advised with the same regularity that talk of a pro-German rising in Irak under Rashid Ali and the so-called 'Golden Square' conspirators was merely foolish exaggeration of a 'purely local' agitation. However other voices, some of them angry, reached the Foreign Office and Sir Basil (as he had now become as a reward for his services) was replaced in Baghdad a week or two before Irak was temporarily overwhelmed by the Rashid Ali rebellion in 1941. Basil Newton was devoted to sport and especially shooting, and Bernstorff used to invite him to shoot duck on

his estate. His purpose was an ambitious one, namely to bring Mr Newton
to some realisation of the danger to the world of Nazi Germany, a task
in which he failed signally.

Newton was expected to arrive on the evening of the day when Shiela
and Adam arrived, and Bernstorff suggested a somewhat conscienceless
game at the expense of his distinguished guest. He planned that in the
course of conversation each of them would ask Newton a prepared question, his answers to which would prove whether or not he was, as Bernstorff maintained, 'bone from the collar-stud up.' The plot was carefully
laid but miscarried as, before the moment for action came, Adam and
Bernstorff became involved in another and unplanned test of the Minister's sagacity, taking the form of a violent mock-quarrel as to whose family
could claim the more ancient lineage, the climax of the argument revol-
ving round the inscription on certain Trott and Bernstorff tombstones.
Mr Newton listened with serious interest, but did not join in this purely
local dispute.[7]

At some time during Shiela's visit to Hamburg Adam proposed marriage to her. She refused. On the day after her return to Paris she wrote to
him as follows on the 2nd of October.

'Perhaps in talking with you I minimised the difference between love
and friendship, fearing the gravity of my answer. If I have seemed insen-
sitive to that gravity, ungrateful for the honour you gave me, unaware
of the consequences of my answer, it is only from the impossibility of
expressing all I have thought, and, if you can understand, from the respect
in which I hold your feelings.

'I know that in offering you friendship for love, I am offering you something which you have not asked for, and refusing something which it
would be an honour to give—but let me give what I have to give, which
is a deep affection for you, a real desire to share in your work and always
to be a warm and steadfast element in your life.'

On the same day Adam wrote to her:

'The new period of my life—marked by your final absence—enveloped
me in a large grey mist in which one does things numbly and without
joy. The autumn in the street where I had brought you so many times

[7]Shiela Grant-Duff. Discussion. The writer had some acquaintance with Basil
Newton.

was empty and cold. Siebert alone had an expression of warmth—I am glad he is here. But to-night I will stay alone.'

The old problem vexed his spirit: how to live, in accordance with his ideal of a German patriot, in a Nazi-dominated Germany. A letter which he wrote to his mother in English on the 10th November, 1935 implies something of the indignities of ordinary life under the nationalist revival. It is written with some artful disguise in case it might have proved useful evidence.

'I should not be a bit worried about the searching idea. Every respectable citizen has been searched some time or other. There is not a thing in my library that I would consider worth confiscating, though quite a number of books that I would very much regret to lose. You might therefore remove those of conspicuously Jewish or Marxist origin. But please look after them well—they are indeed necessary for anyone who is seriously interested in their refutation ... My work is not going too well, I find it difficult to be restful and calm as you should be inside when you want to work hard. And the law is so far from the life that concerns me at the moment ... How is Vera? This is a time to learn calmness and courage both of which I feel rather lacking in. It is nice to think of you nice and quiet together near the stoves and country silences into which you never walk.'[8]

At the end of this month Siebert left Hamburg for Berlin. The firm for which he was working seems to have arranged a transfer. The Siebert case is from its nature one of the least documented episodes of Adam's life, and the deficiency is not always made good by personal memories inevitably distorted by time. What appears likely is that Adam felt uneasy at Siebert's leaving, not only because he could now no longer protect him but because they had both got into some trouble with the police. Siebert could not drive a car and he asked Adam to teach him. This he did, in his own car, but for reasons not now remembered, they did not ask for the necessary licence—perhaps because they were expensive, and

[8]Owing to an intervention in Frau von Trott's favour by the *Landrat* the search did not take place. She had been informed on by a spy at a girls' school where her youngest daughter was studying. C.T.

perhaps because any visit by a convicted Communist to a police station was thought to be unwise. At all events, Adam taught his friend in the woods, driving along the rough paths and in clearings by night. It was not a practical solution as the unusual disturbance in the woods, with shouts of warning as Siebert narrowly missed a tree, could not do other than attract attention. The police came out one night and caught them. They took down the usual details about them but took no further action.[9] At the time Adam inclined to regard the whole thing as a joke, but when Siebert had gone he may have realised that the police had a simple weapon to use against his friend, and possibly against them both, should they wish to.

At the end of December Adam's time in Hamburg came to an end, and after a short visit to Berlin he went for an eight weeks' course held in a Referendaren Lager, a labour camp for young lawyers which was stationed at Jüterbog, about fifty miles South of Berlin. The experience was more congenial than the similar one of two years before, one reason being that this time his fellow-campers were educated men of his own age. His letters both to his parents and his English friends show that in fact he thoroughly enjoyed this break. As mentioned already camps of this kind (at their best, but only then) were one of the few reputable Nazi institutions, and the life appealed to Adam's sociability and his intense deutschtum.[10] He had struck lucky. But he had only been at Jüterbog for a short time when disturbing news reached him. Siebert had been arrested.

On the 28th of January, 1936 Adam wrote to his mother in English: 'As I hear from Kassel to-day my Hamburg friend, the young prisoner, has once more been arrested. There may be trouble ahead for me too, but I am completely calm and have the best of consciences as I am *certain* he did not resume any of his previous trends.' Here Adam was mistaken. He did not understand Communist morality. In fact on going to Berlin Siebert had resumed 'his previous trends' in obedience to party discipline,[11] though how much the police knew about this again remains in doubt. The motoring offence, however, was not raised so far as is known.

Adam announced the news to Shiela as that of Siebert's sudden illness.[12]

---

[9]Siebert. Discussion.   [10]C.T., G.D., D.H. [11]Siebert. Discussion.
[12]The letter is lost but her reply of 9.2.36. allows this deduction.

Thereafter the letters tell us little and from them one cannot know what he did, or indeed whether he did anything at all to bring about Siebert's release. It is the opinion of Herr Siebert to-day that though to do so would have been Adam's natural impulse, he was probably dissuaded by his *Neue Blätter* friends. It proved unnecessary in the event as Siebert was released after two weeks. Again it is not known why, but the opinion of Hans Siebert himself, agreeing with that of his Communist friends at the time, is that he was set free so that he might unknowingly lead the police to the arrest of other and higher-ranking Communist leaders. Being forewarned he acted with extreme circumspection and no one seems to have fallen to the police on his account.

At this point the slight and unclear evidence of Adam's letters, and the memories of those involved are too contradictory as to dates to allow a certain sequence of events to appear. What is important to Adam's story is to bring in one fact: that he arranged for Diana to send Siebert an invitation to stay with her family in London, thus enabling him to obtain a visa and to facilitate his entrance into England.[13] For the moment he passes out of Adam's story, but he was to return to it briefly before the end.

While these events were in early stages, and Adam was still at Jüterbog, he once again found himself the subject of Oxford rumours[14] which reached him. They were again to the effect that he had at last thrown in his lot with the Nazis. To people in England with an imperfect knowledge of how the Nazi system worked, this appeared as the logical inference to make when news came of Adam's attendance at the Referendaren Lager. The rumours had the usual effect of arousing his never simple and always ambivalent emotions about England and English life. He wrote to Diana: 'Sometimes I feel I never want to go to England again, whatever kind of home-sickness I might feel towards it. Happily the world that I love is not moved by these squabbles.'

As usual his anger was short-lived. It was to Oxford, and the world that he loved there, that he turned for counsel shortly before he left the camp in March. An event of great importance had occurred. In early March Hitler proceeded to the cancellation by force of the Locarno Treaty. Less than a year before he had solemnly declared in the Reichstag that he

[13]D.H. [14]D.H.

adhered to its provisions.[15] He now ordered the German army to move into the demilitarised zone of the Rhineland. On the 7th of March the operation was completed.

A letter from Shiela, characteristic of Left-Wing belief in those days, gave Adam an alarming (and misleading) picture of the bellicose response of Great Britain to this fateful challenge: 'This latest news is ghastly. I have just come from a debate in the House of Commons. The Government seems to regard war as inevitable—now the object is to win it. It was heartrending to hear the Government jeers when Morrison and Cripps said there was only one way out—only one hope for peace—a just and equitable world system based on the sharing of wealth and not the competition system. Of course it's not realism—realism now is just to do with guns.'

It may be that this letter moved Adam to seek advice from an Oxford friend. At all events he wrote. His own letter does not survive, but the answer from Maurice Bowra does. It gives a truthful and lucid picture of the British reaction to this sign of the times in the early days of 'appeasement,' before that title had been officially adopted. The letter is from Wadham College and dated the 14th March, 1936.

'My dear Adam,

I was extremely glad to get your charming letter with its many interesting pieces of news. I wish I could see you and have a good talk. Everyone here is naturally excited over the latest situation, and I think there is little doubt that so far as England is concerned some sort of agreement will be patched up. The real factor which will prove decisive is the overwhelmingly pacific feelings of the average man. There is a minor trade boom going on for the bourgeois and they don't at all want to be let in for a war. The young have all listened to speeches from the League of Nations Union for years and regard the idea with horror. It is a very different world from that in which I was brought up which inculcated bigger navies and the splendour of adding to the Empire, so that even if one disliked the idea, one still regarded it as inevitable. The breaking of the Locarno Treaty has not made as great an impression as I should have thought. People think it is part of the Versailles Treaty,

[15]See his speech of 21st May, 1935. *The speeches of Adolf Hitler 1922 to 1939* ed. by Norman H. Baynes. Oxford 1942. Vol. II 1,218—47.

which most countries, England included, have already broken. Against this extreme dislike of the idea of war and a rather cynical desire to patch up any sort of peace, one must put a real fear of war which seems to me to grow every day. Most people one meets speak of it, and when a thing comes to dominate fears like that, it usually, sooner or later, turns into fact since people get hardened to the idea and feel it almost [better] to have the thing itself instead of the terror of it.

'The worst of it all is that England is getting more and more isolated from the intellectual life of Europe than is right or healthy. It is curious to find no important books coming from Germany and the French [are] in such a state that they can only write out of their hysteria. The result is that we too are cut off and stewing in our own juice. This never really suits the English and it is liable to have pernicious results, especially a detached, ignorant and hard-hearted carelessness about what may happen elsewhere and a dangerous tendency to dig our own heads in the sand.

'I see very little of the Germans here. X is a dull fellow and ought never to have got a Rhodes scholarship, and I do not know the others. I feel one can apply what was said of a headmaster of Rugby: "If a Headmaster can't teach and can't preach, he ought to be either a scholar or a gentleman." Zimmer of Heidelberg was here the other day, the most amusing and delightful of men, with an extremely active and imaginative mind, ranging without restrictions over all sorts of fields and expressing itself in the most gay and careless manner. He is very much my idea of what a Prussian man of learning ought to be, and no doubt in the great days there were many like him.

'If I come to Germany I will gladly let you know, but I rather doubt it. I am probably going to lecture at Harvard in September, and before that I have a good deal to do here.

All good wishes
Yours ever
Maurice.'

When the camp broke up Adam went to Berlin, and then once more to Kassel for a last round of hard work before facing his examination for Assessorship which was to take place in stages, beginning in July and end-

ing with an oral session in October. As before he found spiritual consolation in visits from Helmut Conrad. He wrote on one occasion of him 'I
was very much struck by the unbroken clearness of his views though he
spent the last year in comparative isolation from practical affairs . . . (The)
visit did me good. He is intelligent, brave and right-hearted. There is no
reason why I shouldn't be too.'

Helmut Conrad was one of a diminishing band of friends with whom
he could talk freely. Hasso von Seebach had gone, Siebert was about to
leave, and in the spring of 1936 Peter Mayer left Germany for good.

Adam was forced to ask himself again whether emigration was not, after
all, the only sensible course.

He again said No. But there was a great difference in his answer now.
For some time he had been wondering about a very curious plan which
he had devised for himself. It could be described as a qualification of his
feeling against emigration.

Some time in the year before, not later than October 1935, and perhaps
a bit earlier, Adam was moved to write to the hero of his young days,
Gustav Ecke. For several years he had been a teacher in Peking University.
When to his surprise he got a letter from one of his young followers of
twelve years before, he had no clear memory of him. He knew nothing
of Adam's later development and adventures, but he knew his family
and had happy recollections of Imshausen. The subject-matter of Adam's
letter interested him. It was, in brief, that in the world of discordant ideas
in Europe Adam should seek wisdom by the study of Chinese sages,
especially Confucius. Adam asked advice of Ecke and sent him a copy of
his Kleist essay. Ecke returned a friendly reply. The essay told him all
he needed to know about Adam's political position which he found most
sympathetic. He recommended him to undertake his study in China.[16]

On the 19th December, 1935 Adam replied to Ecke in an autobiographical letter. It is a strange vague document in which his intentions
are not clear. It would seem that he was tentatively exploring an impulse
to complement his studies of Hegel with a study of Confucius. This was
a moment in his life when he was much taken with the idea of writing
a critique; in spite of remaining under some Hegelian influence, he had
become prone to misgivings about his former hero. He wrote in this

[16]This may be deduced from Trott's reply of 19.12.35.

letter: 'Hegel's practical philosophy continues to disturb me. Its "dynamic" premises have nowhere else had quite as dangerous an effect as in our country, and their subtle contemplative beatification of an imaginary European order of values is, I suppose, one of the reasons for the tragic impotence of our intellectuals, and even of our whole "civic life".'

In the course of correspondence which continued into the summer of 1936, Adam's purpose began to become clear to himself and his friend. No other detail of his life shows more vividly how extreme was the romantic side of his character than the plan that emerged. Remembering that in 1700 Leibnitz had founded the Academy in Berlin[17] under the influence of what he believed to be the system of learning in China, Adam now conceived the idea of going to the Far East in order to study the works of Confucius from which he hoped to draw the necessary spiritual and intellectual strength to undertake a great work of political reform. Through Confucius, he believed, he would understand the basis of ethical Government and thus be able to give a unique and dynamic contribution to the Germany of the future.[18]

Ecke thoroughly approved the plan. He told Adam he would be welcome to stay with him as long as he liked whenever he could come to China. The plan then remained in abeyance for a few months. Adam decided not to make up his mind until he had passed his Assessor examination.[19]

After the spectacular Nazi success in the Rhineland, Hitler had the sagacity to spend the rest of the year 1936, the year when the Spanish Civil War began, waiting on events rather than initiating them. While he showed his amazing capacity to obtain advantage from any turn that events might take,

---

[17]Strictly speaking the Academy was founded by Frederick I of Prussia as the *Societas Regia Scientiarum* with Leibnitz, the moving spirit in the venture, as first president. The *Societas* grew into *Die Akademie der Wissenschaften zu Berlin* under which name it is commonly known.

[18]A discussion between the writer and Herr Ecke in November 1966. Also a memoir written by Herr Ecke in 1957, referred to subsequently as Ecke.

[19]Between March and October (when he concluded his exam), there are frequent references by Trott in G.D. to a plan to go to the East, but they read as hopes rather than definite plans, and are not usually expressed in serious language.

he avoided extreme provocation in the international field. Though his Luftwaffe help to Franco in Spain is believed to have been vital, he had the advantage here of an issue over which opinions were divided throughout Europe, and his contribution to the nationalists was not massive in numbers, during this year. Even in his Austrian policy he put up a fairly convincing show of moderation. In his own way he practised a policy of appeasement, and, since he wholly neglected the claims of sincerity, he was able to do this with a success that the classic appeasers of the next phase never knew. He reached the end of the year with the Rome-Berlin Axis, the Anti-Comintern Pact, and the weakening of Austria to his undoubted credit.

During this time of sinister quiet Adam's life was relatively uneventful. The Siebert case had seriously endangered him and if he was to obtain his assessorship, and thus fulfil the wish of his father, he needed to lie low, little as this may have been to his taste.

He lived in Kassel as before. He had many visitors, including a few English ones. He travelled round Germany. But most of his time was spent in study for the ordeal which would at last liberate him from the wearisome cycle of examinations. His political life was dormant. In so far as it was active, it centred chiefly on the affectionate and tempestuous correspondence with Shiela.

In July, as Adam was about to sit for the first of his examination papers, Shiela went to Prague as correspondent for *The Observer*, and from the moment of her arrival she unreservedly identified herself with the Czech cause. Her account to Adam of her first encounter with a member of the British Legation makes this plain. 'I felt isolated with him,' she wrote, 'as I have not felt when alone. The implication that we are the English and those are the Czechs sinks into every word and gesture, and in the end one is quite miserable. He was one of those typical Englishmen—very depressed and yet cynical and joking—and cynical not for some disillusion or misfortune, but by nature. I think it is a lack of vitality, lack of spirit in both senses—and yet he was quite nice . . .

'He thinks the Czechs know they are doomed and will be fools if they resist, that the French will not help them, nor will we. He thinks the Poles are sitting on the fence and doing it exceedingly well . . .'[20]

---

[20]Depressing as this person may have been his gift of prophecy was considerable.

Adam's sympathies were far too German to go with Shiela's new enthusiasm. It was not very long before there was a clash. On the 18th August Adam wrote to her:

'Things will go from bad to worse when you make yourself the mouthpiece of our dear neighbours all over the place, because not only will it not fail to make you hostile to the Trott, but—taking your objectiveness for granted—may perhaps bring on more quickly the Spanish state in all Europe[21] ... I am afraid you are becoming very much a Spectator, while Trott, having been allowed the courtesy of a visit in the boxes, is back labouring to produce some of the effects. It's nobler to be a Spectator than a mere producer of effects, true enough—two very separate rôles though.'

Shiela replied five days later: 'I don't know what you mean by saying that I will bring on the "Spanish state" all over Europe if I do what I want to do. Remember who started the Spanish war.[22] Are we just to stand still and let them win over the rest of Europe, because if we do not let them, they will commit the same sort of atrocities here.

'I deny absolutely that any of the neighbours of Germany are a danger to her. Everyone is ready for peace and for the construction of some sort of European system. The only thing they are not ready for are bilateral pacts which leave a very strong spider talking to a very weak fly ... I don't want to be made hostile to you, and am not made because I am not a Spectator and you an actor, as you believe. We are both spectators and actors at the same time and not so very much divided.'

Affection reigned again undisturbed until the beginning of September. In that month Shiela went on a journey to Saxony and wrote to tell Adam how much she had disliked the people there. On this occasion Adam did not spring to the defence, as he usually did, but treated the assault with good humour. There is an odd joke tradition in Germany (incomprehensible to a foreigner) to the effect that the Saxons are the most ludicrous of all the German peoples. Adam showed the letter to his mother who was thoroughly amused, and, as he told Shiela, this took the

[21]The Spanish civil war had broken out a month before in July.
[22]Franco's army in Morocco was transported to Spain by aeroplanes some of which were German and Italian. 'Them' in the next sentence evidently refers to the Fascist powers, German and Italian and Spanish nationalist.

wind out of his sails. But Shiela's remarks rankled nonetheless. Here are
some extracts from a second letter that he wrote to her on the subject.
Her adventures in Saxony, he says, 'made me hate that bloody tribe down
there, which is admittedly our worst and least sympathetic, but also made
me hate this insufferable habit of journalism to pick up "impressions of
everyday life" and elaborate on that substance an equally unbalanced
and painful wrath by which nothing but the general confusion is fur-
thered ... Of course neither of us have very much right to be complacent
about our respective countries, though in some specific aspects we have,
and you to a large extent in the political aspect which gives you an unfair
advantage because it is mostly that aspect one refers to when comparing
countries. (I admit though that I considered ourselves even there in a
relative advantage as long as we were in no more danger of teaching the
coloured comrades what you are teaching them.)[23] The real point surely
is that there is no good in comparing countries in that way and to listen
anxiously to the sentiment of vulgar Saxonians, because that, and I'm
afraid most journalists' habits of thinking and feeling, end with counting
one's soldiers and not only counting them.'

Shiela's reply is undated and was presumably written some five days
later about the 10th of September. It contains a résumé of her feelings
and beliefs after two months as a journalist in Prague. Her opening is
conciliatory in substance but not in tone.

'Well—well—well—I didn't think it was as bad as all that, and I believe
you're unreasonably upset by my (Saxony) letter. If only you knew, I
was feeling most friendly, and meant to talk seriously with you about
the problem . . .'

Adam had accused her of making emotional judgments under the influence of Czech friends. She rounded on him for this: 'The only influence
which made me feel so hostile to your countrymen was your countrymen
themselves.' The gloves were now off and she waded in, but not to a
complete knock-out, for as often happens when one writes from indignation, she 'in rage strikes wide.'

'Now that I have started quarrelling, I will quarrel with the whole of
the rest of the letter, and instead of being distressed or depressed by my

[23] A reference to the Colonies taken from Germany by the Versailles Treaty and
then beginning to be a matter of Anglo-German dispute.

objections, you must answer back, because I am very seriously disturbed by the problem and want to solve it.

'First of all, about journalism—this new attack—(you need only put "foreign" in front of it to be perfectly at one with the leading thinkers of your countrymen). The "insufferable habit of journalism to pick up impressions of everyday life and elaborate . . . an unbalanced wrath"— what do you mean? If you mean I was wrong to find *all* Saxons disagreeable because I found some so—well and good, but that is a personal and not a professional mistake. If you meant it wrong to find out the problem of the German minority by talking exclusively to beggars and waiters, you're quite right again—but you seemed to be condemning the only possible method of journalism, which is to study problems in general, by facts and figures and treaties and policies, and then to see the actual conditions to which all these apply . . . This is all off the main point, which is that your attitude to journalism I find vulgar and unthinking and it infuriates me—there! By this onslaught you need not be bewildered or frightened, for if it is unjustified you can prove that it is, and if it is justified you can mend your opinions.

'Now, I will attack you for not going on with the problem at all, and instead saying (something also very silly) that it is no good comparing countries politically—no, you can't be so silly as that—your English went very much to bits. Writing for the pleasure of the postmen[24] has a shocking effect on style—.' With this angry letter their dispute reached a climax from which it affectionately declined. Greater ones were to come.

In the meantime Adam had been sitting for his examinations the last of which, the oral session, was to take place on the 22nd of October when he would be told the final result. He wrote to Diana from Berlin the day before: 'To-day (and I hope to-morrow) I feel like a bull with a definite load before his horns and quite strong and gay about it.'

His confidence was misplaced. His past caught up on him now. He had bad luck too. The People's Court, one of the most repulsive of all Nazi institutions, by which the party sought finally to crush the independence of the judiciary, had recently been founded, and one of Adam's three oral examiners was an official of this Volksgericht with the rank of Senatspresident.[25] With such a man as an examiner Adam had no hope

[24]Evidently a reference to censorship.   [25]C.T.

of high honours. However he was not failed. He obtained his Assessorship
but his performances was declared to be befriedigend—satisfactory, no
more.

He wrote to Diana soon after.

'The examiners behaved very severely and told me I wasn't good enough
and deserved neither first nor second class and gave me something between
second and third—adding a lot of nasty and rude remarks before I quitted.
"Quitting" this time means I am no longer a state servant—no longer under disciplinary power of the Ministry of Justice—that in fact I am as
much of a free man as one is likely to be under the circumstances. My
first reaction was extreme tiredness and depression (a) because I wasn't
thought as good as I thought I was, (b) because one 35-year old man
was ploughed,(c) because there was nobody to tell me (as there was in
London when the similar blow happened) that really I wasn't so bad! So
I spent a wild night with a colleague and a carpenter in the north of Berlin
and came home after four.'

Later he wrote: 'I was rather unreasonably depressed by my handling
by the examiners. It was a mixture of being disappointed by myself and
indignant at the way I was treated.'

One might reasonably suppose that it was his poor showing in the
examination that finally strengthened his resolve to go to the Far East,
but in fact he appears to have made his decision shortly before, after en-
countering frustration in another form. He had been in some sort of
negotiation for a post with I. G. Farben, and on the 6th of October he
wrote as follows in the course of a letter to his father.

'I saw a director of I. G. Farben. He told me that as regards personnel
in the legal department of I. G. Farben the policy of selection was far
from being unpolitical . . . In view of the fact that even in a business
career one is exposed to the same almost unbearable pressure under which
I have spent the last three years, you will understand why, in spite of my
serious doubts, I shall decide on travel after all because, in my honest
conviction, there is simply no other way.'

He had been confronted with another grief, another example of 'unbearable pressure' during the past summer. His friend Helmut Conrad
had been the victim of characteristic Nazi injustice. In spite of the fact
that the case against him had been quashed, perhaps because of it, Nazi
party headquarters in Bonn looked on his presence in the University as

undesirable. They successfully intervened with the University authorities and they compelled him to leave.[26] By this action he was condemned to a life of poverty and inactivity for the next three years. Here was one incident, and there were probably many others, unmentioned for good reason in his letters, which made him long for fresh air.

Nevertheless his 'serious doubts' remained for a little while yet. One of them concerned his American friend. If he went to China, his plan was to go by way of America and meet her again in California. As appears from his letters to Shiela, he had written and told her of his plan and it seems that her answer had been a refusal to meet him again. He had again written asking her to reconsider this decision and was waiting for her reply. The distressing possibility that if he went he might be near her and yet forbidden her presence daunted him.

But over and above this there was with Adam, as often, a doubt on the ground of principle: was this a patriotic thing to do? Was this pusillanimous? And again he resolved that his ultimate future, whether he went to China or not, was to be in Germany. Evidence of the state of his mind comes from memories of conversations he had at this time with a friend whom he had first met at Oxford. This friend had been, like Adam, a German Rhodes scholar; his name was Fritz Schumacher. He was a year older than Adam, and after obtaining his degree at Oxford he had spent the third year of his scholarship at Harvard. He did not return to Germany till June 1934. He had then gone into business, working in the export trade. Although German policy set a high value on a favourable balance of payments through export, many German manufacturers had the utmost difficulty in finding their way to export their goods through the enormous tangle of Dr Schacht's ingenious fiscal organisation. The latter involved foreign trade in numerous and sometimes very complicated bilateral agreements requiring deep study if they were to be understood. Schumacher and his partners aimed to guide manufacturers through the labyrinth, and in this they were very successful.

In early October Schumacher married in Hamburg and lived with his young wife near Berlin. It was now in the last weeks of 1936 that the friendship between himself and Adam became close. They had numerous conversations and explored each other's ideas.

[26]Conrad. Autobiographical note.

Unlike Adam, Schumacher saw the predicament of his country in simple terms and had none of the other's qualifying second thoughts. He was helped to a clear view by the fact that his wife was partly Jewish. He saw Nazism, and the Nazi government, and Adolf Hitler as purely evil. As a result he was beginning to have a bad conscience about his business success. What he was accomplishing for the export trade could be described as patriotic, but it conformed with the purposes of the Nazi party and thus, he believed, could only have evil consequences. As things stood, so he argued, patriotism, in the ordinary sense of activity on behalf of the country and the Government, was impossible for a German. Patriotic devotion was forced into eclipse. For that reason he intended to leave and take up British nationality. He urged Adam to do the same.

Adam was immovable. Challenged by the other he agreed as to the utter iniquity of Nazism, but he did not, because he could not, believe in the eclipse of Germany. He would explain to the other, sometimes in Hegelian terms which Schumacher could hardly follow, the significance throughout the world, as he saw it, of the events then taking place in Germany, and how they were witnessing something much more far-reaching and of deeper meaning than the mere seizure of power by a crew of desperadoes. At other times he would abandon elaborate argument and merely say, 'Go, if you like, but I'll stay because someone's got to stay.' If he went to China now, he said, it was only so that he could come back better equipped to serve Germany by combating Nazism from within. 'When I come back I will stay here,' he said, 'and lead a double life. I will get some post from where I can work clandestinely against Nazism. But I will do it here, not from abroad.'

Schumacher grieved that he could not change his friend's mind. He thought that what Adam proposed for himself was beyond his or any man's moral strength, and likely to end in confusion.[27]

At some time at the very end of October or the beginning of November Adam finally made up his mind to go to China. He had not yet had an answer to his second plea to his American friend, but the possibility of not meeting her no longer deterred him. His parents approved the idea, his father somewhat reluctantly, his mother very sympathetically: 'It is strange,' she wrote to him, 'that despite all hesitations and mis-

[27]Mr E. Schumacher. Discussion.

givings I am absolutely *for* the journey. I *know* how much I am going to miss you, but in spite of that I do not have a moment's doubt.' With this encouragement his next care was to find the means to enable him to make the journey. For this purpose he went to England. His plan was to ask Rhodes House to allow him to keep his owing third year as a scholar in a Chinese University.

The request was extremely unusual but circumstances were very much in Adam's favour. The secretary of the Rhodes Trust on whom the decision most depended was Lord Lothian. He remains an enigmatical political figure of his time: an ardent Roman Catholic who, with bitter soul-searching, had abandoned his faith and after spiritual adventures had found a second religion in Christian Science, Lothian was a man always open to new ideas and always apt to lose his way; yet at the same time he was remarkable for capacity for work, energy of mind, and unswerving loyalty to his basic principles. In his conduct there was nothing of the weak hesitation of one who finds it difficult, as he always did, to make up his mind. He could speak no German, and knew little about Germany, yet from the influence, it may be supposed, of his first political mentor, Lord Milner, under whom he had served in South Africa, he was strongly disposed towards admiration of Germany. The present turn of events perplexed him. His appreciation of Hitler showed perspicacity at one moment, wishful thinking at another. From Lord Milner he had learned to look on Parliamentary democracy and its squalid party wrangling with some disgust, so he was not greatly appalled at Hitler's suppression of parliamentary rule in Germany. Having not strained at this gnat he found he could swallow some camels. He had been one of the earliest advocates for a supra-national authority in Europe, for a 'World Commonwealth,' during the First World War, and yet he found he could sympathise with the Nazi hostility to the League of Nations. This was not another instance of Lothian losing his faith. It was a natural result of his burning conviction that Germany had been treated with shameful injustice by the Treaty of Versailles. He was a humane man, easily shocked by violence, and in his attitude to warfare not far from pacifism at this time; yet he was not moved to take a definite stand against the violent cruelty and bellicose nationalism of Hitler and the Nazi regime. The reason was simple. From 1917 onwards he had looked on the Soviet regime with increasing horror, and the avowed anti-Communist impetus of Nazism deceived him, as it did many less intelligent people, into some blindness regarding Nazi atrocity, and into fancying virtue where there was none. Though a serious man, he had much sense of humour, but this pleasing characteristic also led him badly astray on one occasion. In self-parody he had himself photographed reading *Mein Kampf*. Such a prank could hardly not give rise to serious misunderstanding.[28]

It is possible that in that element of indecision which was present in Adam through his non-Nazi patriotism, Lothian recognised a disposition which could capture his sympathy. Adam had immense personal charm. So had Lothian. Charmers do not always charm each other, but when their elusive and often suspect quality is not suspect at all but the expression of generous character, then mutual sympathy can be strongly assured. At all events the result of Adam's two meetings with Lothian in London in November 1936 resulted in an affectionate relationship. They had met several times before, as mentioned already, but this seems to have been the first occasion when they had long and serious conversation. Lothian, among other reasons for favouring Adam's unusual proposal, had founded travelling fellowships as part of the Rhodes benefactions, and Adam's proposal fitted in with the spirit of this short-lived experiment.

Lothian, who was the most eloquent of men, persuaded his fellow trustees and they gave their official approval to Adam's proposal, granting him £350 for a visit to China of at least one year's duration on the understanding that he spent most of that time in University studies in the country.[29] The sum might appear quite inadequate for so great a journey, but he did not ask for his passage money. Friends (who prefer to remain unknown) gave him his passage to America as a mark of gratitude for all he had done to help them to escape Nazi persecution, and he received help from Sir Stafford Cripps who gave him his fare from America to China.

Adam returned to Germany and stayed there till mid-February 1937. In the first week of the month he heard from his American friend asking him to visit her in California.[30] He occupied his time before leaving with

[28]This sketch of Lord Lothian is based chiefly on Michael Astor's book *Tribal Feeling*, Lord Brand's article in the Dictionary of National Biography, and Sir James Butler's biography.
[29]Rhodes House Archives. C.T. [30]G.D.

making arrangements for his journey, and in travelling round Germany meeting scholars and men with Chinese experience, and saying goodbye to his closest friends. As before he saw a great deal of Schumacher. But perhaps the most interesting episode of this winter was his dispute about the whole venture with Werner.

The relationship between the two brothers had continued as difficult as at any time during the past year, but in the winter of 1936-1937 it took a sudden turn for the better. Werner had married. Adam went to stay with the newly-wed couple in their home in Marburg, and in letters to Shiela and Diana he described the tranquillity which had come into his brother's life under the influence of his attractive young wife. All the mutual affection of the brothers rose up once more. But this did not mean that they could find themselves in harmonious agreement over their ideas. Werner looked with severe disapproval on this plan to visit China. He looked on the notion of 'travelling round the world to meet yourself' as so much rubbish and self-delusion.[31] In a long letter written to Adam on the 10th January, 1937, Werner explained his objection in detail, though it cannot be said that he shed on it the light of simplicity. Here is the main content, Englished so far as anything so massively German can be.

'I believe that, *seeing the way you have ordered your life until now*, your breaking out of it now is inevitable. You will, I am sure, admit that any form of thinking along broad political lines pre-supposes the universality of Europe in the non-materialistic sense,[32] and further that to see an analogy between China and Germany is an absurdity in the absence of such universality. It is my conviction that such universality may be found no more in Europe but only ranged against Europe, and this means in turn that it is no longer possible to become part of a social structure.

'I am also somewhat disturbed by the suspicion that you expect to encounter (in China) such feudal elements as, in your view, are cruelly thrust aside[33] in present-day Germany, and which in England are too rigid and lifeless; elements which belong to *your* concept of democracy. You expect to meet these same elements in the isolation of China, standing moreover in precisely that dialectical relationship to modernity which you

---

[31]Werner von Trott. Discussion.   [32]'in einem übermechanischen Begriff'.
[33]'Gefangen' literally 'imprisoned.' Werner may be using the term literally, or metaphorically as suggested in this translation.

need in order to live under modern political conditions without betraying your traditions. Added to this is the vitality—so full of promise—peculiar to whatever is exotic and wild and which is attractive to everyone who has chivalry in his blood, and which time and again has led aristocrats to embrace the ideas of Rousseau.

'But since I no longer believe in this country, nor in its sober profundity, but regard it rather as a romantic dream of genuine solidity,[34] and since I believe that the avalanche of 1933 is a European concern, namely the collapse of Christian Europe and of Christian politics, more fateful in its results than the French revolution—especially as the retarding effect on it of the earlier English revolution must now be considered to have failed—I regard your future, with deep anxiety, as the future of a modern Don Quixote.

'It is my dearest wish that you should reflect on this during the next two or three months . . . I also urge you to examine yourself to see whether your private motives have been sufficiently integrated with the more general ones in such a way that you can act out of *both* and that each is not an excuse for the other. You have hardly any option, given your dubious political position with the concomitant impossibility of it giving your private life that shape and form from which alone you may regulate your private life as something temporary and bound to perish.[35] Thus you are bound to waver between over- and under-estimate of your private affairs, and both attitudes war with the other. I quite see that you can only resolve this contradiction, which is basically the contradiction inherent in Christian Democracy, within the kind of social order which you yourself want. But as regards this social order please remember that I no longer believe in its latent reality, in the sense, that is to say, of Bismarck's Policy as the Art of the Possible.'

Although this strange letter was based on the kind of involved argument which appealed to Adam, there is no sign that it moved him to any further hesitation. On the contrary he seems to have been moved to more obstin-

[34]'einen romantischen Traum echter Solidität'. The meaning is perhaps that he sees the intolerant Nazi regime as imposing a fraudulent brotherhood through romantic (or hysterical) impulse.
[35]'Vorläufig und sehr bedingt'. Presumably a reference to the religious concept of individual human life as a prelude to a higher life after death.

ate determination, judging by a letter to Diana. Werner, he told her, 'just cannot understand my wanting to go to China, far from seeing that I must—well, well!' On the 19th February, 1937 he said goodbye to his family and left Imshausen. He was not to see his father again. He went to Paris for a few days (his first visit) and there met Shiela.[36] From Paris he went to England. His first visit was to Oxford where he attended a 'gaudy.'

This visit to England was one of the happiest of all. In Oxford he saw Maurice Bowra and Isaiah Berlin among many other friends. In London he met the Chinese ambassador, Lord Halifax on whom he looked with awe as 'in many ways the person one should try and become like,' and Sir John Hope-Simpson who told him something of his experiences in China where he organised flood relief in the Yangtze valley[37] from 1931 to 1933. His friend David Astor asked him to stay in London as his guest in the family house at 4 St James's Square. He now met David's mother for the first time. As the friend of her son, and as someone approved by her admirer Lord Lothian, she enveloped him instantly, as was her wont, in her affection.

She knew from David about his family background and the Protestant piety of his mother. She asked—or rather demanded—to be put in touch with Frau von Trott so that from her she could learn about the situation of the Protestant Churches in Germany. She asked Adam if he had any riding boots. He hadn't! Did he realise that he would have to do a great deal of riding in China? She swept him off to the right shops and bought him boots and clothes for riding, to which she added a suit, an overcoat and a hat. She gave him the benefit of her views on the international situation in Europe. She declared herself openly *prodeutsch*, Adam told his mother, 'and believes us to be encircled by Roman Catholic powers whom she hates.' Adam seems to have found her delightful and perplexing. 'I got on very well with her,' he told his mother, 'although she is a somewhat wild lady—obschon sie eine etwas wilde Dame ist.'

---

[36]G.D. In a letter to his father he mentions that among others he met Friedrich Sieburg, then Paris correspondent of the Frankfurter Zeitung. He was well known as the author of *Gott in Frankreich*, translated into English with the title: *Is God a Frenchman?*
[37]G.D.

He left England for New York in the first week of March. He received, either in London or on board the *Deutschland*, a letter from Shiela who had returned to Prague from Paris. It contained a very odd piece of news.

'I discovered my position in Prague was really pretty bad. I am quite seriously suspected in a lot of quarters of being a spy of your country. Even my own countrymen and colleagues seem to have let the suspicion pass. On the other hand, Thomas Balogh, who is a Central European, and born in all that atmosphere of intrigue and watchfulness, has been most loyal. I am just beginning to work up venom about it tho' even now I find it more ludicrous and funny than anything else.'

The explanation was simple. As an *Observer* correspondent Shiela represented a paper which, under J. L. Garvin's editorship, took a pro-German line and often showed marked lack of sympathy towards Czechoslovakia. But there was probably a further reason for this new notion that Shiela (of all people) was an agent of the Nazi party, and Adam gave expression to this in his answer written from the boat.

'Do you think your correspondence with a young German may have something to do with it, specially when, after opening it, it must have proved highly unintelligible to the general reader?'

Their letters contained a great many private jokes, and they addressed each other and referred to their friends by all manner of crazy nicknames. Their few references to public matters were often obviously disguised. All this could be mistaken for coded messages. Farcical as it was, this queer and apparently trivial event seems to have had far-reaching results which were to do great harm to Adam's good name.

Chapter 9

INTERLUDE

From February 1937 Adam was away from Germany for just over twenty-one months. It was an escape from the unbearable pressures on him in Nazi Germany, so much so that Adam was at one time tempted to make of it an act of complete escapism by settling in America as an emigrant.[1] But his persistent and deeper conviction against emigration remained and won, as it was bound to do. In a way there was no escape during these two years. His constant and tormenting predicament, how to reconcile his patriotism with his opposition to Nazism, did not diminish; like the fiend that treads close behind, it followed him over the seas.

Yet in another sense, quite different from any suggested above, this was in effect a time of escapism. Without the corrective of experience within Germany, there were moments when Adam began to see Nazism in a softened light.

His sojourn in China had the result of making him a calmer, more mature man in the opinion of many of his friends.[2] It cannot be said to have made him more perceptive politically. In that sense this curious enterprise failed. It was perhaps bound to fail for the reasons implied by his friend Schumacher in their long talks together in the preceding winter. Adam was trying to hold a position which was untenable.

On the 10th of March, 1937 the *Deutschland* reached New York. Waiting for him on the quay were Ingrid Warburg and another friend of long standing, Josias von Rantzau, at that time German Consul-General in New York. As thousands and millions have found on reaching the far side of

[1] A letter of October 1938 in G.D.
[2] Among others Herr von Kessel and Doctor Boehncke both remarked on this to the writer.

the Atlantic, the bewildering experience of a first sight of New York, the sense of being a babe in this modernistic wood, was beautifully cheered by the ancient American virtue of hospitality. He met his cousins William and Louise Schieffelin[3] who invited him to stay in their New York apartment. A little later in March, he was taken up by another family of cousins, the Osborns, with whom he stayed in New York and in the country at their estate on the Upper Hudson. He was invited for a country visit to the Jay family of Bedford, Virginia, where he felt that he could see in full reality the ideal of the conservative revolutionary. When he went to Washington he stayed with Theodore Taft, also a cousin through descent from Justice Jay. As happens to one in America, he met an enormous number of people.

Among old and tested friends there were, beside the Warburgs, three who had a special place in his heart: Julie Braun-Vogelstein, her niece Hertha Vogelstein, and Hasso von Seebach. He saw them in New York and Washington. They were planning to go soon to permanent residence on the West Coast where he was to meet them again.

Of the many new acquaintances which he made in America four stand out because their influence was to be very strong on his later fortunes. Pre-eminent among these was a man with whom he had been in correspondence since November 1936, on the strength of an introduction from Lord Lothian. He was called Edward C. Carter. He was the moving spirit in an enterprise known as the Institute for Pacific Relations.[4] This loosely formed body, founded in 1925, was to some extent modelled on the Royal Institute for International Affairs, and as with Chatham House, departments of State availed themselves of the services which the Institute could uniquely supply. By the mid-thirties it had grown into a research group for Far Eastern affairs without any rival in the world. (The term 'Pacific' in the I.P.R. title did not refer to peace but to the Pacific Ocean.)

A man with Adam's new-found interest, introduced by an eminent personality of Chatham House, was extremely welcome to Carter who

---

[3]Trott's American acquaintance is recorded in his letters to his parents, and in correspondence between Frau von Trott and her Schieffelin cousins. (Letters C.T.) Also in C.T., D.H., G.D., J.B.V.

[4]Carter is sometimes described as the Director of the Institute. In fact the Director was William C. Holland. Carter was the organiser.

hastened to receive him in his consciously bohemian, paper-strewn, scholar's apartment in New York. There was something of the actor about Carter: he enjoyed his exaggerated reputation as a mysterious person exerting hidden influence in many distant corners of the world, and his disorderly den was part of the act. This must not be taken to mean that he was anything but a perfectly genuine man. He was not a first-rate scholar of the subjects with which he dealt, nor did he pretend to be, but he was a first-rate organiser of scholarship, and of the difficult feat of relating learning to action. He liked Adam's idea of studying China with a view to equipping himself for political life in Europe. He was generous with help and arranged for his new friend to attend a brief course of Chinese study at the Berkeley campus in the University of California before crossing the Pacific.[5]

Through Sir Stafford Cripps Adam was introduced to the courageous chief of the Union for Civil Liberties, Roger Baldwin. A liberal of the classic American school, Roger Baldwin had suffered opprobrium and even prison for his beliefs, and he saw in Adam a natural colleague.

In Washington Adam met the editor of *The Washington Post* through a letter of introduction given to him by Paul Leverkühn. He was Felix Morley, a former Rhodes scholar and a student of American policy in the Far East.

In this year they met only once, making each other's acquaintance over a dinner on the 29th March. Felix Morley recorded the occasion in his diary. 'Von Trott, Leverkühn's German Rhodes Scholar friend, proved a thoroughly delightful young fellow . . . He spoke with exceeding frankness of the repressions of the Nazi regime and regards a popular uprising as by no means impossible. It will be a ghastly business if it comes.'

These three new vital friendships, with Carter, Baldwin and Morley were to have happy consequences. It was otherwise with the fourth.

During his stay in New York Adam went for a week-end to Boston and met some of the leading people of Harvard University. The best known of these at the time was, without doubt, Felix Frankfurter, then at the very height of his astonishing vigour and abilities. As a former Rhodes scholar the eminent lawyer and politician was glad to meet Adam

[5]This account of Edward C. Carter and the I.P.R. is chiefly based on a discussion with Carter's friend Professor Lockwood of Princeton University.

through a letter of introduction from his friend Isaiah Berlin. Frankfurter
was one of the most genial of men, of wide interests and easy access.
Differences of age meant little to him and his love of Oxford was one
of the passions of his life. As a Jew his hatred of Nazism was personal
and bitter, but he never abjured his German loyalties and a young German,
educated at Oxford, with a reputation for anti-Nazism, was three-fold
welcome to him. The encounter was the happiest of all those that Adam
made at Boston,[6] though Felix Frankfurter's delight in the young man
was not entirely shared by his wife. She said afterwards that she would
have liked Adam better if he had not been 'so darn good-looking.'[7] It is
possible that her suspicions came to influence her husband and caused him
to revise his first favourable impression.

In New York he met and made friends with the celebrated Colonel
'Wild Bill' Donovan, then fresh back from an official tour of the battle-
fields of the Spanish Civil War, and already beginning to plan the organisation of American military and political intelligence in the event of the
war with Germany which he believed to be certain.[8] A letter to Shiela
tells that Adam stayed with Donovan in Washington and gives the impression that they got on very well together. To meet he was a man of
gentle manners and charm with no external sign of wildness, and every
external sign of overflowing good nature.[9] By rights Donovan, the foun-
der of the Office of Strategic Services, should play a considerable part in
the story, but, surprisingly enough, this was not how things turned out.
After April 1937 the two men never seem to have seen each other again,
nor does his name recur in any surviving document about Adam.

Another meeting with a well known personality was more fruitful.
Through Doctor Visser't Hooft he met the famous theologian Reinhold
Niebuhr[10] in New York. Niebuhr was immediately attracted to Adam
in whom he believed he discerned a rare spirit. He was to stand up for
him in difficult days.

A curious little incident is to be found in his meeting with Mr Hamilton

[6]C.T. and a letter from Trott in G.D. [7]Sir Isaiah Berlin. Discussion.
[8]Allen Dulles. The *Secret Surrender*. London 1967.
[9]The writer met Colonel Donovan in the Middle East during the Second World
War.
[10]C.T.

Fish Armstrong, then a member of the Council on Foreign Relations, and later editor of the influential New York quarterly *Foreign Affairs*. Mr Armstrong took Adam to lunch at the Century Club. He found that his guest made no secret of his anti-Nazi convictions, but he was puzzled by a certain 'tenseness' in his behaviour.[11] The explanation was very simple. Shortly before this, a book by Mr Armstrong called *We or They?* had been published and had caused some stir. It was a brief, vigorous and extremely able polemic against the Soviet, Fascist, and Nazi tyrannies, both in respect of their internal and foreign policies. It was addressed to American isolationists and its main theme was that between such regimes and traditional liberal ones there could be no compromise. The book aroused all Adam's resentment at what he took to be the moral smugness of Germany's critics. He mentioned it in a letter to Shiela written about a month after this meeting.[12]

Quite apart from Mr Armstrong's book, the 'tenseness,' given Adam's disposition, could hardly have been completely avoided in America, especially in New York, with its large German Jewish population. It is sometimes forgotten to-day that up to March 1939, the American reaction to Nazism in the thirties was, in spite of the prevailing isolationism, more hostile, more immediate and more anti-German than in England. To Americans in 1937 (with the exception of such eccentrics as 'Wild Bill') American participation in a new German war appeared remote and improbable, and they could thus afford to look at Nazism as the horror it was. American hostility, being less informed and more indiscriminate than in Europe, tended to affect all Germans in the country, even Hitler's victims. Adam wrote to Diana:

'I have sensed an awful distrust against me over here, which I suppose is only natural in the present international situation and which I was protected against to an enormous extent by my personal friends in England. More and more you are either an emigré or a Nazi, and as neither of them are you liked.'

It was the opinion of his friend, Franz Golfing, whom he now met again as an exile, that in his endeavours to educate himself in American politics his eager questioning was mistaken for a sinister curiosity.[13] In addition to suffering some unpopularity as a German he may have been

[11]Mr H. F. Armstrong. Discussion. [12]G.D. [13]C.T.

suspected of being a spy. If that is true, it can explain much that was to come.

At the end of April he left the United States for Canada where he visited Montreal, Ottawa and Toronto. He stayed for a few days with the Governor-General, at that time Lord Tweedsmuir.

He returned to the United States in the first week of May, travelling from Toronto to Chicago. He then went on to Kansas City and from there to the Californian coast and that reunion with the beloved friend of his Göttingen days who exerted so great and irresistible a spell over him. By what seemed to be a fortunate coincidence she had a small house in Carmel, California, where Mrs Braun-Vogelstein had settled. On arrival on the west coast Adam went to stay with Julie Braun-Vogelstein. He looked forward to meeting his other friend with longing and trepidation.

The little coastal town of Carmel is about a hundred and forty miles south of San Francisco by road. Here Adam stayed for a week or so with his friends. His plan was to await the arrival of another friend of Julie Braun-Vogelstein, a Sinologist called Wolfram Eberhard. Adam had been put in touch with him by Gustav Ecke, and together they had drawn up a plan to study and attend the course at Berkeley. After that they would travel to China together. They had met in Germany but did not as yet know each other at all well. While waiting for Eberhard to arrive in Carmel Adam had much time on his hands as the other was delayed on his journey.[14] A good part of this time he devoted to renewing his passionate friendship.

Very soon after his arrival in Carmel the fateful meeting occurred. Both felt extremely nervous at the first encounter. They decided to go away together for a few days. They went to the little town of Taft which is about a hundred miles north-west of Los Angeles and situated in the mountains of the Coast Range. Their three or four days together seem to have been happy. A somewhat enigmatic sentence in a letter to Shiela tells as much as one may know: 'We had a peaceful and strong quiet time together in these wild hills which I imagine Greece must be like.'[15]

He returned to Carmel where he lived in a garden house on the pro-

---

[14]C.T. and G.D.
[15]The word 'strong' here is typical of Stefan George's idiom and carries some such meaning as 'firm in mind'.

perty rented by Mrs Braun-Vogelstein. It contained a big room which
was used for study by Adam and Wolfram Eberhard, who arrived in the
first week of June. Soon after, the two of them went to San Francisco
to attend the course at Berkeley. It was conducted by Professor Lessing
who had formerly been Eberhard's teacher and was much admired by
Gustav Ecke.[16] They spent every week-end at Carmel. It was a happy
time to all appearances, spent with affectionate companions in the radiant
Californian landscape or on the beaches of the west coast, and with abundant mental stimulus in new and exciting studies. But a dark cloud grew
and obliterated Adam's delight.

His American friend's intuition, distressingly conveyed to him the year
before, that it would be a mistake for them to meet again, gradually
proved to be justified. Their first nervousness was a truer indication of
the case than their later mutual joy. Time soon began to show that their
relationship could not be taken up again with profit, and that after ecstatic
recognition it could not mature again. But the relationship had entered
far too deeply into the emotions of both for it to be relinquished, or for
it to subside and vanish on its own. A certain mutual exasperation began
to grow between them, and with loss of control there was recrimination
and anger followed by all the weariness of bitter regret. Adam was tortured by guilt because he believed that through selfishness he had brought
unhappiness into the life of someone he loved. She deplored her lack of
firmness which had allowed this calamitous meeting to take place. Yet
their mutual love persisted in an agony of spirit. Fault should not be
found or blame apportioned in such a case. An appalling mistake had
been made, and the wonder of it is that in spite of the desolation which it
brought, her love for Adam and his for her ultimately survived, and survived triumphantly.

This is to look into the future. What must be stressed here is that in this
interlude in Adam's life, most of it so free in spirit, the first part ended in
devastating emotional anguish.

In keeping with his obligations to Rhodes House, Adam spent his last
days in America during this 1937 visit in recording his ideas about the
country. In this he was following a well established custom; indeed up to
and in our own time, to cross the Atlantic and not to set down on paper

[16]C.T.

one's impressions of the United States has been looked on almost as an abuse of hospitality. Adam did not fail, but the report which he wrote did not in the end reach Rhodes House. The reason is intriguing. He found, with the mass of ideas which were thronging his mind after four months of travel and encounters, that he could not express himself authentically in English. 'A strange thing happened to me', he wrote to Diana later. 'I wrote a report in German on my time in America and promised Lord Lothian a translation. I haven't been able to put my same ideas into English which indicates to me clearly that I am breaking away from your ways and associations.'

It may have indicated that. But this unexpected failure to be able to use his rarely correct but always fluent English, at a moment when he needed to use it, may have had psychological implications. One must not pronounce on such matters without far more evidence than is available, but the possibility has occurred to the writer that here was an unconscious psychological gesture of escape from the grievous unhappiness of the emotional involvement into which Adam had wilfully stepped.

The report itself, circulated among his friends under the title *Amerikanische Eindrücke*, is a creditable piece of work which, like all but a very few of such documents, has lost its vitality through changes of awareness and understanding, through 'the wrong of time.' It need not detain the reader.

It was now time for him to set out for China. He had left Carmel in the first part of July and was now in Los Olivos in Santa Barbara county on his way to the southern port of San Pedro.[17] There had been some confusion about his passage and instead of travelling to Shanghai with Eberhard by way of Japan, he was given a reservation in a boat sailing the southern Pacific course. This inconvenient arrangement moved him to an ungracious outburst about Sir Stafford Cripps's handsome gift. He wrote to Diana: 'Perhaps, fearing the immediate outbreak of war you would rather have me swim for a whole month in a little British freighter in the South Pacific than know I was in Japan where I might conspire against your Empire?'

At another time he might have behaved with more decorum and patience. The recent emotional experience through which he had passed

[17]A letter to his father in Letters C.T.

had left him with badly frayed nerves. When he went aboard his ship, the Motor Vessel *Maron*, a fellow passenger with whom he had made friends took a photograph of him on deck. He kept it. People who saw it later presumed that at the time Adam was ill, but in fact his physical health was then perfectly sound. He had suffered an emotional shock from which it took him long to recover.

He sailed from San Pedro for Shanghai on the 17th July, 1937.

On the far side of the Pacific the M.V. *Maron* ran into trouble, as was to be expected, for this was an unpropitious time for Far Eastern travel. Nine days before the ship sailed from America, there had occurred, on the 8th July, 1937, aggressive action by the Japanese in China which decisively transformed the character of the Japanese-Chinese struggle. It was now one of war.[18] In the jargon of their own inimitable hypocrisy, the aggressors continued to describe the consequences of their action as an 'incident,' and so the war remained 'undeclared.' This Japanese touchiness in no way modified the savage cruelty with which they conducted operations. As often happens in such crises, the initial aggression was followed by an

[18]To generalise for the reader's convenience, Japanese economic and political penetration of Manchuria took an aggressive line in the summer of 1931 when, not without some Chinese provocation and collaboration, the Japanese occupied Mukden. This led to localised campaigns. China appealed to the League of Nations who appointed a Committee of Enquiry led by Lord Lytton. The Japanese Government refused to negotiate with China through the League of Nations and replied to the mission of Lord Lytton by the establishment of a Manchurian Republic with the boy-emperor Hsuan Tung (known as Mr Pu Yi) as nominal dictator for life. Ceremonial inauguration of the regime took place on 9th March, 1932, six weeks before the arrival of Lord Lytton. In his report, published on the 22nd October, 1932, Lytton asserted that Japan had acted as an aggressor. The British Government shrank from full support of Lytton or the League Commission. Critics of British appeasement policies point to this as the beginning of the decay of the League's authority for the enforcement of peace. The matter is open to argument. What is certain is that from this time onward, after the assassination of the Japanese Prime Minister Inukai, in 1932, the extremist war party in Japan increased its influence. The treasonable nature of the superficially Chinese, but Japanese-directed Government of Manchuko, as Manchuria was now called, and the offensive character of Japanese policy in China became increasingly unmistakable.

interval of parleying. The Japanese attempted to obtain their objective without the trouble of a campaign. The parleys failed and on the 26th of July the Japanese resumed their offensive, after which war and its miseries were to be the lot of China for many years ahead.

The captain and crew of the M.V. *Maron* and the passengers had only been given meagre news from broadcast bulletins, but when they reached Manila they met people who claimed to have first-hand information about what was happening, and they learned that Peking was isolated, and that the Japanese were making a rapid southward advance down the coast. The boat sailed on and at Hong Kong became involved in these events. She was commandeered on the authority of the Chinese Government for the transport of Chinese troops north. The passengers were stranded.

Adam was now in some doubt not only as to what to do next, but whether it was possible to continue farther with his strange venture. However he enjoyed the rare ability of turning disaster to good account, and he did so on this occasion. In fact being stranded in Hong Kong was to turn out a great piece of luck for him.

He telegraphed to Eberhard in Japan telling him of his plight and received an answer making a rendezvous in Hong Kong at the end of August. On the strength of a general letter of introduction from Lord Lothian, he then got in touch with the president of Hong Kong University, Sir William Hornell, who recommended him to take the opportunity to visit Canton. He had a useful connection there in his cousin William Schieffelin who was the Chairman of the Trustees of Lingham University. He stayed in this University and discussed his plans with the provost, Dr Henry, who encouraged him to persist in his venture which he believed was still likely to be of great value to him, even at a time when China was in a state of warfare.[19] Dr Henry's advice seems to have decided him. He returned to Hong Kong where he met Eberhard on the 26th August.

They decided to make a journey together round the semi-autonomous province of Kwangsi. Such an expedition was very much in keeping with Adam's plan, since Kwangsi had been developed into what was claimed to be a model province. This was the work of Marshal Pai of Kwangsi who had retired in dudgeon to his homeland and thrust himself

[19]Letter from Trott to Lord Lothian 3.9.37. Rhodes House Archives.

into the governorship after being disappointed of his hopes of higher promotion by the Republican Government.

They had great difficulty in obtaining the necessary permits,[20] because since the anti-Comintern Pact and the increasingly pro-Japanese tendency of Nazi foreign policy, Germans were looked on with more than usual suspicion.

But they were determined to go and they went. They travelled by Chinese river boat up to the fortified frontier town of Wuchow, and there entered into negotiations with the police over cups of tea in a temple. Much to their surprise the two German travellers were given visas which allowed them to go wherever they wanted in Kwangsi. Adam wrote to his mother: 'Eberhard has a wonderful way with the Chinese police, soldiers and officials, and while these conversations are going on with lots of laughter and jokes I must seem a bit of a bore.' Later, when the journey was over, he wrote: '[Eberhard] was sometimes very cross with me because my natural impatience did not fit in at all well with the Oriental character.'

The next day, the 5th or 6th September, they embarked on another river boat and sailed up the Si-Kiang river on their way to the former Kwangsi capital Nanning. They were given what was described as the *cabine de luxe*, a small wooden cubicle in the centre of the deck round which a large number of their fellow passengers, chiefly drawn from the younger element, congregated and gazed astonished at the spectacle of these outlandish strangers, especially at Adam whose stature made him seem like some legendary being in a fairy tale. When they arrived in Nanning a young banker, whom they had met either in Hong Kong or on the journey, invited them to a feast. For the first time Adam enjoyed lavish Chinese hospitality, and in the ancient style uncontaminated by Western ways. Singing girls clothed in radiant silk performed to an accompaniment of bells, cymbals and drums. The fare was of the utmost Chinese delicacy and included sharks' fins, swallows' nests, doves' eggs, and rice wine. According to the rules of Chinese etiquette the guests maintained the merriment of the occasion by ceaseless giggling, and Adam, when trying languageless to be polite to people who met his overtures with peals of laughter, could hardly not suspect (certainly wrongly) that

[20]C.T.

they were laughing at him.[21] It is a custom that takes time to get used to.

From Nanning they went overland by bus to Liuchowfu. Here lived some people whom they had met on the first river boat and, as Chinese politeness demands, they called on them. Once more, as a consequence, they were involved in festivities, and found themselves taking part in a wedding conducted with all the magnificence of Chinese tradition. From Liuchowfu they continued north by bus to the provincial capital Kweilin, and here they suddenly met with the grim side of Chinese life in the 20th century.

They found a gloomy garrison city in which there was hardly a civilian of the male sex to be seen. They noticed that they were the object of angry looks. There was a troubled atmosphere, like the oppressive stillness before a storm, and wherever they went, to the theatre or to eating-houses, they seemed to find increasing hostility. They met a missionary, a certain Father Glass, and from him and his friends they learned that Japanese radio propaganda claimed full alliance with Germany, for which reason Germans were in positive danger in such a place as Kweilin. Added to this there were rumours of an impending insurrection. According to some this was the outcome of a Japanese conspiracy in the interior, according to others it was a bid for a Communist take-over. Eberhard's diary records, shortly after this, that both these beliefs belonged to war-hysteria and that what was really happening was another phenomenon of war, a scramble for command. Early on the second day of their visit they heard the frequent sounds of shots. They learned later that seventy-two people had been executed. They remembered the warnings of their new acquaintance and those given earlier by Herr Kempe, the German Consul. They decided that Kweilin was not a place in which to linger.

They returned to Wuchow sailing down the River Kwei. 'During the last five days', Adam wrote to his mother, 'we have been travelling in the smallest of boats through landscapes whose sublime grotesqueness is such as you may hardly imagine. Some parts of this river journey are said to lead through the most beautiful scenery in all China.'

This was the end of the Kwangsi journey. It had occupied about three weeks. As soon as it was over Adam wrote a report, both in English and German, about this experience which had led him to take a favourable

21C.T.

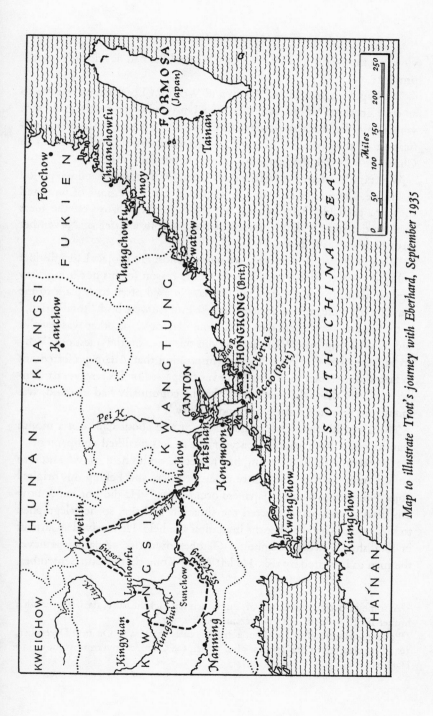

Map to illustrate Trott's journey with Eberhard, September 1935

view, on the whole, of the claim that Marshal Pai had developed a model province.

The happy partnership of Adam and Wolfram Eberhard now came to an end. Eberhard had had an offer for a University lectureship in Ankara which ante-dated his assignment to China. He felt that with the intensification of the Japanese war, and the resultant position of Germans in China, he was free to change his plans. He left for Turkey.

Wolfram Eberhard was a friend of Adam for a short but unique period in his life. Long after this time he set down his impressions of him, and they are particularly interesting for the light they throw on the ideas that were driving Adam forward at the time. In a letter of November 1957 he wrote as follows:

'We got on well and felt that we were friends. His project had a distinct political "point" which may have been the reason for his not being very explicit about it until he reached China. He used often to explain to me that Hitler's State and the ancient Chinese Empire were both "totalitarian," but while one was founded on a religious ideology, the other was racialist and pseudo-religious. What bearing did this have on the question "Why do subjects obey?" I often had the impression that Adam preferred not to talk about certain things, and I never trespassed on his reserve, particularly as I felt that whatever it was that he continually had in mind, was sound and reflected a sense of responsibility.'[22]

Thanks to Eberhard Adam now knew more about China in a month than he could have learned in a year with a less qualified companion.

He was now on his own and had to decide on his next move. Hitherto he had been far from the centre of disturbance, and Peking, his original objective, was now under Japanese occupation.[23] He did not know how this disaster may have affected the situation of Ecke, so he telegraphed to him to discover whether the invitation still held. He received an answer in English: 'Welcome beginning October own risk.' Adam was never the man to be scared by risk. He left Hong Kong on the 14th September,

---

[22]A somewhat free translation of 'zumal ich das Gefühl hatte, dass, was er auch immer im Kopf hatte, gut und verantwortlich war.'

[23]Peking was surrendered without a struggle early in the war. On 13th December, 1937 Nanking fell to the Japanese after which the Chinese Government moved to Hankow.

1937, and travelled by way of Japan and Tientsin to Peking, where he arrived about the 20th.

Gustav Ecke had little preconceived notion of what sort of man his youthful follower had grown into. Adam was of course much taller than he expected, and the high imposing forehead of all the family came to him now rather as a surprise, emphasising his height as it did, and somewhat strangely. His first impression was that this handsome young man was extremely Hessian, and this came out in a way familiar to Ecke: that in contrast to his good manners and elegance there was to be noticed a touch of country roughness very typical of his homeland. Describing his impression thirty years later, Ecke said that this bucolic character in Adam was visible in the way he walked. He had the gait of a man used to going across country in woods in search of game. You could also see at a glance that he came of an ancient landed family, and though aristocracy was so innate in him that he was without self-consciousness in this respect, the obviousness of the fact that he came from such origins 'sometimes set underdogs against him.' Within a few minutes he recognised that here was, to use Ecke's words, a man of 'live imagination and eager, curious mind.' The two became friends, from the first moment when they met again in Peking.[24]

Adam returned the affection and was instantly captivated by Peking. He wrote to his father at the end of October, 'In spite of the persistence of the war, the city gives out an atmosphere of lofty calm, the fame of which drew me here and has not disappointed me.'

To his mother, he wrote on the 20th November, 1937: 'Last Sunday we rode out of the town—my pony threw me once in the sand, and I made my first reconnaissance under a wonderful cloudless sky . . .

'On Tuesday, we made an excursion to Ecke's temple—before the onset of winter makes it impossible . . .

'From a terrace we looked down on to a wide valley where donkey or camel caravans passed like black caterpillars, bringing coal, hemp, or other produce into the city, going as in ancient times through the river, which can be forded in two places. One driver rode a stubborn donkey, another drove a black pig through it and a third was carrying a child, like St Christopher. Camels and their drivers bring the vastness of the

[24]Ecke. Discussion.

Asian steppes into the streets of the town—but I am not the first to feel
or write about this. By the way, apart from the temples and palaces, you
must imagine this town as a huge village, with streets full of cattle, children and filth. As soon as you enter through one of the red, brass-em-
bossed doors, though, you find yourself in a world of absolute peace and
precise refinement, its sole function seeming to be to ward off the invasion of shapeless, chaotic life. As I probably told you already, Ecke is
particularly interested in Chinese architecture and his house is famous
because the interior decoration is to the last detail in keeping with the
style of the building. You can imagine what a contrast this is to the surroundings on my journey hitherto, and how much it seems like the haven
I have been seeking . . .'

The friendship between Ecke and Adam was among the most perfect
which Adam enjoyed in the course of his life. The reasons are not far
to seek. He shared Ecke's passionate interest not only in the pursuit of
knowledge, but as well, and only apparently at a more superficial level,
they shared a ready and robust sense of humour. Adam referred to him as
'my beloved German professor' and said further 'Together we can laugh
at all the world and discuss endlessly our rather different approach to
it. He is a source of real joy and inspiration to me.'[25] And again he tells
of his friend in a letter to his mother: 'Ecke thinks it might be rather better
if I were sometimes a little "sadder," as the opposite emotion echoes from
our little village palace across the roof-tops.' One of the difficulties of
Adam's biographer is that in his writing so little of his laughing joyousness
finds expression, but it is remembered first by almost everyone who knew
him.

Adam stayed with Ecke in Peking for a year, making journeys into the
interior of the country and elsewhere. His friend has left an interesting
description of how he first took up his ambitious self-appointed task.

'Immediately after his arrival, he began to work quite seriously, learning the high Chinese conversational language, reading the classics with
a Chinese student and becoming acquainted with several excellent Chinese, who soon introduced him to Confucian ideas. In the course of several
months, his relations with a remarkable old gentleman, Mr Huang Po-
ch'uan, developed into a close, and, for Adam, very valuable friendship.

[25]G.D.

Mr Huang, then already over sixty, was an antique dealer by profession, with a reputation of being one of the greatest connoisseurs of old bronzes. He not only advised museums abroad but also published excellent books on his subject which have remained standard works for all students of archaeology, and as Mr P. C. Huang or Huang Chun he was famous in the circles of Chinese antiquaries.

'Adam spent many hours every week in conversation with this excellent man, and the three of us spent many a long evening in one of the wine houses of Peking, drinking, chatting and listening to the ballad singers. Thus Adam slowly gained a practical understanding of the Chinese way of life, and the Confucian philosophy that formed its background, while he acquainted himself with the ethical theories of this philosophy by reading the classics and their occidental commentators.'

From Huang Po-Ch'uan Adam bought a seal of which the Chinese inscription read 'A friend of mountain and water.'[26] Remembering the incident long after Gustav Ecke was moved to quote Goethe's lines in the first part of Faust:

'Verstehst Du was für neue Lebenskraft
Mir dieser Wandel in des Oede schafft?'[27]

Adam made two big journeys from Peking. The first was begun on 14th March, 1938. He left for Tientsin and Tanku where he embarked for the southern Japanese port of Moji. Arrived there, he spent some days in the southern island province of Kyushu, going to see the volcano Aso among other marvels. From Kyushu he sailed to the neighbouring island province of Shikoku, and from there to the mainland. He went to Tokyo by way of Osaka and Kyoto. By the time he arrived it was the second week in April.

All the time he was observing closely and studying this new world. He lodged in small Japanese hotels. 'Nothing but Japanese was spoken,' he told his mother, 'which is amusing but not always easy.' Like many others who have had the opportunity to compare the Chinese with the Japanese way of life he found the latter far less pleasing. He noticed that he was at some physical disadvantage among the small-built Japanese.

[26]D.H.
[27]Do you understand how much vital energy this wandering in the desert produces in me?

In a letter to Diana he told her: 'For the first time I feel disliked by almost everyone who looks at me. My tallness seems to increase that dislike and one longs for the benevolent smiles of the Chinese.' He reached the usual conclusions about the major contrast between the two civilisations, but a letter to Diana shows that he did so with more than usual perspicacity. 'The intensity of Japan's technical civilisation,' he wrote, 'coming with fresh impressions from China, is staggering. With a demoniac dexterity they have learned all our tricks—though the whole system seems like a volcano, agitated not by social revolution within but by caprice on top.'

While he was in Tokyo a curious event occurred. A new German ambassador was appointed. He was chosen by Hitler, on representations made by Keitel to him and Ribbentrop,[28] not from the ranks of the diplomatic service but from the army. He was Major-General Eugen Ott, a former senior member of the German General Staff, who had led a military mission to the Japanese army at the end of 1933, after which he was appointed military attaché to the German Embassy in Tokyo. There seems to have been only one precedent for the promotion of a service attaché to ambassadorship, and that had been in the case of Adam's maternal grandfather, in Vienna in 1869. Even so, this promotion from service attachment to head of mission was unique in modern diplomacy as it occurred without any intervening period. Coming as it did a month after Hitler's seizure of Austria, this seemed an ominous sign of the times. It seemed that German policy was now moving rapidly from the Anti-Comintern Agreement of the year before to full military alliance with the Japanese Empire.

At the end of April Adam left Japan and went by way of Korea to Manchuria, or Manchuko as it was now called, travelling as widely as he could, visiting Port Arthur, Mukden, and going north as far as Harbin. He had seen Japanese military occupation in Peking, but here he could see something far more significant: a large province organised by the Japanese through their creatures, their Quislings as such beings were to be known two years later. Here Adam could see something of what the Japanese were aiming at in their bloody career of aggression and war in China.

In spite of his strong preference for the Chinese, and his often-expressed belief both in their national cause and their ability to fight for it with success, and in spite of Manchuko being the classic scene of Chinese humiliation by the Japanese, he greatly enjoyed this part of his travels. His reaction seems to have surprised himself. He wrote to Shiela, 'I was extraordinarily happy in Manchuria and the only reason I can find for it is that I found myself on the colonial soil of a rich undeveloped country where there's room to do things and where I met and made friends with the men who did them.'

He gives other reasons for his interest in Manchuria in a long letter to Anne von Katte with whose husband, Martin von Katte, he had visited Ernst Jünger in 1935. Jünger remained a strong common ground of interest, and Adam read him on his travels and was moved to express new ideas about him to his friend. 'He has an admirable, self-disciplined sincerity of thought', he wrote to her, 'and on my journey I would like to have been able to use his sometimes unearthly power of observation. In Japan I often found him forced upon my thoughts although that country would probably disappoint the expectations he has of it. General Nogi, who is highly esteemed by him, and is indeed a very outstanding figure, has a certain facial resemblance to Jünger. After the surrender of Port Arthur Nogi agreed to be photographed with the conquered Russian naval commanders, and the Japanese have put this picture in the former Russian Casino in Port Arthur, a white wooden house in the Russian country style, and many other relics of the murderous struggle round the fortress . . . .

'It was a very remarkable experience, after this Oriental world of China, Japan, Korea and Manchuria, suddenly to meet the Russian element which outwardly is almost of our world though inwardly it often hides something monstrously (ungeheuerlich) alien to us, something wild and Asiatic—I have watched this in a very fine old official type from Vladivostok and Habarovsk who shows a painful mixture of hysterical pride and unbelievable depravity. A week in Harbin was one of the most interesting experiences of the whole trip and has greatly tempted me to make a thorough study of the Russians one day. You will surely remember how much their books once meant to us.'[29]

[29]Quoted from *Wandlung und Wiederkehr* essays presented to Ernst Jünger on his seventieth birthday.

He arrived back in Peking at the very end of May. Here he was to remain till September, except for brief journeys to Inner Mongolia and Shansi which he made in July.[30]

Before telling of his last adventures in China, it may be convenient at this point in the book to consider two matters. One is Adam's political outlook at this time, and the second is the political situation into which he was manoeuvred by circumstances, and of which he was not wholly conscious.

For the reasons given at the beginning of this chapter, especially the fact that he was living far from Germany, his political ideas became somewhat distorted by defensiveness; they began to lack precision and definiteness more than usual. The tendency increased throughout this troubled year. People whom he met, including Germans, sometimes asked: What side is he on? His answer, if the question had ever been addressed to him personally, would surely have been 'On the side of Germany, and by Germany I mean something infinitely more than the present Chancellor and the wretches who serve him.' The real conundrum was how to combine the undoubted merit of that attitude with the practical political needs of the moment. He had not found the answer. Not by a long way.

His letters are, as usual, the most valuable guide to what was taking place in his mind. On the 8th April, 1938 he wrote to his parents on the subject of the seizure of Austria by Nazi Germany: 'The Austrian business—the greatest success so far of our new policy—as seen from here seems an extraordinarily important departure. By this the general distribution of power seems to have been altered profoundly, and this may become apparent soon. In any case, as it looks from here, the danger of war would seem to have diminished through this German increase in power—but the farther you look in this world, the more you are impressed by the *uncertainty* of most of those factors you have to take into account, and the impossibility of understanding what action the different powers will feel impelled to take. One can only make a study of the conditions which govern their movements, and thus assess possibilities in given conditions. In this context the psychological and moral factors seem

[30]C.T., G.D.

more important than the economic ones to-day. Yet for an assessment of these, the approach practised hitherto by politicians and journalists does not enlighten us much. Again this supports my view that one should study the mind of a people by learning about their typical doctrines.'

For all the complexity of his expression, the attitude of mind shown here is relatively simple. As a patriot he rejoices in the union of Austria and Germany; he protests that this great event will diminish the danger of war but almost immediately after he suggests the possibility of the opposite. He refers to 'moral factors' but by this expression he seems, judging by the evidence of other letters, to refer not to moral factors operating in Germany, but to his hopes that Germany's neighbours and the outside Western world will adopt an attitude free from hypocrisy. From habit he lays a good deal of blame on the Press. Of course he had to be careful what he said in such a letter, and he becomes more revealing in his letters to Shiela since in writing to her he felt no need to suspect the presence of a censor. Yet in another way he becomes less revealing here since, exchanging letters with this passionate Naziphobe, he felt he could not relinquish the sacred duty of the defence of Germany, even at a time when the utter brutality and moral degradation of Nazism was at last plain to everyone except those who wanted to be deceived. This correspondence reached its climax in 1938. Adam first mentions the Austrian crisis in a letter of the 15th of March.

He opens with the remark that her letters 'from the Bohemian hills sound so angry. Time, space and developments hold us apart now very sternly don't they? . . . Hearing in Kyoto of all that is passing in Europe I wish you were in the States already. Maybe when this gets to you it will be too late to remind you of your promise not to continue your trade [journalism] when the things start . . . Be good and don't go hysterical as I quite see one might. I'll give you a few good names in the U.S.A. but don't expect too much of that country anyway. Do you think you could face India? You will see how little England really is in Europe and how equally wicked we all are—the world is like that all over—but to keep the kernel of it sweet, one must not despair or be afraid.'

Shiela was in Prague when Hitler marched into Austria, and left at once for Vienna. From there she wrote to Adam before receiving the last-quoted letter.

'It is difficult to write to you after these days in Europe, especially since

I am sure that from China they appear just and inevitable and long over-
due. I do not know how I can explain to you that now war has become a
certainty and that there is no turning back on either side. It will seem so
just to you that that which the social democrats desired should now be
achieved, that it was so right of them to desire it, so justified now to
achieve it. How can I explain to you . . . that the means by which it has
been achieved has plunged Europe into the gloom of knowing at last
that war is inevitable . . . I visited your legation here and was talked to in
a tone of incredible brutality, a tone new to your countrymen, which
shows not an added bitterness but a growing contempt for every restraint. "We cannot, of course, expect England and France to be pleased
to discover that they did not, after all, win the war," he said, and when I
said how horrible were the arrests and suicides in Vienna, he answered
Wir lachen nur darüber. Oh Adam darling, one feels horribly, horribly
betrayed . . .

'I can hear you thinking out loud "How hysterical she is" and blaming
the Czechs for my behaviour. I remember Mowrer[31] writing me a letter
years ago saying I did not realise the blessings of a pokey life. Well, now
I do, and now it's too late.'

The correspondence remains one-sided for some weeks and Adam
explains the reason in a letter from Peking of the 4th June.

'I know this time I was very bad about writing. There was a certain
amount of hostility in my silence at first, because by becoming aggressive,
I felt you had abandoned being a good European . . .

'We should think still, a little more about avoiding the catastrophe by
constructive means and attitudes than building strategic positions for the
event of its happening. If it does, all is up anyway. Your concentration
on the central European issue with an ideology of uncritical democratic
liberalism will I fear make you less and less capable of seeing the really
world-wide problem of making Europe into a source of order and con-

[31]Edgar Ansel Mowrer, the distinguished American newspaper columnist. Shiela
Grant-Duff worked for him in Paris. Having made his name as a leading war
correspondent for the Chicago Daily News in World War I, he became a free-
lance correspondent first in Rome then in Berlin. In 1932 he published *Germany
Puts the Clock Back*, one of the most remarkable journalistic books of modern
times. For this exposure of the new course in German policy, soon to be put into
full effect by Hitler, Mowrer was compelled to leave Berlin for Paris.

structive lead on a large scale once more—because no other Continent can do this. We certainly are *one* still and most of what our orators and your publicists produce runs against actual fact and the necessary trend of Europe's relation to the world.'[32]

On 20th July Adam wrote Shiela a long letter in which he tried to make his position clear. It is this letter which brings the correspondence to a climax of disagreement, and, at the time, nearly led to an end of this close friendship. The theme of the letter is one enunciated already, 'how equally wicked we all are,' Germany by no means the most. If Adam's letter of the 4th of June is a distressing document, this one is far more so. It could have been written only at a time when lack of information, combined with wishful thinking, had weakened his political judgment.

To understand the two points of view, particularly Shiela's, one must remember that this was written as the German-Czechoslovakian crisis was moving slowly towards a war-situation. At the time of the Austrian coup d'état, the German Government assured the Czechoslovak Government, through the latter's legation in Berlin, that it had no designs on its eastern neighbour. Hermann Göring acted as the messenger pledging his 'word of honour as a German officer.' Immediately after that, Henlein, the German minority leader in Czechoslovakia, began an agitation for German autonomy in the Sudeten districts. The Nazi Government supported him with abusive anti-Czech propaganda, and maintained the fiction, widely believed, that Henlein was acting in total independence of Hitler, though in fact, as many people guessed, he was in receipt of a large Nazi subsidy and acting under Nazi orders. Hitler was manoeuvring for mastery of Europe, using the same repulsive methods that he had found effective when climbing to power in Germany. Here is an extract from what Adam wrote to Shiela on the 20th July.

'I have never hesitated to tell you how I hated your ambition to make a name for yourself in journalism. You have, to a slight extent, taken this objection of mine seriously, but mainly you have put it back to obsolete prejudice and treated it lightly because you knew very well that my affection was stronger than my disapproval.

'I believe that in your own life you want "liberty and truth" more than

[32]It is in this letter that Trott describes to Shiela his reasons for enjoying his stay in Manchuria.

anything else and that your "rage" about oppression and dishonesty is quite genuine and heartfelt. But I do not believe that in judgment (or hard work which it requires) you are capable to apply these principles fairly to the conditions under which they must operate on the "other side." I think very few people indeed are capable of that—but any occupation with current events which fails to reach such fundamental detachment and fairness is bound to be swayed by collective prejudice and the uncritical interests inertly entrenched in it. That's why I think a person like you with your impulsiveness and your strong personal ambition—however sincere your beliefs may be—is bound in journalism to become a prey of forces which you cannot control. There is quite enough cynicism and of sheer love of high life in you to bridge over the first few conflicts which must be traversed—though ultimately you could not be cynical or corrupt.

'Mme Tabouis' book[33] which I have just been reading also is not corrupt or cynical—but I think it is hopelessly shallow in its premises and irresponsible in its conclusions . . . I hope your book will be better than hers.

'Your former employer[34] wrote an article about Canton which you may have seen. It is another example of what I mean. It is no doubt well written (I saw it in a translation) but again hopelessly shallow and without a hint of the real power that is moving China's resistance. I do not mean foreign powers, for them he may have deliberately left out, but what he calls the "solid foundation of a Chinese state." Just big words inflated by a sense of righteousness about the personal preferences he happened to have formed . . . I do feel that a fellow like M with his great talent and sense of justice ought to stick to his home country to try and establish the rudiments of liberty and justice. My friend Roger Baldwin who is the head of the civil liberties union was put in prison, and hounded like a public enemy on other occasions, because he insisted on the reality

[33]In 1938 Madame Geneviève Tabouis's book *Blackmail or War?* (English edition) was published. It was based on her weekly articles in *L'Oeuvre*. Madame Tabouis was among the foremost journalists to rouse public opinion to the international dangers of Nazism. She was often ridiculed as an alarmist and for making allegedly exaggerated claims to secret information.
[34]Mowrer. This evidently refers to material published later in book form under the title *Mowrer in China*.

rather than highflown quotations of human rights, liberty and justice. If M was only compelled to read every day the *local* columns side by side with the idealistic comments and denunciations he writes about Europe, he might be a little humbler about the good he is doing to the world. America—in all a young and wonderful country with a foundation of right and a wide range of possibilities is full of oppression and injustice and his home town leads the way in that. Is it not sometimes just as much an untruth to be silent about certain things as to state them incorrectly? I am sure you will agree that this is true of a lot of the high phraseology used by your Central European friends.

'The more I have seen of conditions in the rest of the world, America, *your* position in the Pacific, the whole attitude of western powers here, the more I feel sick about that whole *spirit* of denunciation against Germany. If it came from God it were sufficiently justified, no doubt. But from you—who are committing the same sins every minute of the day in some part of the world which you prefer not to know—such denunciation raises an awful feeling which I hope you will not minimise when you denounce the "German mentality" . . .

'I agree with Samuel's article in the "XIX Century"[35]—but I resent and consider as utterly hopeless and damaging the high-handed denunciation of a people which contains just as many hardworking and responsible "Europeans" which have been defeated and silenced by economic desperatism and not at least by the leading spirit of Europe wanting to perpetuate Germany's defeat in 1918.

'As long as it is not possible for you to consider all that happened in Germany a *European* phenomenon and responsibility, no step further can be made. If on the other hand you try to hedge in Germany morally and materially the explosion is bound to happen and destroy what foundations of a Europe in our sense may still be left.'

---

[35]An article by Lord Samuel entitled 'The Choice before Us' appeared in the June 1938 number of *The Nineteenth Century and After*. He expressed disapproval of Neville Chamberlain's conduct of affairs, and proposed a different version of the policy of appeasement. This would have included British rearmament, but would have avoided the division of Europe into 'blocs' by refusing definitive guarantees to any State, notably Czechoslovakia. He favoured negotiations over the former German Colonies. 'To be liberal', he said, 'only towards liberal states is not liberalism at all .'

After this letter Adam received none from Shiela for three weeks. He wrote to her again on the 10th of August. Since his last letter of the 20th July the Czechoslovakia crisis had been maintained in a state of crescendo. Adam tried to soften the effect of his earlier letter, though he repeated his main contention. Here are three extracts:

'I hope my letters lately have not seemed like a "stab in the back" when you were just in the thick of fighting to get your book done.[36] They must no doubt have seemed very offensive to you, as apparently you are now shutting up altogether. I often think of you and our little quarrels and how I should blow them away if you were with me in this last beautiful undisturbed summer. I fear that for you it is everything else but undisturbed . . .

'But you must be generous too and admit some justice to the charge I have made against your *spirit* of defending Europe—a spirit I come up against more and more, i.e. one of blind denunciation of Germany's ills which although couched in phrases of liberal rights and progress is fundamentally drawing more and more on socially reactionary motives and those of nationalism which made the last war. Who am I, as a German, to make such a charge you may ask. Unless, again you are generous and admit that Germany was to a large extent (by no means wholly) driven into these ills, you accept by reacting to it on the same plane the entire mess of prewar sentiment and motivation and share in responsibility what will indeed inevitably ensue . . .

'I am not, as you might think, going over to some "other side" or trying to escape or surrender my identity to whatever comes. It is true that this long journey has put me in a rather remote position and this last year in China has given me chance to think of things more objectively than I ever could before.'

Shiela's answer was written on the 1st of September, 1938. This was a week before the opening in Nuremberg of the Nazi party rally which was to be devoted to intensification of the German-Czech quarrel. By this time there were only two reasonable explanations of the European situation: either Hitler was deliberately provoking war with Czechoslovakia, or he and his closest colleagues were only pretending to provoke war

[36]Shiela Grant-Duff was writing her book *Europe and the Czechs* which came out on the 30th of September, the day of the Munich Agreement.

in order to extort concessions from France and Britain. Research by historians has shown that the first of these hypotheses was the correct one.[37]

The letter which Shiela wrote to Adam, in the midst of this ghastly time, came from the heart and is an impressive statement of her ideas.

'Thank you for your letter this morning. It is lucky it came before I sent the passionate letters which had been accumulating in my mind and on paper. We cannot quarrel at a distance and I would probably be sorry if my letters landed you in jail even though I have more than once decided that is the suitable place for you. You are quite right that your letters are "a stab in the back." They are a real betrayal . . . This side *is* more important than any single human relationship—and more and more my only deep and strong affections are for people who care for these things too, and if you do not—then we part.

'In your last letter, you protested against the *spirit* in which I defend Europe, and you attack my attachment to liberal rights as mere phrases.

'I think the only thing—or chief political good—is freedom, and every policy which one approves has some bearing on that . . .

'If frontiers are to disappear, they can only do so if the fundamental attitude to life on each side of them is the same. I think this is the fundamental attitude of the democracies.

'There are many good things in Germany, and even in the Nazi regime, but you know as well as I that fundamentally there is no compromise between the attitude of Germany and Italy and the attitude of England and France. I do not even believe that the two can live side by side, and "respect each other's internal regimes," as my countrymen have constantly exhorted us to do with your country (your countrymen have never once done so). I believe if Europe is ever to be united, one or other of these systems has got to disappear. It seems to me a Europe united under a despotism is not worth living in. Perhaps a new Dark Age has got to come

[37]The matter is ably summarised with reference to documents in Alan Bullock. Op. Cit. pp. 439-71 (Revised Penguin Edition of 1962). Hitler was at times forced by the dissent of certain of his generals and the unwarlike state of German public opinion into some hesitation, but the widely held view of the time that Hitler never had any intention of engaging in war is not supported by contemporary documentary evidence.

before a new Renaissance, but the civilised Romans can hardly have welcomed the Barbarian invasions.

'Therefore I am passionate in my hatred of certain systems. I do not call on "socially reactionary motives." As luck has it, the Right here and in France is the last to turn against you. There is, dear Adam, still approval among the "socially reactionary" for your countrymen.

'Then you reproach me with nationalism and of war-1914 sentiments. You know, I have tried always to make a distinction between Governments and people. Germany is a beautiful country and I have many friends —but what has been done to show there is a distinction between Government and people? Nothing. In moments of anger one thinks, "They are the same, and I condemn them both" or "They are different, and the people too cowardly and weak to say so."

'Then you say, how should I condemn when my countrymen commit these atrocities in the Empire? You know I condemn that, and would work against that too—and started to do so till I realised the greater danger was here at home, in Europe.[38]

'You will remember there was a thing called the War Guilt Clause. It has been disputed. If there is another war, there will be no dispute again. I deny we drove Germany to accept a regime which meant war.

'Now we come to my friends. Of M[owrer] in China I know nothing. Probably in three weeks he did not understand the "real power which is moving China's resistance," but he does care passionately for certain things I care for. I admire him morally and politically and if you accept me you accept him—or neither.'

In the next paragraph she mentions Hubert Ripka, a Czech friend to whom Adam had referred slightingly. Ripka was to enter the story of Adam's life again. He was, at this time, the editor of the Prague daily *Lidove Noviny*, meaning 'the People's News,' by common consent the best informed and most responsible newspaper in the country. To Adam's prejudiced reference she answered with a defence that was not unworthy of her subject.

---

[38]Two years earlier Shiela Grant-Duff had worked for Jawaharlal Nehru. It is curious, and very characteristic of the Left in the thirties, that in this well-ordered defence Shiela takes so little objection to Trott's outrageous suggestion that the Government of India under Lord Linlithgow's viceroyship was the equal in crime of the Nazi Government under Adolf Hitler.

'Your criticism of R. too I despise as jealousy. Even if it is more, this is not the moment to utter it. He has worked more for Czech–German co-operation than any other Czech, and has failed because of the political crimes and follies of your countrymen. He is the most honest, brave, and disinterested man I have ever met. His love of his country and his idea of Europe is far more profound than any other I have met, and goes far beyond mere self-defence against your countrymen. But to-day, that alone requires heroism and unfaltering determination which I admire profoundly. I care for him very much, and he has come nearer than anyone else to replacing what I lost through your country 25 years ago.[39] That Germany again threatens that is not a reason for my feeling very calm about it, or my tolerating criticism of my friends from you. So there it is. Now you can judge whether we agree sufficiently to be friends. I retract absolutely nothing . . .

'I suppose you will go back and be part of it. I cannot condemn you, but I cannot approve either, and perhaps one day I shall think you did wrong.'

A last comment made right at the end of the letter is worth recalling. Shiela describes High Elms, her mother's family home where she was staying and where Adam had once visited her. She goes on to say: 'I wish you would come but perhaps you never will. Many people think there will be war next week. It all depends on one man. I think your proper attitude would be shame and to ask forgiveness. Even I feel ashamed, and I am less guilty than you—but you only reproach me and declaim.'

Before receiving this letter Adam wrote again to Shiela. The occasion was the Munich agreement and what he wrote is revealing and modifies the impression left by his earlier letters. One might expect him, after what he had written so recently, to rejoice in this tremendous diplomatic triumph of the Third Reich, but to expect that is to forget Adam's essential character. It seems that, after Hitler had made himself master of Central Europe, although Adam still indulged some hopes of an international accord rising from this turn of events, he recognised with a shock what this triumph might mean. His letter is dated the 1st of October.

'We have now heard of the Munich accord, a solution which is no

[39]Her father, Lieut.-Colonel Adrian Grant-Duff was killed in action in 1914.

doubt very painful to you in many respects. I wish we could weigh together its probable ultimate outcome. I don't feel at all easy about it yet.
Anyway the thing seems to be settled as a *European* and not as a German-
Czech issue which, if people had sense, might lead on to something really
more satisfactory—but I participate in the fears you have previously expressed about exactly this contingency and I am with you in your present
apprehensions.'

It was in this letter that he confided to Shiela that he wanted to return
by way of America 'to look for a place to work,' as he expressed it, 'if
our continent is really going to be what we both feel threatening now a
conflict has been spared.' Yet he reiterates his belief that he must get home
to Germany because 'the East as a permanent place to live is out of the
question—the European problem is the only one that really concerns
one.'

A day or so after sending this off he received Shiela's letter of the 1st
of September. In his new reflective mood he was prepared to accept much
of what she said and see that he had been wrong in great part to have
written as he did before. He answered her in a long letter written on the
6th of October. He hastened to assure her of his abiding affection. He went
on to say that he felt 'completely to blame' because 'I confess that I failed
to realise the intrinsic turning point which came about with the Anschluss
and which opened up the path for a coercive settlement of the Central
European problem.' Yet though this letter was very much of a peace-
offering, it was not a recantation. He says at one point: 'You do not really
answer my reproach that perhaps capitalist and imperialist democracy
uses liberty as a smoke screen for definitely coercive policies, whereas
some aspects of "authoritarian" systems may mean a more straightforward
assertion of the rights of man in modern industrial society than its radical
opponents realise. With other words, the conflict of ideologies may really
be quite unrepresentative of, and disguise the real nature of the conflict, which may be based on rival but not different ambitions! I do
not agree that the rival dynamic of the European powers is ultimately
incompatible and must result in the bloody victory of one ideology
over the other.' This was a Marxist argument leading to a pacifist
conclusion.

The correspondence continued until the end of October, and was then
renewed after Adam's return. Neither side changed opinion, and after

Adam's letter of the 6th of October no new element enters this remarkable document. But the friendship survived the storm.

During this interlude of 1937 and 1938 Adam's political reputation developed in a way harmful to himself, and this development was directly related to the formation (or one might even say deviation) of his opinions during this time.

It has been noted earlier that Adam wrote with freedom to Shiela because it seemed to him that the last thing he needed to bother about was a prying official eye. Here he was almost certainly mistaken. It is probable that British and American security authorities in the Far East read every letter of the correspondence in transit. In the later part of his time in China Adam came to suspect that his letters were being tampered with, since some that he wrote to Julie Braun-Vogelstein never reached America, or else were unaccountably delayed.[40] Even so he seems not to have realised, at any rate at the time, how much he was surrounded by suspicion. The point is not one that can be proved, but it is likely that the apologia for Nazi conduct in 1938 which he addressed to Shiela, added greatly to a mistrust that began early while he was in China. It has been told already how a similar mistrust may have formed in America.

The softened view of Nazism which he adopted at this time through emotionally misguided patriotism, was known to most people whom he met, and much deplored by some of them. The sister-in-law of his friend Josias von Rantzau was then in Peking where her husband held a diplomatic post. In a brief memoir written long after, Frau von Rantzau recalls that 'he was very well-liked among my Peking friends even though in refugee society he was believed to be somewhat influenced by Nazi thinking.' If his own people could confound his too uncritical patriotism with Nazi-involvement, others could do the same more easily.

Gustav Ecke provides interesting evidence of how suspicion mounted against Adam. As Eberhard remarked about him on their southern journey, he seemed to have a master-thought which he kept to himself. Gustav Ecke noted the same thing in Peking, but found it easy to explain. First of all there was his plan to study Confucius so as to fit himself to

[40]Julie Braun-Vogelstein. Discussion.

exert right influences on German Government. This was not a matter suited to discussion except with the closest friends. Added to his reserve on this subject there was his reluctance to talk about German affairs. He wanted to return to Germany and take part in public life. But, at a time when Germany was governed by Adolf Hitler who had boasted openly in his book about his skill in treachery and intrigue, a German with what appeared to be a secretive manner easily became an object of suspicion. Among people whom he met at Yenching University was the English writer Harold Acton who at that time was lecturing there. He has told the writer that he liked Adam and admired his vigorous intelligence and commanding personality, but sometimes felt uneasy with him because, as he said, he 'could not quite make out what his game was.'

Private suspicion was conjoined to official suspicion and fed it. Most unfortunate for Adam, in this respect, was the coincidence of his arrival in Tokyo with the appointment of General Ott. The General's promotion to ambassadorship was a queer and tangled story, and the facts were not known then. Ott was head of the Army Department or Wehrmachtabteilung in the Ministry of Defence before January 1933, and he owed his position to the patronage of his friend Schleicher whom he greatly admired. After Hitler became Chancellor, Ott was removed from his department and sent to Japan, less as a move to strengthen German-Japanese ties than as a way of getting rid of an unwelcome and non-Nazi Schleicher relic still lingering on the scene. Ott did well in his new mission, and also as military attaché in Tokyo; hence his elevation and return to favour. The appointment was essentially a gesture of conciliation made by the Nazis to the army and the defeated party of Schleicher, but it appeared to be a victory of the Nazi party over the diplomatic service.

The position of Germany in the Far East was extraordinarily confused in 1938, and as such it was the natural subject of alarmed speculation. At the time of Ott's appointment in Japan, a German military mission, headed by General Alexander von Falkenhausen, was still in Nanking acting as military advisors to Japan's dedicated enemy Chiang Kai-shek! The anomaly was resolved a month later when Falkenhausen and his staff were recalled in May 1938. In reality the contradictions of German policy in China and Japan at that time seem to have been due to nothing more mysterious than the fact that preoccupation in Europe gave the Nazi leaders no time to organise a coherent line of political conduct in the

East, but people rightly associated Nazism with deceit and subterfuge and these grotesque anomalies seemed to bode evil. While the main conclusion reached by foreign observers, that Germany and Japan were drawing together for combined aggression, was true enough, the detailed interpretation of events and personalities was wrong, and one of the personalities to be most wrongly interpreted was Adam.

The East is the classic habitat of 'Rumour painted full of tongues,' but only those who have experience of the East can know how the weakness takes hold on the European sojourner as firmly as it does on the indigenous babbler. Strangely enough this does not come through the intercourse of Europeans with Orientals so much as through something opposite, through the fact that since relatively few Europeans wish, or know how to become full members of Oriental Society (where they are not always welcome), they are thrown back on themselves and on the very small societies which they compose when stationed in distant lands. To indulge in gossip and embroider on it is a universal remedy for the tedium of life in an isolated village. In the case of European embassies and large business organisations, physical circumstances often add to their isolation, since by an inherited practice they live not in houses in the streets of the chief cities, as in Europe, but in walled-in settlements, in 'compounds' as they have come to be called. They see few non-Europeans. Western Governments probably owe a very great deal of the misinformation from the East which has misled them in the last fifty years to the simple expedient of compounds, originally designed for the protection of their representatives. Rumour does not only flourish within those walls; it waxes fat and begins to go mad. Wild tales come to be believed not only about indigenous affairs, not only about other Europeans and rivals, but even about each other, by those who dwell in such self-imposed and cannibalistic circumstances of siege.

In such an atmosphere, Adam's strange search for knowledge, and the secrecy with which he surrounded it, appeared to many who peered out of the compounds to be positively dangerous. It was believed in some British Embassy circles in Tokyo that his travelling scholarship was a Nazi fraud, a clever manoeuvre to further the German intelligence network, and no one, so far as the documents show, seems to have taken the trouble to enquire into the case at Rhodes House. His interest in the Japanese 'New Order' seemed to confirm the supposition that here was a

Nazi engaged in some dark and malign exploit. The fact that immediately
after visiting Tokyo at the time of Ott's appointment he went to Manchuria, added further colour and conviction to the picture. It is sometimes
said that a sense of humour can dispel ridiculous legends. It is forgotten
that joking about them can sometimes spread them. One of Adam's
foreign friends in Peking used to refer to him jokingly as 'the German
Spy.' There was no malice in this but, according to Gustav Ecke, it helped
to popularise an idea that Adam's real purpose was political, not scholarly,
and thoroughly undesirable.

One must remember that Adam was only known, outside conspiratorial circles in Germany, by one public political act, and that was the unfortunate letter that he had written to the *Manchester Guardian* four years
before.[41]

In the middle of September 1938 Adam left Peking for his last journey in
China. His departure was marked by a mysterious incident. According to
a belief of Chinese folklore a 'house-snake' appears on certain significant
occasions. In a letter to Adam written on the 18th November, Gustav
Ecke told how when he returned home from seeing Adam off 'suddenly
a large snake with flaming red spots appeared and coiled itself up in the
passage near your house.' The servants were sure that this was a portent,
though of what they could not say.

With Professor Helmuth Wilhelm as companion, he travelled through
the northern province of Shantung, and a letter to his parents gives a
very good description of his feelings and impressions in this war-shattered
place. 'I have not yet got so used to the horror of poverty and filth in the
streets everywhere, that I am not appalled every time anew. The faces
of the people here tell poignantly of the dangers, oppression and raids
that they have lived through. There is something rigid and wild in their

[41]The tale of British disapproval of Trott in certain (by no means all) official
circles in China and Japan has been told to the writer by a person in whose information he has complete confidence, and who wishes to remain anonymous. Since
no enquiry was made at Rhodes House it would seem unlikely that suspicion
was influenced by information about the *Manchester Guardian* letter, except for
the fact that this letter seems to have been officially remembered against Trott
two years later.

glance—one's smile is never returned, and it seemed to me that even the children were in a state of tension.'

He travelled to the port of Tsing-tau and from there sailed to Shanghai where he stayed for about a fortnight. Before leaving he wrote a letter to his father on the 12th October. He had revised his plans. While the Czechoslovak crisis was at its height he had wished to return home soon, but now after Munich, when peace of some sort was assured for some months at least, he considered the advantage of staying on till February of 1939 so as to enlarge and deepen his studies. He wrote of travelling from Shanghai to Hong Kong, and on to French Indo-China, visiting Haiphong and travelling from there to the Chinese border province of Yunnan, after which he would fly from Yunnan to Chung King.

To help him in this ambitious undertaking Sir Stafford Cripps had made Adam another handsome gift, but the new plans came to nothing, and the money was used for the speediest possible return home. It is improbable that Herr von Trott received Adam's letter of the 12th October. On the 28th, in Hong Kong, Adam heard by cable that his father was dead, and his mother asked him to come back home.

By chance there was a boat of the P. & O. Line in Hong Kong at that time, the steamship *Randi* which was due to sail the next day. He reserved a passage and sailed to Europe by way of Ceylon and the Suez Canal. As on his journey from San Pedro to Hong Kong he followed the news from the radio broadcasts and the Reuter bulletins pinned up with other notices on the green baize board. He learned thus of that fatal sign that Adolf Hitler was in no way appeased by the Nazi triumph at Munich: the 'Kristallnacht' anti-Jewish pogrom of the 9th of November. He was moved by this hideous event to write to Diana, remembering his friend Wilfrid Israel.

'My thoughts have been with him very much these last weeks—do you know where he is, how I can reach him? Give him my love if you can. You know that it is we who are humiliated by what has passed and it is for us to wonder whether our former friends wish to have anything more to do with one who, after all (in my case through my very absence) has to accept his full share of responsibility. I know that our friendship is too deeply rooted to be affected by all these developments, but I know of hardly another one I have abroad that in some way or other is not. This

I think will be my hardest discovery on returning to Europe after these eventful months . . .'

He reached the end of his sea journey in the later part of November, disembarking at Marseilles and from there going to Germany by way of Paris where he met Shiela. They were glad to see each other again, but the meeting was inevitably marred by the great differences which had arisen between them. In an affectionate letter written afterwards Shiela said she was sorry that he had 'felt angry and defensive in Paris,' but she added that she was 'glad it is not permanent.'

But though the friendship survived, the breach was in a sense permanent. No more did Adam take this friend into full trust when it came to political interests. She was aware of what had happened. 'I suspect that we are enemies,' Shiela wrote on the last day of the year, 'I do not know what you really care for and admire, but I suspect it is not what I care for.'

Early in December he returned to Imshausen. He could now feel, amid the scenes where he had most often been with him, all that he had lost in the death of his most honoured father, but he rejoiced to see his mother, sisters and brothers again, and, in the grey-green silver of the winter, that Hessian landscape from which his thoughts had never been very far in the last two years.

Chapter 10

CLIVEDEN 1939

Soon after his arrival home Adam wrote to Diana from Imshausen. 'At first the pleasure of being in familiar surroundings again was a stranger sensation than almost any of the upsetting changes I found here. In your letter about his death you seemed to prove exactly that you know in what way I miss my father. He kept the peace in our house and prevented it from running into the extremes to which it is tending. His presence seemed to intervene between wrong tendencies and a final break and now it seems very much as if I should perform this function and yet am not quite up to it . . .

'I am still happy when I walk over the hills and woods and their presence with every familiar place is like the presence of one's whole life and youth and dreams. But the folds of the valleys seem to have become smaller and more by the way . . .'

The troubles of the house were largely due to a familiar circumstance, namely that the family had to argue their claims on the inheritance. This never agreeable moment in life was complicated by the legal situation. In some respects Nazi Germany followed the Weimar Republic, and was in step with progressist administration throughout Europe. Inheritance was liable to an elaborate system of taxation aimed at breaking up large family estates into small holdings. Adam, as a Leftist, approved of this defeudalising course, but, as he said in another letter to Diana, 'you would understand that we want to preserve the home in which we have been for more than seven hundred years.' In a family of high-spirited people, some of whom, especially the two elder brothers, were highly strung, such a moment of loss and transition could hardly pass without a high degree of friction. But from his Chinese learning Adam also detected a deeper cause of the unhappiness which he found at Imshausen.

Referring to this time (at a later date) he quoted an ancient Chinese saying that when the Emperor is good there is peace between the cities, harmony between the communities and within the family, but that when the Emperor is evil the cities wage war one with another, the communities give themselves over to strife, and husbands quarrel with their wives.[1]

With his long apprenticeship over, Adam wanted now to find employment in the service of the State, in keeping with his family traditions, but he found this even more difficult than he had expected. More and more, state service was being reserved to members of the Nazi party.

Adam found positive discouragement in the fate of his friends. Helmuth Conrad was still living at Waldersee, without hope of employment, and in straitened circumstances. Almost all his Berlin socialist friends had left and those of his Corpsbrüder who disliked the regime and had the good fortune to be 'landed gentry,' had retired to their estates to be away from Nazi pressure. Most of his Jewish friends had emigrated, one of the rare exceptions being Wilfrid Israel who, protected by his British passport, valiantly battled on for his people. He was one of the few people in Germany whose circumstances allowed him to lead a life of opposition, of a strictly legal and therefore utterly inadequate kind it is true, but one of opposition nonetheless. Albrecht von Bernstorff was still working in the Wassermann Bank in Berlin, *his* only protection being that he was looked on as a ridiculous aristocratic eccentric whom it was politic to leave alone. Triumphant Germany under its successful and squalid leader was a dismal place in which most people who retained civilised values had to choose between martyrdom and a life of spiritless discretion and escapism.

One should remember here the commonest and easiest form of escapism, of which Adam had a bitter experience. His friendship with Lugowski had been one not only of stimulating intellectual vigour, but of sweetness and tenderness. It can be described as the last sentimental, essentially boyish relationship that he enjoyed. But now it was no longer a part of his life. By 1939 Lugowski had surrendered to Nazism and became a member of the S.A. Weary of the ceaseless demands of mental strife, he had accepted the whole nauseating doctrine of Teutonic racial superiority and (notwithstanding his Polish origins) of the German right to trample

[1]C.T.

on Jews, Slavs, and other sub-men.[2] Exactly when this apostasy took place
is not remembered, but it seems to have been during Adam's absence in
China. It may have been in part due to the withdrawal of Adam's influence.

Adam's first aim was to be given a post in the Ministry for Economic
Affairs but in this he had no success. He knew more people in the Foreign
Ministry than in any other department, and here some openings appeared
—rather vaguely it is true—in the spring of 1939. But before this Adam
had conceived a new and original way to serve his country, independently
of defined official position, and this new plan occupied most of his energies
from February until September. He aimed high. He had returned to
Europe and the oppressive atmosphere of expected war. He set himself
no less a task than to prevent the outbreak of war in Europe.

1939 was at once the most successful and the most disastrously unsuccessful period in Adam's life. When one considers how young he was,
and that he had no political advantage beyond intelligence, wide acquaintance and great charm of manner, it is extraordinary how far he contrived
to go along the difficult path which he decided to follow. But the aim
which he had set himself was quite impossible of attainment, politically,
psychologically and spiritually. Eventual failure was inevitable.

Adam's political beliefs and aims remained those of a conservative
revolutionary, opposed to the Nazi regime, patriotic, determined that
foreign anti-Nazism should not be used by Germany's enemies as a means
by which to harm Germany. The old problem remained. How was a
patriotic German to serve Germany without giving any moral surrender
to Hitler? The fiend had followed Adam round the world.

He clung to two political convictions, one of them open to doubt, the
other almost certainly true. The first was that there was no greater political
folly or disaster than full scale war between great nations equipped with
modern industrial resources.

His second conviction was that avoidance of war in Europe depended
on one factor alone: on peace being firmly maintained between Germany
and Great Britain. It followed, so Adam argued, that every effort must
be made to influence the British and German Governments towards the
kind of action on the part of both likely to lead to an accord. There can

[2]C.T. quoting another source. Lugowski was killed in the war.

be no doubt that Anglo-German agreement was in truth the key to peace. The flaw in the argument was that agreement with Germany, while Hitler ruled, was only possible on intolerable terms.

Adam was aware of this flaw but he believed that he could get over it. He was impressed by the persistence of anti-Nazi feeling among civil servants and among officers in the army. He was further impressed by the fact that some party members were becoming disturbed in mind about the recklessness of Hitler's policy. He believed that if war could be prevented, Hitler would fall, and he came to believe that this would happen soon and inevitably. His judgment was led astray once more by the natural optimism which was so strong and attractive a part of his personality.

He had been thinking long about this question of how to bring about Anglo-German accord. While he was in China he drew up the outline of a scheme for practical action. He did this in a very curious document which he wrote for Rhodes House in English and German and sent to Lord Lothian and Edward Carter.[3] The German version is entitled *Ostasiatische Möglichkeiten—Possibilities in East Asia*. The document is a full indication of the surprising trend of his thoughts.

British and German interests, he explained, were not in conflict in China and Japan; in fact they coincided in one important respect, namely both Britain and Germany had an interest in bringing the Sino-Japanese war to an end. Britain saw her large commercial investment in China threatened by Japanese expansion, and by the increase of Russian influence within the country. Only peace could remove this double threat. Germany on the other hand must desire an early peace because Japan was on terms of close friendship[4] and the war could only weaken a potential ally. With Britain she shared anxiety at the increase of Russian Communist influence on China. Though acting in concert with Great Britain, Germany rather than Britain should take the initiative for two reasons. First because the German Government was on more sympathetic terms with the Japanese

[3]The German version is dated 'Beginning of July 1938', the English one 'September 1938'. In the English version the expressions are occasionally toned down.
[4]Trott uses the word 'freundschaft', referring to the loose partnership established by the Anti-Comintern Pact of November 1936. There was in fact no formal Treaty of Alliance between Germany and Japan until the Tripartite Pact (Germany, Italy and Japan) of 27 September, 1940.

military party in power; secondly, German initiative would be diplomatically correct in view of the Anti-Comintern Pact. Great Britain would occupy herself with the economic and political aspects of the negotiation. If such a combined move succeeded, the advantage to Germany would be considerable. It would undo those 'tendencies' in Great Britain and America which sought an alliance with Russia aimed at the 'Have-Nots.' It would give Germany a more wholesome reputation in the Anglo-Saxon world, and of course it would be beneficial to German trade. The paper covers other subjects, but this, very briefly, is what he had to say on joint German-British action.

The whole proposition has an air of unreality about it, but this was not the impression of readers at the time.[5] Edward Carter was moved by the paper to invite Adam to attend a meeting of the I.P.R. scheduled for the autumn.

The major significance of the whole paper, evidenced by letters to his parents, is that the prevention of war between England and Germany was his chief political preoccupation, and that he recognised that mutual ill-feeling had gone so far that the normal approach was no longer possible. He set to work to organise other approaches.

From the beginning, and throughout his attempt, he was under a misunderstanding which was widely shared not only in Germany but in Great Britain. Since 1935, there had been so much talk about rearmament in the British Parliament, and so much protestation from the Labour party that a rearmament policy was being carried out to excess, that the idea naturally spread that Great Britain was very strong from a strictly military point of view. For this reason British acceptance of diplomatic defeat at Munich had caused much surprise. In England it provoked Neville Chamberlain's enemies to believe that he was a secret Fascist sympathiser; in Germany, to English surprise, it caused fresh suspicions, carefully fostered by the Goebbels-run press, that Great Britain was playing some deep and treacherous game against her. A letter from Adam to Shiela of the 30th December, 1938 shows, or may be held to show, for

[5] In *Harold Nicolson Diaries and Letters 1930-1939* p. 302 a somewhat similar suggestion is reported as having been made by Nicolson to Hugh Dalton and Albrecht Bernstorff in June 1937, and well received. Trott's paper was read with approval by the British Ambassador to China (Letters. C.T.).

it is very cryptic, that Adam was sensitive to both these suspicions, though, as his friends the Bielenbergs recall clearly, he had not yet made up his mind.

The first part of the letter, which is so purposely obscure that for ordinary reading it might as well have been written in cypher, is interpreted by those same friends, and by Dr Margaret Boveri, as evidence that he had learned about the conspiracy of Generals Witzleben, Halder and others, in which they planned to arrest Hitler in September 1938 on the day that the Führer gave the order to invade Czechoslovakia. By the few in the anti-Nazi opposition in Germany and the anti-Chamberlain opposition in England who knew about the plot, it was believed not that the generals missed their moment through hesitation, but that Chamberlain's successful manoeuvrings for a conference destroyed the opportunity. Accepting the foregoing interpretation of Adam's letter, he evidently agreed with this view of the event, and found his respect for the military hierarchy confirmed. The key phrase in the letter runs as follows: 'The attempt to couple the venture with a general overhaul and readjustment of the inner gears of the machine was frustrated by your clever Neville and the only alternative is another venture or an overhauling in the garage . . .'Also: 'At present the door is shut, the engine stinks and puffs the evilest poisons, suffocating all the more sensitive lungs while everybody gets more and more uneasy.'

In the next paragraph he tells of a meeting with Hjalmar Schacht whom he had met before and for whom he had some admiration.

'Schacht whom I saw said there is no chance at all for a European war, now no longer as clever Neville had been forging ahead with the other hand while holding out the one, and that the other with all it could pull with it was ever ready and probably stronger already than both of ours . . . I have been told his predictions are often wrong. Anyway all that is only two days in Berlin before Christmas and certainly only one side of the matter. The country is magnificently industrious, full of amazing achievement, but painfully resigned and spiritually asleep, if no worse.'

Early in the year Adam made the first move in his plan to make new political approaches by renewing his English friendships. He had as yet no more distinct design. There was no difficulty about 'cover.' He owed a visit to Sir Stafford and Lady Cripps to thank them for their generosity; he owed another to Lady Astor who had given him the clothes in which he fell from his pony in the sand of Peking; he owed another to Rhodes House.

He came to London on the 12th of February, arriving in the early morning. He planned to go to Oxford the same day and the first English friend he met was Diana Hubback with whom he had breakfast at Paddington Station Hotel. They then went for a long walk in Kensington Gardens and gave each other an account of their lives during the past two years. In her memoir Diana recalls that 'we realised then with joy that—on the eve of the war that was surely coming to separate us once more—and just before my own wedding—we had at last reached that true confidence in each other and emotional stability in our relationship that we had so long sought.'

He found revisiting Oxford, where he stayed at All Souls, a somewhat uneasy experience. He described it to his mother. 'It would be difficult for me to-day to get into the life of Oxford again, although the unchanged friendliness of the older men gave me cause for joy, I mean especially four heads of colleges, Balliol, New College, Wadham[6] and All Souls. On the other hand my contemporaries here have become rather remote from me, and the atmosphere of their thought and activity is no longer pleasing to me.'

The truth was that the very reaction against Germany which Adam had foretold to Diana, the result of the Kristallnacht pogrom, met him in England, though evidently in mild form. He met many of his friends again: the Cripps family, Geoffrey Wilson who was now Sir Stafford Cripps's secretary, Shiela, Goronwy Rees, Diana again with her fiancé David Hopkinson, Professor Tawney, and other old acquaintances of London and Oxford. He went to Kent for a party arranged by Shiela at High Elms, near which she now lived.[7] It was all highly enjoyable, but he was troubled in spirit. 'It was quite harmonious,' he wrote to his mother, 'but I succeed less and less in finding my way into the atmosphere of the carelessly excited and thoroughly disobliging ideas which are current here, and indeed into the atmosphere of this country which at present is dispirited (dieses gegenwärtig aufschwunglosen Landes). All my travels seem to have led to the conclusion that first and foremost I want to live

[6] In 1938 Doctor C. M. Bowra had been elected Warden of Wadham College.
[7] Account to his mother. Letters C.T.

and work in Germany. But England is in the process of a profound re-assessment and one should not be deceived by the confusion on the surface. The country has deep moral reserves, and representatives, who are both courageous and intelligent, of her finest traditions. With such people I should like to remain friends always, although I believe that to-day the conditions for this are quite different from what they were in your time.'

Diana recalls a painful episode. At that time German brutality and the inadequate humanity of British immigration policy resulted in an Anglo-German agreement that 10,000 German and Austrian Jewish children, but not their parents, would be given shelter from persecution in Great Britain. Thereupon some thousands of Jewish men and women, at an emotional cost hard to imagine, sent their children away to refuge in the knowledge that they were unlikely ever to see them again. Diana was working for the committee handling the reception of the children in England. The office was in Bloomsbury and she once asked Adam to meet her there. He said he could not. Since his ultimate purpose was to under-take political work he could not risk such an indiscretion. But also, he said, he could not bear to go to the office because as a German he felt so utterly ashamed that such a reception committee was necessary.[8]

He saw a great deal of David Astor, and during the last part of his visit he stayed with David's family in their house in St James's Square. From the point of view of his new ambition, this was the most important event of his visit. Lady Astor was not a person of great political influence except indirectly, in these immediate pre-war years. She and her husband were close friends with many personalities who were dominant in the luckless British political world of 1939, and, as they were generous hosts, their London home in St James's Square and their magnificent country house, Cliveden, became frequent meeting places of Parliamentarians and jour-nalists devoted to Neville Chamberlain's policy of world-wide appease-ment. The two great houses resembled those luxurious political strong-holds described in Disraeli's novels, and the whispers about a mysterious and all-powerful 'Cliveden set' added a touch of melodrama entirely in Disraeli's taste. It was a decided advantage at that time for a young man with political ambitions to be regarded with favour by Nancy Astor.

She was the most loyal of friends. Once she had fixed her affection

[8]D.H.

she grappled the subject 'with hoops of steel.' Friendship with her was always for life, and Adam was given this remarkable and (as some found) even alarming honour. In frequent talks together she asked him about his adventures since their last meeting, and he told her about them and his present ideas. She found these entirely congenial. Anglo-German accord was of the essence of Neville Chamberlain's policy in which she and her husband so passionately believed. It can be assumed that Adam told Lady Astor about his ingenious, his all too ingenious design for an Anglo-German common policy in the Far East which would lead to a gradual restitution of peaceful Anglo-German relations in Europe. Nancy Astor decided anew that this friend of her son was a person of consequence whom she would help to success.

As before she was concerned about his clothes. It is possible that since his return Adam had had neither the time nor the money (because he had overspent in China) to get himself a suit worthy of his presence. At all events Lady Astor declared that he must go to the best tailor in London and fit himself out at her expense.

Adam returned to Berlin on the 1st or 2nd of March. Less than a fortnight later the German army marched into Prague. On the next day, the 15th of March, Hitler proclaimed from the Hradschin Castle that 'Czechoslovakia has ceased to exist.' A week later, on the 22nd of March, Germany occupied Memel. The Munich Agreement was in ruins, and a new era opened in Europe. Adam recognised these facts, but he never fully appreciated their fell political consequences. He saw the greatly increased need for a German counter-revolution, and if, as seems likely, he knew of the frustrated Halder-Witzleben conspiracy, he found in it additional evidence that such a movement was both possible and ready. For the moment his ideas regarding the foreign policy needed to help the movement forward appear to have been the same as those of the military conspirators: to encourage Britain and France to stand firm. Later, under new influences, Adam's ideas about foreign policy changed, and the reason seems clear, namely that he did not grasp the fact that the events of mid-March had destroyed not only the Munich Agreement, but Neville Chamberlain's policy of appeasement for ever.

The month in Adam's life after his return to Germany in the first week of March was important, but remains obscure in many details. He was occupied with secret activity, such as should leave only meagre evidence behind. His purpose was to search out the opposition.

It seems probable that his experiences in England, the coldness towards him that he had suspected among his Oxford contemporaries, and among Shiela's friends in London, added a new spur to this search. Certain it is that the anti-German feeling which he had detected rankled in his mind. He wrote to Diana more than two months after his return: 'I have a growing suspicion that a number of my friends identify the evils of Europe with Germany as such, and base their continued relationship to me only on the degree to which I happen to fit into your English life. I consider that verdict as profoundly untrue and unjust and I do not wish to compromise with this kind of acceptance which I consider both sterile and irresponsible.'

In Berlin Adam saw much of Albrecht von Kessel at this time, and through him met many persons in the Auswärtige Amt who looked with anger and alarm at the aggressive course which Hitler had taken since the seizure of Austria.[9]

At some time in the spring and summer of 1939, and it may well have been now, Adam met General von Falkenhausen, the withdrawal of whose anomalous mission to Chiang Kai-shek had occurred while Adam was in the Far East. At this time Falkenhausen was living in retirement (very much out of favour following his protest against the suppression of his mission) in Dresden and it was there that Adam met him. It seems from what occurred later that they quickly discovered the anti-Nazi sympathies they had in common and that early on in their acquaintance the General made no secret of his opinions. This and other meetings confirmed Adam in a welcome opinion. It is evident that by April he believed himself to be in the midst of a great, unexpressed and secret opposition, a movement covering all Germany, and of which foreign opinion was unaware.

The evidence for this comes in large part from Geoffrey Wilson. After meeting again in England he and Adam planned to do a journey together travelling to the Black Forest and round Bavaria before returning to Berlin. They met early in April at Imshausen.

[9]Herr von Kessel and Mr and Mrs Bielenberg. Discussions.

Geoffrey Wilson was very impressed by Frau von Trott whom he had not met before. He found her awe-inspiring, not least because of the regality of manner which was natural to her. There were other guests staying in the house, and she liked them to come to her room separately and by appointment. When his turn came, he was warned not to smoke in her presence. He found her sitting very upright in her chair like a queen receiving at an audience. Nevertheless there was nothing of excessive formality in her conversation with him. He found her extraordinarily intelligent and with a wide curiosity about the world outside; he found a person who belonged to a past time but was in no way lacking in sympathy for those who belonged to a new and worse one.

Adam and his friend set out by car, going first to Heidelberg, then south to Baden and the Black Forest, eastwards to Munich and then travelling north through Franconia and Saxony to Berlin where Adam remained, while Geoffrey Wilson returned to England. For him it had been an illuminating experience.

As they travelled round together, Adam told his friend what he and his associates were planning. He was quite certain there would be a war. He was also quite certain that if Britain and France held firm and met further Nazi aggression by military force, then Germany would at last suffer a military reverse, and then Hitler, with his prestige tarnished beyond restoration, could and would be removed from power and a respectable regime, military in character, would be instituted. This plan must not be understood as one aiming at a military débâcle such as had shaken William II from his throne. Such an idea is completely out of character with Adam's continual and sometimes extreme patriotism. The suggestion that he should be party to such a thing would have shocked him to the depths of his being. His hope was for such a military set-back as Germany would probably have suffered if Great Britain and France had acted forcefully in 1936 against the military reoccupation of the Rhineland. It was hoped that a military reverse in 1939, assumed to be inevitable if Great Britain and France showed resolution, would not discredit the army, but rather would allow the service leaders to take over Government from a maniac who liked to play at soldiers. It was necessary, however, that the new Government should enjoy goodwill abroad, especially in England. This last opinion was to remain with him, but his ideas about foreign military opposition to Nazism were to undergo much change.

At many points in the course of the journey Adam met friends by pre-arrangement. They usually met in hotel bedrooms, and their discussions were conducted in low voices with the radio-set turned up loud in case the room had been 'bugged' by the Gestapo. One would greatly like to know who these friends were, but there is no record. 'I can't remember the names,' wrote Geoffrey Wilson in a letter of 1957, 'and anyhow they may not have been the real ones.' Sometimes Adam insisted that the two of them should stay at separate hotels to throw off Gestapo suspicion.

One very dramatic encounter is remembered by Geoffrey Wilson. He and Adam drove up a mountainous hill in the Black Forest, and at the top of it they met his younger brother Heinrich who was with a small hiking party of boys in the neighbourhood. The meeting had been pre-arranged in order to discuss a certain matter. This was to do with plans which Adam had for Heinrich in the event of war. He was to go, following various moves which they discussed, to Switzerland, his task there, so Wilson gathered, being to maintain contact between conspirators within Germany and German and foreign sympathisers without.

The air of intrigue and clandestine assignation continued throughout the journey till their arrival in Berlin where Adam introduced his friend to Wilfrid Israel. At the end of it Geoffrey Wilson was left with an impression that Adam had taken him on this journey for a definite reason: he wanted his friend to see for himself that there was a vigorous and active anti-Nazi movement going forward in Germany, and that foreign powers would be well-advised to take account of it in the making of policy. Such a definite purpose, if it did exist in Adam's mind, would have been perfectly consistent with his slowly-forming plan.[10] As the spring turned to the radiant summer of that fatal year, Adam took his plan a step further.

At the end of April Adam was offered an official post in the Foreign Ministry. On the 29th he wrote to his mother in English: 'The foreign Amt has offered me—conditional to the minister's approval which is highly doubtful for party reasons—the post of a secretary (Legationsse-kretär) which would mean skipping the rank of Attaché and open a prospect for relatively favourable promotion. But I cannot yet say I

[10]This account of Trott's tour with Geoffrey Wilson is taken from two letters from him to Frau Doktor von Trott of 1947 and the discussion previously referred to.

want this type of work and career which will keep me abroad most of my life and tie me to people that have always had a damping effect on me. Yet, there it is—here is probably an earlier chance for useful influence than any other proposition I am likely to find and it really is a choice between relative evils. I wish you would write and tell me soon exactly what you think about this. I think Father would probably have wanted me to go in for it. What do *you* feel?'

He did not obtain an official appointment, but this was probably not due to ministerial disapproval but to his own wish: as a fully accredited member of the German foreign service he would be without the freedom of action which he needed if he was to carry out his design. What he needed was an informal relationship with the Auswärtige Amt, and this he found.

It is here that a strange figure comes into Adam's story, that of Walter Hewel. He was more than ten years older than the other and had had an adventurous life. He had become a friend of Rudolf Hess in the war and through Hess he became a member of the Nazi party in the early days of the movement. He took part in the Hitler-Ludendorff putsch of November 1923. He was arrested, stood his trial, and was among the forty or so Nazis who shared Hitler's mild imprisonment in the fortress of Landsberg.[11] On his release in 1925, although he retained his faith in the Führer, he also believed that he had no future in Germany, and made plans to emigrate. This he did with two companions, Hubertus von Weyrauch and Eduard Bonhoff, both of whom were related to the Solz branch of the Trott family. The three of them sailed to Australia with the intention of making their fortune in lemonade. They acquired a manufacturing plant and a sales agency and looked forward to great and speedy success. However, they made some miscalculation in the manufacture, with the result that one day all the bottles of an enormous consignment exploded at the same moment throughout Australia. Not surprisingly confidence in the lemonade weakened, sales-resistance set in, and the venture was forced into liquidation. Soon after this lemonade fiasco, Weyrauch and Bonhoff returned to Germany, but Hewel found some success in other directions and remained in Australia till after January 1933. He then came back and as an early member of the Nazi party he was given interesting

[11]Ernst von Weizsäcker. Errinerungen. Munich. 1950.

employment in Government service. He had the advantage of being remembered and liked by Hitler who did not blame his years of expatriation.

Through his cousin Adam met Hewel in 1939, probably at the Garde-Kavallerie Club in Berlin, to which Hubertus von Weyrauch had obtained Hewel's election.[12] At this time Hewel was a member of Ribbentrop's personal staff in the Auswärtige Amt with the rank of Geheimer Legationsrat which may be translated as 'Confidential Counsellor, second class.' His duties were those of a senior liaison officer, and he operated in this capacity between the Chancellery and Ribbentrop's personal office, and between the latter and the Auswärtige Amt. It may seem odd that a Minister should require a liaison officer between himself and his own Ministry, but that was the Ribbentrop way. The Minister had not had uniformly happy relations with members of the foreign service, and he suspected that a majority of them looked on him as a mischievously incompetent amateur in the realm of international affairs, and (very painfully) that they mocked his pretensions to high birth and his questionable use of the aristocratic prefix 'von.' (His anxieties were wholly justified.) For these light reasons, and also for a dark one, that he was as extreme and fanatical and murderous in his aims as his master, and so did not want interference from people of sober mind, Ribbentrop surrounded himself with a group of party members, most of them not professional diplomats, and kept all but a chosen few members of the service at a distance. There was also in him a good deal of the aversion to familiarity and the peppery insistence on his position usually found in a man who has risen high and is not used to command.

In practice Hewel's duties consisted largely in attending Hitler's late-night sessions, and listening to those lengthy disquisitions on art, architecture, race, war, and many other vast subjects, in which Hitler expressed views that he believed to be of astounding originality, and which were, in fact, not untypical of the half-educated lower intelligentsia of thirty years before. According to Adam's account of what Hewel told him, the liaison officer's main difficulty in this part of his assignment was to stop himself falling asleep. But though he could not disguise from himself that the man was a colossal bore, Hewel retained the veneration he had felt in

[12]C.T.

his young days, and looked on the Führer as a statesman of genius guided by insight of a superhuman kind. He proved his devotion and was to be among Hitler's last companions in 1945.

Although Hewel's preferences in politics were undesirable, he seems to have been an agreeable person in himself, one of those whose seduction into Nazism was due to simplicity and not vileness of character. In spite of his idolatrous admiration of Hitler he was not without independent judgment, and he found that he shared an important conviction with Adam: that whatever the next move in Nazi policy, an Anglo-German war must be avoided at all costs. What he heard from Ribbentrop and his colleagues in the Minister's entourage disquieted him in this respect, and when they grew to know each other he confided to Adam the anxieties of his mind. This must not, however, allow the reader to forget that as a truly dedicated Nazi Hewel was no oppositionist. If he had for an instant realised that Adam was an anti-Nazi, he would have denounced him on the spot. Of all Adam's closer acquaintances he was the most dangerous.[13]

In his fear Hewel had a sympathiser within the walls of the Foreign Ministry. This was Ernst von Weizsäcker, a somewhat enigmatical figure. At this time Weizsäcker, a man of fifty-seven, was the senior Staatssekretär in the ministry, a post corresponding to the Permanent Under-Secretary in the British Foreign Office. He was one of the regular service members of the ministry whom Ribbentrop was obliged to see quite often, whether he wanted to or not. Weizsäcker was not a Nazi and later claimed to have been an active anti-Nazi. The claim was not accepted, but not absolutely rejected. In 1948 he had to stand trial as a war criminal, was condemned, but later set at liberty on an appeal which concluded a legal process which had lasted nearly two years. There was both justice and the reverse in these proceedings. Weizsäcker was not a hero of the anti-Nazi opposition as he suggested in his memoirs; he was a 'trimmer.' That is no condemnation in itself, and it should be remembered that the first subject of this opprobrious political description turned the tables on his enemies.[14] As a trimmer, Weizsäcker had inevitably changed his

[13]This account of Hewel and his relationship with Trott is drawn from C.T. and a discussion with Mr and Mrs Peter Bielenberg.
[14]George Savile, 1st Marquess of Halifax (1633-1695) 'The Character of a Trimmer.' The interested reader should consult the last pages of this great pamphlet.

tactics, and to some extent his policy, since 1938. In that year he had played boldly, conveying to the British Government, through the intermediary of the brothers Erich and Theodore Kordt, both members of the foreign service, intelligence of the Halder-Witzleben conspiracy. He gave the advice that France and Great Britain should stand firm. The advice was not taken.[15] He was quite certain that there was no prospect of remounting the Halder-Witzleben conspiracy in 1939. The aim, the removal of Adolf Hitler from German affairs, was unaltered, but, the accompanying policy and the method of attainment were changed.

The new policy had to take note of two facts of major importance. The first was the success of Hitler's Czechoslovakia policy; the second was the extraordinary weakening of the French and British position in Europe as a result of Munich. One feature of the tactics remained constant: the sending to London of emissaries who, at risk to themselves and those who sent them, would explain the secret policy of those who opposed Hitler.

Before Munich the policy following a successful putsch would have been simple. Assuming that the persecution of minorities would be abandoned by the succeeding government, the incorporation of Austria into the Reich and the military reoccupation of the Rhineland would be the outstanding matters for negotiation, and neither of them at that date were conceivable causes of war. But after the seizure of Czechoslovakia, and with Germany worked up into a state of national indignation over the ever-popular cause of the Prussian-Polish frontier, then it was going to require the greatest ingenuity and statesmanship to formulate a new exterior policy which, when carried out by a post-Nazi Government, would command popular assent and at the same time soothe the anti-German feeling in Europe which Nazism had aroused.

From Adam's later activities (and it can be assumed that he was briefed by Weizsäcker) it appears that the State Secretary believed that he saw the hope of a solution. As a bright signal in the increasing dark, he saw

[15]Party enemies of Chamberlain and many German apologists ascribe the failure of the plot entirely to Chamberlain's decision to go to Munich, as mentioned before. In the writer's opinion more acceptable and well-researched views are to be found in Wheeler-Bennett, O'Neill, and William L. Shirer. *The Rise and Fall of the Third Reich*. London 1961.

the appeasement policy of Neville Chamberlain still glittering with promise. A continuation of Chamberlainite appeasement would in the end, so it was believed, take away Hitler's political *raison d'être*, and he would be followed by men capable of being appeased, such as the former Chief of Staff, Ludwig Beck, Carl Friederich Goerdeler, or Weizsäcker himself. With such men ruling Germany, the grand object of European pacification would be achieved.

The foregoing seems a reasonable deduction from the evidence. What is certain is that the British guarantee against aggression which Chamberlain extended to Poland on 31st March was deplored by Weizsäcker and his confidants as likely to give Hitler and the Nazis an emotional advantage in stirring up a German war against Poland and her allies. They recognised that time was short and every conceivable effort must now be made to get the British Government back into the giving mood of Munich.[16]

They went further and drew up an ingenious plan within which a new appeasement effort could be undertaken. The plan was that Germany should restore the independence of Czechoslovakia, exclusive of the Sudetenland, and receive compensation for this act of generosity at the expense of Poland, presumably by a readjustment of the Corridor frontier. Some time about the end of May or the very beginning of June the plan was the subject of calculated indiscretions which reached the Polish press: a reference to it appeared in *Polonia*, a newspaper published in Katowice. Reactions to the plan were, according to reliable witnesses, sought secretly in Paris. They were now to be sought in England.[17]

One must again indulge in some guess-work. The new appeasement plan, presumably drawn up by Weizsacker and those around him, is in striking contrast to the ideas Adam confided to Geoffrey Wilson in April. How then was Adam converted to the plan, and where lay its attraction for him? Perhaps in the simple fact that it had one effective advantage over Adam's ideas, namely that unlike them, it contained, however impractically, a shape and a distinct and defined purpose. It certainly appears that once it had been put to him, Adam fell in with it, and for the time being his activity was attuned to it.

---

[16]Wheeler-Bennett p. 449, also Weizsäcker and Kordt memoirs.
[17]Letters of Madame Ripka (9.6.39) and Hubert Ripka (16.6.39) to Shiela Grant-Duff.

The anti-Nazis of 1939, and of the war years, have been much criticised, notably by Sir John Wheeler-Bennett, for wanting to enjoy not only many fruits of Nazi aggression but even additions to the booty.

The argument is forceful, and it certainly represents an almost inevitable reaction abroad to these anti-Nazi pleas for further generous treatment of Germany. But it does overlook the realities which the opposition would have had to face in the wonderful event of their taking power from the Nazis. No German politician could forget the lesson of the Weimar Republic: that it stood not for parliamentary freedom, for effective measures of social progress, for remarkable diplomatic triumphs under Gustav Stresemann, all of which it had to its credit, but for defeat; whereas the Hohenzollern Empire in spite of its criminal folly, in spite even of having lost a world war, stood for memories of triumph. Hag-ridden by the libel that the men of the Republic had stabbed the allegedly victorious paladins of the Kaiser in the back, Weimar lacked for friends, and so for loyalty in hard times, and for that reason above all it fell. What hope had anti-Nazis of being able to form a German Government enjoying massive popular support, if they appeared before the people as men who really had stabbed the truly victorious Führer in the back? Would it not seem that they had deprived Germany of a great leader, and just at the moment when he was about to solve the most pressing of Germany's problems, the Polish Corridor? And if they appeared, moreover, as men pledged to foreign powers to cancel and reverse the incredible and triumphant achievements of Nazi Germany during the last eighteen months of Hitler's rule, would one have to be a bloodthirsty monster of conscienceless chauvinism to look on them as traitors to the Fatherland? But if they could come with gains in their hands, above all with the gain of a rectified Polish frontier, that subject of artificially stimulated but nonetheless burning anxiety,—then surely the leaders of the counter-Revolution had some chance of democratic acclaim. Such was the argument on the other side. It was not a trivial one.

After discussion with Weizsäcker and Hewel, it was decided that Adam should go to England at the beginning of June, and through his Oxford friendships, especially through the Astors, make contact with British men of influence. The evidence leaves no room for doubt that Adam was charged with the task of putting forward the Czech-Polish scheme. It was a most unfortunate decision.

During the same month of June Weizsäcker also sent Erich Kordt, *Chef de Cabinet* in the Auswärtige Amt, to London to give additional authority to the pleadings of his brother Theodore Kordt, Counsellor in the London Embassy. Concurrently two officers, Fabian von Schlabrendorff and Colonel von Schwerin, came to London on secret missions from the opposition group in the High Command. The evidence suggests that the civilian and military oppositions were much less closely co-ordinated in 1939 than they had been in the year of Munich, but the heads of policy were maintained in common. They revolved round two interdependent propositions. An Anglo-German war was to be avoided at all costs; Hitler lived on conflict and thus to deprive him of the occasion of war was to deprive him of the very essence of his rule. In the preceding chapter Adam's tendency towards pacifism has been noted, and it will be seen that it fitted in well with the views of Weizsäcker. It was in some disagreement with the ideas of the military opposition of this time.

Adam received his instructions to go to England, not from Weizsäcker, but from Hewel. This gave him a great advantage as it meant that embarrassing questions were unlikely to be asked in the Ribbentrop entourage. On the 1st of June he set out on the first of the journeys he made to England in the last summer of peace. On arrival he rang up David Astor who immediately arranged for them both to go to Cliveden on the next Saturday, the 3rd, when he would find among his fellow guests the Foreign Secretary Lord Halifax, Lord Lothian, and Sir Thomas Inskip who at that time was Secretary of State for the Dominions, and in 1938 had been Minister for the Co-ordination of Defence.

Adam left a detailed account of his political adventures at Cliveden during that week-end. The record is to be found among the published documents relative to German Foreign Policy.[18] It was written by Adam a week later and intended for the eyes of Hitler himself. For that reason it has to be read with much reserve. Adam seems to have had two purposes, one to acquaint British leaders and later Hitler himself with the Czech-Polish scheme, the other to influence policy by making Hitler aware of the great change in Governmental belief, intention and prepared-

[18]*Documents on German Foreign Policy 1918-1945.* Series D (1937-1945) Volume VI. *The Last Months of Peace March-August 1939.* H.M.S.O. Trott's memorandum is on page 674.

ness which had occurred in England since March 1939. In order to do this he had to present himself not only as a German patriot, which he was, but as a fervent admirer of Hitler and Ribbentrop, which he was not. Knowing the intolerance and obstinacy of the Nazi mentality, he could not have followed any other course if he hoped to achieve anything, and he was intent on achieving an ambitious aim. Study of this curious document leaves a reader (and certainly this reader) with the certainty that the self-portrait that emerges is a grotesque caricature, and indeed there is something absurdly comic about it, for if Adam had really behaved as he said he did, he would have tried the patience of his host Lord Astor, of Lord Halifax, and his friend Lord Lothian so sorely that the meeting must have ended in angry embarrassment, whereas in fact it led on to further successes. By good luck there is an independent eye-witness account of Adam's conduct at Cliveden during this week-end, and it disposes of the official caricature.

But however much Adam falsified the picture of himself, there is no reason to distrust his account of what other people said to him. He may have put in a flattering remark to the Führer here, or softened an expression there; in the case of Lord Lothian he may even have given a fallacious idea of the form taken by their talk together, but it is unlikely that he radically misrepresented him. Indeed to have gone further than this in falsifying the views of the Anglo-German situation which he heard from Astor, Halifax, and Lothian, would have been nothing but ridiculous and self-defeating intrigue. However there is nothing in what he reported that is inconsistent with the known opinions of these three. (He makes no mention of any exchange of views with Sir Thomas Inskip.) It seems reasonable therefore to treat his record of what was said to him with seriousness, and the rest as of light account, except where it suggests interesting speculation.

This was Adam's first visit to Cliveden, and the splendour of the scene must have delighted him: the house, in its 19th century restoration magnificently evoking the original palace of the Duke of Buckingham in Charles II's day, approached on one side by a straight half-mile drive headed by a baroque fountain; on the other side overlooking from a height formal gardens and a distant view of one of the most graceful curves in the whole course of the Thames! A fitting scene for great decisions in world politics.

The dinner party on the Saturday evening was large, in the Cliveden fashion, and it is perhaps possible to take this sentence in Adam's report literally: 'Being the only German among some thirty guests, and supported only by my host, who is still as markedly Germanophil as ever, as well as by his like-minded son, I sensed that the general attitude towards me was one of unusual embarrassment.'

At dinner Lord Halifax sat on Lady Astor's right hand and Lord Lothian on her left. Adam sat next to Lord Lothian. Again we can take Adam's account literally when he says: 'At first Lady Astor with her aggressive and mocking manner made it rather difficult for me to obtain a hearing, but I succeeded at last, and when the rest of the men gathered at our end of the table, after the ladies had left us, I was able, in about three hours, to put the German point of view clearly and unreservedly, and to register the nature of the British reaction to it.'

Three hours is a long time to linger over the port, and Lady Astor would be unlikely to tolerate absolute neglect of the ladies for so long. What in fact happened, as David Astor remembers, was that after half an hour or so the men joined the ladies on the terrace, at one end of which Lord Halifax continued his conversation with Adam.

To go back a little.

Immediately after the departure of the ladies from the dining-room, Adam, according to his account, went 'over to the attack' and asserted that 'bitterness and hostility' prevailed in Germany as a result of the British guarantee to Poland, Greece and Rumania, and as a result of the 're-newed attempt at an Anglo-Franco-Russian combination.' He mentioned encirclement and the readiness of the Germans to fight against this long-feared threat to 'the foundations of their whole existence.'

The report takes on new interest when Adam comes to outline Lord Halifax's answer.

'Lord Halifax, indeed, admitted that among the British people also there prevailed a definite emotional readiness for war but that they would fight only "if forced to do so by Germany." Although they were ready to make the utmost sacrifices and would not shrink from a necessary war, nevertheless they were, even now, prepared to take any really reasonable way out.

'After the Munich Conference, he had seen the way open for a new con-solidation of Powers, in which Germany would have the preponderance in Central and South East Europe, a "not too unfriendly Spain and Italy" would leave unthreatened British positions in the Mediterranean and the Middle East, and with pacification in the Far East also becoming possible. After Munich his confidence in the sincerity of Germany's desire for understanding had lessened, and after the occupation of Prague people in Britain had been asking in consternation "who is going to be attacked next?" It was only in sheer "self-defence that he had then adopted the new policy of guarantees and alliances".'

Adam then represents himself as protesting the views which (as he told in his letter to Shiela) he had heard from Schacht about Britain's rearmament programme. 'This new armament fever,' he reports himself as saying, 'had necessarily led our Führer to the conclusion that he must solve Germany's vital problems without consulting Britain.' As regards Prague, if this had shattered England's confidence, then he could only say that England's 'lack of understanding' and hostile policy had long before that shattered Germany's confidence in Britain. And so on. The debate was then taken up by Adam's host.

'Lord Astor remarked in reply that he and his friends had, even after Munich, advocated concrete concessions to Germany's right to live. He was convinced, and had repeatedly pointed out, that Germany had never, in the past, been accorded the position due to her as a great nation, and that she had no one to thank other than her present leaders for the change in this state of affairs. Hitler's greatness, which must be recognised, lay in the very fact that he had maintained Germany's real vital rights against all opposition from outside, and it would have been possible to uphold this just cause of his even in Britain as long as he had not "destroyed" the vital rights of another independent nation. By the occupation of Prague, Germany had deprived her friends in Britain of the weapon which would have enabled them to support us.

'The British people unfortunately regarded Prague as a first step to further conquests of a similar nature. It was only because they felt that every further German step in this direction increased the threat of a violation of their own national integrity, that the British public began to take an interest, unexpected indeed, but now passionately alive, in the threat hanging over Poland. If he or his friends were still to try to defend German policy publicly in Britain they would be regarded as traitors and hounded down. For by doing so, they would be defending, as they were now reproached for doing, the first steps in a German policy which must inevitably lead to the "destruction" of all Germany's neighbours and ultimately to the annihilation of Britain herself.'

Adam answered this, (so the report asks us to believe), by protesting the inevitability, and thus the innocence of the rape of Czechoslovakia. He compared the German-Czech situation of March 1939 with what would be the Anglo-Welsh situation, if Wales was independent, hostile and strongly armed. We may perhaps give some credence to the self-portrait when he relates that he complained that the Press acted as an anti-German mischief-maker. After summarising a further plea by Adam for 'understanding,' the report then comes to a very interesting passage which does seem to reflect in crude fashion what Adam really said:

'Germany's neighbours had again and again . . . by the whole post-war policy of the Powers, and by the recent attempts of British diplomacy, so restricted Germany's natural development—for which every German had within himself an elemental feeling derived from historical experience —that in the end, the only way left to us was the use of force.'

Adam's words, however he said them, provoked Lord Lothian to take up the argument.

'Lord Lothian, who, it seems to me, has not yet gone over to the anti-German, Anglo-American camp, gave a turn to the conversation of the highest interest to us. The following is roughly the gist of his remarks.

' "He admitted that, within certain limits, the use of force and self-help had represented the only and therefore legitimate means for the Germans. The Western powers had not succeeded in evolving from the post-war state of affairs an order which really conceded to Germany her vital rights. Germany had only been able to assert herself by unilateral actions; that this way out was inevitable for the German leaders could not be denied. In his personal opinion this also held good for the military occupation and disarming of Czechoslovakia as being an unavoidable necessity for Germany in the long run. Thus far he was prepared to follow the German argument.

' "But he regarded the continuance of administrative measures of oppression and the 'destruction' of the Czech nation as the decisive turning point at which he, too, had felt obliged to fall in line unreservedly with the change in British public opinion. Germany, by this policy, was destroying the only basis on which a powerful development of German life would have been reconcilable in the long run with the continued existence of Europe. With this 'liquidation' of an independent nation—going beyond the limits of strategic requirements warranted by her own vital rights—Germany had called forth the passionate opposition of all independent nations of the world, and not least of Great Britain. The use of force against the vital rights of other nations must inevitably turn the tide of national feeling in all countries against Germany. And this was also the real reason why the British people had become so deeply incensed against the Germans—only now had the decidedly anti-German feelings of hatred and violence, formerly confined to small groups, penetrated to the masses. Only now had the 'man in the street' become convinced of the necessity, and possible imminence, of a struggle for the vital rights of independent nations, hitherto preached only by isolated agitators. Although to some this might have appeared a mere pretext, had it not been for Germany's march through Belgium the ordinary man could not have been induced to fight in 1914. 'Prague' had the same meaning for the mass of the British people; this explained the readiness for war and death of the average Briton, who was still to-day passionately peace-loving, a readiness which was perhaps difficult for us to understand". '

In this account of what Lothian said, the report is probably reliable, but his remarks may have been made in agreement with Adam, rather than in any spirit of contradiction. Apart from a conventional remark by him about the great loyalty of the German people to the Führer, the report gives no further information on the conversation after dinner. At this point it may be illuminating to give the independent account of the conversation to which reference has been made. It was written by William Douglas-Home and published in an autobiographical sketch entitled *Half Term Report*.

' . . . I recall an evening, in the summer of 1939, that I spent at Cliveden, staying with Lady Astor, the mother of my friends Michael and Jakie . . . One night, over the port, . . . I heard a discussion about international politics between a British Cabinet Minister and a young German called von Trott. Von Trott, as passionate an anti-Nazi as he was a patriot, spoke with a perfect mastery of English, of the aspirations of the German nation as a whole. While allowing for the mistrust engendered in the British mind by the activities of the Nazi leaders—a mistrust which he fully shared—he seemed to be trying to impress upon the Minister the necessity for an immediate adjustment to the *status quo*. He argued that some gesture of goodwill, not verbal, but actual, should be made towards Germany, not only to satisfy her just desire for a revision of the Versailles Treaty, but also—and this might be decisive—to remove some of the planks from Hitler's political platform and thus pave the way to power for those who had the interests of the world, as well as Germany, at heart. This young man, who a few years later was to die a martyr's death in opposition to the Nazi regime, spoke with a deep sincerity and a sense of urgency. Listening to him, I understood how it was that so many Germans, loathing and despising Hitler as they did, yet felt that in his insistence on the rights of Germany, he was voicing the wishes of his people . . .

'Be that as it may, it was the future, rather than the past, with which von Trott concerned himself that night. He saw the disaster ahead, and he felt that, with mutual co-operation and sacrifice, the danger might yet be averted, and the problem solved by peaceful means. Implicit in this was the essential qualification that the *status quo* should be revised.

'When he had finished speaking, the Minister stubbed out his cigar in an ashtray and said, "Yes, it's a fascinating problem." And it seemed to me, sitting at the other end of the table, that, in the hopelessness of that answer and that gesture, he stubbed out Germany, and Europe, for many years ahead.'

It is to be supposed that Mr Douglas-Home only heard the earlier part of the conversation. His record is very interesting as it so clearly indicates the anti-Nazi element in what Adam said, and which he had to hide so completely in the report. But this account of Halifax is not only at variance with Adam's narrative, but can be shown to be completely erroneous. Mr Douglas-Home's memory may not be at fault however. Halifax was a classic charmer and 'Yes, it's a fascinating problem, isn't it?' is just the sort of vague remark he might have made in a sympathetic and dovelike tone when at a loss for something definite to say, and as Foreign Secretary he had to be careful what he did say. But this apparently aimless rejoinder did not represent what was going on in Halifax's mind. There is no reason to doubt that he also gave Adam the lucid explanation of the British position quoted already, and in fact, so far from stubbing out the future, he took Adam's remarks very seriously indeed, as appears later.

To this independent account one should add another by David Astor. 'During the course of Trott's talk with Lord Halifax,' he wrote in an article printed in *The Observer* in 1956, 'Trott warned him of whispers among officials in Berlin that the Nazis were "up to something with the Russians," but he did not know what. It proved to be the Hitler-Stalin pact.' In this connection it may be remembered that the Russo-German negotiations which culminated in the pact had begun in a chance remark made by the Russian ambassador to Weizsäcker on April 17th.[19]

The most remarkable of Adam's political adventures at Cliveden occurred after the dinner party of Saturday night, probably some time on the Sunday, and concerned the plan which he had been commissioned to try out on English opinion.

He had a conversation with Lord Lothian, and if the report is to be believed at this point Lothian without prompting made a proposition more or less exactly similar to that with which Adam had been entrusted. This is surely a hardly credible coincidence: what seems more likely is that Adam put forward the proposition, and then reported its favourable reception as though the initiative had been Lothian's. It should be remembered that, so far as can be ascertained, neither Hitler nor Ribbentrop knew anything about this plan except possibly from the article in *Polonia*. The report introduces the conversation as follows:

'[Lothian] asked me on no account to mention him as the originator of the idea that he was now about to unfold to me. In view of his mission to the United States[20] and the present atmosphere there L obviously wants to avoid the suspicion that he has not yet been converted from his idea of reconciliation with Germany. This idea was not a proposition which he felt himself entitled to make to Germany, but simply a way out by which, in his opinion, the German Chancellor could triumphantly point out to the world at the present moment the further idea of development. He would be glad to hear the views of a German on this, but again asked me not to mention him publicly in this connection—because he had previously been reproached with intending to secure new victories for Hitler.

'He started from the assumption that at the present moment Hitler was engaged in consolidating his Reich in Europe. He had already pointed

---

[19]Wheeler-Bennett. p. 439.
[20]Lothian had been appointed ambassador to the United States but did not go to Washington till August 1939.

out that, in his own personal opinion, the strategic elimination of Czechia had also been absolutely necessary for this. The Czech nation was to-day surrounded by Germany on nearly all sides; the national political (reichspolitische) need to continue a struggle against the Czechs therefore no longer existed. Any attempt by Western European powers to find military or political bases there against Germany was now finally barred. If, in these circumstances, it was within the bounds of possibility for the Führer to give Bohemia and Moravia their full national independence back again, on condition of an effective limitation of their armaments, and economic co-operation with Germany, such an action would, in his view, have a revolutionary effect on British public opinion, and consequently on the freedom of action of the British Government and on world opinion in general. Hitler would, with one blow, disarm his bitterest enemies abroad, restore confidence in Europe, and thereby lend to the British desire for understanding, which was still honestly felt, a unanimity it had never known before. On this basis he thought that the general elimination of all moral and material differences still existing between Germany and Britain was possible.

'Economically the German living space would naturally have to extend far beyond the present limits. But, if recognition of the national identity of the small Czech people, surrounded by Germany, could actually be made an indisputable and demonstrable reality, it would seemingly guarantee in European politics the possibility of reconciling the expansion of German power with the continued existence of the individuality of other nations. On this assumption he was firmly convinced that nothing would any longer stand in the way of the splendid rise of Germany in the world.

'Danzig and the Polish question would find an obvious solution as soon as the Poles no longer had the slightest justification for asserting that increased economic and geographic dependence on Germany was equivalent to national subjection to her.'

About the proposition itself, A. L. Rowse, whose last meeting with Adam was soon to occur, made a comment of remarkable penetration in his book *All Souls and Appeasement*. It contained, he writes, the best advice that could have been given to Hitler, but, he goes on 'fortunately he was too far gone to take it; evil men are betrayed by immoderation more than anything . . . If Hitler had had the decency to hand back a simulacrum of independence to the Czechs, he would have had the British

Government eating out of his hand; he could have got away with Danzig, without opposition; he would have had Poland at his mercy, and not only Poland, but all Europe.'

To return to the report. Adam's self-caricature reaches heights of incredibility at this point. 'I replied,' it runs, 'that the first feeling that I, as a German, had had when listening to him had been that it was actually up to Britain, being less confined, to restore confidence by a generous gesture.' He then went on to suggest the restitution of the Colonies, to assert that Prague was 'an old German city which could not be given away again,' and to enlarge on the martyrdom of the Sudeten Germans at the hands of the Czechs which made this 'problem' all the more intractable. Then having more or less declared Lothian's recklessly generous proposal to be insufficient, Adam, so he himself related, declared that the proposal was superfluous since national autonomy was in fact the goal of the Führer's policy, as shown by his speeches (though precisely which is not indicated.) This grotesque passage ends as follows: 'In this respect the Führer really had a better claim to be trusted than had world opinion and the British people, in their turn [a claim] to be given tangible demonstrations.'

These alleged expressions of contempt for the scheme can of course be dismissed as fantasies adopted for the purpose of disguise. In a later passage Adam urged acceptance, and the terms he used make painful reading, but only if we forget again that this was written for the eyes of Ribbentrop and Hitler. 'From our point of view,' wrote Adam in this part of the report, 'the step envisaged by [Lothian] would really only complete the humiliation of Britain. For the more demonstratively Germany makes respect for foreign nationalities in Eastern Europe part of her political programme, the more clearly will any claim to protectorship, hitherto assumed by Britain, pass to Germany.'

Lord and Lady Astor were so favourably impressed by Adam on this visit that Lord Astor arranged for him to meet Neville Chamberlain. He was received at No 10 Downing Street on Wednesday the 7th of June. The Prime Minister's Parliamentary Private Secretary, Lord Dunglass,[21]

[21]Later Earl of Home, at present Sir Alec Douglas-Home, M.P.

was also present. 'I emphasised to [Mr Chamberlain]', Adam reported, 'that I was in England in an absolutely private capacity, but that I would be glad to explain to him the feelings of an average German, in which rôle I stood before him.

'To this he said that the average German was not totally unknown to him because of the many letters which he received from them. Immediately after Munich he had received grateful and enthusiastic communications from Germany, but now there arrived nothing except bitter accusations, reproaching him for wishing to encircle Germany.'

Adam then, according to his account, repeated these reproaches and deplored the 'rearmament directed against Germany.' The report would have us believe that he even went so far as to say that the Germans 'could not help feeling that every friendly act by Britain towards us had as its only object the gaining of time, in order to fight us more successfully later.' The report regains credibility in the next paragraph.

'I repeated what I had told Lord Halifax, especially about the "guarantee" of Poland and the bitterness towards Britain which this step had created among the German people.

'He said, and here I quote: "Do you believe that I enter into these obligations gladly? Herr Hitler forces me to it." We had forced Britain on the defensive by the occupation of Czechia, and now the British regarded every concession as a capitulation to an aggressor, caused by weakness.'

Adam, so he said, 'explained to him' that British rearmament could only have an aggressive purpose, in the German view, since German plans for the East could not possibly threaten the United Kingdom. He referred again to the wrath of the German people at the new British policy of encirclement, and this aroused Mr Chamberlain in turn.

'Mr Chamberlain said—he spoke in great excitement at this point—that the British people too were "passionately stirred"[22] and that they would fight if another independent nation were "destroyed." He had tried again and again after Munich to prevent the development of such a crisis. But his efforts had been rejected by Germany.' Chamberlain then repeated the familiar arguments about the inevitable change in British outlook which had been caused by the German seizure of Prague. The report tells of Adam repeating his argument against the iniquity of an

[22]In English in the original.

encirclement policy by which 'German confidence had been shaken.' As regards the policy itself Adam represents himself as informing the Prime Minister, 'This would have to be discontinued.'

At the end of the paragraph which contains the above, the report again for a moment begins to ring true, as Adam artfully introduces the theme of Weizsäcker's proposal. 'If Germany', Adam asked the Prime Minister, 'could furnish proof that she respected other people's national identity (Volkstum) more effectively than her own minorities were being respected, would Britain then in her turn help to remove German distrust by coming to meet us halfway in a generous and practical manner (durch ein grosszügiges und praktisches Entgegenkommen)?

'Mr Chamberlain replied that he personally tended to regard such proof as practically impossible, but that, if furnished, it would have to be taken very seriously in Britain, and would also restore to the British Cabinet a public platform for their policy towards Germany.'

Neville Chamberlain, who was revered by the British electorate as the personification of straight dealing, was fiercely and indiscreetly mean and disloyal in his treatment of those who disagreed with his policy, especially when they were members of his own party. The report is only too easily believed in this passage which is the last to record what the Prime Minister said on this occasion: 'He stated to me that the small group of Conservatives who are rebelling against him—Eden, Churchill, Duff Cooper—could be completely ignored, and that because of his large majority he need not pay any great attention to the Opposition.'

Before leaving, Adam had some words with Lord Dunglass. According to the report Lord Dunglass 'promised to influence Oliver Stanley, the President of the Board of Trade, in the sense of my statements noted above, with the result that, on the day after the speeches by Halifax and Chamberlain, Stanley also spoke in Parliament in favour of a more practically accommodating attitude towards Germany.'

This alleged promise by Lord Dunglass to influence Ministers is of course not to be taken seriously, but the report is not mere invention at this point, and the evidence is that Lord Dunglass told Oliver Stanley the gist of the conversation.

On the day after Adam's interview with Neville Chamberlain, Lord Halifax spoke in the House of Lords, and one passage in his speech does seem to reflect the conversation at Cliveden. 'British policy,' he said, 'seems to ourselves straightforward and plain, but it is perhaps not difficult to imagine how differently it may appear to many thinking people in Germany. There must be many such who are not less shocked than ourselves at the treatment of the Jews . . . But, feeling all this, such people in Germany may . . . feel too that Germany would never, in fact, have secured consideration for [her] claims . . . unless she had been prepared to back them by threat of force. And it is no long step from this for the patriotic German to accept the gospel sedulously preached to him that British policy consists in the blocking of any and all of Germany's legitimate aspirations.'

On the next day, the 9th of June, Oliver Stanley made a long speech in the Supply Committee. It is probable that at the time of writing Adam had only read a brief evening newspaper report of the speech, and this contained Stanley's reference to 'a more practically accommodating attitude towards Germany.' Hansard reports him as speaking as follows with reference to trade in the Balkans: 'Let me make it clear, as I have done before, that there is no desire on our part to exclude the great industrial country of Germany from the natural markets which she enjoys in the Balkans.' This passage may well have been influenced by Lord Dunglass having told him of Adam's comments on German opinion.

But Adam was quite mistaken if he believed the speech to have been friendly to Germany in its general character. Stanley forcefully indicated that trade set-backs in the past six months had been mainly due to recurrent political crises deliberately provoked by the Axis powers.

The results of Adam's meeting with Chamberlain were not such as one might guess from the report. Sir Alec Douglas-Home's memory of the occasion (as he has told the writer) in no way corresponds with this picture. He recalls Adam putting forward his ideas with moderation and winning courtesy. Neville Chamberlain's own reaction to the meeting is believed to have been very favourable to Adam. He is said to have declared that this was the sort of man whose services as a go-between should be much encouraged, because here was someone who could be sure of a sympathetic hearing on both sides.[23]

[23]Sir Isaiah Berlin. He has told the writer that he heard this from a friend of Neville Chamberlain. He is certain of the information but not of the identity of his informant.

Some time during the week which had begun with the party at Cliveden, possibly on the same day as he met Neville Chamberlain, probably earlier, Adam had another and not agreeable encounter in which again he tried for approval of the scheme which had apparently originated with Weizsäcker in agreement with Hewel. It would seem that having received a favourable response from Lord Lothian, and very guarded approval from the Prime Minister as well, he determined in the bold way that was typical of him, and criticised by professional colleagues such as Kessel and later Hans-Bernd von Haeften, to seek the opinion of those most closely concerned, the Czech leaders.

At the house of Shiela's mother in London he met Hubert Ripka by arrangement. Since the German invasion of his country, Ripka and his wife had lived as exiles between London and Paris, and he acted now as Eduard Beneš's principal adviser on foreign affairs. It is fair to add that when in 1936 he and Adam had met in Prague with Shiela, Ripka had conceived a distrust of Shiela's German friend[24] Ripka may have had an exaggerated notion of the other's anti-Czech prejudice, as appears later.

There were present at this meeting in June 1939 only Ripka, and his Alsatian wife, with Mrs Grant-Duff, Shiela and Adam. After conventional remarks had been exchanged Adam took Shiela aside and said that he had something he wished to say privately to Ripka alone. Not without some protest this was agreed, and the protest was the stronger because the three concerned felt that Ripka would hide nothing from them which concerned the cause of Czechoslovakia. The precaution was reasonable nonetheless. Secret proposals are best kept secret. In this case they were not.

When the ladies had withdrawn, Adam put forward his proposal, basically the same as that which he had given to Lothian at Cliveden (as appears) and put to Lothian's exclusive credit in the report. One may legitimately suppose that Adam based his hopes for a favourable response from Ripka to this proposal for a Nazi withdrawal from Bohemia and Moravia at Polish expense on a not unreasonable conviction that Beneš and the Czech leaders must have retained bitter memories of the shortsighted and contemptible behaviour of the Poles in the crisis of 1938. These were wrong calculations, and at the end of the conversation Ripka

[24]Shiela Grant-Duff. Discussion.

told the other that he would have nothing to do with the proposed transaction. After half an hour or so Ripka or Adam went next door to tell
the ladies that they might come back. Adam left soon after.

When he had gone Ripka burst into a passion of indignation and he
told the three of them what had passed. At the end of the next week, on
the 16th of June, Ripka wrote Shiela a letter from Paris which shows that
his angry mood was if anything more violent than before. 'Je déteste
votre Ad,' he began, and went on later in the letter to denounce him both
on personal and political grounds. 'Il me dit ce qu'il veut (sans doute il
en dit plus qu'il ne veut étant très bête), et il n'aurait pas néanmoins de
conscience en se servant de votre amitié pour ses obscurs buts politiques.
Il suit une politique qui peut-être est plus dangereuse pour nous tous qui
aimons la liberté que la politique brutale d'Hitler. Je suis nettement dé-
primé en voyant tant d'allemands qui sont pénétrés jusqu'au fond par le
culte de force et par la mystique du pangermanisme. Je ne vois aucune
autre issue que d'écraser militairement l'Allemagne et de faire voir aux
allemands qu'ils ne peuvent plus conter sur la force. J'avoue, j'ai considéré
Ad plus honnête et plus européen qu'il n'est.'

Though in his indignation Ripka wrote as though he believed that the
plan was Adam's own, he was fully aware, as he told Shiela at the time,
that so far-reaching a proposition must have come from highly placed
German authorities. His own belief was that it had originated with
Göring. It seems most probable that when he referred, as he did during
his talk with Ripka, to influential circles in Germany he meant those
around Weizsäcker.

On the same day as this meeting, or very shortly after, Ripka was
moved to write an account of what he had heard to Winston Churchill.
He was careful to shield Adam, not mentioning him by name, referring
only to 'a very reliable friend', and conveying an impression that this
friend had warned him of a dangerous intrigue, and had not recommended
acceptance of the plan. The latter Ripka outlined as follows: 'Hitler would
evacuate Bohemia and Moravia; in exchange he would be given the
Corridor and Danzig, and eventually Upper Silesia.' He commented on
the dreadful consequences which would follow British agreement. 'In
exchange for this seeming concession,' he wrote, 'Hitler would carry away
glittering success as to the Polish question and Poland would find herself
as enfeebled as Czechoslovakia after Munich.' Churchill did not reply till

the 15th of June. He thanked Ripka for the information, giving his opinion that the proposed plan would come to nothing. The absence of Ripka's manuscript from Churchill's papers suggests that he sent it to the Foreign Office, possibly to Vansittart.[26]

By some means Adam came to know that Ripka had informed Winston Churchill about their secret discussion. A day or two after he met Shiela at a party and said bitterly: 'I hear you betrayed me to your friend Churchill.'[27]

According to Adam's collaborator in the writing of the report, Mr Peter Bielenberg, the intention of the Czech–Polish proposition was not at all as Ripka understood it. The hope of those who originated the plan was that if such a matter came into open discussion, and that if 'a solution of the Danzig and Corridor question was in sight on condition of a restitution of Czechoslovakia,' then Hitler's aggressive and inevitable intransigeance would put him in the same unpopular position as he had occupied when he spoiled for war during the crisis of 1938. This would give a fresh opening to the conspirators in the army.[28] Adam could not mention this hidden design and Ripka took his proposal for Nazi intrigue. Adam made a great mistake in broaching the plan to him at all.

The meeting with Ripka stands out as a striking reverse in a series of encounters which otherwise compose a remarkable story of success. Before he left England Adam had another successful meeting which had positive results. This was with a famous political personality of those days, Doctor Thomas Jones, invariably known as 'T.J.' in the political world. A. L. Rowse describes him as having 'all the tingling liveliness of the Celt,' and of being a 'great busybody and contacts-man.' He had been an indefatigable agent for Baldwin, and though now growing old and losing his influence, he was still a confidant of Ministers and something of a power behind the scenes. He was a close friend of the Astors and was one of the most extreme of the appeasers. He met Adam through David Astor. The introduction was made at the request of Lord Halifax, who

[26]The copy of Ripka's letter in Churchill's papers is undated but refers to Halifax having been told of the plan 'during the last few days' meaning presumably the Cliveden weekend. Trott told Ripka that certain British politicians approved the plan, but he mentioned no names.

[27]Shiela Grant-Duff. Discussion. [28]A letter to the writer from Mr Bielenberg.

let it be understood that he wanted 'T.J.' to question Adam more closely on his ideas, as he intended to incorporate them in a speech on foreign affairs that he was to make at the end of the month.[29]

It would be most interesting to know what occurred at the interview between Adam and Doctor Jones, and in the latter's book, *A Diary with Letters 1931-1950*, a book whose candour is remarkable, there is an entry under the 6th of June 1939 which purports to tell just that. Adam is represented as urging 'the unexpected formation of a Coalition government representative of [British] "War-mongers" and of [the British] Left because this might convince the German Government that [the British] cannot be relied on to remain passive and ineffectual. This he feels might stay their hand.'

The above is in contradiction to everything remembered by his friends of what Adam said at this time. The explanation is simple.[30] The published entry of the 6th June is not in fact a report of Jones's interview with Adam but of his interview with Colonel von Schwerin. There is textual indication of confusion of identity because Jones describes Adam as a 'young officer serving on the German General Staff.' It would seem that neither Adam's nor Schwerin's name was on 'T.J.'s' original note and that when, many years after, he put these papers together for publication, he suffered a very natural slip of memory, as both men had been introduced to him by David Astor. In fact Adam seems to have had no contact in England with Schwerin or Schlabrendorff. So far as can be known, he was in only tenuous relationship with the military conspiracy backed by the former Chief of Staff, Ludwig Beck, the Chief of the Counter-Intelligence Service, Admiral Canaris, and the latter's principal staff officer, Major-General Hans Oster. He was to be associated with them later.

[29]C.T. quoting David Astor.
[30]It is taken from a letter from David Astor to Dr Clarita von Trott and quoted in C.T.

Chapter 11

THE APPROACH OF WAR

Adam flew back to Berlin on the 9th June, and immediately set to work on the report with his Hamburg friend, Peter Bielenberg. They had met as legal colleagues during Adam's brief period of duty in Hamburg, and a close affection had immediately grown up between him, Peter Bielenberg, and Peter's English wife. In 1939, Peter and Christabel Bielenberg had been planning to leave Hamburg in order to emigrate to Ireland, but they were dissuaded by Adam. He was quite convinced, he told them, that the day of liberation was close and that they should not be out of Germany when the Nazi regime fell. He persuaded them to leave Hamburg, not for Ireland but for Berlin and the centre of the approaching counter-revolution. They fell in with his reasoning and, shortly before this time, Peter Bielenberg had thrown up his promising career in his family legal business in Hamburg and, at considerable financial loss to himself, had taken a post in the Ministry of Economic Affairs. Adam at the time was living in the home of an aunt, Frau von Schweinitz, in the Pariserstrasse, situated in the Kurfürstendam area, and the Bielenbergs had moved into a house in the Berlin suburb of Dahlem. A little later, in July, Adam took up quarters with them.

Adam and Peter Bielenberg wasted no time and, not without merriment at the Nazism with which Adam credited himself, the report was ready and typed by the early hours of the 10th.[1]

Adam then wrote to his mother.

'So that you may rejoice with me, and be able to pray for a fruitful continuation of what I am doing, I will tell you briefly that the phase in

[1] Mr and Mrs Bielenberg. Discussions at various times.

Anglo-German relations which is now opening is due directly to my intervention. At Cliveden, a week ago to-day, I had four hours' conversation with Lord Halifax, on Wednesday one of half an hour with Mr Chamberlain. Nor was I idle in the interval. To-day I worked till three o'clock. In a few hours I shall be seeing Herr von Ribbentrop, perhaps Hitler too. I am *very* glad to know that you are well provided for. (In English) Bless you, love.'[2]

Adam did not see Ribbentrop, nor Hitler, nor anyone of importance in the German Government. Though Weizsäcker recommended the report to be seen by the Führer, there is no reason to suppose that it ever reached him. There can be little doubt as to what happened. Ribbentrop wanted no competing claims about understanding of England, and no interference in his English policy. It was his belief that he was a supreme expert on British affairs, and with an intuition second to none (except the Führer's) he had decided that the English would not fight in defence of Poland or anyone or anything else, no matter what English politicians might craftily or hypocritically say to the contrary. He had no intention of allowing smart young aristocrats with Oxford connections to propose different notions to the Führer. He and he alone had the answer to the English riddle. Ribbentrop is something of a riddle himself. The above is not a caricature of his English policy and of how he spoke of himself in that connection, for which reason it remains a matter for puzzlement how a man in whom vanity and stupidity were so pronounced could have brought off so great a diplomatic success as the Russo-German Non-Aggression Pact. He had a remarkable ambassador in Moscow, Count Werner von der Schulenburg, it is true, and it is also true that Ribbentrop did not know what do to with his achievement once he had accomplished it, facts which make the enigma a little easier to unravel.

So far as Adam was concerned, events, or what are perhaps better called non-events, moved quickly over the week-end of the 10th to the 12th of June. His hopes of seeing either Hitler or Ribbentrop seem to have been effectively blasted by the end of the morning of Saturday the 10th, for on the same day he set about making contact with another member of the Nazi hierarchy, Hermann Göring. (This is the only evidence that Göring may have been interested in the Czech-Polish scheme.)

[2]C.T.

He succeeded, and was given an appointment for Sunday the 11th. He was in the act of preparing to set out for Göring's country house early that morning when a message came that the appointment was cancelled. Ribbentrop, it seems, had learned about it and had hastened to remind Göring that foreign affairs were not within his competence, and Göring did not choose to fall out with Ribbentrop over this affair.[3] In such circumstances Adam decided to go back to England. He left either on the 11th or 12th by air.[4]

It is difficult to understand at first sight why Adam made this second visit. His most advantageous course, so it would seem, was to remain in Berlin, for the moment at least, there to pursue an intrigue, acting through Hewel, with the object of circumventing Ribbentrop so as to achieve the object of the report, namely of bringing the Weizsäcker proposition (now disguised as Lothian's) to the notice of men in power, and above all of Hitler. This of course, is assuming that the plan was Weizsäcker's, and to get it across was the main objective. There may have been other factors, now unascertainable, which persuaded Adam to go on a second visit to England. He may have received orders from Hewel. One thing is certain: the return was a mistake.

Obstinately Adam continued to think in terms of an appeasement policy. Obstinately he refused to be influenced by advice. Lord Lothian had accurately informed him when he said at Cliveden that the news of violated Prague had roused British anger against Germany in the same sudden way that the news of violated Belgium had roused it in 1914. As his letters show, Adam's long absence in China had put him out of touch with the changes and directions of mood in British opinion, and indeed in all European opinion. He had the information about this, but emotional appreciation was lacking. This was not altogether surprising as the revolution of British feeling which had occurred was immense, as anyone who lived through those days in England will remember.

Apart from his long absence in China there was a second reason for

---

[3]C.T.

[4]A letter to his mother announces his departure 'in one hour' by air for London. It is dated the 10th. This must be a mistake. There are mistakes as to day of the week and date in Trott's report. Expert advice recommends that in matters reporting very recent events the weekday is the surer guide.

Adam's failure to grasp this fact. It seems that, arising out of his ambivalent feelings about England, he was convinced that the English national vice of hypocrisy was irremediable. The moral fervour of British political determination in 1939 (meaning the general political disposition of the whole people) seemed to him nothing better than disguised anti-German nationalism. In addition there was that other basic reason for the failure of this mission: that he had also misjudged the situation in Germany, again perhaps through long absence and loss of contact, whence his belief in the speedy collapse of the Nazi regime.

On arrival in London, perhaps as early as the evening of Sunday the 11th, he again went to stay with the Astors in their London house. He spent the first part of the week in London, and then, probably on Wednesday the 14th, went to Oxford, staying at All Souls. He spent the week-end with Shiela and her mother at High Elms. Here he was confronted with a singular opportunity.

In her days as a newspaper correspondent in Prague Shiela had met Winston Churchill on a visit to London. He was impressed by her judgment and asked her to see him whenever she was in England, to keep him informed about Czech affairs. This she did. Already she knew the younger Churchill generation and she became a close friend of the family. To this week-end she invited among others Winston Churchill's daughter Diana and her husband Duncan Sandys. Most of the talk consisted of lively political discussion and Duncan and Diana Sandys urged Adam to meet Churchill, but he refused firmly.

On Monday 19th he went to Cliveden. In the same week he returned to Berlin.[5] This visit, unlike the first one, had not been a success. It had, in fact, been a total failure, politically unproductive and personally disastrous.

A day or two after his arrival Adam had written to Diana who was in hospital recovering from an operation, 'Shiela whom I saw for the first time to-day tells me that there is infinite suspicion spreading about me— nice fools!'[6] Suspicion was very typical of the 'period of awakening' in England, which besides being one of lofty idealism was also a period of strenuous gossip. First publicised by Claud Cockburn in *The Week*, the notion of a sinister 'Cliveden Set,' working for the triumph of the

[5]Letters to his mother, and in D.H. and G.D. [6]D.H.

Nazi cause in Europe, was now widely accepted, and Adam's friendship
with the Astors, and his being given access to the Foreign Secretary and
the Prime Minister through them, inevitably gave him a dark reputation.
Shiela had given Adam a timely warning. He did not take it.

In London he met Peter Mayer again, once with Professor Tawney,
and once in Mayer's own flat. Neither meeting was a success, and the
second one was painful. It was Adam's endeavour to persuade him on
both occasions of the imminence of the German counter-revolution, and
he went so far as to assure Mayer that opposition to the regime was to
be found in the ranks of Himmler's SS. On both occasions Mayer assured
him that he was certain from the information reaching him and his friends
that there was not the smallest hope of such a welcome movement until
the Nazi Government had met crushing failure. At their last meeting the
conversation became acrimonious. Adam gave way to his prejudice
against emigrants. 'You do not understand the situation in Germany,' he
said, 'and how can you, since you have been out of the country for three
years?' Peter Mayer replied,'While you have been in China.' They parted
angrily, and Mayer was left with the impression that Adam was giving
way to escapist dreams. Incredible as it may seem, Adam's belief that
opposition circles existed in the SS was founded on fact.[7]

The same disagreement, but without bitterness, was in his meeting with
Fritz Schumacher sometime during this second visit. They met again with
David Astor. Their main topic, on this occasion, was Adam's paper
Ostasiatische Möglichkeiten, which Schumacher had been privileged to
read as a former Rhodes scholar. He thought that it erred on the side of
fantasy, but that even if the extraordinary political manoeuvre which he
proposed in the paper could be put into operation, it would only benefit
Nazism, so long as Adolf Hitler ruled. There then ensued the familiar
argument that Hitler was on the verge of political extinction, a view with
which Schumacher, like Mayer, could not agree.[8]

Strong and even painful as the disagreements were in discussions with
compatriots, they were at least candid. An emigrant from Germany knew
well enough the need for discretion, and was conscientious about this.

[7]Mayer. Discussion. Margaret Boveri. A letter to the writer.
[8]Schumacher. Discussion.

It followed that Adam could speak freely with Mayer and Schumacher as regards his anti-Nazi beliefs and intentions. But with his British friends, some of whom were notable for indiscretion, he met the fatal difficulty of his mission, that he could not take them into his confidence on this vital matter. Had his temperament been less combative—less liable to take up the patriotic point regardless of the ideological one, then he might conceivably have succeeded in his aim of persuading those whom he met that there were alternatives to the fierce war-like enmity towards Nazi Germany of the new mood. But, even so, to achieve real success in this difficult field he needed some experience, and it must never be forgotten that the younger among those on the German side who strove for good, amid so much evil, had no political experience of any practical kind. The opportunity for it had been taken from them by the tyranny under which they lived.

At Oxford Adam stayed at All Souls as the guest of Warden Adams. It was at All Souls, on his visit in 1937, before he went to China, that Adam had met Helmuth von Moltke who was to mean much in his life. They had been introduced to each other by A. L. Rowse. The disturbed friendship with Rowse had never been restored to its early condition of mutual understanding and affection. He and Adam met now on polite and distant terms. 'At a certain point,' A. L. Rowse writes in his book, 'on both public and private grounds, I decided that the relationship should end. Though I am ashamed to say so, I was not sure that he was not reporting back to Berlin what our opinions and attitudes were.'

A dinner in Hall at All Souls is remembered by several of those whom he met during this mistaken visit to Oxford. The talk soon turned towards politics, and Adam contributed the same kind of arguments as he had used at Cliveden for a continuation and intensification of a policy of appeasement, but with the important differences that he did not, as he had done with Lord Halifax, strongly indicate that the purpose of appeasement should be to take away Hitler's political raison d'être. As a result he appeared to be an apologist for the Third Reich; he appeared indeed as being in reality that caricature of himself which he had projected into his report for the benefit of Ribbentrop, and an impression was reluctantly received that Adam, once so exemplary in his hostility to Hitler, had now surrendered to Nazi success. Professor Stuart Hampshire who was present at the dinner, and at the discussion which followed in the

Common Room, has told the writer that the occasion was among the most painful he remembers.[9]

A very similar incident took place in his own college. He dined in Hall at Balliol and again gave the impression of a defender of Nazism, and of putting forward the preposterous suggestion that Hitler, having got into a bad temper on account of English criticism of his criminal action against Czechoslovakia, should be soothed by further concessions in Poland, Danzig and Africa. The impression seems however not to have been so unhappy as at All Souls. Something in the way Adam spoke also allowed his hearers to understand that he was not telling his real mind, and that he was not doing more than acquainting them with the official German argument.

Among those in Hall was a contemporary friend, Christopher Hill who had become a fellow of the College. He and Adam had come up as undergraduates together and a friendship had grown between them. When dinner was over Hill asked Adam to come to his rooms for a chat. He asked no one else, to enable the other to speak freely. He was surprised and hurt when over their whisky Adam repeated the same arguments as he had used in Hall. Greatly against his inclination, Hill found himself forced to the conclusion that Adam was no longer the genuine opponent of Nazism he had once known.

This opinion, formed already in All Souls, was rapidly relayed through Oxford by its almost African celerity in the dissemination of gossip. It is easy to take up a disapproving attitude towards a false judgment based on the vagueness of impressions made in conversation. Two things should be remembered. First that remorse for 1938 appeasement had caused hysteria, so that any appeasement of anyone anywhere was thought wicked. Secondly one must remember the Lugowski case. There were few opponents of Nazism inside or outside Germany who did not, at some time in the thirties, suffer painful disillusionments at the surrender to the victorious Third Reich of people in whom they had formerly reposed absolute trust.

The last point needs to be borne in mind regarding the best known of Adam's encounters in Oxford. This was with Maurice Bowra in Wadham

[9]Professor Hampshire. Discussion.

College. The episode has been described in detail by Sir Maurice in his autobiographical book *Memories*. What Sir Maurice might have stressed more in his account, and of which he was perhaps not conscious, is the extraordinary pathos of the occasion. At an early moment in the recurrent crises of loyalty which afflicted Adam, he had turned, in 1936, to Maurice Bowra from whom he had received a welcome assurance. He had not seen him for a long time when he met him again in February of 1939, and that reunion was evidently agreeable. Adam now sought him out again. 'I was very glad to see him', writes Maurice Bowra in his book, 'since I had always thought that he was firmly against Hitler.'

Adam was more candid with Maurice Bowra than he had been with the fellows of All Souls and Balliol. He told him, what he had apparently not told Halifax or the Prime Minister (though it may be assumed they were apprised of the fact), that he was working for the Auswärtige Amt. He then confided to him, and to him alone at Oxford, that he was also working for the enemies of the regime. He went so far as to say, 'I represent the German opposition!'[10] Maurice Bowra wanted to know the policy which this opposition proposed to follow in the event of achieving power. He was distressed and angered to learn that Hitler's potential successors planned not only to hold on to all the Nazi gains, but to seek readjustments in Germany's favour in the areas that had now been forced into dispute by Hitler. Bowra wanted to know what these people were proposing at the moment. 'My suspicions became worse', writes Sir Maurice, 'when he went on to argue that we should let Hitler keep all his conquests, and so remain at peace with Germany . . . As an Englishman I was strongly opposed to letting Hitler keep his gains, and I did not see why any possible successors to him should enjoy them. I decided that Trott was playing a double game and trying to weaken our resistance just when at last it was beginning to grow stronger.' In anger he requested Adam to leave the house.

In the course of conversation Adam had told Maurice Bowra that he was going to America in the autumn in order to attend a meeting of the Institute for Pacific Relations. Convinced that Adam had come to England with the agreement of the Gestapo, Bowra wrote to influential American

[10]Sir Maurice Bowra. Discussion.

friends warning them against him. One of those to whom he wrote was
Felix Frankfurter.[11]

'Adam seems to have had no satisfactory meeting with anyone in Oxford. Lord David Cecil was disturbed by a conversation he had with him
in Isaiah Berlin's rooms in New College. Cecil had never had political
conversations with him and now he found himself drawn into one, rather
to his puzzlement at first, until he realised with some uneasiness that what
was being said to him was intended for the information of Cecil's brother
Lord Cranborne.[12]

In less dreadful times nothing could be more blameless than Adam's
wish to convey to an important politician, through his non-politician
brother, a clear picture of how average German opinion viewed a
crisis which was oppressing Europe, but in the days of violent British
reaction from appeasement, only a declaration of anti-Nazism was acceptable. It is the tragedy of this part of Adam's life that both he and his
friends in Oxford presumed to excess on the loyalty which Oxford men
give to each other. Adam had to be careful to avoid becoming a proclaimed anti-Nazi, and he thought his Oxford friends must understand
this; they believed that in this matter they were owed the truth and
nothing but the truth.

Isaiah Berlin who had known Adam longer, and with the added insight
which comes after a quarrel which has been healed, shared the distress
of his Oxford friends. But with his closer knowledge of Adam, he could
discern where the root of the misunderstanding lay: not in opportunism,
not in a love of intrigue, not in a blindly patriotic desire to further Nazism
and its persecutions and mad philosophy, merely because these things
happened to be German, but because Adam had come under the influence
of Hegel and could never be quite free of it.

[11]This account of Trott's meeting with Sir Maurice Bowra slightly departs from
that given in *Memories*, and follows an account given in conversation. The account
in his book is evidently not based on any contemporary document as the meeting
is there dated May 1939, and in fact could only have taken place in mid-June.
In one or two details in addition it does not agree with unanimous evidence from
other quarters. This does not in the least apply to the general impression of the
incident so vigorously conveyed in *Memories*, on which this account is chiefly
based. It is to be noted that Sir Maurice makes no mention of a proposed restoration of Czechoslovakia. The plan may have been dropped by this time.
[12]Lord David Cecil. A discussion.

He saw Adam's predicament somewhat as follows: as Hegel had recognised in the French Revolution an immense fact of history, although its influence ran against so much that he believed in, so men living in 1939 must recognise the same claim in the Nazi Revolution, and see it not only as a German but as a European phenomenon. It was, in the earlier period, mere shallow Bourbonist blindness to declare the French Revolution a 'bad thing' which, as a punishment for its sins, must be abolished. In the same way, merely to rush into a war with the object of abolishing the Nazi Revolution, as a punishment for its sins, was merely to rush against the process of history. What was needed was not uncompromising antagonism, but perceptive manipulation of the facts of the case; not bigoted denial of the facts, but constructive response to the challenge which they offered. The constructive response in this case was not rearmament and guarantees, but an imaginative and authentic persistence in a Europeanisation of the entire problem until a genuinely tranquillised Germany would move with her fellow European states to the next historical stage. The programme might be vague, but so was Hegel. Such in outline was the state of mind which Isaiah Berlin thought he detected in Adam.[13]

That this or something very like it really was in Adam's mind is almost proved by a record of a conversation, held some time in London during this visit to England, between Adam and Mrs Bosanquet to whom he was related through his Schieffelin cousins, and whom he had first met in the United States. Barbara Bosanquet's record runs as follows:

'The talk I remember best was . . . in a dark hotel in Bloomsbury . . . Hitler had by then consolidated his power and had committed many crimes. Adam's loyalty to the National Socialist revolution was being questioned—by himself as well as his friends. I remember his saying,"You know, Barbara, the National Socialist revolution is necessary for Europe, and it has come to stay. It means real social justice—a truly classless society. I suppose" (I thought he seemed a trifle rueful here) "it means that our class will have to lose its privileges and most of its property—but I think we are prepared to give them up." I said,"I don't doubt a word you say, Adam, but how is it that a people's movement that has so much good in it can generate crimes such as the Purges and the Jewish persecutions?" He thought a moment, and then, as nearly as I can remember, answered:

[13]Sir Isaiah Berlin. Discussion.

"These things are poisons which seem to rise to the top. They are bad and they must be eliminated." I said,"That means getting rid of Hitler." He was silent a long time and then nodded. "Yes. That means getting rid of Hitler".'[14]

It has been said often enough, and with truth, that Hegel was not the apostle of bloodshed that anti-Nazi propaganda tried to make out later; indeed something of the opposite is true: Hegel had so little sympathy with, and grasp of the passions loosed by war that he made a radical error in his political philosophy by underestimating and even ignoring the suicidal character which large scale conflict was soon to acquire.[15] This opinion may be open to argument, but what seems beyond dispute is that in the fateful crisis of 1939 Hegel was no reliable guide. It has been shown already, in the writer's opinion, that Adam had long fallen out of love with Hegel, but the influence was still with him. In moments of intense and painful moral crisis a man does tend to go back to the thought and belief that first formed his mind. It can be a calamitous move

There was another friend of Oxford days, whom Adam saw at this time, who could instinctively grasp the character of his predicament. This was Richard Crossman, at that time assistant editor of the *New Statesman*. He met Adam in London. Their conversation together had none of the inhibition and embarrassment of Adam's meetings in Oxford. On the contrary Dick Crossman, as always, was quite fiercely outspoken, and he could act thus without endangering their long and tested friendship because they shared an ardent love of Germany.

Crossman had no patience with any Hegelian idea that Nazism was 'necessary to Europe' because it had egalitarian and indeed admirable qualities which, in other circumstances might be welcome to men of the Left. Nazism was evil in itself, he believed, and only contaminated the good with which it might be accidentally associated. He had yet further

[14]*Berichte über Trott*. Original papers and notes on interviews collected by Mrs Bielenberg. Referred to subsequently as *Berichte*.
[15]In paragraph 338 of *Die Rechtsphilosophie* Hegel asserts that the presence of idealism in international conflict makes war innocuous. 'Modern wars', he wrote, 'are therefore humanely waged, and person is not set over person in hatred . . . In the main body of the army, hostility is something vague and gives place to the respect of each side for the duty of the other.' As Bertrand Russell might say, truly a professor's war!

grounds for dispute, more radical even than this. He did not agree with the need for a British policy which would scrupulously avoid a second World War, even in the hope that this might give time for the organisation of an anti-Nazi counterstroke. If the counterstroke came, well and good, but it was only a diminishing hope, and not the concern of British policy. 'You come along,' he said to Adam, 'with all this damned peace of yours, but you don't realise that we don't want peace with the Nazis. We've tried it and it doesn't do. We're out for war. That's our interest. If it can be a bloodless war so much the better, but we don't want to make pacts and alliances and agreements with any more Nazis. We are hostile to the Nazis. We think they're a lot of bastards. We want to defeat them, push them down, smash them.'[16] The disagreement was absolute, but Dick Crossman retained the friendship, and never lost faith in Adam.

One meeting which was kept secret is remembered from the visit. It was with Hans Siebert and was subjected to heavy and grotesque disguise. They arranged (how is not remembered) to meet in the Mummy Room in the Egyptian section of the British Museum, and there, sitting on a bench on a hot afternoon, surrounded by those ghastly figures, Adam and Siebert renewed the long dialogue which had opened in the prison-house of Kassel. Adam stuck to his opinion that Germany's hope lay in the leadership of an enlightened aristocracy, and Siebert to his more conventional and extreme Left-Wing view. Adam still retained faith in the military hierarchy and Siebert his prejudiced distrust. Siebert noticed that though Adam still held the same opinion, he had grown more open-minded than he had been, and was less doctrinaire; he was still influenced by Hegel and Marx in the old way, but was somehow less dependent, more self-confident; he seemed to have become an empiricist. They talked long. They both had newspapers with them in case they were interrupted and needed to adopt the attitudes of two strangers, but except for the slowly patrolling attendant they were left alone. This was the last time Siebert saw Adam, and the last episode of their friendship was in keeping with its whole course: he was left with a memory of intense disagreement and intense affection. [17]

This visit marked the last time that Adam saw most of his English friends. He had only met Diana once; she was still recovering in hospital

[16]Mr R. H. Crossman. Discussion.   [17]Siebert. Discussion.

during all this time.[18] He never saw Shiela again nor any of those he had met at Oxford.

If Adam's enterprise could be said to have had any effect commensurate with the bold ambitions with which he had set out, this appeared a week or so after his return to Berlin, on the 29th of June. On the evening of that day Lord Halifax made an after-dinner speech at Chatham House, broadcast by the B.B.C. on its national and overseas networks.

Since 'T.J.'s' account can be dismissed as a confusion of personalities, and Adam misrepresented himself in his official report, it is impossible to know for certain what he contributed, but it is easy to guess, especially in a passage where Halifax referred to the Anglo-German colonial dispute. 'Whatever may be the difficulties of the Colonial problem, or of any other, I would not despair of finding ways of settlement, once everybody has got the will to settle. But unless all countries do in fact desire a settlement, discussion will do more harm than good. It is impossible to negotiate with a country the leaders of which brand a friendly country as thieves and blackmailers and indulge in daily and monstrous slanders of British policy in all parts of the world. But if this spirit gave way to something different, His Majesty's Government would be ready to pool their best thought with others in order to end the present state of political and economic insecurity, and if we could get so far what an immense stride in the world we would have made!'[19]

Adam, for some reason, was not able to hear the broadcast. The speech was not published in the morning press in Berlin, probably because Dr Goebbels's Ministry had not yet had time to decide what to do with it, but it was reported in the midday and evening papers. Another Hamburg friend, Fräulein Clarita Tiefenbacher, was with Adam when he at last got the news. 'I have a very vivid memory,' she recorded later, 'of Peter Bielenberg and Adam standing on the Wittenberg Platz and reading the latest newspaper report of Halifax's speech, delighted at finding in it the arguments which Adam had put forward to him.'[20]

A day or two later Adam received the full text from his cousin-in-law

[18]D.H.   [19]Royal Institute for International Affairs. Reports 1939-1945.
[20]C.T.

Charles Bosanquet. Adam had seen him on his two summer visits, and on both occasions Bosanquet had been at pains to impress on him that in British opinion the behaviour of the German Government was bound to lead to war in which British people would gladly join rather than persist in the shameful and miserable course of material and moral defeat that they had known in the last years.[21] In sending the Chatham House text he sent a covering note to make sure, one may suppose, that at least one man in Berlin knew how dangerous the political situation between England and Germany had grown.

'You may be interested to have the text of Halifax's speech last night. Both Alexander and Layton[22] who followed declared that their people (Labour in one case, Liberal in the other) stood squarely behind Halifax on his two main points:

'1. England fights with Poland if Danzig is forcibly annexed.

'2. England will share colonies with Germany when the latter decides to co-operate in the way that civilised people have co-operated for a hundred years.

'You must know that opinion in England has hardened still more since you were here last. The speeches made by your leaders and the tone of your press has convinced most people that Germany wants war and won't listen to any idea of negotiation.

'The general attitude may be summed up in the words "We're fed up with Germany" and the general impression is that Hitler will force a war this summer. This idea is becoming familiar; indeed people now look forward almost with relief to getting it over. "It's got to come so let's get it over . . ."

'It is essential that responsible people in Berlin should know that England will fight over Danzig in order to stop this gangster era in international relations.'

This was a vigorous assertion of anti-Appeasement policy, and one might expect Adam to have found it unwelcome. On the contrary, he

---

[21]A letter from Mr Bosanquet to Trott of 7.6.39.
[22]A. V. Alexander (later Viscount Alexander), Labour politician and First Lord of the Admiralty in the first Churchill Administration, and Walter Layton (later Lord Layton), Liberal politician and chairman of the principal Liberal newspaper *The News Chronicle*.

was delighted to receive such evidence of British determination, and the Bielenbergs remember him brandishing the letter and the press-cutting and crying: 'Charles has done the best thing he could! Now I've got it on paper—now I've got something to show them!' He had copies made and distributed. He was never an easy man to predict, especially if, amid his complications and wildest inconsistencies, one lost sight of his integrity.

One very strange episode of the summer of 1939 should be remembered. In the first days of July Adam asked David Astor to visit him in Berlin, his object being to introduce his English friend as 'an important British political contact.' For some reason Adam especially needed at that moment to impress Hewel. In vain David protested that his only official position in Great Britain at the time was that of the manager of a concert party, with headquarters at Whitby, which was then planning a pantomime for the coming winter. Adam would take no refusal and insisted on him appearing as the guest of honour at a political cocktail party arranged for the purpose. David went to Berlin in spite of the protests of his father Lord Astor, in whom Adam had confided his oppositional work, and who feared for his son's safety. 'With feelings of acute embarrassment,' David Astor has related, 'I went through this performance, hoping it would help.'

During this visit, Adam arranged another meeting for his friend, this time involving no deception. It was with Professor Johannes Winckelmann, from whom Adam wished David to hear 'the German plans for the avoidance of war.' The plan which Winckelmann unfolded to the young Englishman was, judging by Winckelmann's own account,[23] (written twenty-four years later admittedly) far more unreal and fantastic than anything which Adam had put forward at any time. 'Germany,' the Professor told David Astor, 'should obtain a definite rectification of her Eastern frontier, and for this there should be established in exchange an English supervision and control of the Hitler administration (dafür sollte eine englische Aufsicht und Kontrolle der Hitler-Regierung eingetauscht werden).' It is to be presumed that by 'Hitler-Regierung' he meant some German condominium in border areas.

David Astor replied that if such was the only plan on which any hope of peace reposed, then there was nothing more to be done. 'That means

[23]Berichte.

war,' he said. He added that the premiss on which the argument depended was itself impractical, as England was not prepared to withdraw from the guarantee to Poland. The argument seems to have grown somewhat heated, and, according to Professor Winckelmann, Adam was moved to make a threatening remark: 'The British Commonwealth is no more than an Alliance on its last legs, [24] and Germany has contributed strongly to its breaking up.' Professor Winckelmann does not relate how it was proposed that this unstable British position, threatened moreover by Germany, was to be reconciled with the unprecedented responsibilities which he hoped to see Great Britain undertake in German external affairs. His report gives the impression that the conversation turned back, perhaps on his initiative, to the immediate subject. 'We would try in the meantime,' he reported, indicating presumably what was said next, 'to maintain peace at any price, even if we knew that, with the help of the Army, it would be easier to overturn the regime in time of war.' It was a crazy time and it would seem that this conversation was appropriately crazy.

On the last day of the visit Adam drove David out of Berlin to a concentration camp. They stayed watching from the road until an official began to show some interest in them. Adam wanted to remind his friend what he was fighting against. David Astor was back in London by the 9th of July when he wrote a memorandum of his conversations with Adam and his friends in Berlin, and sent it to Lord Halifax. In the covering note he said: 'I found the minds of ordinary members of the German public still dominated by the same two main ideas, one positive and one negative—that Germany must some day have easier access to raw materials, like every other industrial country; that nobody can tell what the Führer will say or do.' [25]

Adam paid another visit to England, his last, a day or two after this. He spent the night of the 18th of July at Cliveden. This was the last time

[24] The original German is 'eine Gemeinschaft auf Abruf', which is not open to literal translation. 'Auf Abruf' is a near-slang expression most commonly used of an employee who is 'under notice'. A literal equivalent in English 'on call' unfortunately has the opposite meaning to the German expression, but is sometimes found in English-German dictionaries.

[25] A.P. The memorandum itself has been lost.

he saw David Astor. During one of their talks together, and it may have been on this July night, Adam asserted more fully than he had done before, the pacifist trend of his ideas in these days. Whatever happened peace must be preserved. Even if it meant taking wild and even seemingly foolish political risks, nevertheless peace must not be sacrificed. 'Why don't you like Hitler?' he suddenly asked, and before the other could answer he said, 'For the same reason as me; because he is a fanatic nationalist, because he's cruel and is guilty of the murder of his fellow men, because he is blind with hate. I agree with you in all that—but can't you see that if we have war, then everyone will become a nationalist fanatic, everyone will become cruel, and you and I will kill our fellow men and perhaps each other. We will do all the things we condemn in the Nazis, and the Nazi outlook will not be suppressed but will spread. Is that really the solution?'[26]

Judging by the dating of a letter Adam was back again in Berlin on the 13th. He was moved to write to David Astor on the next day, and the occasion was an odd one.

It will be remembered that in the late 'thirties Commander Stephen King-Hall edited a weekly 'newsletter,' similar in some ways to Claud Cockburn's *The Week* of which it might be described as a Right-Wing version. Like *The Week* its main purpose was to rouse British opinion to the dangers of Nazism and the approaching war, but unlike the rival paper it insisted on the need for intense and rapid rearmament. The Nazis never believed that the British press was free of Government control, and it seemed impossible to suppose that a paper, run by a retired officer of the Royal Navy and a candidate for parliamentary election, was an entirely free venture, as was the case. The newsletter prompted many protests from the German Embassy. Then in those dreadful summer days of 1939, Commander King-Hall decided to use his weekly newspaper as a means of telling the German public about British opinion on the latest Nazi-organised crisis, and on the Nazi regime in general. A German edition was published early in July and sent by post to German citizens, mostly professional men and other *prominenten* in the main towns, their names and addresses being taken from German telephone directories.[27]

---

[26]David Astor. Discussion.
[27]Mr Harold Kurtz. He took part in the operation.

What was the effect on the majority of King-Hall's readers is not possible to know. He received, of course, many gratifying letters, as he told in the course of a news reel interview, and probably many angry ones too. The effect on Doctor Goebbels was to throw that unpleasant man into a violent temper, and he devoted much space in *Der Völkischer Beobachter* of the 14th of July to a lengthy refutation admixed with much personal abuse and anti-Semitism in the approved style of his Ministry.

Adam did not read the newsletter but he read the article in *Der Völkischer Beobachter*, and—most unexpectedly—was moved to write indignantly to David Astor. For the moment suspicion and anger blinded him. He only saw the danger to Germany, right or wrong. But there is something else in the letter which makes it poignant reading to-day: it shows how a strong emotion could throw him back on the hope of appeasement. It must never be forgotten, whatever its party opponents may say, and for all its political blundering, that the policy of appeasement had a noble aim.

'Every German, it is my impression at the moment,' he wrote, 'feels rather pained by this sea captain's letter affair and its aftermath. It came most untimely and just when all should be done to prevent further mutual irritation. And it serves, I am afraid on balance, only to solidify bitterness in this country and a feeling that a similar attempt as in 1917 is being made to disintegrate Germany's fighting spirit in potential battles. Nobody here doubts that should another war break on Europe we are faced with a world-wide hatred certainly no more lenient than in the last war.[28] Reaction to methods of this kind is instinctive distrust and self-defence. This is perhaps the deepest motive in the reaction over here, but there are further ones. There is an equally widespread conviction that Britain has no right to imply in her address to us that we are her moral inferiors or that she is in a position to assume the function of a judge in international morality. You have no idea how deeply the average German citizen, strong-headed, industrious, and law-abiding as we are on the whole, resents the easy moralising tone which treats his decent and

[28]This probably refers to a not tactful or defensible passage in the newsletter quoted in the *V.B.*, 'After such a war a peace treaty will be concluded compared with which the Treaty of Versailles was child's play.'

hard effort to earn a living as an unenlightened and slightly immoral affair.'[29]

And so it goes on. It is absurd to deny that Adam was both a patriot and a nationalist; as absurd as to deny that he was capable of seeing through patriotism and nationalism, as absurd as to deny that his love of his country made his opposition to Nazism all the more admirable.

Adam often perplexed his friends by his changes of mood, and these were sometimes so extreme and swift that they could give the impression of total changes of idea and conviction. His friend Herr von Kessel compared his character to that of Shelley, saying to the writer: 'If you had to describe Shelley and there was no poetry to help you, how would you do it?'

Albrecht von Kessel enters the story again at this point. In July, probably within a few days of having written his letter about Commander King-Hall to David Astor, Adam asked Kessel to come with him to Dresden so that he might introduce him to General von Falkenhausen. Kessel was at this time private secretary to Weizsäcker. He asked his chief for a day's leave as he wished to make a visit outside Berlin. 'Where?' asked Weizsäcker. 'Dresden', replied the other. Herr von Kessel records that, hearing the word Dresden, Weizsäcker smiled sympathetically. He knew what was meant.

He knew, that is to say, that the two of them were up to opposition work, but not of its particular and dangerous character. At this time Falkenhausen had been given employment again and commanded the Dresden military area, and Adam and his friend saw in this an opening for drastic action. They agreed that on arrival Kessel, as the holder of an official position, should act as the spokesman. The meeting was brief and to the point. In the course of preliminary talk, the three of them agreed that the outbreak of war must be prevented. Kessel then put forward the specific proposal: Falkenhausen should invite Hitler to inspect an air-raid shelter, and then in the course of the visit assassinate him. The two men

[29]This refers to a passage in the newsletter quoted in the *V.B.* in which King-Hall compares the better labour conditions in Great Britain with those in Germany, referring to the prevalence of the 5-day week in the former.

had put their lives into Falkenhausen's hands. There was a pause. When the General answered he addressed Adam with a smile: 'And this is the sort of thing,' he said, 'that I get from the Foreign Ministry—Und so etwas kommt aus dem Auswärtigen Amt.' The whole conversation did not last for more than half an hour.[30]

Soon after this dangerous attempt to arrest the course of events by violence, Adam wrote again to Charles Bosanquet, and once more, it would seem from the answer which has survived, he wrote in the appeasement vein and in a spirit remote from the frightful events then developing. The generous character of the letter moved the other to reply as follows:
'Dear Adam,
        Thank you for a magnificent letter . . . I want you to know first of all that I entirely agree that the way out of our difficulties is to bind our people together in joint adventures against famine, disease, unemployment, ignorance, and boredom! There are plenty of enemies left, Lord knows, for us to crusade against, and I agree that we in Britain should start the ball rolling.
But not until the nightmare is ended.
        'Preparations, press agitation and mere vulgar spying have provided sufficient evidence to convince men in authority in London that your Government has made up its mind to include Danzig in the Reich and to make Poland, Hungary and Rumania into protectorates. The move is expected within the next eight weeks. Now if this move is made it means a World War because Chamberlain is not going to Munich in 1939. The British people has willed that there shall be no more unilateral changing of maps, to speak in the current jargon.
        'In this situation, a ludicrous one when so many people in both countries would agree with your letter, it is politically impossible to launch the great design . . .'

During the first part of the tortured summer preceding the war Adam had seen much of his friend Wilfrid Israel in Berlin. Protected by his

[30]Berichte. Also discussion with Herr von Kessel.

British passport Israel continued his patient and sometimes successful efforts to facilitate the emigration of Jews from Germany, his purpose, as a
Zionist, always being to enable them to reach Palestine in the end. It
seems that, like so many people at that time, he could not bring himself
to believe that a second World War really would break out, and for long
he delayed making arrangements for his own safety. In May however he
disposed of his business and came to London, taking to safety his private
secretary, a great friend of Adam, Fräulein Rita Lüdecke, who was half-
Jewish. Adam rallied his English friends to good effect on her behalf and,
much later, in August, he wrote to Shiela who appears to have asked him
who Fräulein Lüdecke was. Adam replied with elaborate circumlocutions
so as to avoid trouble with the censor, using the word 'gypsy' for 'Jewish',
and, as in the old days when Shiela was in Prague, he could not resist
the opportunity for some complicated private joking. For the last time
in their correspondence, and like a gleam of light in gathering darkness,
one hears his laughter.

'Rita is very high-born indeed,' he wrote; 'she comes from a high-up
gypsy family and I think her father was a Count or even a King in their
community. The family got involved into the wars and revolutions of
the last and this century, and Wilfrid finally rescued her when she was
living in a castle of waggons, taming lions on the outskirts of Berlin.'

If the letter was examined by the censor, this nonsense duly fuddled
him, and it reached its destination. When Fräulein Lüdecke left for England Adam had said to her: 'Remember this, that no matter what happens,
no matter what crimes are committed or what horrors are in store, no
matter what people say, even if what they say is true, never lose faith in
our country.'[31]

Wilfrid Israel did not finally leave Berlin till July.

During the war he made a remark which should be remembered. It
was at the time when the earlier mood on the western side was passing,
when it was no longer thought admissible to say that the struggle was
being waged against Nazism and not against Germany in her essential
character. It was the time when Sir Robert Vansittart lent his considerable
gifts to grotesque outbursts of hatred unworthy of his name, or of any
name except that of a racialist fanatic. It was also a time, it should be

[31]Mrs Rita Hodge. A discussion.

added, when the atrocities committed by Germans under Nazi leadership, especially against Poles and Jews, gave more than ordinary excuse for such uncontrolled hysteria. Wilfrid Israel said something of this kind one day: 'As a Jew I am sometimes tempted to hate Germany and Germans, but then I remember Adam von Trott and that stops me.'[32]

This is to go beyond the date of Adam's last moves in his efforts to do something to prevent the outbreak of war. The story must return to the middle of August. Though Adam seems still to have underestimated the sincerity and passion of the British mood, he was aware that correct information about British opinion and policy was not reaching Hitler, and an incident which occurred on the 14th of the month may have intensified his alarm in this respect. General Georg Thomas, the head of the Armed Forces Economics Department, and a courageous opponent of the regime, drew up a memorandum pointing out that aggression on Poland could only result in a long world war, and that Germany was not in a strong enough economic position to endure such an ordeal. He presented the memorandum personally to General Wilhelm Keitel and read it to him aloud, or rather he attempted to do so, but was cut short by Keitel who snapped at him that the contents of his paper were merely 'academic' as the danger of a world war did not exist. France and Britain were too decadent to fight, he said, and the United States would never go further than disapproval of Germany's action. Keitel had no voice of his own and faithfully echoed Hitler. This was undoubtedly how the Führer was thinking.[33]

The interesting point about this incident, so far as Adam's story is concerned, is that Thomas had drawn up his memorandum in consultation with Goerdeler, Beck and Schacht. With the latter Adam continued on a friendly footing, and it seems likely that through Schacht he heard of Thomas's attempted intervention. This would account for his being suddenly overtaken at this time by fresh anxiety that Hitler was being kept in ignorance about Britain. It also seems likely, and perhaps certain, that Adam then consulted with Weizsäcker.

A certain air of mystery surrounds what followed, and it is not possible to know now precisely who prompted whom, or if events were the result of coincidence.

[32]David Astor told this to the writer. [33]Wheeler-Bennett and O'Neill.

The evidence of his memoirs shows that Weizsäcker shared the same anxieties as those of Thomas and his friends. The account of Mr Ian Colvin[34] shows further that for some time he had ideas as to how it was possible to deal with the problem of informing Hitler about Great Britain, namely by the use of the right kind of intermediary. Mr Colvin has this to say in his book on Vansittart: 'Those who knew Hitler well, such as Weizsäcker, were in favour of imposing envoys. The Baron[35] once advised that "some general with a riding crop" should be sent. To hand Mr Chamberlain [in 1938] had Sir Robert Vansittart, a broad six foot one inches and with perfect German. He chose Sir Horace Wilson, a slim five foot nine and no German at all.'

This belief in the value of prominent intermediaries, speaking fluent German, was not only held by anti-Nazis. Among the documents of the time published by the Foreign Office there is a curious telegram sent by Sir George Ogilvie-Forbes (then Chargé d'Affaires in Berlin) to Lord Halifax on the 23rd of April 1939.[36] On the evening before, Walter Hewel had dined privately with Sir George and had told him (presumably on official instructions) Hitler's ideas on Danzig, the Polish situation, President Roosevelt, and Anglo-German relations. The last paragraph of the telegram reads as follows: 'Herr Hitler has not yet given up hope of permanent good relations with Great Britain, one of his oldest and dearest ambitions. He has expressed a desire that some really prominent personage with a fluent knowledge of German should come and have a man-to-man talk without the intermediary of an interpreter as has hitherto been the case.'

There seems no reason to doubt that Hewel reported Hitler's wishes accurately. It would appear certain that Weizsäcker shared Hewel's knowledge, and it is probable that Adam did too. Nothing came of Ogilvie-Forbes's telegram at the time, but the evidence is that a memory of the proposition remained, to be acted on four months later.

According to his own account Weizsäcker, in the summer of 1939,

[34]Ian Colvin. Vansittart in Office. London 1965.
[35]In German usage a Freiherr is often referred to by the more familiar title of Baron.
[36]Documents on British Foreign Policy 1919-1939 Third Series. Volume V. No. 268.

suggested to the British Ambassador. Sir Nevile Henderson, the idea of
'bringing in an Englishman, preferably a general, who would be able
to talk to Hitler, man-to-man, as privately as possible,' and this appears
to have happened on the 18th of August. On that day Henderson wrote
to Lord Halifax telling him that he considered it essential that a letter in
English and German should be sent by Chamberlain to Hitler to make
British intentions absolutely clear. Then, on the same day, and very shortly
after writing his despatch, he sent a telegram to Halifax reporting Berlin
rumours of France and Britain abandoning Poland at the last moment.
The telegram contained the gist of his despatch, including his recommendation of a dual-text letter, but adding (though not mentioning his name)
Weizsäcker's proposal. 'I have reason to believe,' Henderson said, 'that it
would be far more effective if this letter were taken direct to Hitler by
someone such as General Ironside who could explain verbally where
we stand and where Germany stands.'[37]

To return to Adam. The reason that it seems virtually certain that Adam
consulted with Weizsäcker is that, at exactly the same time as Henderson
began to act thus, Adam began to act in much the same way. But it is
clear from what followed that Adam had no notion that he and his friend
Peter Bielenberg were acting in concert with Sir Nevile Henderson.

Adam devised a refinement on the Weizsäcker scheme, very much in
keeping with his romantic streak, namely that the emissary should not
be an envoy from the British Government but a personal representative
of the King, and thus fully entitled to access to the Head of the German
State. For this purpose, and to make absolutely certain that the information
should reach Hitler himself and not be burked by Ribbentrop, he
believed that the British envoy should be a member of the royal
family.[38]

His four visits to England had drawn some unwelcome attention on to
Adam, and he had his visit to the United States for the meeting of the
I.P.R. in view. In these circumstances the mission to England in search

[37]The whole episode of Chamberlain's letter and Henderson's proposal regarding
General Sir Edmund Ironside can be found in Documents on British Foreign
Policy 1919-1939 Third Series Volume VII Nos. 56,58, 68, 69, 73, 78, 83, 84, 93,
101, 118, 142.
[38]C.T.

of a suitable envoy was entrusted to Peter Bielenberg. There were plentiful risks for him too, as he was a reservist with the rank of Lance Corporal and as such not allowed to leave the country without permission.

Taking a chance (a very narrow one as it turned out) that at most one more week-end would pass without further mobilisation in Germany, Peter Bielenberg flew to England arriving in London on the morning of Saturday the 19th of August. He went to David Astor's house where he stayed, and his host immediately wrote a personal letter to Lord Halifax. In this he explained that Adam was prevented from coming himself to England, but that 'he feels that it is so urgent that some message should be conveyed of the tendencies he sees in Berlin that he has sent over his closest friend Peter Bielenberg who is at present in my house.' He went on to say that Adam's 'message is, briefly, that doubts as to England's intentions are again growing in Germany. From this he foresees in the very near future grave dangers.' He told Lord Halifax that Peter Bielenberg was available for interview throughout the Saturday and until Sunday evening when he had to return to Berlin. If Lord Halifax had no time for an interview, he and Peter would write a memorandum embodying Adam's message.

The letter was delivered by hand to the Foreign Office, and the two young men then waited for the telephone call which never came. David made discreet enquiries and it appeared that Lord Halifax was away for the week-end. At intervals Peter rang up his wife in Berlin to enquire in the guarded language of a prearranged code whether his calling-up papers had been delivered to his house. Here at least his luck held out. As Sunday evening approached, the two friends composed a memorandum to Lord Halifax to be delivered to him on the Monday.

Peter Bielenberg's ideas were at some variance from Adam's. He was in full agreement with Adam's main proposition but he had more prosaic views, identical with Weizsäcker's, as to the right kind of emissary. He thought that what was needed was a military figure of fine presence, a member of the House of Lords if possible, and with a somewhat spectacular record, rather than a royal duke whose oppressively aristocratic character might only call forth the screaming envy of the former scruffy Bummler of the Vienna doss-houses. After discussion the two friends decided to put forward the name of Lord Gort as their recommendation. They finished their memorandum, and groaned at the English addiction

to the week-end which seemed to hold the Foreign Secretary in thrall
even at this fateful moment.

In fact Lord Halifax had not been away and, as one might expect, was
in the Foreign Office the whole of that week-end. Much of his time there
had been spent in dealing with this very question of a message to be sent
to the Führer by an 'imposing envoy.' Sir Nevile Henderson pressed
the idea as strongly as he could, and between the 18th and Monday the
21st he urged it four times on his Minister, three times by telegram and
once by letter. Halifax was consistently and strongly opposed to the plan:
he argued to Henderson that the purpose of sending a special envoy was
to convey the severest possible warning in strict privacy, so that a withdrawal by Hitler would not involve him in humiliation, and that the
mission of such a person as Sir Edmund Ironside could not possibly be
kept secret, and the whole purpose of sending a letter rather than making
a public pronouncement (which Henderson deprecated) would be frustrated. He put the matter before the Prime Minister who agreed with
him. Inevitably his views prevailed, in spite of strenuous support of Henderson by the British ambassador in Rome, Sir Percy Loraine, who suggested that while General Sir Edmund Ironside was sent to Germany for
a straight talk with Hitler, Field-Marshal Lord Cavan should be sent to
Italy for a straight talk with Mussolini. This element of competition is
one of the oddest details of the story, especially as both ambassadors
were asking for their normal functions to be taken over!

On Monday the 21st Lord Halifax formally instructed Henderson to
draft a dual-text letter from the Prime Minister to the Führer, and on the
next day, the 22nd, he further instructed Henderson to take the signed
document personally to Hitler.

Peter had returned to Berlin on the evening of the 20th, and he and
Adam fade out of this episode.[39] Lord Halifax's apparent callousness to
him and David can be explained in several ways. The fact that Adam's
and Peter's mission was concerned with 'doubts as to England's intentions'
made it otiose, since this was also the theme of Sir Nevile Henderson's
representations. Since he was unlikely to learn more from Peter than he
was being told already, Lord Halifax may also have been moved by a

[39]This account of Peter Bielenberg's mission is based on discussions with him and
on David Astor's letter to Lord Halifax which enables the incident to be dated.

wish not to get the young man into trouble, for a visit to the Foreign Office might well be noted and reported by a Nazi spy. Had he received Peter, he was unlikely to have been in favour of his plan, for Peter wanted to suggest that the emissary should arrive in a blaze of publicity so that the German people should be able to see who was intent on war.

In fact, the proposal, seen from a distance, was doomed to failure, whether acted on in the form proposed by either Adam, Peter, or Henderson. It was based on two serious misunderstandings, the first concerning the Hitler-Ribbentrop relationship. It was true to say that Ribbentrop misinformed Hitler about Great Britain, but he could do so only because Hitler wanted information which accorded with his predilections. Herr Walther Hofer has described perfectly Hitler's preference for wishful thinking over reasoned calculations. 'The fact has to be faced,' he says in his book *War Premeditated*, 'that in spite of dozens of assurances, Hitler refused to the very last minute to believe in the seriousness of these British declarations . . . He did not want to believe in them because he refused to admit to anyone, even to himself, that his whole judgment of the situation was wrong—wrong because it was based on the amateurish conceits of his own imagination rather than on the objective realities which any normal statesman takes as his authority. Hitler's calculations were not based on indisputable facts: he projected onto the outside world the product of his own instinctive and intuitive visions. His calculations were not adapted to the world of real facts: on the contrary, the world had to fit into his plans—and when this did not turn out as he expected, there was fury and destruction and woe betide anyone who dared to upset him by offering some objective facts and insights.'[40]

The second misunderstanding concerned what was in Hitler's and Ribbentrop's minds when they asserted, personally or through Keitel, that there would be no World War because France and Great Britain would not fight. They were not only thinking of decadence, though it suited them to say so, but of the great State secret of the hour, the Russian-German non-aggression pact. Late in the evening of Monday the 21st of August, the day after Peter's return, the Auswärtige Amt released the information that negotiations had been successfully concluded with Molo-

[40]Walter Hofer. 'Die Entfesselung des zweiten Weltkriegs'. Stuttgart. Translated by Stanley Godman *War Premeditated* (London 1955).

tov, and that on the 23rd Herr von Ribbentrop would fly to Moscow for the final ceremony of signature. On the 23rd, while Ribbentrop flew to Moscow, Sir Nevile Henderson, accompanied by Weizsäcker and Hewel, flew to Berchtesgaden where he delivered the dual-text letter on the 24th. The letter did not alter Hitler's mind in any way. A senior liaison officer on Hitler's staff, General von Vormann, gave the following account of the Führer's reaction: 'Hitler refused to believe in a war with England and France. He reckoned quite firmly on having a free hand against Poland. In his conversation he dragged in every conceivable argument to try to prove that his interpretation of events was correct, and repeated them again and again in all kinds of variations.'[41]

Ribbentrop's reaction, when he returned from his triumphant visit to Moscow, was more agitated. When 'the second Bismarck,' as Hitler described him, learned of Henderson's visit to Berchtesgaden, and that the main content of Chamberlain's letter had formed the subject of speeches in Parliament by the Prime Minister and the Foreign Secretary on the 24th, and later of a broadcast address by Lord Halifax, he flew into a hobble-gobble fit of temper; and when he learned moreover that there were those in the Auswärtige Amt who rejoiced that instead of the fall of Chamberlain's and Daladier's Governments, hourly expected by Ribbentrop and Hitler, Great Britain and France were standing firm this time, then in his rage he issued the following order to the personnel of his Ministry:

'If the Führer decides to reply to Polish provocations and to solve the Polish problem, he will destroy the Polish State within twenty-four hours. Britain will never dare oppose him: if she did she would be beaten and lose her empire, while France would bleed to death on the Siegfried Line if she interfered. If I hear that any official expresses a different view, I will shoot him myself in his office and be responsible to the Führer for my action.'[42]

It is impossible to believe that any envoy, no matter what his skill or force of personality, and even if he was welcome, could have made headway against the opinionated dementia of Hitler and his Foreign Minister.

[41]Vormann's notes are not published but a copy exists in the *Institut für Zeitgeschichte* in Munich. Hofer.
[42]Hofer. He relies on the accounts of Erich Kordt and Weizsäcker.

But if it must be admitted that the last minute efforts of Adam and his friend ended in failure, as they were bound to do, one must admire the tenacity and courage with which they were made. If their plan (like the plans of Weizsäcker, Henderson and Loraine) had something of fantasy and absurdity about it, that is nothing against it. The times were fantastic, and the men who controlled human destiny at that moment were close to madness, and, *sub specie aeternitatis*, utterly absurd.

Adam made one more attempt to influence the course of events before the outbreak of war. Through a friend in the British Embassy he sent a memorandum to David Astor on the state of the opposition since the conclusion of the Ribbentrop-Molotov pact. The paper is dated the 24th of August. It is short, running to about 750 words, and is in two parts, the first dealing with the opposition at the moment, the second with 'the new opposition' of the future. It is this part of the paper which holds interest to-day, as it shows how Adam was thinking. He had evidently still not abandoned his hopes of some kind of appeasement policy towards Germany being pursued by Great Britain, and he warned against the bellicose attitude of German emigrants living in England. 'The force of the Popular Front, especially in France, grew up in the fight against Fascism: this is only a negative force. When they gained power and a positive programme it did not allow a policy with a long view. The New Opposition in Germany is a) developing on the ground of unity and organisation, b) on the basis of political unity not only in the negative sense of the fight against Fascism, but also in a positive sense.'[43]

Right to the end Adam maintained optimism, but it is the belief of those who saw him at the time in Germany that in his heart he knew that hope was dead. Several times he said: 'We will have to go through the mill.'[44]

There remained only to say goodbye to his English friends. He wrote to Diana that he hoped to visit England in September on his way to America. 'All this is said', he wrote, 'as if the streams were continuing to run smoothly—if they don't, I do not feel that there is anything very particular to affirm. That seems as simple and sure as the continuation of the planets—

[43]A.P. [44]C.T.

and there is no fear and crime attached to them except what the astrologists manufacture. And our friendship will continue to live among the stars even when we are both dead and gone. Love always.'

He wrote on the 24th of August to David Astor, using ornamental Chinese paper with a print of a branch in leaf on it. The letter is full of complicated allusions of forgotten or doubtful meaning to-day. It ends: 'Whatever happens to you and me, we'll remain friends, anyway, I know. Ever yours. A.'

He wrote his last letter to Shiela on the same kind of paper. It is undated. 'I have a feeling my last letter was rather inadequate and somehow don't want to leave it at that just now, especially as it is becoming highly doubtful whether my August trip to England and America can still come off. I hate this constant pathetic leave taking, but when we finally cut off, I do not want the smallest drop of bitterness to poison our mutual memory —let's bury the best European friendship deep in the soil, so it cannot be harmed by any winter or surface destruction, and may blossom out again like these Chinese ones.'

On the 1st of September Hitler invaded Poland and the war began.

Chapter 12

NOT NEUTRAL AMERICA

At the beginning of September Adam went to Heidelberg on the second of two visits he made that summer. He went to see his brothers and a certain Doctor Wilhelm Kütemeyer whom Werner greatly esteemed. Adam told them about his English adventures, and the last endeavour of Peter Bielenberg on his behalf. He found Werner critical, and as usual he listened to his brother's disagreement with respect, though with some distress on this occasion. Werner thought that Adam was placing excessive trust in the value of spectacular action as a means of influencing world events towards peace and virtue: this was not the way, he believed, and insisted that the right one lay in a renewal of the spirit, something which could only be brought about by collective endeavour in small communities, not to be translated into public life till it had reached a high degree of perfection. They had a long talk about Freiherr vom Stein whom they both passionately admired, and discussed with increasing disagreement the nature and purpose of State institutions. Adam, true to his enduring belief in the merit of conservative revolution, saw such institutions as the guardian of free development, while Werner asserted that institutions only became valuable when informed by the renewed spirit.[1] They argued thus, and it is typical of both that the outbreak of war found them arguing, Adam in a Hegelian sense, Werner in a Tolstoyan sense, about the wider philosophical implications of the moment.

Soon after the declaration of war by Britain and France, Adam returned to Berlin. He wrote to his mother on the 11th of September: 'I have

[1] C.T. At the earlier meeting in July Trott and Kütemeyer had decided to visit England together to study the relation of British State organisations to civic freedom.

volunteered but cannot count on being called up in the next weeks and in the meantime will be employed in the Auswärtige Amt (at least probably). Most of my friends and the people I know show a calm and clear resolution in the face of what has happened. We must be prepared in any case for grievous years ahead.'

For some weeks Adam had been in correspondence with Carter about his proposed attendance at the I.P.R. autumn meeting, and Carter had asked Lord Lothian for a grant of $1500 from the Rhodes Trust to enable Adam to undertake the journey. Lord Lothian had persuaded his fellow trustees to agree and the money had been remitted to Carter's office a few weeks before the invasion of Poland.[2] Adam in the meantime had obtained the necessary permission from Walter Hewel to travel to America. With the outbreak of war the permission was automatically cancelled, and it was doubtful whether the invitation still held until, on the 12th of September, Adam received a cable: 'Institute exploring possibility expanding Far Eastern inquiry to relate unofficial scholarship to general postwar settlement. In view your knowledge present inquiry regard it utmost importance your coming this country earliest possible moment for consultation. Hope this can be regarded as your first national service cable Edward Carter.'

As Edward Carter explained later in a letter to Mr Allen Dulles, the last sentence of the message was cunningly devised to cause an impression that the I.P.R. was not unfavourably disposed to the Nazis, thus facilitating a travel permit from Germany. Weizsäcker and Kessel both strongly represented to Hewel that a mission by Adam to the United States could be of great value to Germany in whose foreign policy American neutrality was a major objective.[3] In presenting the case they did not have to descend to falsehood for in fact no one believed more in the value to Germany of American neutrality than Adam himself. As appears later, his reasons were not such as to appeal to Nazi minds.

The permission was renewed and arrangements were made immediately. Adam was given a temporary attachment to the 'Information Department' of the Auswärtige Amt which met his expenses. These proved to be heavy as the circumstances of war made it dangerous for him to cross the Atlan-

[2] A letter from Carter to Mr Allen W. Dulles of 11.10.46.
[3] Herr von Kessel. Discussion.

tic twice and so he was again involved in a journey round the world. He
left Berlin on the 19th of September and travelled by Munich to Genoa
where his boat, the Italian steamship *Vulcania*, was due to sail on the
22nd.[4] While walking along the quay before going on board he caught
sight of a fellow passenger whom he knew. Like Adam this man, Fritz
Caspari, was a former Rhodes scholar. They had known each other for
some years, but they did not become close friends till early 1937. Caspari
was now returning to America, having been given the status of expatriate
or Auslandsdeutscher, in order to complete a University course. On this
September day of 1939 he caught sight of Adam walking along the quay
dressed in a very elegant mackintosh. 'I thought you were in California,'
said Adam. 'And I thought you were in China', said Caspari.[5]

He told Adam that he was in some doubt as to what to do. He explained
the predicament: that morning the captain had summoned all the German passengers to the First Class saloon. He had told them that there was
no question of Italian ships, as neutral vessels, failing to make the Atlantic
crossing, but he warned that he would probably be obliged to enter
British territorial waters at Gibraltar, in which case the British navy would
insist on right of search, and of taking German passengers off to internment. He asked them to decide whether they were prepared to take this
risk and appointed a time limit before which they must tell him their
decisions. Caspari was trying to make up his mind, and finding it difficult
to do so, but Adam brushed aside his fears. If they had the bad luck to be
interned, he said, he knew how to get them out. He had influential friends
in England, notably Lord Halifax, who would soon restore them to
liberty. They had no need for anxiety, he said and seemed almost to look
forward to the adventure. They embarked.

The *Vulcania* began the crossing of the West Mediterranean by way of
the Balearic Islands, and then sailed on the South West course towards
the new dangers of the Pillars of Hercules. Among the German passengers
there was one whom both Adam and his friend knew to be a Nazi party
functionary of some prominence, and as the ship neared Gibraltar, this

[4]C.T.
[5]Herr Fritz Caspari. Discussion. Unless otherwise stated, the whole of this account
of Trott's voyage to America and the first stages of his visit are taken from Herr
Caspari's account.

person began to give way to nervousness. He came to ask Adam's advice as to what he should do if subjected to British interrogation. He had, he admitted with a shame-faced air, taken the precaution of throwing his party badge overboard. Adam was 'overjoyed by the spectacle of a Nazi in difficulties because of his party membership,'[6] and proceeded, in consequence, to give him the required advice with relish and recklessness.

'You did quite right to throw away your badge,' he said, 'and all you have to do now is to keep up the act. Don't let them think you really are a Nazi. If they ask you say No, certainly not, Hitler's an absolute bastard.'

The party functionary was deeply shocked. 'It's very difficult to do that,' he said.

'Not in the slightest,' said Adam. 'Look, you want to do it like this. A British officer comes to me and says, "Are you a Nazi?" I reply like this: "Me a Nazi! Good God—I should think not! Hitler's an absolute bastard!" And then if he still suspected me I should go further'—thereupon he treated the functionary to denunciations of the grossest kind, after which he put him through a rehearsal.

As a loyal servant of the line, the captain of the *Vulcania* was determined to avoid search by the British. When the boat was close to Gibraltar a destroyer steamed out towards her. The captain set his course southward and sailed fast towards the Spanish territorial waters of the North African shore, and he was helped by numerous little craft painted bright red and yellow to mark the way. It was a race between the *Vulcania* and the destroyer in which the *Vulcania* scored the victory, reaching Spanish waters before the destroyer could hail her. There the *Vulcania* anchored and lingered while the destroyer stood by on watch to overtake her when she sailed on. In the morning the destroyer had gone and a cruiser was in her place. The *Vulcania* still lingered on and won the trial of patience. Presumably other and more pressing duties were assigned to the cruiser, for on the second morning she had gone, without relief. The *Vulcania* then sailed past Gibraltar, cut across British waters and reached the open sea. She sailed to Lisbon and from there began the Atlantic crossing.

Great was the rejoicing of all the German passengers at their escape. Their relief from the prospect of internment must have been enormous indeed, but looking back on the incident to-day one cannot but regret

[6]C.T. quoting Herr Caspari.

that the gallant captain so successfully outmanoeuvred the British naval authorities, and that as a result of a search Adam was not forced into expatriation. What would have been his career then taxes the imagination.

Soon after departure from Lisbon the Nazi party functionary sought out Caspari. He had recovered much of his accustomed confidence and addressed the other with markedly less friendliness and more authority than before. He asked Caspari about 'this Baron von Trott.' What was he doing going to America, and what sort of a person was he? Caspari replied that he was a very loyal German.

'Are you sure of that?' replied the Nazi. 'I am not. I did not like his behaviour when I asked his advice. I had a feeling that when he acted the part of a disaffected person he really meant what he was saying. As I think about it I become more certain, and I am going to say so.'

'You want to have a talk with him?'

'I did not mean that. I meant that I am going to report the incident to my superiors in Germany.'

'You are going to do nothing of the kind. If you feel uneasy about the incident, you will raise the matter with Herr von Trott and no one else.'

'I don't trust Barons and I don't trust him.'

'I said you will raise the matter with *him*.'

The Nazi grumblingly assented. Caspari went to Adam and warned him. The latter recognised immediately that he had allowed himself to be carried away by his delight in the rôle he had acted for the functionary's benefit and that it was important to undo the effect of his charade. So he met the Nazi and in the course of a long talk, in which he projected all his charm of manner, he adopted the pose of a sincere admirer and adherent of the regime. The functionary appeared to be satisfied.

It is the belief of Herr Caspari, and others of Adam's German friends,[7] that the functionary did nevertheless send home an adverse report. Later events do not bear this out.

Adam had set himself a definite task. His aim in America may be described as the same as the one he had followed in England, adapted to the new circumstances. Since the war had broken out, the aim of preventing it was now translated into terms of confining it and bringing it to an end

[7]C.T.

as soon as possible. This end was envisaged as being marked by an anti-Nazi uprising in Germany. This uprising needed the encouragement of outside approval and support, taking the form of a close and generous definition of 'war-aims,' in which neutral America would be associated. Unless the aims showed generosity, they would inhibit even extreme opponents of the regime from contributing to a course that might involve the ruin of Germany. There must be the strongest guarantee that anti-Nazism would not be rewarded by Draconian terms of settlement. (Never did he forget the lesson of Weimar.)

The success of this course of action depended largely on the character of American involvement. The United States was the only power in the world with the moral prestige and the material resource to impose its will, and if it was known that the administration of Mr Roosevelt, and the President's opponents of the Republican Party too, favoured a prosperous Germany, purged of Nazism, enjoying 'her rightful place among the nations' and so forth, the powerful and ever-increasing anti-Nazi interest in Germany would not hesitate to take the initiative, depose Hitler, disperse the Nazi party, and set up a civilised regime. America would then be the political leader of the world, but the whole of this movement depended on America's moral prestige, and this prestige in turn depended on American neutrality. Such in outline was the plan of whose practicability and wisdom Adam wanted to persuade leading men in the United States.

During the voyage Adam discussed these and others of his ideas with Caspari. He was convinced that a great resistance movement to Nazism existed within Germany, and his optimism in this respect seemed in no way dashed by the absence of any manifest opposition on the outbreak of war. He spoke about the kind of international policy which he thought that the new de-Nazified Germany ought to follow. He thought that the independence of Czechoslovakia and Poland ought to be restored in full, but the union with Austria maintained and the Polish corridor frontier redrawn to remove a perennial grievance.

He spoke of the sort of anti-Nazism he wanted to strive for. He saw no merit in substituting one fanaticism for another. It was undeniable that Hitler had exploited the German people mercilessly and ruthlessly, but for all that it should not be forgotten that he had also led them to great achievements: the realisation of those items in the Social Democrat pro-

gramme, notably the Labour Corps, which had swiftly relieved the misery
of unemployment in Germany; the masterly network of the new two-
way roads; the revitalised social services and the slum-clearance—these
things, he said, had been attained 'by the sweat, energy and courage of
the German people'; they were a subject of just pride, but fanatic anti-
Nazis tended to denigrate them along with the injustice and the atrocities.
'No one has the right to try to take such things from the German people,'
he said.

The enterprise began with a mishap which was never to be put straight.
It began by chance from the fact that while Adam was a first class passenger, Caspari was travelling second class. When the *Vulcania* berthed at
her quay in New York the two friends were separated, as disembarking
passengers in the two classes were directed to different customs sheds.
They arranged to meet later at Adam's hotel. By the time Adam arrived
there, Caspari had gone out, leaving a message that he would be back
later. Adam in turn went out, probably to see Edward Carter, and he also
left a message, a written one. In this he said what time he would be back,
regretted the missed appointment, and ended with a sentence explaining
his lateness: 'Die Kontrolle dauerte lang.'

Either the Federal Bureau of Investigation had an agent in the hotel,
or the concierge's suspicions were aroused by a message written in German. At all events Adam's innocuous note soon found itself in F.B.I.
hands. The last sentence struck the authorities as sinister. They translated
it correctly enough as 'The control lasted long,' but they seem to have
been unaware that among the many meanings which the word 'Kontrolle'
can cover in German, a usual one, and the most obvious in this context, is
'customs examination.' The German specialist who handled this matter
in the F.B.I. preferred however to translate the word according to a very
uncommon usage, as 'Radio-code.'

One cannot know precisely what happened. It may be that the American authorities had already been warned about Adam by British Intelligence who were active in still neutral Italy, and would easily find out the
names of German passengers to America. Or it may be that the F.B.I.
now made enquiries, leading to further enquiries from England, yielding
the answer that this mysterious traveller from Nazi Germany was the
subject of Czechoslovakian, British and American suspicions, originating
in Germany, Great Britain, the United States, Japan and China—a world-

wide operator! All that can be known for certain is that at some time about now British Intelligence informed American authorities that in their opinion Adam was a dubious character who should be watched,[8] and that the F.B.I. believed that he spent his first hours on American soil sending messages to Berlin by the aid of a cleverly concealed wireless transmitter.[9]

Two or three weeks after arrival the two friends separated, Adam remaining on the east coast, and Caspari leaving for California. From the beginning Adam hastened to renew his contacts in the United States, and also to meet certain German expatriates. As with his adventures in England, it is possible to know a great deal about what happened, but very difficult, owing to contradictions in memories and the absence of a diary, to know the chronological order of events. It would seem that Adam spent most of his time in New York till the beginning of November, then went to Washington, attended the I.P.R. November Meeting at Virginia Beach, and then returned to New York where he stayed till his departure for the west coast to catch his boat at San Francisco in January. During his first stay in New York he went to Washington on several short visits. His time on the east coast is not precisely divisible into three neat episodes, though that is the rough shape of events.

Among his closer New York friends he found, of course, Roger Baldwin and Edward Carter who had made this journey possible and now gave him an office in the I.P.R. rooms on East 52nd Street. He rejoiced to find Julie Braun-Vogelstein, her niece Hertha and Hasso von Seebach, three people whom he loved and who had gladdened his earlier visit. He renewed his affectionate acquaintance with his cousins William and Louise Schieffelin, and made himself known again to Doctor Reinhold Niebuhr. Through Mr Hamilton Fish Armstrong he made acquaintances in the Foreign Policy Association and the Council on Foreign Relations, including Whitney Shephardson, like Adam a former Rhodes scholar.[10]

Another acquaintance of great significance to Adam's endeavours at

[8]The writer relies on the same authority to whom he owes the information given on page 218.
[9]Herr Caspari was informed of this whole 'Kontrolle' episode by F.B.I. officials on an occasion to be mentioned later.
[10]George M. Merton. Berichte.

this time was Alexander Böker, also a sometime Rhodes scholar. They had met as guests of Bernstorff, but did not become at all close in friendship till now. At this time Böker was Assistant to the exiled German Chancellor, Heinrich Brüning, whom Adam sought to meet through this friendship.[11] Brüning seems to have heard something of Adam's bad reputation and was at first reluctant to meet him,[12] but when he did so he took to him immediately. Nevertheless he found himself critical of Adam's political ideas though he soon modified his opinion as appears later.[13] If Adam came near his goal it was through Brüning. Reinhold Niebuhr, who saw much of Adam in New York, remained critical, though like Brüning he recognised that, despite wanting in sense of reality, Adam's ideas were the product of a generous nature and mind. The eminent theologian was somewhat dismayed at the unpractical character of the 'Prussian idealism' (so he described it later) which informed his reasoning and which he found quite unmodified since his first talks with him in 1937. He could not see how the kind of new Germany he envisaged, ruled on a Left-Wing Parliamentary basis, under a limited British-style monarchy, could possibly emerge naturally in a state corrupted by a unique retrogression from civilisation. Niebuhr was perplexed by Adam's romantic faith in the moral stature of the German military hierarchy, and could not understand how he saw in Hjalmar-Schacht a centre of anti-Nazi opposition and resistance.[14]

For all their criticism Brüning and Niebuhr never doubted Adam's integrity or his aversion to Nazism, but it was otherwise among many of the German expatriates. It is not possible to know to what extent his damaged reputation in certain official circles became known to his fellow-countrymen from leakages of official information, or to what extent growing suspicions were due to puzzlement at Adam's equivocal position: it was natural for people to ask how it was possible for a 'good' German to visit the United States with the agreement of the Auswärtige Amt, and Adam was not able to defend himself by a public avowal of anti-Nazism. On the contrary he had to be extremely cautious in speech and action,

---

[11] Alexander Böker. Berichte.
[12] Edward Carter. A letter to Mr Allen W. Dulles of 11.10.46.
[13] Sir John Wheeler-Bennett. Discussion. Also Carter-Dulles letter.
[14] Dr R. Niebuhr. Discussion.

and went out of his way to soften the anxieties of the German Embassy. In that connection Edward Carter has left some interesting evidence in a letter.

'One day, prior to a visit to Washington,' he wrote, 'as a hedge he arranged for me to lunch with Thomsen[15] at the Hotel Gladstone on East 52nd Street, just across from the I.P.R. offices. Thomsen was, I believe, Chargé of the German Embassy in Washington at that time. We discussed ways in which German scholars might profit from the researches on Asia of Asian and Western scholars. Of course some of those who were sceptical about Adam could not understand why he had to maintain contact from time to time with the Nazi officials here.'[16]

One of the few Germans in America in whom Adam was able to confide without reserve was Kurt Riezler. He was a very interesting man and one who was likely to appeal to Adam's imagination. Riezler had had a career as a civil servant, a political theorist and an author. He was for many years senior personal secretary (Referent) to Chancellor Bethmann-Hollweg, and after the war he acted as State Secretary to President Ebert. Between 1912 and 1914 he wrote two books. The first had the intriguing title, *The Necessity of the Impossible* (*Die Erforderlichkeit des Unmöglichen*). The second was published under a pseudonym (J. Ruedorffer) with the more conventional title *Principles of World Policy* (*Grundzüge der Weltpolitik*). Everything that has been said in condemnation of the spirit of William II's rule can find an excuse in these two books and in the degenerate Hegelianism of Treitschke and his followers to which they give expression. The Referent seems to have exerted a congenial influence on the German Chancellor.[17]

Like Bethmann-Hollweg, Riezler was of ambivalent character, but in

---

[15]Hans Thomsen had graduated from journalism to a senior post in the German Embassy, and was acting as Chargé d'Affaires at this time. (Mr W. F. Bell, a member of the British Embassy Staff in Washington at the time.)

[16]A letter of 8.7.49 from E. Carter to Mrs Hopkinson.

[17]In an essay by Imanuel Geiss published in 1965 as part of a series *Hamburger Schriften* edited by Fritz Fischer, he gives an interesting quotation from Riezler's diary, to the effect that Bethmann-Hollweg had 'the typically German and idealistic conviction that the people needed a war.' One may add that this idealistic conviction was not unknown among non-German European politicians of the time.

a way that shows more honourably in his case than in that of the much whitewashed Chancellor. After the war he experienced what can best be described as a religious conversion. He totally rejected the quasi-Hegelian, quasi-Nietschean philosophy of aggressive nationalism in which he had so passionately believed, and in 1920 wrote a book, *Die Drei Krisen*, announcing this recantation. He suffered for his new opinions, and after 1933 he found himself with no alternative but to leave Germany and migrate to the United States.

How he met Adam remains uncertain. What is known is that they met frequently and that Riezler was one of very few of Adam's compatriots in America in whom he confided his association with men who were prepared to conspire for the overthrow, if necessary by violent means, of the Nazi regime.[18] When Adam was suspected by his fellow Germans he assured them of their mistake, but, as appears later, he (like other of Adam's friends) had to use great caution in his defence.[19] He remains an intriguing and important figure in the background about whom one would like to know more at this point.

The suspicion increased, and Adam continually came on fresh evidence that he was being followed. He noticed in the apartment hotel where he stayed in New York that whenever his telephone rang, the telephone in the room above rang simultaneously, and ceased when he had picked up his own instrument.[20] Until quite late in his visit he assumed that he was being followed by Nazi agents. Julie Braun-Vogelstein remembers how he used to come to see her in her hotel, usually late, and how she warned him that he must be careful about these visits to a Jewish expatriate. 'They will be spying on you,' she said. He laughed. 'They are at it already,' he said, 'The fellows have just followed me right up to your door.'[21] It was only slowly that he realised that this shadowing was the work of the F.B.I.

His main task in New York was writing, in collaboration, a memorandum which Adam and his friends wished to transmit to President Roosevelt. The distribution of authorship has been the subject of varying accounts, but the origin of the memorandum is not in any doubt. In

[18]Mrs White (née Riezler). A discussion.
[19]Hermann Graml *Der Deutscher Widerstand gegen Hitler*. Cologne. Berlin 1966.
[20]Carter-Hopkinson Letter. [21]J.B.V. p.388.

dramatic circumstances Adam made friends with Paul Scheffer, a former
Berlin editor, and at this time American correspondent of the Right-Wing
Deutsche Allgemeine Zeitung. The time of their meeting was in the last
week of October. In a letter to Doctor Margaret Boveri Scheffer recalled
what happened: 'He visited me. I knew him from Berlin days when he
was a Lehrling (apprentice) in the office of Doctor Paul Leverkühn. Carter
had spoken to me of the occasion of Trott's journey. His success [in
reaching America] had brought him no mean prestige in Nazi eyes.[22]
Since Trott came on an official mission, I was reserved in my talk with
him at this first meeting. With some warmth Trott promised to come
again. Two days later we had a further conversation, still with the same
reserve. I went out with him. In the darkness of the street I tried the effect
on him of a critical remark, and in his lively way Trott seized my meaning
immediately with a cry of "At last!"'

With confidence suddenly established, Paul Scheffer then told Adam
in detail about his ideas and asked him to read an article he had written
for the *Atlantic Monthly* some three months before on the need for a clear
statement of war aims by France and Britain in consultation with the
United States.

The ideas in Paul Scheffer's article (which had not been published) were
in complete agreement with Adam's,[23] and his new friend proposed that
this essay should form the basis of a memorandum to be presented to Mr
Roosevelt.[24] In a letter to David Astor Adam described himself as the
'author . . . only in parts.'[25] According to Paul Scheffer, Adam did little
beyond editing, and writing the last two paragraphs which are certainly
his.[26] In spite of the mounting suspicion against him, he was nevertheless,
to their credit, chosen by the group as the most fitting person to undertake
the task of confiding this document to the political leadership of the
United States. It was agreed that he should present himself as the sole

[22]The reference is to a legend, still repeated, that the *Vulcania* was searched by
British officials and that Trott escaped internment by posing as an Englishman,
wearing a Balliol tie—no easy feat without a well-forged passport!
[23]Correspondence between Dr M. Boveri and Paul Scheffer.
[24]Vierteljahrshefte für Zeitgeschichte. Deutsche Verlags—Anstalt Stuttgart.
The issue of July 1959 contains an essay by Professor Rothfels 'Dokumentation,
Adam von Trott und das State Department.' Referred to later as Rothfels 1.
[25]A.P.   [26]Rothfels 1.

author since Scheffer, as the correspondent of a (supposedly) Nazi paper, might not be an acceptable name.

The memorandum is in five sections of unequal length, and contains about five thousand words. It is very typical of the western liberal mood of the autumn of 1939. The outbreak of world war, for all its inevitability, came as an appalling shock, and a spontaneous reaction among a great number of politically minded people was to set them thinking about the destiny of our age, to provoke them to 'spiritual stock-taking,' as it was called, to drafting plans for the reformation of the world, no less. Friends everywhere wrote long letters to each other about their beliefs and intentions. The memorandum portrays the spirit of the time very clearly.

The opening section, of about 700 words, is commendably outspoken. Two foreign views of Germany are discerned and outlined: one 'starts from the proposition that Germany has now given final proof of her inability to live on equal terms with other European States; consequently it considers it imperative to weaken Germany beyond hope of recovery . . .'; the other view 'starts from the proposition that the Versailles Treaty and especially the spirit of its application was too harsh, and that the present war is its natural outcome.' The section ends as follows: 'Even though the German people are increasingly opposed to the National-Socialist Government and embittered by its policies, it is clear that only a negligible minority of Germans will deny their support even to the present regime, if the preservation of the German nation is at stake.'

The short second section sets forth the main purpose:

'Most . . . considerations . . . support an early declaration of the Allied peace aims, if a departure from the Treaty of Versailles and its philosophy could be envisaged. The practical purpose . . . would be:

1. to finish the war quickly;

2. to reduce . . . friction in Europe . . . by a negotiated peace.

3. to set moving machinery for European co-operation.

'The extreme importance of a timely clarification of war aims derives not merely from the fact that it would reassure and consolidate opposition in Germany and thereby contribute to the discrediting and undoing of Nazi domination. It is of vital importance also for the future internal situation of the Allied States themselves.'

The third section describes, with excessive optimism, the state of opinion among the various classes of the German public to whom this declaration of aims would be addressed. The proposition is that though all classes in Germany have been kept in ignorance of the causes of the war, they are all potentially hostile to the rule of Hitler. In the penultimate paragraph the whole subject is summed up as follows: 'Taking Germany as a whole, the following can be stated with certainty: Hitler came into power by promising the destruction of Communism to all who had something to lose, and by promising the restoration of Germany's greatness without war.[27] In August 1939 Hitler finally destroyed these two fundamentals of his power.' The conclusion is drawn that an anti-Nazi rising is imminent, but in the last paragraph a note of warning is heard. 'If, on the other hand, the German people—groping for some bearable alternative to Hitler—are met with continual vagueness and intransigence from the Western powers, their desperate hopes are bound to turn eastwards once more.'

This leads to the subject of the fourth section. The proposition here is that the Second, as opposed to the First World War, opened in all the engaged countries without traditional appeals to 'Glory,' but as a grave and considered step taken by the whole people. As the burden of war makes itself felt, there may be a general turning against Governments, and a 'people's war' may lead to 'a kind of semi-religious revival with chaotic social consequences . . . and revolutionary tendencies, already latent, may manifest themselves in a more chaotic and destructive form the longer the war lasts.' Such dangers were in fact only narrowly averted in post-war Western Europe, as readers will remember, and in Eastern Europe they were translated into reality.

The last section is likely to have prompted the most disagreement. It concerns practical measures: how to convey these terms in such a way as to capture German confidence. German scepticism stemming from the memory of Wilson's Fourteen Points is stressed. Although it is stated (one of the few concrete points made) that Germany should accept her 1933 frontiers as sufficient, the main proposal is a peace of compromise. 'The contribution,' a key passage runs, 'from both sides will have to be substantial; but even large sacrifices, if made on the basis of negotiation, must

[27]A preceding passage suggests Trott and Scheffer were here accurately reflecting military opinion. See Wheeler-Bennett pp. 464-6.

be considered as infinitely preferable to the indefinite toll of life and treasure which a drifting on of the European catastrophe will necessitate.' The authors of the memorandum overlooked that at that moment, after the barbaric breach of the peace by Hitler, no Polish, French or British Government could make a 'substantial contribution' with the purpose of soothing the susceptibilities of any German regime whatsoever, and hope to remain a Government for more than a few hours after. Although the passage is followed by one insisting that Germany's main contribution must be to acquire a civilised and trustworthy regime, this was the language of appeasement, rational and easily defended as it was. As an author of the memorandum, Adam was once more overtaken by a tragic fate which pursued him. In all this activity, he was too late.

The memorandum ends with an implied appeal to the United States, tactfully conveyed, to take part in peace moves. 'America,' a passage runs, 'not divided as we are by social and national boundaries, may well raise the standard of all peace discussion above our complex prejudices of the past.' As mentioned already, the concluding passage is known to be by Adam.

About the middle of October, while Scheffer and he were still working on the text, Adam went to Washington to keep an appointment which had been arranged for him through secret negotiations by Edward Carter with the British Embassy. The negotiations were successful and the aim was a bold one, for Adam to meet the British ambassador, his friend and benefactor Lord Lothian.[28]

The arrangements were made by Carter and carried out with the help of Roger Baldwin. The rendezvous was Carter's room in the Mayflower Hotel in Washington. Fitting circumlocution was maintained. Roger Baldwin took a room in the hotel too. Sometime before Lothian's time of arrival Adam went to the hotel and asked for Mr Baldwin and on being told the the latter was expecting him he went to Carter's room. There he awaited Lothian. When the ambassador arrived Carter stayed only five minutes and then left him and Adam alone. They had a long conversation, according to Carter. The four men in the plot dispersed separately as they

[28]Very rough dating is possible from correspondence between Trott and David Astor. In an undated letter Trott tells David Astor 'Philip I shall see day after to-morrow'. David Astor replies to this on the 27th of October.

had arrived.[29] The ruse was successful, so far as appears, and the meeting did not become known, at that time at any rate, outside the British Embassy.

No.available minute has survived of what was said, but in a letter written some time after to Charles Bosanquet, Adam seems to indicate that he pressed on Lothian the main recommendations of the as yet incomplete memorandum.[30] According to one memory of the time, that of a member of Lothian's Embassy staff, Sir John Foster, with whom the ambassador discussed this meeting, Adam took the occasion to revive some of the ideas he had expressed in *Ostasiatische Möglichkeiten*. That the memory is not at fault is strongly suggested by the fact that a month or so later Adam's address to the I.P.R. meeting hinted at similar trains of thought. One should also remember that Lothian had read *Ostasiatische Möglichkeiten* and it would be natural for the two men to discuss its ideas. Sir John Foster remembers from Lord Lothian's account that Adam argued that since an end to the state of war in Europe seemed a very distant possibility, there was all the more reason for following up those interests for peace shared by Great Britain and Germany which he believed he had discerned in the Far East, and whence conditions for general peace might stem. The proposition did not impress Lothian or members of the Embassy as realistic and it was not pursued.[31] But Lothian's affectionate interest in Adam persisted nonetheless.

Soon after this meeting Adam was back in New York. By the time he and Scheffer had the final text of the memorandum ready and typed into two copies, it was November. Before leaving for Washington Adam consulted Mr Fish Armstrong, and though he did not show him the text, he outlined the contents of the memorandum to him and gained his support. Mr Armstrong put him in touch with the Washington representative of the Foreign Policy Association, a certain Mr Stone. On arrival in Washington Adam went to see Mr Stone and gave him one of the two copies of the memorandum to read. Favourably impressed, Stone called on the Assistant State Secretary, Mr George S. Messersmith, on the 13th

[29]Carter-Dulles letter and a discussion with Mr Baldwin.
[30]The letter written from the Barbizon-Plaza Hotel New York is undated, but a letter in answer suggests late October or early November.
[31]Sir John Foster K.B.E., Q.C., M.P. Discussion.

of November, and gave him the copy in turn. A note of the 14th of November from Messersmith to Sumner Welles shows that the Assistant Secretary had two further copies made, one for Secretary Cordell Hull, the other for Welles, and a pencilled note on this document shows that Welles had already been shown the memorandum, presumably by Cordell Hull.[32]

It looked at first as though things were going very well indeed for Adam. Messersmith was not only favourably impressed but, according to Paul Scheffer, was 'all fire and flame' for the ideas expressed in the memorandum, and in spite of the need for keeping its existence a closely guarded secret, he had twenty-four copies made and distributed to influential persons. The White House, Adam learned through Stone, had shown a 'lively interest,' from which Adam concluded naturally enough, and rightly it seems,[33] that the President himself had read the paper with approval.[34]

Adam's American venture bears a resemblance to his English one in the last months of peace. The pattern of events is similar: initial success despite an undercurrent of mistrust, followed by a reverse which might have been avoided if he had left well alone.

The initial success was remarkable, for the great and very difficult goal of acquainting Roosevelt personally with the propositions of this German memorandum had been attained. The moment was in some ways propitious. The Presidential plan to send Sumner Welles on a mission of enquiry to the countries of the Western Allies and the Axis was under discussion, and though Roosevelt made no secret of his anti-Nazi sympathies, he had not abandoned the ambition of achieving historical greatness as the peace-maker of the world. His 'lively interest' was to some extent a logical reaction to the arrival of this unexpected document in

[32]Rothfels 1.   [33]This is also the conclusion of Rothfels 1.
[34]The story of the memorandum's adventures is told in a series of letters (referred to subsequently as Scheffer-Boveri) addressed to Dr Margaret Boveri by the late Paul Scheffer in a correspondence which lasted from April 1951 to August 1958. (Quotations have appeared on page 297 above.) He relies on memories of his own experiences and of what Trott told him. He asserts that Trott presented the memorandum personally to Messersmith, but the documents quoted in Rothfels 1 make it clear that Trott presented it through Stone and did not meet Messersmith till the 20th of November. Stone is not mentioned in the correspondence.

November 1939. But there was no certainty in the matter. Roosevelt had not made up his mind. He felt war-like one day, and saw himself as a pacificator the next.

Whether or not Adam might have avoided disaster by leaving well alone, the fault for his not doing so did not lie with him in America. It lay with Messersmith who (through Stone) encouraged him to visit those to whom he had sent copies of the memorandum.

It was natural for Messersmith, once he had decided on the indiscretion of circulating the memorandum, to send a copy to Felix Frankfurter, a close friend of Sumner Welles and a man much esteemed by the President. It will be remembered that Adam's meeting with him in Boston in 1937 had been particularly happy. He greatly looked forward to meeting him again, but did not like to propose himself directly as he knew how bitter this leading Zionist had become against Germany. Edward Carter made enquiries and Judge Frankfurter replied that he would be glad to see him.[35] On receiving the news Adam was overjoyed and, as he was liable to do, gave way to over-optimism. He forgot Frankfurter's sensitiveness and remembered only that they were both Oxford men. He did not know that Frankfurter had been warned against his activities by Maurice Bowra.

The meeting went very badly. Frankfurter did not like the tone of the memorandum, with its implied argument that the Treaty of Versailles had led to the rise of Hitler. In the course of discussion Adam expressed himself candidly and without the least inhibition, and this had the unhappy effect of causing Frankfurter to find his remarks intolerable and insulting. There are three different versions of what was said. According to what Frankfurter told Isaiah Berlin, he was exasperated when Adam asserted that there was still hope of restoring peace so long as Neville Chamberlain was British Prime Minister and Lord Halifax Foreign Secretary, but that such hopes could not be realised while the British Government contained such a bellicose figure as Winston Churchill and employed another in Duff Cooper.[36] Adam's accounts made no mention of any remarks about British Ministers. Paul Scheffer remembered him telling how the meeting broke down when Adam said something of this

---

[35]Carter-Dulles letter.
[36]Sir Isaiah Berlin. Discussion. Shortly before this Alfred Duff Cooper (later Lord Norwich) had concluded a lecture tour in America.

kind to Frankfurter: 'Would you react so strongly against the plan (put forward in the memorandum), if you were not a Jew?' Herr Caspari remembers Adam telling him that the fatal moment arrived as he argued to Frankfurter that the United States should give open support to the non-Nazis, but that if the accompanying propaganda was to be effective in Germany, American Jews should not take a prominent part. It is perfectly possible that all these remarks were made in the course of the conversation, and the authenticity of the one recorded by Herr Caspari is suggested by a curious sequel which belongs to a later paragraph.

Whatever the precise sequence of events on this occasion the end was calamitous. Edward Carter recorded later that 'Frankfurter lashed out at him and gave von Trott the impression that Frankfurter thought he was a double-crosser.'[37]

From this time on Adam's mission began to fail. Mistrust increased. Undoubtedly this mistrust was helped on by an agitation against him maintained strenuously by Felix Frankfurter, but it would be a manifest mistake to conclude that he was the unique or even major cause of Adam's misfortunes. It is more likely that Frankfurter acted as he did because he was impressed, not only by the disturbing account which he had had from Maurice Bowra, but by a host of disparaging rumour. He had probably asked to see Adam so that he could judge for himself. In his hypersensitive state a tactless remark confirmed all his worst fears.[38] But the theory, which has often been expressed, that, had it not been for Felix Frankfurter, Adam's mission would have succeeded is inadequate to account for the depth and intensity of the suspicion which grew against him.

It is hard to exaggerate how immense was that 'wall of mistrust,' as Professor Rothfels has described it, which rapidly enclosed Adam's reputation. To this day the mistrust persists in America. It came from many different quarters. Its main origin was that F.B.I. conviction that Adam was not only a Nazi agent but Hitler's master-spy. As usually happens

[37]Carter-Dulles letter.
[38]Dr Niebuhr told the writer that he pleaded Trott's innocence to Frankfurter in vain, but came away with an explanation of the incident different from that given by Trott himself. The judge, Dr Niebuhr said, was class-conscious and retained as well an Austrian aversion to the aristocracy of North Germany. It was his belief that Frankfurter was influenced towards a bad opinion of Adam by his 'baronial manner', rather than by anything he said.

when a name is blackened by rumour many chance circumstances seem to afford proof of iniquity. Adam's enforced secretiveness as to what he was doing seemed to mark him out as following the trade of espionage, but his openness in moments of indiscretion pointed, in the eyes of the F.B.I., to the same conclusion. If, they argued, this man could talk so freely in an apparently anti-Nazi sense, and yet be planning to return to Germany, then surely his apparent hostility to the Nazis was no more than a well-organised 'cover' for his real employment. It is true that Adam's indiscretions were of an extraordinary kind, and Riezler was moved to complain to Paul Scheffer that he found Adam's conduct 'hair-raising' when he addressed well over a hundred people, gathered in Mr Schieffelin's house, on the subject of what the aims of an opposition should be regarding the formation of a post-Nazi Government.[39] He made other indiscretions in telling people about his real beliefs and intentions, but this address to more than a hundred people, the great majority of whom he could never have seen before, was the high-water mark of his rashness!

F.B.I. suspicion continued to be nourished by non-American sources. There is good reason to believe that when news of his visit came to some of the former *Neue Blätter* group, now exiles in the United States, they asked their old colleagues in England for an opinion on this mission whose purpose was said to encourage American neutrality, and from England they received unreassuring replies.[40] Many German refugees in New York listened to a rumour that Adam was a Gestapo agent whose object was to find out, for purposes of ultimate vengeance, which of them were active in propaganda against the Nazis,[41] and this also reached the F.B.I. who were as diligent in the collection of information as they were weak in judging it. Unhappily Adam gave gratuitous cause for the enmity of the refugees. He knew that many of them suspected him, and his nerves became distraught, as those of a man will when continually followed and shadowed. He felt sure that a certain young German poet, who had a room in the house of a friend of his in New York, was watching his movements and reporting them. One day when Adam was alone in the house he went to the young man's room and looked through his papers. He did so inexpertly and when questions were asked Adam confessed to his

[39]Scheffer-Boveri. [40]J. P. Mayer. Discussion. [41]Wheeler-Bennet p. 487.

friend what he had done. He regretted his deed which he admitted was
due to angry impatience. The incident was smoothed over, but it had
become known and had its inevitable effect.[42]

It became increasingly difficult for his friends, notably Roger Baldwin,
Felix Morley, Dr Brüning and Reinhold Niebuhr, to calm the suspicion
which surrounded 'the Trott case' which soon became a favoured topic
in the gossip of Washington.[43]

There was one reason for suspicion which was perhaps the most fatal
of all, and originated in Adam's own predilection. The name of Hjalmar
Schacht has already been mentioned as that of a man in whom Adam
trusted as a leader against Nazism.

It so happened that in October Schacht was taken with the idea of
making a personal approach to President Roosevelt to urge the value
of American peace-moves.[44] He wrote to a former business associate, the
American banker Leon Fraser, asking him to arrange a lecture tour, under
cover of which American national sport Schacht would pursue high-level
discussions in person.

The State Department regarded Schacht as a sinister individual, and,
for all his disagreement with the Führer, they saw little of the non-Nazi
and nothing of the anti-Nazi in this man who had rescued Hitler's regime
from economic chaos. His proposal was ill received. His friend was asked
to reply that should Doctor Schacht visit the United States there was no
question of his being officially invited to Washington. With this affront
the incident passed, but it left an afterglow which threw an uncomfortable
and deceptive light on Adam. For among letters of introduction Adam
carried one from Schacht to Leon Fraser.[45] At no time had he made a
secret of his admiration for the great financier, and his purpose in visiting
the United States was on examination identical with that of Schacht. Inevitably an idea grew up that Adam was in the United States as Schacht's
representative, and by those who were not careful to consult the dates,
Adam was seen as a second choice of envoy after the rebuff to the former
miracle-worker of the Reichsbank.[46]

[42]A first-hand account. [43]Dr Felix Morley. Discussion.
[44]Wheeler-Bennett describes the incident, relying largely on Cordell Hull's
memoirs.
[45]C.T. [46]Wheeler-Bennett.

It was probably due to this exaggerated notion of Adam's genuine association with Schacht, that when a copy of the memorandum was given by Mr Wheeler-Bennett to the British Embassy and from there conveyed to the Canadian Government, its proposals 'were regarded with profound suspicion' in both places.[47] Hopes of meeting President Roosevelt vanished.

Adam did visit the White House, however, but on second-best terms which brought no compensation. Through Roger Baldwin he had met one of Mrs Roosevelt's closest women-friends. She told Mrs Roosevelt about Adam, whom she admired, and this resulted in an invitation to bring him to see her one afternoon. On the day in question Adam found himself ushered into a reception room to be greeted by the First Lady surrounded by a large gathering of women whom she was entertaining to tea. He was by no means put at his ease when she greeted him by loudly proclaiming to the company, 'Why now this is Mr von Trott who is going to tell us all about Mr Hitler.'[48] It is not recorded, unhappily, how the situation developed from that point.

Adam seems to have realised, possibly from the advice of one of his American friends, though evidence is lacking, that the growing mistrust around him came from a belief not only that he was a loyal servant of the Nazi Government, but that he was seeking to revive the policy of appeasement, which now, if it was to be effective, had to include the acceptance of Hitler's gains in Poland, and the prolonging of the life of the 'thousand-year Reich' by allowing Hitler to escape the consequences of unleashing a second World War. At all events, though the contents of the memorandum had so strong an appeasement-character, Adam decided to make it

[47]Wheeler-Bennett Op. cit. p. 487. Sir John Wheeler-Bennett has told the writer that he saw Trott, whom he had first known as an undergraduate, frequently in Washington. He was never tempted to believe stories of Trott's conversion to Nazism and respected his honourable intentions. Nevertheless he looked with increasing misgiving on Trott's political ideas which seemed to him quite out of touch with events. Trott, at this time, frequently expressed admiration of Neville Chamberlain and deplored the influence of Winston Churchill. This leads Sir John to believe that Felix Frankfurter correctly reported the conversation to Sir Isaiah Berlin, though this does not mean that he reported the whole. Discussion.

[48]A contemporary document shown to the writer by Dr Clarita von Trott.

clear that he was not now advocating a policy of further concession. This is brought out by Messersmith's record of his conversation with him.

The two of them met at last on the 20th November. Here is Messersmith's account which he addressed to Mr Cordell Hull on the same day.

'When Dr Brüning was my house guest recently, he spoke to me about Adam von Trott and said that he was convinced that Trott was an honest man and really represented responsible, potentially powerful, conservative opinion in Germany . . . which would have to be depended upon to form eventually a respectable and responsible Government in Germany. He suggested that he thought it would be useful if I would see von Trott while he was here. I told him I would be glad to do so, but I did not give expression to Dr Brüning of the doubts which I myself had concerning him.

'Justice Frankfurter spoke to me some time ago with regard to Trott whom he has known in the past. He was highly suspicious of von Trott, and I gathered that his suspicion was based on information which he may have received from some of his friends in England. My own attitude was inclined to be one of scepticism, as I think experience has taught us how difficult it is to determine whether these people, pretending to speak for conservative elements in Germany, are really doing so, or whether they are acting for the present German Government.

'Mr von Trott came to see me this morning, and the impression he made on me was on the whole good, and I am now inclined to believe that he is an honest man and does represent the thought of certain responsible elements in Germany. I referred to the memorandum which he had furnished to Mr Stone . . . Mr von Trott said that while the memorandum represented on the whole his views, he was not so sure that the time had come for a statement of the Allied peace terms or conditions. He was not so sure that this would serve a useful purpose at this time. This was not an idea that he was pressing himself, for the most dangerous thing, he said, which could happen was a premature settlement which would leave the present Government, or something similar to it in power in Germany. Such a solution would be as much a catastrophe for Germany as it would for the rest of the world. It was the last solution which those whose thoughts he represented in Germany would wish . . . He was all the more concerned about this because there was still a very powerful group in England which he felt could not be altogether trusted and which might

be prepared to make peace on terms which would be disastrous all round
—as much for Germany as for the rest of the world.

'I was frankly astonished to hear Mr von Trott make this point with the
emphasis he used, as I had been under the impression that he was pressing
just the other way—that is, using his influence here among certain people
in order to encourage the movement towards forcing the Allies to a statement of peace terms now. It was my understanding that it was Mr von
Trott who had been responsible for Mr Lippmann's article some weeks
ago which was so surprising. Perhaps Mr von Trott's own views have
undergone some change in recent weeks.'

On 10th October Mr Walter Lippmann had contributed an article to
the *New York Herald Tribune* under the title *The Third Alternative*, in
which he cogently argued the possibilities of 'a decent peace' and the need
for an immediate declaration of war aims to help the process on. Mr
Lippmann had met Adam in Washington before the article appeared, but
has since most emphatically denied that he wrote under Adam's influence.[49]
The article and the memorandum are similar in purpose and to some
degree in content, but it must be remembered that in the 'spiritual
stocktaking' mood of late 1939 the ideas in both were very typical of the
time, however surprising to Mr Messersmith.

It cannot be said that Adam made deft political use of his opportunity
with Messersmith. He did not specify whom he referred to as an untrustworthy 'very powerful group in England,' and it is not possible to obtain
precise knowledge now, but to raise the matter at all was a digression.
Adam clearly did not appreciate how important it is on such an occasion
to stick rigorously to the subject in hand, and the subject was not
lingering British Naziphilism.

To return to the interview, Adam in a manner typical of his impetu-
ousness showed some further inconsistency. Having 'astonished' Messersmith by an apparent volte-face from the attitude shown in the memorandum, he proceeded to astonish him yet more by coming nearly if not

[49]Rothfels 1. In 1965, when the writer met Mr Lippmann in Washington, the
famous columnist said that he met and admired Trott in 1939 but questioned his
political ability. He added that he had been told later that Trott was a Nazi agent.
'I suppose that is all rubbish,' he said, indicating that suspicion lingered, though
not with him.

quite full-circle. Messersmith's paragraph following the one last quoted shows Adam expressing views in contradiction to what he had said a moment before. He also added to the idea (of course quite unconscious of its danger) that he was Schacht's representative.

'Mr von Trott said that it would be extremely important, sometime before the spring of next year at the latest, for the conservative elements in Germany to have some idea of a definite character as to what the Allied peace objectives and terms were. The uncertainty in which they were was making it more difficult for them. I remarked that there was information that some of the industrialists and financiers in Germany who had been opposed to the regime and its objectives were now getting behind it on the basis that it was a complete disintegration of Germany which was the Allies' objective. Mr von Trott said that he doubted whether the views of the industrialists and financiers had changed to that degree, because it was their thoughts that he represented, but one had to keep in mind that there was that possibility growing out of their uncertainty, and that such a change, of course, would be unfortunate.'

Adam then proposed the compromise with which to reconcile the apparent contradiction.

'He realised,' Messersmith's report continues, 'more than ever the difficulty in the Allied peace terms being formulated and stated at this time, and the danger which lay therein. He was wondering, however, in what way some information could be conveyed to the conservative elements in Germany as to what the Allied objectives were, in order to give that movement the strength and support which it needed.'

Although Messersmith had not, by his own account, made up his mind about Adam, he allowed him to suppose he had made a good impression. He asked him to let him know when he returned to Washington from the imminent I.P.R. meeting. He listened sympathetically to his complaints about being shadowed by Nazi or F.B.I. agents. But of the recent 'fire and flame' there was now no sign, and Adam's new, complicated, inconsistent approach to his own memorandum was not likely to revive it again.

The meeting of the I.P.R. took place from Wednesday the 22nd of November to Sunday the 3rd of December when the conference dispersed.

The sessions were held in the Cavalier Hotel in Virginia Beach. On the instructions of Lord Lothian who remained intrigued by Adam's mission, and hopeful of its meaning, Mr Wheeler-Bennett obtained an invitation to attend the sessions and accompanied Adam southwards. Adam attended the conference as a member of the 'International Secretariat' of the I.P.R.[50]

Adam's performance at Virginia Beach was admired by everyone who has left a record of it. Yet in spite of remarkable success in challenging circumstances, and of capturing much sympathy, he was still unable to allay suspicion. An American diplomat, Mr Robert W. Barnett, has left this account of his memories of the meeting:

'Inasmuch as Germany was not a member of the International Committee of the Institute for Pacific Relations, Adam's presence at the conference immediately prompted considerable speculation. Mr Carter had a penchant for drama and was deeply devoted to the principle of public controversy, freely expressed among people of the most widely differing prejudices and viewpoints. There was no Japanese representative at this conference; I recall that Mr Carter assigned one very able American scholar to represent as best he could the Japanese position in the Pacific area. We all assumed, therefore, that Adam had been invited to present ideas and adopt positions which would balance the preponderantly Anglo-American attitudes towards Pacific area problems, and towards the European conflict as it had a bearing on the Far East. In a sense, therefore, he was a spokesman for the "enemy" because, although the United States was still neutral, the Americans, as well as others at the conference, were overwhelmingly pro-English and anti-Axis. Adam was also regarded, of course, as a valid specialist on the Far East, on the strength of his period of study in Peking.

'I remember very well the impact upon the gathering of his physical presence—tall, suave, considerate, fluent in several languages, quick to make friends, a good listener, and a comfortable, relaxed conversationalist himself. He made no obvious effort to seek the public eye, but he was never without companionship socially, and he never failed to capture the full attention of the conference when he spoke out in public discussion.

[50]Official record of the meeting.

'The reputation of the Nazi espionage system was such that all of us felt certain that nothing he said privately or publicly would fail to get back to Berlin. This may or may not have been the case, but we assumed that it was, and tried to assess, as best we could, what purpose he was attempting to achieve for Berlin by being at the conference. As time passed, several themes began to emerge from his contributions to discussion. He kept insisting that Germany was a society belonging to the Western community. He kept warning against the disastrous consequences for the West of a spread of Communist influence. He pled for understanding by the United States and Great Britain of a common need to save civilisation from dominance by forces of brutality, and he tried to relate the crisis in Europe to conflict in the Far East between Japanese militarism, China, and all the factors of change and stability to be seen there. If all of this sounds somewhat abstract, that corresponds with the general impression he produced. It was hard, if not impossible, to actually pin down where he stood. At the same time, his fairly frequent interventions were anything but dull, but rather, with intimations of mature insight into the operation of world-power, open-minded, undertaken with a pleasant combination of modesty and self-confidence. His rôle at the conference was, perhaps, the most interesting and impressive of any played by its participants.

'. . . After conclusion of the conference, a good many of its participants tried to construe Adam's purpose to have been to help to soften the will of the Allies, and thus make easier Germany's strike through to the Channel. Others construed his purpose to pave the way for a quick settlement between Germany and the Allies leading towards a joint assault upon the U.S.S.R. Some considered Adam to be a most ingeniously successful emissary of Ribbentrop, while others feared for his safety once he returned to the German Foreign Office in Berlin. There were very few who did not form a high opinion of his intelligence and subtlety.'[51]

Even the faithful Carter was just a little shaken by the immensity of

[51]Letter from Mr Barnett to Dr Clarita von Trott zu Solz of 5.1.59. The accuracy of this description has been entirely confirmed for the writer by an independent discussion with Professor Lockwood who was also present at the meeting, and by the brief synopsis in the official record of the principal speech by 'A German member.' This is given in an appendix to this chapter.

the distrust around his friend, and in this he may have been influenced by his colleague Whitney Shephardson who had taken a violent dislike to Adam.[52] That Carter had grown a little uneasy is shown by Messersmith's record of a meeting with him a few days after the I.P.R. conference had dispersed.

'Mr Carter called to see me on December 7th to say that he was glad that I had seen Mr von Trott. He said that Mr von Trott was active as his "German associate." He asked me to what degree I thought confidence could be put in von Trott. I told him that von Trott might be an honest man, and probably was, but no man coming out of Germany these days was altogether a free agent. Mr Carter said he was conscious of all this and asked, if I had at any time information that von Trott was not trustworthy, to let him know.'[53]

Adam had a second meeting with Messersmith on the 8th of December. From Messersmith's brief memorandum on the meeting it is clear that, while maintaining his reservations, his final judgment on Adam was favourable. 'My net impression,' he wrote, 'at this time is that Mr von Trott is an honest man who is in touch with the conservative elements in Germany, not in sympathy with the present Government, and who would like to see a change of Government. I am, however, of opinion, that he is not an entirely free agent, as no person who is permitted to leave Germany and to return, as is true in the case of Mr von Trott, can be entirely a free agent.'[54]

Mr Messersmith proved his favourable opinion by writing to the American Chargé d'Affaires in Berlin, Mr Alexander Kirk, telling him that Adam would visit him. He wrote: 'I am inclined to think he is an honest man who is deeply concerned over the future of his country.'[55] It was a kind note, but not an enthusiastic one.

Soon after Adam's second meeting with Messersmith on the 8th he went back to New York where he appears to have remained till he left for the west coast. Some time during mid-December he attended a dinner of the Yale Club, arranged by Edward Carter, the plan being that he should address them on his political ideas. This was another act of quite extra-

[52]Mr Shepardson. Discussion. [53]Rothfels 1.   [54]Rothfels 1. [55]Rothfels 1.

ordinary boldness on Adam's part. About thirty guests were invited, which meant that thirty people had to observe complete secrecy as to what was said, if Adam was not to be placed in the utmost peril![56]

For several weeks two F.B.I. agents, by now easily recognised by Adam, had followed him round Washington, Virginia Beach, and New York. This Yale Club dinner seems to have made no difference to their instructions and the two men continued their wearisome shadowing duties.

Conscious that the memorandum had failed, Adam thought hard about how he could recover lost ground, and presently he hit on an expedient. His cousin by marriage, Charles Bosanquet, happened to be in America at the time and was due to return to England. He agreed to take a memorandum from Adam to Lord Halifax. The subject was the same as that of the previous memorandum, though simplified, and set out with reference to Great Britain alone.

The memorandum was put in a sealed envelope, and taken to England by Mr Bosanquet who delivered it to Ivone Kirkpatrick at the Foreign Office. Its further fate is not known.[57]

After his return to New York Adam again found consolation in his loving friendship with Julie Braun-Vogelstein. 'The hours he chose for his visits,' she has related in a memoir, 'may well have aroused suspicion of a political conspiracy in our apartment. His days were crowded, and he often phoned about midnight: "May I come to see you now?" Loving him as a son, I always answered: "Naturally. You are welcome at any time." These meetings were always well worth waking up for, much more satisfactory than the breathing-spells he occasionally found during the day. Of his activities he never told me any details. "You must not be involved in such a game." he reiterated. "It is a most precarious game." Instead of reporting his talks with other people or divulging his plans, he spoke to me about his inner conflicts and dilemmas, about the reorientation essential to a world so hollowed and undermined. It pained him that Werner, his elder brother and mentor in former years, strongly disapproved of his "too secular" aims, thus depriving Adam of a much needed partner and challenging friend. Furthermore, since Hegel was no

[56]An account of the meeting. *New York Herald*. October 1945.
[57]Vierteljahrshefte für Zeitgeschichte Heft 3/64, 'Trott und die Aussenpolitik des Widerstandes' referred to subsequently as Rothfels 2.

longer his intellectual guide, Adam, having adhered for so long to such
a comprehensive system of thought, now doubted the validity of any
philosophical system. This meant he had to steer a course through the
dark in a raging gale, without a chart or compass save his own conscience
and his belief in God. "I am completely alone," he said. "I share parts of
myself and fragments of things with others—there is no one on whom I
can call . . . and my immediate return is imperative. Despite all my efforts,
my main purpose over here has been thwarted."

'Those were his words; they cut me to the heart and are still ringing in
my ears. As he shuddered at the memory of the hideous crimes the Nazis
had already committed, I implored him: "Stay here, and represent another Germany." "I must return," was his immediate answer, "to help
to make Germany a place that can be represented." He sprang from his
chair and striding across the room he broke out indignantly: "You talk
just like my English friends whose letters warn me against returning to
Germany . . . You would be the first to urge my return were you not
ignorant of what is at stake. Every minute I delay I become an accomplice
in an unspeakable horror. I know what I am talking about, and that I
must be back before March. I must."

'There was a tone in his voice, a fierce flash in his eyes which forbade
further discussion. The words quoted here may give an impression of
arrogance, but his presence ruled out any such assumption.'[58]

Julie Braun-Vogelstein often wondered afterwards to what he was
referring when he spoke of 'an unspeakable horror,' and has never found
the answer. She thought at one time that he may have had some fore-
knowledge of the Nazi genocide policies, 'the Final Solution,' but this
is most unlikely. The probable explanation does not rule out concern
with genocide, however. By December 1939 the Nazis had done such
deeds of cruelty in Poland, in a methodical attempt to destroy a whole
nation, that if they had committed no other crime against humanity
they would have blackened the German name for a generation. It may
well have been such knowledge and such thoughts and the certainty
that more such horrors were to follow, that gave Adam his impatience
to return to conspire against the regime. All the stranger, if so, his continuing faith in the German military commanders who had lent themselves

[58]Memo B.V.

to Hitler's designs. It was a strange delusion, whatever the explanation, shared by many people in the world then.

Adam's remarks about his English friends and their warning letters refer to correspondence which had been going forward almost since his arrival. Before sailing Adam had written to David Astor telling him of his journey and also of the likelihood of his being 'snatched off the boat by either your or the French marines.' This letter he posted in Genoa. He wrote to David again soon after arrival in New York. Three letters came back in answer, two in October, one in mid-November. Adam had also written to Diana on the 11th of October. The news of his presence in America spread to his friends in England, and they were astonished and overjoyed, hoping that this meant that he had at last taken the step of emigrating. Several of them, including Lady Cripps and Geoffrey Wilson, wrote to him during November, urging or implying their hope that he would not return. Another of these friends was Wilfrid Israel, and his plea was among the most eloquent and, since he knew Germany as his country, the most likely to have influenced his friend. 'How grateful I am,' he wrote, 'to know that you are in the U.S.A. I pray to God you will be prompted to stay there . . . Had you left the country long before the war, I might waver, but the situation you have created for yourself, consciously and unconsciously, is a *definite* one. You are an Ambassador of all those within who are of good will, and at the present moment they by all means need a permanent intermediary and interpreter of their attitude and motives. We have both felt the burden of our time too ardently. All suspicion that I am only thinking and expressing myself as a friend must be excluded.'[59]

The most interesting letters to have survived from this dramatic correspondence are those between Adam and David Astor. In the latter's first reply he told how he had joined a group whose purpose was to 'study the desired shape of things to come in Europe.' The members included Lord Astor, Lionel Curtis, Sir Arthur Salter and Warden Adams. They would like, he told him, to have Adam as one of their number. His second reply, written a week later on the 27th of October, urged Adam in stronger terms not to return to Germany, especially after having met Lord Lothian, and he repeated the invitation from himself, Lord Astor

[59]Letters C.T.

and Tom Jones to join their 'peace-planning committee.' He indicated the subjects of their discussion: whether Germany should return to a federal rather than a centralised polity; what should be the future of such valuable and misused organisations as the Arbeitsfront; what should be the future settlement of Central Europe and Poland; the attitude of Germany and the West to Russia, and how to achieve a united anti-Nazi front. The third letter, written on the 10th of November, is mainly concerned with personalities.

For some reason Adam did not answer till the 26th of December. He then wrote a long letter, running to over 3,000 words, in which he set forth his ideas. David had told Adam that his hope was for no decisive victory, but a compromise peace after the fall of Hitler and before the outbreak of full scale war, but that his anticipation was a long struggle and the fall of Hitler as a consequence of German internal exhaustion, after which Europe would have to rebuild slowly from the ruins. Adam touched on these opinions in the course of rejecting David's appeal for him to remain outside Germany. He wrote: 'If a real exchange of ideas on the basis of actual conditions and possibilities, and a real growth of a common and workable aim for the whole of Europe and the contingent parts of the world can develop out of this, all the better. I shall do my best to keep this hope alive inside Germany, but I do not entirely disagree with your prediction of the probable course of events, which will force us to start again from humble beginnings, less inspired by advanced liberal formulas than by economic problems, arising from a shattered or at any rate infinitely dislocated society.'

He gives further and more personal reasons for returning to Germany. 'You never gave any importance,' he wrote, 'to the fact that during this summer I seemed to develop the ill-deserved reputation of an "appeaser" in certain quarters in England. They have, apparently, proceeded to warn some Americans against me . . . by way of establishing me in the minds of some of those worthies as undoubtedly "out of another Munich".' A reference which occurs a little later is less guarded and makes it clear that he had been told of Maurice Bowra's letter to Felix Frankfurter.

The passage quoted above may strike a reader as rather odd, and perhaps as a piece of self-deception; as though Adam was trying to convince himself, as he had tried to convince Messersmith, that contrary to appearances he was no appeaser in any sense whatsoever. There may have been an element of self-deception at work here, but Adam's protest was in essence consistent with the ideals of his life. The British appeasement policy of 1938 and 1939 was open to condemnation because its ultimate aim was peace at any price, even if this meant the strengthening, perhaps the perpetuation of barbarism in the midst of Europe. The policy which Adam pursued followed similar lines, even to the extent of yielding to Hitler over the question of Danzig,[60] but its aim was to ensure the breakdown of barbaric rule in Germany, moreover in such a way that its revival would be psychologically frustrated. This is not to say that Adam showed political grasp and foresight in this matter. This is not to say that those who were perplexed and made suspicious by the over-elaborate subtlety of his political dialectic were to be blamed; but it is to say that those who saw him as a man eager to take advantage of the appeasement line of policy, regardless of whether this was to the advantage of Nazism or not, gravely wronged his character.

He enclosed a copy of the Trott-Scheffer memorandum, and another written by Mr Wheeler-Bennett. Its subject is the same as that of the memorandum conveyed from Adam to Lord Halifax by Charles Bosanquet, but far better expressed because written with experience of Whitehall and of what impresses British Governmental departments. It concentrates on one point, that the war had but one aim: to restore 'the rule of law and the quality of mercy in dealings between man and man, and in the great Society of civilised states,' a quotation from one of Lord Halifax's recent speeches. From that the memorandum draws a conclusion that 'in a sense the present struggle is a war for the liberation of the German People.' With forcible logic, and illustrating the theme with concrete proposals, Mr Wheeler-Bennett moves the argument to the vital need of a German 'reign of law,' of a Rechtsstaat, as a necessary and major war-aim.[61] 'He understands,' wrote Adam to David Astor, 'as you will soon discover, one essential rôle of Germany probably better than anyone in your country at the moment . . . He should be very carefully listened to.' He urges that he should meet 'your uncle Edward' by which not over-baffling evasion they used to indicate Lord Halifax.

[60]He stated this in the letter to David Astor of 25.8.39 and to Felix Morley. (Diary.)
[61]The memorandum, from a carbon copy which Trott left with Miss Braun-Vogelstein, is reproduced in Rothfels 2.

*With his wife and their
daughter in* 1942

At Imshausen, Whitsuntide 1944, with mother, wife, two children, his brother Werner with wife and two children, his sister Ursula, Freifrau von Arnim with her daughter and in air force uniform her husband Harald von Arnim

In the People's Court

Immediately after hearing the death sentence

The memorandum was received and handed over, and, as with its predecessor, no more is known about it.

As the time for his return drew near, he received yet another appeal to remain. Sir Stafford Cripps sent a message to Reinhold Niebuhr asking him to tell Adam not to return to Germany on any account as his life was in danger.[62] His precise meaning remains doubtful. It is likely that Cripps sent the message because he had heard of Adam's meeting with Lord Lothian. Adam was moved, but he remained firm and stuck to his decision.

His reasons for returning have already appeared clearly: his belief that émigrés could do little if anything for their country, and least of all in such a case as his, after attempting political action and failing. But there was another more personal reason for returning which he never mentioned. If he had remained, as surely he must have been tempted to do, then re- tribution for an act of treason would have fallen heavily and perhaps even fatally on those who had facilitated the journey, on Weizsäcker, Kessel and Hewel. The situation caused by Adam's remaining would have been especially dangerous for Weizsäcker and Kessel whose dislike of the regime was known.[63] It might also have been dangerous for his family.

On his last night in New York Adam again visited Julie Braun-Vogel- stein. She has told how at this last meeting he seemed to take her into his inmost confidence as never before and let her share his secret plans and hopes 'without their being once mentioned.' One can be reminded of how A. L. Rowse had found his gift of sympathy uncanny in its acuteness. 'In view of our approaching separation,' records Julie Braun-Vogelstein, 'he was calm and collected. We spoke little. Suddenly he gave me a look such as I had never seen on his face before. He kept silence while still looking at me with concentration. So we remained until he asked me in a voice full of anguish, "No matter what you hear about me, will you always believe in me?" His gaze remained fastened on me. I answered him with all frankness: "It may happen that I shall not approve of what you do, but I will always trust the purity of your reasons for acting and of your intentions." He looked serene and seized my hand in a firm grip. So we parted. The next morning he rang me up from the airport: "Leben

[62]Dr Reinhold Niebuhr. Discussion. [63]Herr von Kessel. Discussion.

Sie wohl, auf Wiedersehen—nachher!" "Afterwards!" Here was a bless-
ing to cheer me on the way ahead. Then grief overwhelmed me. This was
goodbye for ever—I knew it.'[64]

Before leaving he received an affectionate farewell letter from Mr
Wheeler-Bennett.

'First let me wish you, in every sense, the greatest of good fortune in
the aim which we have in common. May it be achieved sooner than we
hope, but, in any case, eventually!

'Then I would like to say how much I admire your courage and determination under very trying circumstances. I hope that under similar conditions I could match you in them, but I am pretty sure I couldn't.'[65]

He flew from New York to California in the second week of January
1940. He was met at the airport of San Francisco by Fritz Caspari. His
friend noticed how weary and depressed he looked. Among his very
first words Caspari remembered him saying, 'My mission has been a complete failure and it is my fault. I made an appalling blunder when I went
to see Felix Frankfurter in Washington.' He then told him how he had
tactlessly urged that Jews should not take much part in propaganda from
America to Germany.[66]

From San Francisco the two of them drove to Taft and there Adam
met the friend of his youth for the last time. The meeting was calm and
the long affection between them was serenely affirmed.

On their drive back to San Francisco some days later Adam found that
Fritz Caspari's car, in which they were travelling with Adam at the wheel,
was being followed. Unwisely and understandably Adam decided that
the time had come to have some sport at the expense of the F.B.I. He
asked his friend to give him the details of the car: its make, number etc.
This he did, showing surprise at the request, and Adam then told him of
how he had been followed by agents since his first days in New York. In
his indignation he even suggested to Caspari that the F.B.I. was in some
sort of league with the Nazi party. And now as they drove he played his
practical joke. It was dark; he lowered his lights and darted down a small
side road where they waited. Sure enough the shadowing agents came
along after and passed them. The two friends waited. Soon, as expected,
the F.B.I. party came back, to be stopped on the road by Adam with a

[64]B.V. Memo .J.B.V.　　[65]Letters C.T.　　[66]Herr Caspari. Discussion.

torch. To their bewilderment he gave them the details of the car, told them the address to which he was going in San Francisco, and recommended that they should drive on ahead of him if they found his speed not to their taste, while Caspari fought wildly to suppress his giggles in the background. The F.B.I. vanished into the gloom and the two friends went on their way, followed in due course.[67]

Edward Carter had given Adam a letter of introduction to Professor Karl Brandt. A former civil servant of high distinction, Karl Brandt had a fearless honesty and a contempt of party politics which had made him equally unwelcome to the regimes of Papen and Hitler. Circumstances forced him to become one of the earliest exiles from Nazi Germany to the United States. He was then (as now) working in Stanford University, near San Francisco. It so happened that Walter Hewel was Karl Brandt's brother-in-law.

One of Brandt's colleagues in the University, the well-known Alsatian chemist Dr Carl Alsberg, had attended the I.P.R. meeting with his secretary, an Englishwoman called Mrs Young. Alsberg had been given Government employment and did not return to Stanford, but Mrs Young did and in time she went to work for Karl Brandt. He asked her about the proceedings at Virginia Beach, and she told him that a feature of particular interest had been that 'there was a German spy there,' and she went on to say that this was not mere rumour, as the F.B.I. had particularly warned Alsberg that he was a dangerous man. A day or two after this she showed Adam into Brandt's study. While Brandt was reading Carter's letter, Mrs Young took up post behind Adam and before leaving the room strenuously gestured to her chief that here was the spy in person.

After a few minutes' conversation Karl Brandt felt quite certain that a mistake had been made and that this man was no Nazi agent. They had a long conversation at the end of which he asked the other to come home with him to dinner. After dinner they had another long talk, now in complete freedom and mutual trust, and Adam told him about his beliefs and purposes. Karl Brandt was in strong disagreement.

They spoke about American neutrality and Brandt found Adam expressing views that seemed to him to show the influence of Paul Scheffer. With the latter he had argued for over a year, so he recorded, that Amer-

[67]Herr Caspari. Discussion.

ica was bound to come into the war as the enemy of Germany, sooner or later, and Scheffer had insisted obstinately that America would remain isolationist and never take an active part.[68] To Adam Karl Brandt repeated the arguments that he had used, adding that when America did come into the war she would do so with a terrifying thoroughness giving no quarter to the Germany which had disturbed the peace of the world and repudiated the moral standards on which Christian civilisation relied.

Adam then told Karl Brandt his belief that Germany was on the verge of a decisive anti-Nazi revolution. 'He sought to reassure me,' Brandt wrote later, 'that countless numbers were in movement to prevent the continuation of the war. This made me so wild that I was driven to say: "If you and Fritsch (sic) and all your friends (about whose activity I knew a good deal from Arnold Brecht, von Borsig, and several other friends); if these people had wanted to prevent the catastrophe, then something would have happened before the invasion of Poland. Now it is too late. I know too much about them and about what goes on here. The United States are already in the war and will annihilate Germany. You and your friends are such procrastinators (cunctatores) that the greatest Antichrist and the greatest criminal of all time will before very long get hold of you and all your friends—some of whom are my best friends too —and he will hang you"!'

In his anger Karl Brandt raised his voice and was now shouting. He and Adam were in the library and Frau Brandt called to her husband from outside. He went to her and she remonstrated with him. 'You cannot treat a guest in our house in such a way. You must apologise', she said. Karl Brandt returned to the library and told Adam that he was sorry if he had appeared to lose his temper. 'But I said also,' he wrote of the scene, 'that the events which had taken place since my hurried departure from the "thousand-year Reich" on the 4th of September, 1933, had oppressed my thoughts in exile, by day and by night, and it seemed to me that this was a time for a candid exchange of ideas and not for courtesies.'

Adam did not attempt to answer Karl Brandt's arguments, but said, 'You will see. You will find that you take your pessimism much too far. Things are going to happen which will deliver us from the worst. Have

[68]Dr Margaret Boveri has questioned the accuracy of this account of Scheffer's views, but Professor Brandt reasserted this impression to the writer in 1965.

patience.' This roused Brandt to urge on him again the necessity for immediate action. He reminded him again of the terrible retribution awaiting Germany if the war persisted until America joined in. 'The Puritan character is still alive here,' he said, 'and once the United States is roused to war, you will see it in all its harshness and fury. In such moments they judge men as the children of light or the children of darkness, with no half shades. They will be merciless to Germany unless you act now.'

Next day Adam sent a message from his hotel saying, 'Thank you for dinner. I now disappear from the scene. Please say nothing about our talk.' He sailed that day for Japan, travelling by way of Honolulu where his F.B.I. shadows left him at last.[69]

Karl Brandt has told how in later years he often looked with grief at the chair on which Adam sat during that evening in January 1940. He would remember with pain how he had told his young guest 'he will hang you.'[70]

Brandt's sorrowful recollections are of a kind with the feelings which overtook Maurice Bowra when he heard of Adam's end. He says in his book of memories: 'My main reason for suspicion was quite unfounded. Von Trott was not only against Hitler, but after the failure of the plot of 20th July, 1944, he was arrested and hung with a horrifying brutality on a wire cord. When I heard of this, I saw how mistaken I had been, and my rejection of him remains one of my bitterest regrets.'

Adam may be said to have made one more appearance in America. After he left in January an article, about 1,250 words in length, appeared in a magazine published under the auspices of the I.P.R. The magazine was called *Amerasia* and Adam's article entitled *Euramerasia*. It was another plea for American neutrality, following familiar lines. If the United States became involved in the European war, it was argued, then they would have to reach an agreement favourable to Japan, and would in any case be too weakened by distant commitments to be able to play a

[69]C.T.
[70]This account of Trott's meeting with Professor Brandt follows a letter written by him to Dr Margaret Boveri in June 1964 and a discussion with the writer in May 1965 at Stanford University where he gave a somewhat fuller account. The reference to Fritsch in the letter to Dr Boveri is a slip for Brauchitsch who succeeded Fritsch as Commander-in-Chief in February 1938. The anti-Nazi party in the army had hopes of Brauchitsch which were regularly disappointed.

decisive rôle in the Far East. This would give the U.S.S.R. its opportunity to dominate China. The article concludes: 'Beyond neutrality, however, America's position suggests that she should use her natural leadership and responsibility in devising sounder solutions of the conflict between order and revolution than war.' This was what he went to America to say, and here he expressed it in a nutshell.

The last letter he wrote while he still had freedom to make contact (always at risk) with his English friends, was to Diana. He posted it at Hawaii.[71] His ship reached Japan without incident. He stayed there for a few days only, and some time in February travelled once more to China and Peking. Once more he stayed with Gustav Ecke in the little house where the ominous snake had appeared. His former companion in travel, Helmuth Wilhelm,was also there. He noted how happy and relieved his friend was to be in China again, but in the course of much talk together Adam confessed to him that he felt disturbed in mind by the moral problem which he could not escape. As an anti-Nazi where did his duty lie at a time when his country was at war? His experiences in America had not given him the answer.[72]

At the end of February Adam left Peking for the trans-Siberian journey to Moscow and home to Germany. Unhappily there is no record of his impressions, the reason being that he did this exacting winter journey in a state of ill-health. He caught cold in Peking and by the time he reached Moscow he was suffering from a bad attack of influenza. He travelled on to Königsberg by which time he had developed jaundice. He was too ill to go farther and some good friends, of the name of Selle, looked after him.

Contacts were planned between Adam's friends in America and himself, to be maintained after his return to Germany. These could never be put to effective use, and so far as is known Adam never knew what were the ultimate consequences of his mission. For that reason it is convenient to consider the sequel here.

The suspicions of the F.B.I. continued and, as said already, to an extraordinary extent they inform American opinion about Adam to this day,

[71]D.H. [72]Professor Wilhelm. Discussion.

nearly thirty years after. He had taken on a task which might have proved beyond the skill of the most experienced of professional diplomats, and in this endeavour, where his every move was watched with hostile anxiety, his faults loomed large in exaggerated prominence, and his rashness and inconsistency were not seen for what they were, but as the sinister marks of a man intent on a dark design. Karl Brandt had warned him justly of the unforgiving fierceness of the Puritan spirit which tends to rise suddenly to the surface when American public emotions are stirred. Adam enjoyed love affairs during this as during most periods of his life. Had he been a welcome guest to the United States these gallantries would have been regarded with an indulgent smile. In his circumstances as a supposed creature of the Nazi regime, they provoked further belief in the turpitude of his character.[73] After his departure his reputation seems to have taken on almost legendary proportions, and it is hardly an exaggeration to say that he became the centre of a mass delusion.

This mountainous disapproval weighed heavily on his German friends in December 1941 when on the 11th, four days after the Japanese attack on Pearl Harbour, Hitler declared war on the United States. The F.B.I. were ready for such a moment and they acted swiftly. They believed that in one operation they could reduce to impotence the whole German espionage system in their country. All Adam's German friends in America were visited by the police, and, with few exceptions, interned or condemned to live under rigid supervision. Paul Scheffer found himself in an alarming situation. To appearances he was fortunate. The American authorities believed that in spite of his association with Adam he would, as a journalist, be more profitably exchanged for an American correspondent in Germany, so he was chosen for repatriation. Scheffer was quite certain that his anti-Nazi activities were by this time known in Germany, and that to return was death. He asked for political asylum. It was refused. While interned, awaiting repatriation, he contrived to fall down a high and steep stairway. He broke his hip and so was enabled to remain at the price of a grave permanent injury.

Fritz Caspari was interned and frequently examined by the F.B.I. His case was typical of many. He might have cleared his own and Adam's name if he had spoken freely and told the whole truth, but he rightly

[73]Mr Roger Baldwin. Discussion.

believed that he could not do this. He feared that anything he might say might find its way into the Press, and so ultimately back to Germany with frightful consequences for Adam.[74] As a natural result of such reticence the suspicions multiplied, so much so that even so improbable a subject for suspicion as Julie Braun-Vogelstein was kept under specially rigorous surveillance and obliged to report to the police at frequent intervals. Many such stories could be told.

No counter-move in favour of Adam, or of exonerating his friends, came from the State Department or from the British Embassy. Between December 1939 and the end of 1941 Adam's reputation in America had grown black. Messersmith's cold note to the American Chargé d'Affaires in Berlin was answered by an equally cold note from Mr Kirk: 'I shall be glad to see him when he reaches Berlin. We occasionally meet persons of his persuasion and have already indicated to the Department the kind of view they are prone to express.'[75] Though people in the state service might pity his predicament, they did not go farther. It was the same in the British Embassy. If Lord Lothian had not died in December 1940, the story might have gone differently, yet his successor Lord Halifax knew Adam also and had presumably received his memorandum two years before. No move against the prevailing belief that Adam was a subtle Nazi agent is recorded on his part, or that of Mr Wheeler-Bennett whom Adam had so much admired and trusted. Hard things on that account have been said against both by Adam's friends. Two things must be remembered. By 1941 the Nazis had all Europe in thrall as a consequence of aggression upon aggression, and the internal rising against Hitler promised by Adam and 'persons of his persuasion' had not happened, and to the outside world showed no feeble sign of happening. The inevitable consequence was an exasperated and often wild reaction against Germany and Germans, not least against those Germans formerly associated with the appeasement policy. This was the time when appeasement (not only the Chamberlain kind but of anyone or anything) was held to be the root of all ills and Vansittartism was in fashion.

The second thing that must be remembered is what Adam was doing at the moment when Germany declared war on the United States. To all appearances (carefully contrived by himself) his activity was such as to

[74]Herr Caspari. Discussion.   [75]Quoted in Rothfels 2.

put him in high favour with the regime, and it would be extraordinary if this information was not known to London. It must have seemed that Adam had, like so many others, given in to Nazism and decided for the 'New Order' after all. The Lugowski story again.

There were a few people in America, however, such as Edward Carter, Felix Morley, and Roger Baldwin, who did not, because they could not, withdraw their trust, no matter how damning the evidence might appear. Another was Reinhold Niebuhr.

While the measures against Adam's friends were going forward, he made many efforts to restore a sense of perspective. In vain he appealed to Frankfurter to think again, and at length wrote to his friend Sir Stafford Cripps asking for help to undo a cruel injustice. He gave him a list of the names of people who were in trouble on Adam's account. The answer he received was very typical of Cripps. He said that he did not know and had never heard of any of the people mentioned, but that Niebuhr might use his—Cripps's—name to help them in any way he saw fit.[76]

Only after the anti-Nazi attempt of 20th July, 1944, and its terrible sequel, did the American authorities fully relent and withdraw restrictions on Adam's friends. It should be said that long before this the restrictions had in most cases become little more than formalities, but it was only after July 1944 that the victims of the delusion were able to talk candidly about Adam. It was now that Fritz Caspari was told about the 'Kontrolle' scare.[77] Julie Braun-Vogelstein asked the security officer in charge of her case why she had been under irksome surveillance for so long. He told her that though the examining magistrate had been impressed by the straightforward manner in which she had defended both herself and Adam's reputation, the authorities had all the same reached the conclusion that she was one of the most dangerous Nazi agents in America. Astonished, she asked him how so crazy an idea could have arisen, and furthermore, if this was believed, how it came about that she had ever been let out of close arrest!

The officer replied in some such words as these: 'We saw that you had a very special relationship with Adam von Trott, and we were quite convinced that he was the top man in the Nazi spy-system in this country. We believed that, unknown to you, he had used you as a screen behind

[76]Dr R. Niebuhr. Discussion. [77]Herr Caspari. Discussion.

which he conspired for the Nazis. But once he had left the U.S., so we thought, his influence weakened and you no longer carried out his plans, especially as you are a member of the Jewish people. It seemed to us that as an officer of the Nazi Foreign Ministry this man could not, as some supposed, be conspiring against his own Government.'

She answered: 'He was conspiring for his country against its evil Government,' adding: 'You do not still believe these things about Adam von Trott.'

'Oh no,' he said, 'not now.'[78]

But others did, and still do.

When all was over, Reinhold Niebuhr was moved to ask the same question as Julie Braun-Vogelstein had put to the security officer. He wrote to Cripps asking how so enormous and foolish a mistake could have been made as to suppose that Adam was the head of a Nazi spy-ring. The reply he received from his friend was again very typical. It consisted of one sentence: 'Our secret service is better than yours. Stafford.'[79]

It should be possible for a friend of Adam to forgive the F.B.I. their blunders. In 1940 they saved his life. All the evidence points to the conclusion that the sheer enormity of F.B.I. suspicion and hostility towards him lulled the official, unofficial and clandestine Nazi authorities in America into a belief that he was a faithful servant of Ribbentrop and Hitler. No information about his rash anti-Nazi activities, his addressing anti-Nazi speeches to two large audiences in New York, the anti-Nazi memorandum under his name, his discussions with Messersmith, Lothian and Wheeler-Bennett, seems to have reached Berlin.

One last scene may be remembered because it seems (in the writer's opinion) to have an ironical connection with Adam's mission. The story was told to the writer by the distinguished American journalist, Miss Kay Halle. Some time after Hitler's declaration of war against the United States, a small semi-official meeting was held in Miss Halle's house in Washington to discuss propaganda policy. There were present among others the President's son Elliot Roosevelt and Felix Frankfurter. At one point in the discussion Frankfurter intervened to say something of this kind: 'Here is a thing which the rest of you might not wish to mention, but which I can tell you without embarrassment. In all these pro-

[78]Mrs Braun-Vogelstein. Discussion. [79]Dr R. Niebuhr. Discussion.

paganda ventures you should be careful not to give too much prominence to Jewish speakers and writers, because there is a very real danger that if you do so you will encourage Germans to believe the Nazi myth which Goebbels has promulgated from the beginning, namely that this is a war promoted by Jews, and that in reality this is a conflict between Germans and Jews, not between Germany and the United States and the Allies of the United States. I have thought over this matter for some time, and discussed it, and I make the recommendation very confidently.'

APPENDIX I

Adam von Trott's address to the I.P.R. meeting of November 1939. He is not described by name in the official report but only as 'a German member.' His address is reported as follows:

'If the war in the east continues then we will find a progressive re-arrangement of the world powers, but if there is peace in the east soon then the position of the world powers in the Far East will be much the same as in the last few years. It is true that Germany has sacrificed her economic interests in China to gain the political co-operation of Japan. Germany however did not imply hostility to China in the Anti-Comintern Pact, in fact she considers the war a mistake and waste of military power in China which could be used elsewhere.

'If there is peace soon (in the east) German opinion will not favour a China dominated by Japan, because German commercial interests in China have found that they have a difficult time in Japanese-controlled areas. The partial domination of China is not a realistic concept. The predominantly German peaceful opinion would favour a free China and this includes also being free from domination by the western democracies.

'Insofar as western Imperialism is in control in China, the situation is not favourable to Germany, because German economic development is based on barter and a planned export-economy. If the eastern war continues Germany will be subjected to a siege and will be forced into an eastward policy. The western powers will be less able to assist China in the Far East and a real chance will arrive for the formation of a common bloc of interests among Germany, the Soviet Union, and China.

'The attitude of Japan towards an agreement with Russia may depend on the fact that the co-operation which Japan desires from the western powers is no longer of much value. Japan might find it useful to regain a free hand outside of China. Germany favours a peace settlement between Russia and Japan, with Japan taking over a commercial interest in China.'

APPENDIX II

In a recent book *Roosevelt and Frankfurter* (London 1968) there is an interesting reference to Adam von Trott's wartime mission to the United States. The President sent the following memorandum to Felix Frankfurter on January 17th,1940:

'For Heaven's sake! Surely you did not let your Trott friend get trotted out of the country without having him searched by Edgar Hoover. Think of the battleship plans and other secrets he may be carrying back. This is the height of indiscretion and carelessness on your part. F. D. R.'

The bantering tone of the message suggests that the warnings he had evidently received both from his friend and the F.B.I. were not taken by the President with great seriousness. It is conceivable that the paper reflects a favourable view of the Trott-Scheffer memorandum in which the President had persisted despite representations against it by Frankfurter, but this can only be a guess.

The explanatory note accompanying the memorandum in the book contains the following: 'The F.B.I. thought that Trott wanted to enlist the aid of Americans in the dangerous enterprise of overthrowing the Nazi Government, and so reported to the President in a voluminous document.'

This voluminous document would appear to be anomalous and not in keeping with the main F.B.I. recommendation on the case. Otherwise the President's memorandum, taking full account of its joking character, is obscure beyond interpretation. Jokes between old friends are often obscure, but if the elucidatory note is to be accepted it raises the question: could precisely the same obscurity be reasonably expected to appear in the public activities of the F.B.I. after the 11th December, 1941? If the explanation offered in the book is the whole truth, then the F.B.I. of that time must be credited with mental and political contortions in striking contrast to the picture of crude F.B.I. appreciation of the Trott case which emerges from the evidence available before this publication.

Without exception, Trott's friends who were interned in the United States were given to understand by their captors that they suffered this treatment because through him they had come under suspicion of being engaged in a Nazi, not an anti-Nazi conspiracy.

Chapter 13

RETURN

After Adam came back from America there occurred an interval in his life; he went through a period of inaction while slowly and painfully regaining his health. Recovery was slow and he was an invalid for the best part of four months. He remained with his friends in Königsberg till the latter part of the winter and then moved back to Berlin. He suffered a relapse and on two occasions had to go to hospital, otherwise he lived, as he had done before, as the guest of his aunt Frau von Schweinitz, and it was in her home that he took a very important step in his private life.

While in Königsberg he had written almost daily to a friend, the thought of whom, so he told his mother in a letter written at a later time, had been continually with him on this journey round the world. She was Fräulein Clarita Tiefenbacher.

In the last year of peace she and Adam had been on terms of friendship, which (to quote her own account) 'though very warm-hearted remained, owing to our different ages and circumstances, quite unexpressed,' and so she was much surprised at these attentions. When he fell ill the second time in Berlin he asked her to come and visit him. Even now she was not sure what his feelings for her were, and she remembered a thing he had once said to Fritz Schumacher, that 'men who marry are lost to politics.' By 1940 he had abandoned this grotesque belief and when she visited him in the hospital on the 14th of April, 'the decision to marry' as she has recorded, 'somehow came about when we first met again.'[1]

Five days before this, he had written to his mother telling her that he was going to ask Clarita to marry him, and Frau von Trott was disturbed

[1]C.T.

at the tone of his letter: it did not read like the outpourings of a man in love, or of one at peace with the world. She wrote to express her disquiet, and he answered her in English on the 21st of April by which time he and Clarita were engaged. 'My last letters,' he said, 'were written while I felt acutely sick and conscious of my lamentable lack of power to cope with my own and the general situation. This is deeply upsetting, though I don't tell anyone but you and C. For some weeks now I seem to be passing through a crisis of which all these sicknesses are but external outbreaks; you always look at illness this way and will not mind the exaggeration in any such view. And there is not very much more that I can say about this in a letter. One of the certainties, however, that crystallised itself more and more clearly in my troubled mind was the fact that, since I unhesitatingly decided to return to this country I now needed a wife, a home firmly rooted in the loyalties I accept, and [a wife] able to struggle with me for their continued realisation.'

The suggestion in this letter that his illness was in large part psychological is interesting. He told Clarita, and his mother in another letter, that during his journey in feeble health through Siberia, and from Moscow to Königsberg, he had suffered what he described as a 'freezing up,' a 'Vereisung.' By this he did not merely mean the low spirits that go with influenza and jaundice, but rather what theologians describe as *accidie*, and what our ancestors used to call 'the noon-day devil': a withering sense of the nullity of existence and a loss of all zest for life. He had for long been liable to the onslaught of this desolating mood in moments of loneliness and unhappiness, and it afflicted him now.

He saw another cause for his illness, one that can only be described as telepathic, though that is not how he would have described it. During the journey across China and Siberia, so he told Clarita later, he had the sensation of becoming aware, with the suddenness of shock, that during his absence something had gone wrong in Germany, with the result that the doom of the country was sealed.[2] Something had in truth gone wrong. Appalled by Hitler's decision to attack the West through an invasion of Belgium and Holland on 12th November, 1939 Generals Beck, Oster and Halder formed a conspiracy for a military coup d'état, and into this the Commander-in-Chief General von Brauchitsch was drawn, with

²C.T.

much difficulty. With the object of meeting Brauchitsch's scruples, it was agreed that the first move would be for him to try to persuade Hitler of the folly of an attack in late autumn, failing which the Commander-in-Chief would throw in his lot with the conspirators. He applied to see the Führer and was given an audience in the Chancellery on the 5th of November. Hitler, after hearing the objections to his plan, flew into one of his paroxysmal rages and roared out a scolding whose violence was infinitely too much for the tortured nerves of the ever-vacillating Brauchitsch. He abandoned the conspiracy which quickly faded out, but not before Oster, helped by Adam's friend Albrecht von Bernstorff, had warned the Dutch and Belgian legations of Hitler's intentions.[3] With the abandonment of this attempt went one of the last remaining chances of bringing the war to an end in such a way that it could be followed by a lasting peace with a Germany purged of Nazism and not shorn of greatness.

Adam's suggestion (which he never took seriously) that his illness was the consequence of telepathic communication may have been fantasy, based, perhaps, on a sudden recognition of the truth of the hard words spoken to him by Karl Brandt, or it may have been precisely what he supposed. Telepathy is an area of experience as yet unexplored by science, and one cannot know.

Recovery came to him in April. He went to Hamburg to make the acquaintance of Clarita's parents, and to make arrangements for the marriage in her home town of Reinbeck. Here there occurred a grotesque incident, not untypical of life in the Third Reich. Adam sent the necessary papers, including his birth certificate, to the registrar for publication of banns. The registrar was evidently not an erudite person and he feared to publish Adam's nomenclature in full, under the impression that the

---

[3]Wheeler-Bennett pp. 469-72 and Rothfels *The German Opposition to Hitler* (New York 1948) pp. 81-2. The Gestapo seem not to have suspected Bernstorff who was shortly after removed to a concentration camp and held there for six weeks, but as the result of a quite independent intrigue by a Gestapo official who wanted his estate. The bomb attempt on Hitler of 8 November, 1939 seems to have been a hoax contrived by the Gestapo, though it remains 'one of the unsolved mysteries of the war.' (See Wheeler-Bennett pp. 479-84.)
Gerhard Ritter in *The German Resistance* (translated by R. T. Clark London 1965) differs from Wheeler-Bennett in interpretation of these events.

name of the father of mankind indicated a person of Jewish birth. Adam only knew about this farce much later, or he would certainly have put it straight. As it was he appeared for the first and only time under the name of Friedrich von Trott zu Solz. In May he took Clarita to Imshausen for the first time. 'It became clear to me,' she has written about this occasion, 'how much he saw his marriage as something to be integrated with his Hessian traditions, when he led me to the grave of his father in the forest cemetery at the end of the old village, before bringing me to the house to meet his mother and sisters.'

It so happened that Tracy Strong was staying at Imshausen at the same time. Though somewhat inhibited from entering into anti-Nazi activity, much as this was to his taste, by the fact that his son in the Red Cross had the task of assuring the rights of prisoners of war in Germany, this old friend of the family was not prevented by scruple from furthering the plans which Adam had made quite openly with Edward Carter for maintaining contact between Germany and America through the I.P.R. The main plan was to co-ordinate the work of the I.P.R. in America with existing German groups of scholars devoted to Far Eastern research, and Tracy Strong agreed to the use of his address in Switzerland as a postal centre.[4] As mentioned in the previous chapter, little came of this ingeniously organised contact, but it can be said that it facilitated Adam's later journeys to Switzerland.

Tracy Strong was in no doubt as to the real intentions behind Adam's concern for Oriental studies. When the time came for him to leave he asked Clarita to drive with him to the railway station at Bebra. Petrol rationing meant that they did the journey by carriage, and this gave them time for a talk together. Tracy Strong told her that he was very worried about Adam, and he earnestly implored her to use all her influence with him to stop him becoming involved in 'dangerous undertakings.' He was not made for such things, he said; he was essentially too open and straightforward in character to be able to fit himself into the life of conspiracy, and if he did so nothing but harm would come of it.[5]

[4] C.T. Dr Clarita von Trott mentions letters written by Trott to Carter, Herr von Strempel of the German Embassy in Washington, and Herr Rahn of the German Diplomatic Service, organising this co-ordination.
[5] C.T.

On the 8th of June, 1940, Adam and Clarita were married in the church of Reinbeck near Hamburg. His joy at marrying a partner who was a rare friend, a comrade-in-arms, and one whom he passionately loved, was clouded on this day. The time was one of inconceivable German success: the army had occupied Belgium and Holland, forced the evacuation of the whole British Expeditionary Force from Dunkirk, and had seized the Channel ports. Inside France they were within a week of the occupation of Paris, and less than three weeks from the French surrender. Not since Napoleon had such gains been won by an army on the continent of Europe, and it is only prudish to censure the joy and pride which these events gave to Germans of every kind. In Adam, fiery patriot as he was, the German victory prompted sombre thoughts, nonetheless. The British defeat and evacuation had been completed only four days earlier. Many friends had endured that ghastly experience and already the annihilation of Great Britain by air bombardment was being promised by the Nazi propaganda services. In her account of her husband Clarita has told how the realisation of this, and of all it must mean to friends of Oxford and London who could not be there to share his joy, 'lay like a cloud even over this day and in his speech to our gathered relations, it found expression.'[6]

By this time Adam had completely recovered in health and he had been able to take up work, though in a limited capacity, some time before. After a short honeymoon he returned to his official employment which was in the new war-time department of the Auswärtige Amt known as the Informationsabteilung, to which, it will be remembered, he had been attached for the purpose of his American journey. In Berlin, in the spring, he had met an old friend of University days, Alexander Werth, and the latter had recommended him to apply for a permanent posting to this organisation which he expected to join himself later in the year when he had arranged a transfer from the army. Adam took the advice and was engaged as a Wissenschaftlicher Hilfsarbeiter, or 'Research Assistant.' The official archives show his official posting as dating from the 3rd of June, 1940.

[6]C.T.

Adam made no objection to his very low grading as an assistant. He was aware that since his 1939 journeys to England, Ribbentrop looked on him with increasing dislike and irritation. Thus the more inconspicuous his position, the better for Adam, for the time being anyway.[7] By the nature of things he could not know how much the F.B.I. had saved him from Nazi suspicion, and it seemed to him at this time that his position was perhaps more threatened than it had been since 1933. He concluded that not only did he need to avoid the limelight, but to assume a plentiful amount of protective colouring. He had already sought the latter in the report on his journey which he wrote some time in the first part of 1940. The surviving copy is not dated. It is called *Bericht über eine Kriegsreise nach Nordamerika Winter 1939/1940.*

For some reason the British and American collectors and editors of German official documents of the Second World War overlooked this paper. If they had not done so, it would probably have caused even greater commotion than Adam's famous report on his Cliveden week-end. The protective colouring is laid on thick and with even more disfigurement. He writes as a convinced Nazi anxious that German policy should avoid antagonising the United States and bringing about a state of affairs in which the powerful anti-German interest would take the leadership. The main danger to Germany is seen as the malign union of British propaganda with the Jewish press. Remembering the polemical lectures which had genuinely shocked him, he depicts British propaganda as personified at its most ruthless and hateful in the person of Mr Alfred Duff Cooper; *das amerikanische Judentum* is seen as a compound of the established American-German Jewish element and the refugees. The 'frightful will to revenge' of Jews in America is referred to as something peculiarly shocking, and it is stressed that their voice is heard in the inner counsels of the White House.

The extravagance is artfully mixed with sense, and the implied advice is sound. To summarise much detailed exposition, Roosevelt is reported as anti-German but chiefly concerned to retain his hold on the American electorate; not unwilling to lead his country into war, but anxious to play a 'beau rôle' as the representative of the deepest American passions. Adam stressed the prevailing wish of the American majority for non-

[7]C.T.

involvement, peace and neutrality, but (perhaps remembering Karl Brandt) he insisted that this disposition could change swiftly and radically. He indicated that the anti-Nazism of the Left-Wing in America had been modified or confused by the 'drawing together' of Nazi Germany and Soviet Russia, but that other influences could fully restore and intensify anti-Germanism in America, notably if Germany were to inflict an apalling humiliation on Great Britain and her Eastern Empire. 'Essentially,' he concluded, 'the German position can only be upheld in America by the course of events in Europe.' Insofar as this was a serious document, it was a cleverly guarded plea for restraint, addressed to people ignorant of that virtue or of why it was held to be one. In that respect it resembles its predecessor. The fate of the report is not recorded.

For all its manifest disguise, some people may feel tempted to ask whether this Nazi-charactered account by Adam of his adventures in America did in fact really represent something—if not the whole—of his mind. One answer to that question may be found in his heart-cry at parting with Julie Braun-Vogelstein, 'whatever you hear of me, believe in me!' A factual answer is contained in a record of him written fairly close to this time (in 1946) by one of his colleagues in the Auswärtige Amt, and whom Adam met very soon after he returned to his office in June.

His name was Franz Josef Furtwängler. He wrote two main accounts, one in a long letter written in 1946 to Ricarda Huch, another in an autobiographical book entitled *Men whom I saw and knew*. [8] Furtwängler, who was fifteen years older than Adam, was a Social Democrat of long standing who had worked from 1923 to 1933 in the central office of the

[8]Ricarda Huch (1864-1947) was one of the most distinguished German writers of her time. Her books include fiction, history and poetry. She enjoyed some vogue in the English-speaking world in the late 'twenties, but since 1931 none of her books has been translated. Throughout the Nazi period she openly disapproved of the regime. Elected to the Nazi Kulturkammer she refused to join. In the latter part of the war she collected material about German resistance to Hitler under cover of historical research, but only lived to write a fragment of an intended work on the subject. Her survival was probably largely due to sheer strength of personality and presence. Mr Harold Kurtz who knew her describes her as 'a feminine oak tree and in appearance the nearest to Cosima Wagner that Germany then possessed'.
Männer die ich sah und kannte by J. F. Furtwängler. Hamburg 1951. Referred to subsequently as *Männer*.

German Trades Union League. Through a colleague in this office, a certain Doctor Ohle, he met Count Helmuth von Moltke who was at that time forming a secret group of friends which used to meet at the Moltke country house of Kreisau with the object of establishing an all-party opposition to Nazi rule. Through a member of this circle, probably Moltke himself, Adam learned about Furtwängler and invited him to come to see him in his office. The Informationsabteilung was situated in the Kurfürstenstrasse away from the main Auswärtige Amt in the Wilhelmstrasse.

An introduction from Moltke or his friends was taken by Adam as a guarantee of good faith, and from the very first moment of their acquaintance he made no secret to Furtwängler of his sympathies and intentions. His visitor has described how Adam impressed him at this first meeting. 'There before me,' he wrote in his book, 'was an elegantly dressed young man of thirty-one, nearly two metres tall, and with clear blue eyes under thick dark brows. His forehead was so astonishingly high that I involuntarily called to mind the so-called Droeshout portrait of Shakespeare. At first sight Adam von Trott looked older than he was, but when he laughed with boyish high spirits, as he often did, then he showed how much of youthfulness there was in him. Unusual intelligence and an impressive integrity of spirit—that was the first impression.'

During this first meeting Adam was packing a large brief case. He said: 'I am just off to Paris, to-day in fact. They have arrested some Jews there whom I know. I have written all sorts of testimonials to the effect that these people have indispensable special knowledge, and this will make it possible to conscript them into Auswärtige Amt service. Then they'll be out of the hands of the Gestapo. What they do after that is anyone's guess. At all events it's better than letting the Sicherheitsdienst bump them off.'[9]

How he succeeded in this endeavour and what became of these Jewish friends in Paris later are matters which remain undocumented, like so much of what Adam did throughout the war. On the other hand his cover-plans often left evidence behind, as is in the nature of the conspiratorial life. Herr Furtwängler made this interesting point to Ricarda Huch: 'I do not believe that there was another man in the whole [opposition] activity through whose hands ran so many different threads of

[9]Letter to Frau Huch.

conspiracy. What was most remarkable about him in this connection was that he went forward with all his tireless activity in silence and without recourse to grand gestures.'[10]

Not long after this first meeting Adam persuaded Furtwängler also to be 'conscripted' into the Auswärtige Amt. Herr Furtwängler explained in his letter to Ricarda Huch how it was possible to 'conscript' such suspect beings as proscribed Jews and Social Democrats into the German foreign service. 'You must realise,' he says, 'that at this time the Auswärtige Amt was like nothing so much as a teeming antheap pulsating with futile activity, and you could smuggle every kind of person into it provided you had the necessary confidant in the personnel department.'

Ribbentrop's grotesque notions of how to preside over a Ministry were of great advantage to his enemies.

This sketch of Adam's behaviour at a moment when, as mentioned already, many stalwart opponents of Nazism found the excitement of great victory impossible to resist, agrees with all contemporary evidence and leaves no room for any idea that his opinion underwent an important change after his return. He did, however, remain the same contradictory being as before. His patriotism was as ardent as ever, and his sincere and deeply studied belief in an international order did not mean that he had lost a tendency towards nationalist thinking (of a civilised kind) which all his hatred of the evil nationalism of the men in power could never quench.

Partly by accident, partly by design, he was joined by friends in the Informationsabteilung. Peter Bielenberg was persuaded by Adam to come into the department, but he stayed only a short time. He came to help in the section which supplied information on Great Britain while the invasion of the British Isles was still being planned by the naval and military authorities, the hidden purpose of the section being to help British friends and to start a new resistance group operating from England. Peter left when this section was disbanded on the cancellation of the invasion plan. He was glad to go. He found that the life of ceaseless disguise and conspiracy was one in which he was quite unable to take part, given his

[10]There is no documentation to show that Trott was connected with the activities of Oster, Canaris, Beck, and the Service conspirators till later, but there was probably an undisclosed connection through Moltke.

direct temperament and personality. So far as professional life was concerned, he and Adam parted but the friendship continued to be among the first, and perhaps the most intimate in Adam's life.[11]

Another member of the department, Adam's immediate superior, became a close friend from having been an acquaintance. He was Hans-Bernd von Haeften. It has been mentioned that they first met at an Anglo-German meeting held at Oxford in 1932. Haeften's career dated from that occasion. Among those who came to Oxford was a former German ambassador who had known Haeften's father. He was favourably impressed by the son and recommended him to the selection committee of the Auswärtige Amt. Knowledge of this encouraged him to compete for election, and he was successful. Owing to Haeften's frequent service abroad, he and Adam had met little during the intervening years, but Adam knew of a signal if ineffective gesture which the other had made against ascendant Nazism in 1937. At that time Haeften was a member of the German Embassy in Vienna. It came to his knowledge that one of the numerous Nazi agents operating in the city was guilty of fraud. As the man was a German Haeften reported the case to his diplomatic superiors, and this caused the greatest embarrassment as the swindler belonged to that highest Nazi élite, the first seven members to have joined the party.[12] Representations, some of a threatening kind, were made for the case to be dropped, but Haeften persisted. The swindler was withdrawn from Austria and a black mark was earned by Haeften who, soon after this, was posted to Bucharest. There he remained until the summer of 1940 when he was posted to Berlin to take a senior post in the Information Department which, by all accounts, was sadly deficient in professional direction.

He immediately struck up an ardent friendship with his young subordinate. He said to his wife: 'Now I don't feel lonely any more.' He loathed Nazism but had been unable to do anything against it apart from one

[11]Mr Bielenberg. Discussion. C.T.
[12]By German law a political party had to have seven members before it could be legally registered. This the German Workers Party (the parent body of the Nazi Party) had by the time Hitler joined it in 1919. In February 1920 Hitler announced the change of the party's official title. Angered by Hitler's usurpation of his authority, the chairman, a journalist called Karl Harrer, resigned and Hitler was accorded his number, 7.

fruitless gesture three years before. Now he felt that he had a comrade in arms at last. Adam returned the affection. It is the opinion of Frau von Haeften that in his friendship with her husband Adam saw and delighted in a tranquil reflection of his ever-affectionate but ever-troubled relationship with his elder brother. As she has described it, in Haeften he saw a Werner 'whom he could manage,' while at the same time he appreciated the other's steadying influence, that of one who could act 'as a brake' on Adam's impetuosity. Clarita remembers how the first time Haeften rang him up at their home, Adam held up the telephone saying to her, 'Just to hear that man's voice does me good.'[13]

Late in the year Alexander Werth joined the department. Since the days when they both had studied together under Kraus at Göttingen, their friendship had remained very much alive, though they had met rarely. Their careers had gone along different roads. Like Adam, Alexander Werth was anti-Nazi from the first days of the regime, and like Adam he was indiscreet in the matter. As a result he was arrested in 1934 and imprisoned in a concentration camp. On being liberated he was deprived of his passport, but he contrived to leave the country and made his way to England where he qualified and practised as a member of the English Bar. From 1934 till the spring of 1939 he remained in England where he and his sometime fellow student occasionally met on Adam's visits.

In the spring of 1939, after the German invasion and destruction of Czechoslovakia, Alexander Werth determined to go back to Germany. He was ill at ease as an expatriate and hated the impotence of life in exile, so he asked the German Embassy to issue him with an amnesty and a new passport. They told him they would do so if he undertook to join the army on arrival in Germany, and he agreed to the condition.[14] He received his passport and appeared to return to the Nazi fold as a penitent. He in fact returned in an opposite spirit. He had abated no jot of his enmity to Nazism. His case was not dissimilar to that of Adam.

He served in the German army according to his undertaking. As mentioned already, in the spring of 1940 he began to manoeuvre for a second-

---

[13]Frau Barbara von Haeften. Discussion. C.T.
[14]Herr Alexander Werth. Discussion. Herr Werth's long residence outside Germany has on occasion led to his being confused with the eminent journalist of the same name. The identities are wholly separate.

ment to the Information Department and persuaded Adam to apply for a posting.

As usually happens when a new office is grafted on to an ancient institution, the first task was to get the office established as a working machine and not allow it to be pushed into a corner by older and jealous sister-departments. 'Our first objective,' wrote Alexander Werth, 'was to bring regional sections of the Auswärtige Amt together (Great Britain, the Empire, the U.S.A., the Far East), then sift the personnel of these sections and establish cross contacts to the corresponding geographical and political sections of other departments.'[15] In these complicated and tedious administrative manoeuvres they were helped by the fact that the first head of the Department was a civilised senior diplomat of pre-Nazi days, Legation-Minister or Gesandter von Altenburg.

Neither Adam, nor Haeften, nor Werth, nor Furtwängler, nor Peter Bielenberg while he remained with them, forgot for a moment the 'darker purposes' of this activity. Alexander Werth wrote: 'Our preparatory work was essential if we were to carry out the various tasks we envisaged for the future, and our plans were organised with the object of enabling Trott, while carrying out official missions, to undertake simultaneously "unofficial" that is to say illegal ones.'

Their official tasks were far-ranging and may be roughly described as a mixture of political Intelligence work and what came to be called psychological warfare. They were charged with analysing the enemy press, making recommendations as to the psychological value of bombing civilians, publishing books containing derogatory remarks (always quoted out of context) by British authors on their native land (an easy game in which vice-versa the British had preceded the Germans) and speculating about the political reactions to the war in enemy countries. There exists a grotesque document, which has survived from these labours, on a probable schism in the Church of England following German occupation: Cosmo Lang, Archbishop of Canterbury, is represented as likely to lead an emigration of reactionaries to Canada, while the Leftist William Temple, could be relied on to stay behind. It is difficult to believe that the appreciation was written in a very serious spirit. In addition the department was instructed to cultivate and keep in good humour writers and

[15]Berichte.

broadcasters, notably William Joyce, P. G. Wodehouse, and the Nor-
wegian poet Hamsun, who were known or supposed to entertain pro-
Nazi sympathies.[16] The members of the department all felt that they were
condemned to pass their time in a very fatuous way at a great crisis of
history. 'It must be obvious,' Herr Werth has written, 'that a normal man
with any degree of self-respect could not but find the kind of work that
the Information Department demanded quite unbearable, and of course
we found it so. Had not other tasks come our way, legal and illegal, I
doubt if any of us would have still been there by the summer of 1944.'

The 'other tasks' are the main subject of the last four years of Adam's
life. Circumstances compelled a slow start.

After the failure of November 1939, resistance had still persisted, chiefly
taking the modified form of secret negotiations with Vatican and clandestine British authorities, with the object of assuring acceptable peace
terms.[17] Adam took no part in these manoeuvres, being prevented by
absence and illness. It is possible that his dangerous position after the
American journey reasonably inhibited conspirators from seeking his aid
then. After the victories of the summer of 1940 all this secret anti-Nazi
activity virtually came to a stop. Resistance did not cease but sank to a low
ebb and remained there till Nazi policy ran into defeat in the latter part of
1941. The resisters had from 1934 looked to the Army leadership as the
sole instrument capable of destroying the Nazi regime, but 'from June
1940,' to quote Sir John Wheeler-Bennett, 'until the defeats in Russia "the
German Army in Politics" had ceased to have meaning. If ever there was
a non-political army in Germany it was at this time, when in the full
golden tide of glory and conquest, the Generals were more than content
to leave politics to the Führer who had brought them to such heights of
victory, and to accept his decisions uncomplainingly.' This 'close season'
in resistance has been held against Hitler's opponents in Germany both

---

[16]Thanks to the violent counter-propaganda against Mr Wodehouse organised
by the late Lord Norwich when he was Minister of Information, the establishment
of this great English humorist as an enthusiastic Nazi may be considered one of
Dr Goebbels's enduring triumphs. The facts of the case, leading to an entirely
different conclusion, have been put forward many times, notably in a B.B.C.
broadcast by the late Evelyn Waugh in 1961, but the libel on the master persists.
[17]For details see Gerhard Ritter's biography of Goerdeler English version *The
German Resistance* (London 1958), 160-8.

by anti-German opinion abroad and sometimes by opinion within Germany. To have struck at Hitler in his full golden tide, it is argued, would have given resistance the mark of sincerity; to wait for Nazi failure showed a vulture character, a disposition to leap onto bandwagons.

The argument is easily understood, but is surely fallacious. In this matter the views of no man living have more right to respect than those of Herr Fabian von Schlabrendorff, one of the few surviving resisters who personally attempted to assassinate Hitler. As he says in his book: 'There cannot be the slightest doubt that a coup by the army against Hitler after the victorious campaign in France would not have been feasible. The fact that France had collapsed morally as well as materially was plain for all to see and made a deep impression on the German people, especially in view of earlier Nazi predictions of French "decadence".'[18] The fact of the matter is that in the summer of 1940 Hitler had won the war, but mercifully he was so lacking in real statesmanship that he could not consolidate his victory.

In these circumstances not too much blame must go to such a man as Weizsäcker who, in terms of practical politics, now fades out of the story of German resistance, and great honour to Carl Friedrich Goerdeler who in July 1940 wrote an anti-Nazi memorandum, originally addressed to the whole German officer corps and clandestinely distributed to a select number: 'It is not to be imagined', he wrote in this remarkable document, 'that by means of a system which lives in Germany by financial madness, economic coercion, political terrorism, lawlessness and immorality, there can be built up a creative and constructive co-operation of free peoples under German leadership.'[19] He declared, in other words, that the whole spectacular victory was hollow and could lead nowhere except to final defeat. At the greatest possible risk to himself he insisted, at this most unpropitious moment, on the need to rid the world of Hitler and all he stood for.

In this statement of his beliefs Goerdeler, that consistent and in some ways fantastical man, spoke for a dedicated minority whose purpose, in

[18]*The Secret War Against Hitler* by Fabian von Schlabrendorff. Translated by Hilda Simon, London, New York, Toronto 1956. In discussion Herr von Schlabrendorff has strenuously restated this opinion to the writer.
[19]Ritter p. 171.

victory or defeat, was to secure the return of German leadership to civilised hands. Adam was of that minority, but, as with all but a very few of
them, and those not the most practical, he recognised that there was
nothing he could do except prepare for a moment of opportunity, and
maintain his individual opposition. He entered gradually on to that long
period of frustration with which his adventurous life closed.

A note on Adam's superiors may be useful at this point. Before the end of
the year a certain Stahlecker, a senior officer in Himmler's Schutz Staffeln
took over the department from Herr von Altenburg. Clarita has told of
the 'drastic measures' which Adam adopted to counter the efforts of the
SS leader to overawe the staff. Summoned for interview one day Adam,
in striking contrast to his usual politeness, threw off his jacket in the
general's office and put his feet on his desk. The treatment was entirely
successful, even, in Clarita's words, 'miraculous.'

His under-secretarial chief was Weizsäcker, but in the course of organisation the supervision of the department came in practice under Weizsäcker's colleague, the State Secretary 'for special duties,' Wilhelm Keppler. This man was an early member of the Nazi party. He had acted as its
chief economic adviser in the years of the struggle for power, and had then
served as adviser to Göring for the Four-Year Plan from 1936. He had
taken a leading part with Seyss-Inquart in the political manoeuvres leading
to the Anschluss in 1938 and was the first Reich Commissioner for Austria.
By such means he moved from economic to foreign affairs and was
appointed to the Auswärtige Amt in the July of 1938.[20] But in spite of
his success in the Austrian intrigue, he proved to have little if any talent
for the pursuit of his new interests. This was of considerable advantage to
Adam. Keppler came to rely more and more on consultation with him,
and there grew up a relationship not unlike that of Adam with Hewel.

Like Hewel, Keppler was a full-blooded Nazi, a fervent believer in
the movement and in the Führer's nobility of soul, but, as with Hewel,
this did not prevent him from being an agreeable sort of person, of dulled
rather than evil morality. An Indian friend of Adam wrote of Keppler
that 'he was not entangled in the usual Nazi intrigues and not so com-

[20]Wheeler-Bennett p. 272.

pletely a careerist as the others.'[21] It would have been easier for Adam to deceive a man for whom he could feel no respect at all, but not much easier.

This was a distressing time, but it would be wrong to think of it as one of great melancholy. Early married life is rarely that, and one must remember in addition that his joy in life never deserted him, and his youthful sense of humour often came to his rescue. In his short and moving essay Franz Josef Furtwängler has told of how, during these early days of conspiracy, Adam continued the good work that he had begun in Paris, and he has described the spirit in which he acted. 'It is often said,' writes Furtwängler in his book, 'that politics corrupt character, but the personality of Adam von Trott zu Solz emphatically contradicted any such idea. Trott had the art of suggesting to his Nazi superiors, by the cunning use of their own words, orders which enabled him to take out of the concentration camps Jews who would otherwise have been executed, and then as usual he would employ them for supposedly higher political purposes. This was a game which could have brought him to the gallows every time he played it, and yet whenever he pulled off a trick of this kind, it caused him to shake with amusement.'

Early in the next year, 1941, Adam's fortunes took a new turn and, not for the first time in his life, his activity became so complex that his intentions are sometimes hard to follow. At this stage accounts of him become contradictory, and the reason is not far to seek. He found himself involved in a fantastic tragi-farce which resembled nothing so much as a drama written by a playwright of outstanding incompetence who is not quite sure what the subject of his play may be.

[21]Berichte A.C.N. Nambiar.

Chapter 14

THE STORY OF BOSE

The career of Netaji Subhas Chandra Bose is most easily seen as a cautionary tale about the dangers of a narrow mind, of dedicating life to one obsessional hatred, of the blindness induced by fanaticism and irrational self-confidence, but in the illogical way of nationalism his story has suggested very different conclusions. He has been elevated to the status of a political sage. Streets and squares have been reverently named after him in cities of India. Some of his countrymen compare him to the greatest statesmen of whom we have record.

He was born in 1897 of a Brahmin family of Bengal. From childhood he was noted for intelligence and courage, and as soon as he reached manhood he entered on a political career, having passed high into the Indian Civil Service after which he almost immediately resigned. He showed the effect of two influences in his early political life, one personal, and one general. The former came from Jawaharlal Nehru who in the post-war period was a very different character from the moderate statesman of his later years; he was reckoned in those days as one of the most dangerous of the nationalist extremists. The impersonal influence on Bose came from the terrorist traditions of Bengal, traditions which had murderously opposed authority from long before the days of British rule, and had usually acted in the service of religion. In the days of the British Empire, Bengal terrorism had found a new impetus in the new religion of nationalism which Bose personified in all its intense faith and ruthlessness.

He succeeded quickly in political life, perhaps too quickly with the result that he was not able to take account with himself of the immense responsibilities that fell on him as the leader of millions of people. In the nineteen twenties he became the idol of nationalist youth in India. In

1924, when he was only twenty-eight, he became one of the chief municipal officers of Calcutta. He could easily have enjoyed an honourable and influential career within the British Empire had he been capable of compromise. But he was a man of integrity who could not be false to his passionately held beliefs, defective as these were.

His dedicated hatred of Britain and British rule made him one of the most disruptive forces in India, not only from the point of view of the ruling power responsible for law and order, but from that of the nationalist movement as well. He led that part of the Left-Wing of Congress which styled itself the Congress Socialist Party, and from which later grew the 'Forward Bloc,' the most extreme faction of Congress. As the Left-Wing Leader, devoted to violence and averse to negotiation, he waged ceaseless political warfare against Gandhi and then against his former political teacher Nehru. The Mahatma Gandhi was revered as a saint by his immense following, and the open hostility of Bose cost the latter much popularity; yet so powerful was the younger man's force of personality that he rose to great prominence and influence in the very movement in which he had most enemies, and in 1938 he was even elected President of Congress, though he was only able to retain office for a year.

Eleven years before this, in 1927, there occurred a little incident which was to have interesting results much later. Like most of the activist national leaders Bose was from time to time arrested and imprisoned. In May 1927 he was liberated after spending over two years as a prisoner in Burma and returned once more to his inflammatory political career. Once again his name began to figure in newspapers and his unusual character attracted the attention of a journalist and student of Indian affairs in Germany. His name was Franz Josef Furtwängler. He wrote two articles about Bose, and they were both translated and published in American papers. In this form they were read by Bose in India and he wrote to Furtwängler thanking and congratulating him. They were not to meet until fourteen years later, in 1941.

Between 1933 and 1936 Bose travelled in most of the countries of Europe and first made acquaintance with Nazi Germany and Fascist Italy. He was received by Mussolini. Bose has sometimes been described as a keen sympathiser with Nazism. His cult of hatred and nationalism certainly harmonised very well with Nazi philosophy. 'If the Burmans have any faults,' he wrote in a remarkable give-away sentence in his auto-biography, 'it is their extreme *naïveté* and absence of all feeling against foreigners.'

Yet the evidence is that Bose was not a Nazi and had no predilection for the Nazi way of life. Though he believed that his three years in Europe had enabled him to master the political facts of the modern West, his writings indicate that he was and remained too ignorant of the world outside India to understand what Nazism was. He was drawn to Italy and Germany because they were at enmity with Britain. He shared the Left-Wing affection for Soviet Russia for the same reason. He especially esteemed Germany because he recognised that Hitler's policy was moving towards war with England and he looked on a war as providing India with a magnificent opportunity to achieve liberation and independence. His preoccupation with India and her national need was so intense as to exclude any more general principle. He did not care what happened to other people. He had no objection to Empires as such. He admired the Japanese career of conquest; he was undisturbed at the thought of Russia subjugating smaller nationalities, and he recommended that after the defeat of Great Britain, her African colonies should be taken over by Germany. He had one enemy, British rule in India.

When the war came his anger with the Congress leaders at not seizing opportunity was intense. He wanted rebellion *à outrance*. 'The Indian people', he wrote at the time, 'should not be hampered by any philosophical notions like Gandhian non-violence, or any sentimentalism like Nehru's anti-Axis foreign policy.' Bose invariably referred to his followers as the Indian people. In his angry, narrow dedication he seems throughout his career to have believed that he spoke for the whole sub-continent.

In 1940, when the German army was triumphing over France, Bose was conducting an agitation for civil disobedience in Bengal and vainly trying to convert Gandhi and Nehru to his policy. In July he was imprisoned for the twelfth time. He had by now reached his conclusions which he expressed thus: 'Firstly, Britain would lose the war and the British Empire would break up. Secondly, in spite of being in a precarious position, the British would not hand over power to the Indian people and the latter would have to fight for their freedom. Thirdly, India would win her independence if she played her part in the war against

Britain and collaborated with those powers that were fighting Britain.'

His chance came early in 1941. He began a hunger strike in prison and this alarmed the Government into liberating him. Late in January he escaped from India into Afghanistan. The journey took him a long time and the Afghan authorities were embarrassed by his arrival. He was compelled to live in secret but his circumstances became easier when eventually, towards the end of March, he found a patron in Signor Pietro Quaroni, Italian Minister in Kabul. Quaroni reported an interview with Bose by telegram followed by a despatch written on the 2nd April to Count Ciano. The news was relayed to Berlin and machinery rapidly put in motion to convey the firebrand to Europe by the U.S.S.R.[1]

His arrival in the West was well-timed. At the beginning of 1941, when Bose fled from India, certain of the senior officials of the Auswärtige Amt came to the conclusion that Germany was not making the most of her Indian opportunities. There were numbers of Indian exiles living in Germany, and there were increasing numbers of Indian troops serving with the British forces in North Africa from whom prisoners of war were taken. On capture they were shipped to Sicily and Italy and it was assumed that among them there might be disaffected persons. Yet nothing was being done about this situation, either in the sphere of military action or that of psychological warfare. It remains a curious fact that whereas Nazi propaganda was very effective over a large part of the Arabic-speaking world and in Persia, it was never pursued with thoroughness or comparable effect in India. The possibilities of infiltration were less, but another explanation appears later.

[1] This sketch of Bose's character and career is based on his two autobiographies, the first published in 1935 under the title *The Indian Struggle*, the second in 1964 by the Netaji Research Bureau under the editorship of Bose's nephew, Sisir Kumar Bose, and under the title *The Indian Struggle 1920-1942*. The latter book is a continuation and elaboration of the first and includes interesting relevant material such as Quaroni's report. The sketch is also based on Herr Furtwängler's chapter on Bose in *Männer*. A biography of Bose by a former Intelligence officer in the Indian Service, Hugh Toye, with a foreword by Mr Philip Mason, was published in 1959 under the title of *The Springing Tiger*. Mr Toye's book, which is laudatory in approach and tone, contains valuable information on the formation of Bose's military force and its subsequent adventures, but is not so well-researched as Herr Furtwängler's on his political activities in Germany. There is a conflict of dates in all the books mentioned above.

Though they suffer from many handicaps, new official departments of mushroom-like growth enjoy more than others openings for the spirit of initiative. Someone had to deal with the newly recognised Indian opportunity and the eyes of overburdened departments turned towards the Informationsabteilung. It contained in Franz Josef Furtwängler a member who had travelled in India and was an authority. It contained in Adam someone who had studied China, and that was more than enough for the purpose. 'Overnight,' as Clarita says in her memoir, 'Adam found himself an expert on India.' His qualifications were a distant view of the Indian coast on his way home from the East, and two hours in Ceylon where the boat stopped during the same voyage. His predicament was not peculiar to German conduct of war. At the same time as Adam's appointment, and on the strength of some small proficiency in Persian studies, the writer was invited by a G.H.Q. to undertake an expert position on Slavonic and Arabic affairs in succession, being finally designated as a specialist on all things pertaining to Italy. The latter country he knew briefly as a tourist though without acquiring a knowledge of its language, history, modern politics, or geography. Late in the day he was invited to make use of his knowledge of Persia. To be given incredible appointments is one of the compensations of war.

From the Informationsabteilung a special sub-department dealing with Indian affairs was formed, and known as Das Indienreferat. It came directly under Keppler and seems to have retained a close relationship with its parent body so that the association of Adam and Haeften was not disrupted. With Adam went Alexander Werth and Franz Josef Furtwängler among others to the new organisation. Their first two or three weeks were occupied with study. The establishment of the office seems to have occurred in late February.

The duality of Adam's life became more marked at this period than at any other. To understand this phase one must again remember that he still stood in a position of the very utmost danger, and that the possibility of news reaching the SS or the Gestapo of his anti-Nazi activity and his secret meeting with Lord Lothian in America had in no way receded. His need for protective colouring was as strong as ever and he was not squeamish in the use of it. Soon after his return, nearly a year before the inception of the Indienreferat, he had decided that he must take a bold, radical and painful step if he was to allay suspicion in order to work for the great cause he believed in. He applied for membership of the Nazi party and was finally granted it about this time, in the spring of 1941. If he thus succeeded in convincing a few that he had capitulated, those who really knew him such as Peter Bielenberg, Alexander Werth, and his new friend Hans-Bernd von Haeften, never gave the matter a thought and were perhaps glad that Adam was safeguarding himself against the consequences of his frequent rashness.[2]

Yet the matter was not so simple as all that. With Adam things never were. It may be said that when a man pursues an objective under a disguise, there is a shadowy borderline where the disguise and the real man merge. That Adam joined the Nazi party without a shred of respect or sincerity need not be argued. The proofs are abundant, his life being the most impressive one. But that does not mean that he had lost that vein of nationalism which, in very different form, he shared with his brother Werner, and which lay in (sometimes uneasy) juxtaposition with his never dimmed sense of the need for a European and ultimately wider unity. As stated before, he remembered the lesson of Weimar, and he was always certain that no greater political error could be made than for a de-Nazified Germany to appear before its own citizens and the world, stripped not only of Hitler's loot but of the rightful German heritage. From Paul Scheffer there comes remarkable evidence of the strength of his nationalist feeling in early 1941.

Adam had an American friend, Thomas Harrington McKittrick, who was President of the Bank for International Settlements in Basle. He used to make frequent visits to Berlin. In February or March 1941 Mr McKittrick, on returning from Berlin, sent a message to Paul Scheffer, at that time on a brief journalistic visit to Switzerland from America, asking him to come to see him urgently. When they met, McKittrick, to quote Scheffer, 'complained that Trott, for whom he had the highest esteem, had declared to him that German war-aims must include annexations in the East and West. McKittrick said that Trott had spoken to him with emotion about this matter and had repelled all his counter-arguments.'[3]

Was this a cleverly laid cover-plan? If so why should Adam have chosen McKittrick of all people as the recipient of views damaging to himself, knowing they were likely to be repeated to his acquaintance in

[2]C.T. and Bielenberg discussion.   [3]Scheffer-Boveri.

England and America? Or was that precisely why he did so, to discourage truer American reports finding their way to Germany? Yet if
the ruse were to succeed, what was the effect on his mission as a secret go-
between likely to be? Or had he not thought of any of this and was merely
giving expression to a mood of patriotic enthusiasm? Perhaps in touchy
reaction to some remark of his American friend not reported? There is a
hint of jealousy of Adam in some of Paul Scheffer's comments, and it is
possible that he represented the conversation in more disturbing colours
than the subject justified. The incident probably belongs to that shadowy
region in which a researcher may lose his way, and in which Adam may
sometimes have lost his way too. The question can have no clear answer,
but the events of early 1941 can suggest influences on him which made
him feel able to take part in the German war effort as he had not done
before.

His letters to Shiela show how he had swallowed the Leftist notion of
those times that British Imperial rule in India was nothing but an abom-
ination, not less steeped in crime than the Nazi regime. With his new
mission in the Indienreferat he could see his position, as the citizen of a
state at war with a country to which he was attached by loyalties and
affections, in much clearer and less painful terms. By encouraging the
Indian enemies of Imperialism he was helping people who shared beliefs
and principles with him, and he knew how much those beliefs were shared
also by English friends in England. He saw himself in a position similar to
that of many people he knew, men such as Goronwy Rees, Dick Crossman, or Stephen Spender, friends of Germany who remained friends and
yet who joined whole-heartedly in the war against Nazism. He saw himself being able to do active patriotic work with a good conscience. Such
was the impression which his state of mind made on Alexander Werth.[4]
From a similar impression Professor Winckelmann deduced a political
theory. He has given his opinion: 'Trott was led to pursue the Indian
affair with so much conviction by the thought that damage to their
Commonwealth might make the English more ready to talk. He hoped
that thus they might become ready to negotiate, not with Hitler, but with
the other Germany.'[5] An anonymous memoir written by one of Adam's
colleagues in the Auswärtige Amt stresses the fact, without suggesting

[4]Werth. Berichte and discussion. [5]Berichte.

any complicated political plan, that Adam threw himself into the work of the Indian sub-department with energy and sincerity.

Given Adam's tendency towards complexity, there is nothing incredible about such an ambivalent state of mind as is indicated by these testimonies. But was this in fact his state of mind? That it was is emphatically denied by Wilhelm Melchers, an acute observer. He worked in the original department covering the Near East, India and Ceylon in the Auswärtige Amt. He was thus in official contact with Adam's activity throughout, and he has recorded that for Adam the Indienreferat was merely a useful contrivance which enabled him to travel and to maintain secret contacts with English and Americans. He has told how 'shortly before the 20th of July, 1944, Trott told me this in definite terms, but from former talks with him I had guessed that behind all his official activity lay other things such as could hasten on what we had long hoped for.' Adam was scrupulous about not bringing his family into any conspiratorial intrigue, but his two brothers and Clarita were both left with an impression similar to that of Melchers. Yet the fact remains that Adam's official work was undoubtedly pursued with considerable effect, certainly in the earlier stages. It is difficult to decide exactly where the truth lies, or to escape from the enigmatical world to which conspiracy may condemn those who have the courage to follow it.

The Indienreferat was in early stages of study and self-organisation when the incredible news burst upon the official world that Subhas Chandra Bose was proceeding immediately by air from Kabul to Germany via Moscow. On the 3rd of April, 1941 he arrived in Berlin.[6] As noted already the venture was well-timed; not only was there now a competent department in Berlin to deal with Indian affairs, but four days before the man's arrival, on the 31st of March, General Rommel had led the Afrika Korps in the great offensive which was to carry German arms beyond the frontier of Egypt. The army opposing him was largely composed of Indian troops. Unless unforeseeable reverses were to afflict Rommel there should soon be many Indian prisoners for this famous and successful demagogue and agitator to work upon.

The opportunity appeared considerable, but there was a snag, as it turned out a fatal one. No matter how keenly Adam and Werth and

[6] Auswärtige Amt Archives.

Furtwängler might toil at their assignment, the matter depended ultimately on ministerial decisions, in this case by Ribbentrop. His major
weakness as a statesman has been remarked already: though Ribbentrop
sometimes showed considerable astuteness in getting great diplomatic
advantages, he never seemed to know what to do with them once he had
them, and his touch in making enemies of friends was unfailing. He had
not been prepared for Bose's sudden appearance in Berlin and he showed
no grasp of the possibilities of this sudden and exciting development.

Less than a week after Bose arrived he sent a message to the German
Government which in this case meant Ribbentrop via Keppler. It took
the form of a brief statement of the position of the British in India and
the state of Indian opinion and aspiration (which Bose, true to form, identified without qualification with his own ideas and feelings) followed by
six sections on how to attain Indian independence with Axis help, and an
'explanatory note' elaborating some of the ideas contained in the main
statement. The propositions were that Germany should accept Bose and
his party as 'The Free Government of India,' on the model of the exiled
Governments in London; that the Axis should proclaim the independence
of India as a major war-aim, and that the German army should supply
a force of 50,000 men whose appearance on the Indian-Afghan frontier
would result in an immediate revolt by the Army of India and the end of
the Empire. After this memorandum the next move was up to Ribbentrop. He was slow to make it.

On arrival in Berlin Bose was given accommodation in the Exzelsior
Hotel and put in touch with the Indienreferat. Early in this phase of his
career he met Adam who immediately found himself involved in many
tedious questions of protocol. The first difficulty which Bose encountered
and Adam endeavoured to straighten out lay in the crude fact that people
indoctrinated with Nazi teaching about race had no idea how to behave
towards an Indian Brahmin. The hotel staff at the Exzelsior treated him
in an off-hand master-race manner. Complaints were sent to the Auswärtige Amt after which orders were issued that the Indian leader was to
be addressed as 'Your Excellency' and treated with the respect normally
extended to a Portuguese notable.[7] But Bose was not at ease in the hotel,

[7]Bose travelled from Afghanistan to Berlin under the name of Mazzotta, and
throughout this stay in Europe a weak pretence was maintained that he was a
Portuguese diplomat. *Männer.*

even after this amelioration; and on the representations of the Indienreferat he was moved to a handsome villa in the Lichtenstein-Allee near
the Tiergarten.[8]

Outside the Indienreferat, his experiences with the official world in
Berlin were not encouraging. Soon after arrival Adam took him to see
Keppler, an encounter which Adam found horrifyingly embarrassing. In
the true Ribbentrop style, Keppler treated his visitor to a long and wholly
uninformed oration on the subject of India, the British Empire, Congress
and kindred matters, never stopping to allow a reply and never thinking
of inviting the other's views, until he declared the interview at an end.[9]
As for Ribbentrop himself, not having the remotest idea what to do with
this prize, he declined to meet him, on the plea of other pressing business,
and in spite of many requests for interview. Bose became so enraged at
this insulting procrastination that he declared that he would not again
ask to see Ribbentrop and furthermore would ignore an invitation if one
arrived. Adam hoped that he would remain true to this decision, but in
the event he gave way.[10] It appears from a remark in one of Ciano's
papers that Ribbentrop condescended to meet Bose some time in May
1941, and his decision was probably influenced by a second memorandum
from Bose in which he again pleaded for a German policy of support for
the independence of India, and also (a new proposition) of the Arabic-
speaking countries. In this second paper, he also argued that the success
of Rommel in Africa and of the German armies in Greece and Jugoslavia
made this a moment when such a policy could hardly fail.[11] In giving
Bose an interview Ribbentrop showed all his inimitable gaucherie. A
messenger was sent to the Lichtenstein-Allee at midnight, and Bose was
obliged to rise from bed to go to the Wilhelmstrasse.[12] There, to judge
from Ciano's reference, Bose was told that while he would be helped in
propaganda work, 'any public declaration on the part of the Axis on
the subject of the future settlement in India' would be 'premature.' It has
been suggested that one reason why Ribbentrop was so laggard in taking
up the cause of Bose was that by the secret terms of Ribbentrop's diplomatic masterpiece, the Russo-German pact, India was treated as a Russian

[8]*Männer.* [9]C.T. [10]C.T.
[11]Quoted in *The Indian Struggle 1920-1942.* The memorandum is dated 3.5.41.
[12]C.T.

sphere of interest, and the last thing Ribbentrop wanted was any action likely to excite Russian suspicion during the last days of preparation prior to the destruction and abandonment of the aforementioned masterpiece.[13]

In the meantime the Indienreferat was planning, in consultation with Bose, to take advantage of the fact that Rommel's advance was inevitably increasing the numbers of Indian prisoners of war in German and Italian hands. Among the very few Germans with whom Bose became at all intimate were Adam and Furtwängler, but even with them there was so little intimacy that elementary exchange of information was lacking. 'It was natural,' wrote Herr Furtwängler in his book, 'that in the sinister environment of a confusing foreign country in which he could trust no one, and never feel that there was ground beneath his feet, Bose should, like a cuttle-fish, have hidden himself in an impenetrable cloud.' The Indienreferat remained in ignorance of his policy beyond what he had written in his two memoranda.

In these circumstances Adam requested Furtwängler to use his special relationship with Bose to find out something about his hopes and proposals, and so Furtwängler went to the villa and had a long talk. The cuttle-fish cloud did not lift for a while. 'Nevertheless,' records Herr Furtwängler, 'I soon noted that Bose had not left his differences with the Congress majority behind him at the Afghan frontier; moreover he was busying himself with the question of how to work these differences into his propaganda scheme, and this seemed to me the worst thing that he could do. He insisted that though Gandhi, Nehru and Congress had refused to give the sympathy of India to the war against Germany, they had at the same time no wish to adopt either an attitude of forcible resistance to the English nor one of collaboration with Germany—and of course he meant with the Soviet Union too. For that reason he would fight Gandhi from Germany. That was the upshot of what he said during a conversation lasting two hours and conducted from the first with the utmost care.'[14]

Furtwängler did not allow Bose's preposterous notion of a sound political programme to pass unchallenged. He addressed him 'in a friendly way but without reserve' and thus reported what he said: 'It seems to me that you have no choice but to do this: to support the struggle for in-

[13]Toye p. 62.   [14]Männer.

dependence of the Indian people as a simple publicist and broadcaster. Make this struggle intelligible to the world, and without identifying yourself with the Hitler regime in any way. Tell our friends—your friends and my friends—over the air that for the duration of your exile all conflict between you and the Congress majority must be set aside. But to do battle, under the protection of Hitler, with the old and revered Mahatma to whom all India is indebted—you should not even dream of such a thing.' Furtwängler and Adam were in close consultation over the Bose policy and this may exactly represent Adam's thinking, besides Furtwängler's. The same advice was given to Bose by an eminent Orientalist, Gesandter von Hentig,[15] and by Wilhelm Melchers. But Bose's conceit and arrogance knew no bounds. The advice, whose wisdom is beyond question, far from altering his mind, angered and offended him. 'The only effect,' Herr Furtwängler records, 'of my words was something in the nature of a declaration of war. He definitively closed himself in, as it were, as though he began already to feel that he was part of Rome-Berlin-Japanese World Fascism; so much so that he looked upon my friendly objections as an unbearable instance of "knowing better".' He never again felt the need of a discussion with his former friend.'[16]

The tragi-farce went on. The next stage appears, from surviving accounts, to have taken the form of a visit to Italy. Alexander Werth flew to Sicily on the 10th of May to examine the situation of the Indians in the prisoner-of-war camps, and it may have been that Bose went with him, returned to Berlin, from where on the 20th he sent a message to his supporters via the Italian Legation at Kabul,[17] and then went back to Italy. Or he may have followed Werth after the 20th. It is certain that he was in Italy in June and during the first part of July. Adam's movements are likewise not to be followed with exactness. There is a gap in his letters to Clarita and to his mother and one can only know for certain that during this time he travelled in Italy and was in Berlin on the 22nd of June and the 13th of July.

---

[15]Hentig had been a member of the small German party which under Oskar von Niedermayer crossed Persia to Afghanistan in World War I with the intention of raising Afghanistan and Persia against the British.
[16]This and the foregoing two quotations are from *Männer*.
[17]*The Indian Struggle 1920-1942* where the text is given.

The main task of Bose and his German collaborators was to raise an Indian force. The method employed was to separate the men from their officers and N.C.O.s, and then subject them to propaganda. Recruitment was not the simple matter which Bose anticipated: the 'Indian Legion' proved a very sluggish starter. The reception of Bose and the Indian exiles of Rome and Berlin who accompanied him on visits to the prisoner-of-war camps was lacking in warmth and often hostile. Sometimes he was shouted down.[18] Nevertheless thanks to the energetic efforts of Werth and Adam a start was made. Bose helped with his persistent self-confidence. He remained unshaken in the belief that inspired the whole of his life and which could not be daunted by the direst calamity: that he and India were one, that he and he alone spoke for the Indian people.

But if his faith in himself was immovable, his faith in Nazi Germany was continually and sorely tried. What Herr Furtwängler has rightly called the 'Psychopathentyrannis' of the regime made the German official world irremediably incapable of dealing with Asiatics, and Bose was subjected to endless humiliations both small and great. For instance, while in Rome Adam helped him to buy clothes, of which he was in much need, and of course, familiar with Asian hospitality, he took this honoured guest of the state to the best tailors and was not sparing in the number of suits he ordered for him. He also took the opportunity to buy some needed furniture for the villa in the Lichtenstein-Allee. When he and Werth returned with Bose to Berlin, Keppler was moved to question these expenses and thereupon opened an enormous row whose reverberations could not but be heard and noticed by the ever-sensitive Indian, the subject of the row being, to say the least, remarkably unflattering to himself and his mission.[19]

A more serious matter for offence was occasioned by a failure in communication and co-ordination between the Ministries of War and Foreign Affairs. In July Adam, Werth and Bose returned to Berlin where they found a monstrous surprise awaiting them. Fifty Indian soldiers had been persuaded to renounce their allegiance to Britain, and instructions were obtained from the Auswärtige Amt for them to be set free and brought to Berlin to form the cadre of an army of liberation; but no sooner did the luckless fifty arrive at the railway station than they were arrested and

[18]Toye. Chapter IV.   [19]C.T.

imprisoned in small, noisome cells. Werth had better contacts in the Ministry of War than any other member of the Indienreferat and he spent a week-end telephoning. He was able to get the Indians transferred to a less loathsome prison, but to achieve their manumission took several weeks.[20] It is only fair to say that there is nothing particularly German about this story, and the odious treatment on the other side which was occasionally but too often meted out by hysterical authority to potential allies remains a matter for enduring shame. It can be imagined what sort of impression this episode made on Bose. Some of his German colleagues, including Adam, suspected him of vanity because he maintained a ridiculous parade of state in his villa and was insistent on his title of 'Excellency.'[21] They may have been right, but it must be remembered that he had reason to assert his position.

The worst shock which Bose suffered from Nazi policy occurred some seven weeks after his arrival, on 22nd June, 1941. He was without the support of Adam. He was in Rome at this moment and did not return to Germany till the middle of July. On the 17th he was received by Staatssekretär Woermann who did what he could to set Bose's mind at rest about the new blundering course which at last made Hitler's ultimate defeat certain. Bose explained to Woermann how the German invasion of Russia was likely to disturb the kind of Indian opinion on which he relied, and which for him was the only opinion worth troubling about. He told him of the excellent effect on this opinion of the Russo-German pact of 1939 but how, at the present time, 'the sympathies of the Indian people were very clearly with Russia because the Indian people felt definitely that Germany was the aggressor and was for India, therefore, another dangerous imperialist power.' He cleverly put to Woermann the added necessity now of a German declaration of Indian independence as a war aim, and pointed out, in support of the argument, how much more vulnerable India was now to British reformist and compromise approaches. 'It was clear,' reported Woermann to Ribbentrop, '. . . that Bose, having been far from Berlin, is strongly influenced by the Soviet thesis on the question of the origin of the German-Russian conflict. It will therefore be one of our first tasks to put him right in this respect.'[22]

[20]C.T. and Werth Discussion. [21]C.T. and *Männer*.
[22]*The Indian Struggle 1920-1942* in which Woermann's report is reproduced in full.

Whether or not Bose was 'put right in this respect,' he was not long in abandoning his former quasi-loyalty to the U.S.S.R. According to his English biographer, Bose now saw himself in the rôle of a triumphant general, as the commander of the Indian Legion, three battalions strong, marching with the German army to Afghanistan. From there Bose and the Legion 'would leap ahead of the German advance and disrupt the British-Indian defences in North-West India . . . Then Bose would lead his Legion into India and found on it, as the Indian Army turned on its old masters, the ever-growing Army of Free India. From here too he would draw Government officials and administrators, as he took possession in the name of India and founded the Congress Raj.'[23]

Bose's followers never fought on the German Eastern front. The whole raising of the Indian Legion and its accessories was an elaborate failure. The interest for this book is Adam's association with it. For the sake of convenience the rest of this melancholy tale, and Adam's part in it, may be told briefly here though it advances the chronology.

After the breach with Furtwängler, Bose found in Adam a favourite companion and confidant, but the affection was not returned. Two revealing remarks in letters written to Clarita in August 1941 suggest a relationship which could not develop. 'He is extremely gifted,' wrote Adam on the 8th, 'but our personal relationship remains decidedly cool. At every meeting we have to start right from the beginning.' With a touch of satire he wrote a week later: 'It is high time that I (or he) set off on a trip, as I am becoming indispensable to him. His inner point of departure is too negative to allow of a rewarding relationship.' Apart from the company of a few Indian exiles and his Austrian secretary (whom he secretly married)[24] Bose was a lonely man in Berlin but he could not make a friend of Adam. One day Adam told Clarita that he was sure Bose had detected that he was not a Nazi at heart, and so looked on him with secret suspicion. Nevertheless, as his letters show, he accompanied Bose on many of his journeys: to Vienna, Rome and Paris.

As mentioned already, it is difficult and perhaps impossible to know precisely how Adam viewed his assignment with Bose and the Indienreferat. What is certain (and strengthens the view that he entered on this task with some conviction) is that in March 1942 Adam's work caused

[23]Toye p. 63. [24]Toye p. 75.

him to feel a sudden bitter sting of conscience. The occasion was the mission of Sir Stafford Cripps to Delhi with the purpose of obtaining agreement with Congress for the prosecution of the war under acceptable political terms. Cripps left London for India on the 12th of March and arrived in Delhi on the 22nd. Superficially it looked as though he was likely to succeed. While Ghandi had new recourse to his mystical-nationalist practice of pacifism and non-resistance, Nehru and the Moslem leader, Mohammad Ali Jinnah, declared for full resistance to Japan. Nevertheless the mission of Sir Stafford Cripps failed because the British Government refused to consent, at an hour of such danger, to that sudden establishment of full Indian Governmental independence, which, in spite of its threat of a widespread religious civil war in India, Congress demanded.

This was a moment when the Indienreferat seemed to be achieving something at last. An agreement had been concluded with the Ministry of War that Indian prisoners who were considered promising should be assembled in Germany, recruited into the Legion and trained; a radio station directed at India was set up under the name of 'Free India' from which Bose broadcast for the first time on the 19th of February, 1942.[25] The German and Italian Governments still refused to make a declaration on Indian independence, or to recognise Bose as the head of the Indian State, but this did not prevent him from declaring 'war on England' by means of 'Radio Azad Hind' on the 28th of February. A fortnight later, on the 13th of March, again by means of radio, he denounced Sir Stafford Cripps and his mission in unmeasured terms. The diaries of Doctor Goebbels show how it was believed in Germany, not least by Goebbels himself, that Bose's propaganda efforts were having enormous effect in London and India.[26] Of all the leading men whom Adam had met in England there was none he respected and loved so much as Stafford Cripps, nor to whom he felt so much gratitude. 'I have a very clear memory,' writes Clarita, 'of how dejected Adam was when he found himself in this constrained position during Cripps's visit to India. His conscience was burdened and he found no way out of the conflict in his mind. The account by Alexander Werth does not indicate how bitterly he felt that he might have been instrumental in the failure of Cripps whom he respected and looked

[25] *The Indian Struggle 1920-1942* where the text is given.
[26] Goebbels diaries 2nd and 4th March 1942.

up to.' He need not have worried. Bose's activities made no impression
on opinion in India or Britain during the whole course of the war. His
enormous fame came after, when he was no longer alive.

In May of 1942 Bose's luck appeared to turn. Although Hitler and Mussolini had decided not to espouse the cause of free India in April, Bose was
able to convert Mussolini to the need for a declaration of Indian independence when he was given an audience with the Duce on the 5th of
May. [27] The German Government were informed that Mussolini favoured
public support of Indian independence and Goebbels's diary tells how the
news was received with disapproval. It would appear however that the
Duce's initiative forced the hand of the Führer; it was difficult now for the
latter to refuse to receive Bose. So it followed that on 29th May Bose was
conveyed to Hitler's field headquarters, the gloomy 'Wolf's Lair' situated
in the forests of East Prussia. Franz Josef Furtwängler has left a pleasing
account of this occasion.

'From this event a period might be supposed to have opened in which
Bose was given the opportunity of a great "turn out" and of undertaking
notable deeds, but later in the *Wochenschau* [weekly newsreel] one could
see pictures which told how Bose made his entry into Headquarters: an
officer on the Headquarters staff cordially greeted another officer who
accompanied Bose, while the guest and ally from Calcutta crept unnoticed from the depths of the limousine. The conversation with Hitler
passed in the most ludicrous manner. I read the official report in Adam
von Trott's office. Bose began the conversation with the customary
assurance that this was a very significant day for him, the day when he
made the acquaintance of the great leader of the German people. That was
the end of his contribution to the talk. The rest was occupied by Hitler
with one of his famous monologues. He did not wish to set a wave of
propaganda in motion prematurely, he said, for by such means he had
had a very bad experience in Irak. He then read the unfortunate Brahmin
a long lecture on the cultural capacity of the English master-race in India
and remarked as follows: "According to my calculations about a hundred
and fifty years will pass before India is ripe for self-government." He
then gave Bose the well-meant advice to make himself useful to the
Japanese after their invasion of India. Never once, as he ranged from praise

[27]Ciano Diary.

of the English to advice about helping the Japanese, did he take the trouble, if only by a sentence, to bring the other into the conversation. The Indian was an object of indifference to him, and the tactless imbecilities to which he treated Bose are in marked contrast to those conversational arts which he well knew how to practise when he had something to gain from the success of an interview. This untoward soliloquy must have lasted about an hour according to the official minutes, and I only marvel that when it was over the staff did not have to carry Subhas Chandra away from the huts of the Führerhauptquartier in a swooning condition.'[28]

At least the Führer had made clear the main reason why Bose could never get satisfaction from Germany.

Apart from Hitler's distaste for the ideal of Indian independence, two other troubles beset Bose's enterprise during his increasingly weary months in Germany before his departure in February 1943. The first one was that although he was now ecstatically hailed as Netaji or Spiritual Leader by some two thousand of his legionaries, he could never raise the Legion beyond that number to full brigade strength, except by the inclusion of numerous persons of questionable reliability. But to obtain operational employment he had no alternative but to do this. As a result the force was confused and weakened by feeble morale which often turned to desertion. The second trouble was obviously conditioned by the first. Even when he had the men, he was unable to find anything for them to do, for no German commander on the Eastern Front wanted this dubious force. Then came a fitful ray of hope. In July 1942, when Rommel and the Afrika Korps seemed poised for their final triumphant assault on Cairo and Alexandria, the German War Ministry, in consultation with Bose, proposed that the Indian Legion should be placed under Rommel's command for use in a combined political and military rôle, their main purpose being to demoralise the four and a half Indian divisions under General Auchinleck. Rommel would not agree to this.[29] He was non-political in mind, and like many German soldiers of his time he preferred to have nothing to do with Nazi policy, and the horrors it entailed, though forwarding it with all the power of his ability.

With this refusal by Rommel went the last opportunity of finding front-line employment within the Wehrmacht for the Indian Legion

[28]*Männer.*   [29]Toye p. 70.

and for a smaller élite body under Bose known as the Special Company. From this time on he sought to escape from the predicament he had so joyfully walked into when he established contact with Signor Quaroni. Since the events of December 1941 by which Japan placed herself in a state of war both with the United States and Great Britain, Bose looked to the Far East as a more promising area from which to launch an attack against the British Empire in India. The Germans were by now bored with the whole of this Indian enterprise and put no obstacles of their own in the way of his proposed journey to Japan. He was friends with the Japanese military attaché in Berlin, a certain Colonel Yamamoto, and this man on his return to Japan in November 1942 obtained Japanese agreement to the journey. The arrangements took a long time. In the end Bose left Kiel by U-boat on the 8th of February, 1943. Their course was round the European and African mainlands, keeping at a great distance from the shores, to a meeting place four hundred miles S.S.W. of Madagascar. Here Bose and his one Indian companion were transferred to a Japanese submarine on the 28th of April. They then made for Sumatra whence they flew to Tokyo, arriving on the 13th of June, 1943 after a journey of eighteen weeks.

In Germany the Indienreferat, the 'Free India Centre' and the 'International Union of Indians in Exile' (both founded in Berlin by Bose with the help of the Indienreferat) continued to play a part in Adam's plans, but if Adam felt a sentiment of loyalty towards the Indians whom he had helped to recruit, he felt little or any for the departed Netaji. During the last part of Bose's time in Germany his relations with Adam had become even less congenial than earlier, so much so that, very untypically, Adam was perhaps guilty of some harshness at the end. When Bose set forth on his most arduous and perilous journey Adam, though he could not but know that he was the other's favourite companion among the Germans, delegated the duty of saying goodbye to him at Kiel to another member of the Indienreferat.[30]

Reading accounts of Bose, including his own and that of his English biographer who regards the deeds of that very questionable life not only with sympathy but much admiration, Bose's character seems to have

[30]Werth. Discussion.

deteriorated swiftly and horribly under the challenge of war. This is chiefly discernible in the records of his last two years, from 1943 to 1945, the years of his greatest success and supreme failure, when his merciless and often bloodthirsty ruthlessness, his mounting and finally almost insane egotism, seem to have taken possession of a once lofty spirit and degraded the ideals for which he had stood. This degeneration may not have occurred in the twinkling of an eye, and it seems reasonable to suppose that the evil strain, a sinister mixture of levity and megalomania, was growing obvious before he left Germany, and that it was this that repelled Adam into a state of hostility.

Bose's successor as the head of the Free India Movement was an Indian journalist, A. C. N. Nambiar, who had followed his profession in Europe for nearly eighteen years. Like Bose, Nambiar singled out Adam from his German colleagues. In this case the affection was mutual. Nambiar admired in Adam 'a power over men through which alone he seemed predestined to become a political leader.'[31] Adam took Nambiar into his private life and his new friend was impressed by the happiness of his family circle, but Adam never took the other into the recesses of his secret life. Nevertheless, as Nambiar says in the short account he has left, he could often 'feel Trott's unrest, his doubts about the political course and his hatred of the Nazis.'

One reason why Nambiar could detect these hidden matters is probably to be found in the fate of the Legion. After Bose's departure it lacked leadership and there were no more moments of transient high morale following a visit by the Netaji, but a continuing state of dissatisfaction, indiscipline, and frequent desertion, as it became increasingly clear that the Legion had no rôle to play. During 1943 and 1944 it was moved to France and employed on the coastal defences, and among many German officers, especially those without devotion to the regime, a posting to the Legion was sought as a refuge from the horrors and miseries of the Eastern Front.[32] Adam found such a refuge for his younger brother Heinrich.[33] To the end Adam found the Berlin premises of the Free India Centre and the Union of Indian Exiles invaluable meeting places in which to hold conspiratorial discussions, but true to his principles he was careful not to

[31]A. C. N. Nambiar. Berichte.   [32]Toye pp. 73 and 74.
[33]Herr Heinrich von Trott zu Solz. Discussion.

compromise people outside the anti-Nazi secret movements, so Nambiar could only 'feel' and not know.

After his departure from Kiel Bose himself passes out of this story. The tale of his subsequent adventures has been told in detail elsewhere, but the reader's curiosity may have been aroused and an outline of what came after, though admittedly something of a digression, may end this chapter.

The Japanese received Bose with acclaim. In contrast with Hitler and Mussolini they instantly gave him all the public support of his independence policy that he asked for. In Singapore he formed a provisional Government of India, elected himself Head of the State, declared war a second time on Great Britain, and accepted from himself the principal Governmental offices including that of Supreme Commander. This time he had something to command. He found that an Indian National League and an Indian National Army (again recruited from prisoners-of-war) had been formed the year before, though not with great success. He infused his own dynamic nationalism into these organisations and gave them life. In a short time he commanded about 25,000 men. His immediate success was enormous, but it contained a great flaw. The Japanese army was of a different mind to the Imperial Government. They had no confidence in this turncoat force, and following their traditions they despised the disloyalty of these soldiers. When the Japanese took the offensive against the British 14th Army in Assam in 1944, the soldiers of the Indian National Army were used in the operation largely as porters and as expendable reserves to cover withdrawals in the immense disaster which then fell on the Japanese. The Netaji remained at his Headquarters in Rangoon and was never allowed near the front. In Rangoon the Japanese authorities had little difficulty in deceiving him by propaganda about great victories against the British in Burma and Assam, and his force was represented as the spearhead of the general assault. Corrupted by power, totally ignorant of all things military, Bose lived in a dream world and in remote Rangoon lost all contact with his men and all power to influence them. As the campaign developed his army suffered indescribable privations. Thousands died of starvation in the jungles of North Burma and there were mass desertions. Bose's army melted away. So little had his movement succeeded in its task of subversion that the British Army Commander, Sir William Slim, felt compelled to issue a stern order of the day to his Indian troops reminding them that it was their duty to treat prisoners-of-war from the Indian National Army with humanity. When the catastrophe at last reached Bose and he in turn was compelled to flee from Rangoon, he only recognised a temporary set-back. He dreamed of migrating to the U.S.S.R. and of staging a new Russian-sponsored independence movement from there. Fortunately for himself, he was killed in an air-crash in Formosa on the 18th of August, 1945.

He enjoyed a posthumous success and an historical revenge. In 1945 his name was forgotten in India, and his movement and the existence of the Indian National Army were virtually unknown to the civilian population. In 1946 the Government of India decided, on political grounds, not to proceed with court martials of Indian National Army men except in the case of senior officers who had voluntarily deserted, and of those who had been guilty of atrocities against their fellow prisoners. (There was a concentration camp, instituted before Bose's arrival in the Far East but maintained by him, in which prisoners were persuaded to join the National Army by the use of torture.) Congress leaders were in agreement with this sensible and humane policy which was criticised as too lenient by men of the Army of India and returning prisoners of war who had resisted threats, maltreatment and inducements. But agitators got busy with remarkable effect. A man who, among other misdeeds of the kind, had flogged a fellow prisoner to death, was due for trial in Delhi, and this was the occasion for a wild outbreak of mass hysteria. Screaming mobs declared and even believed that those due for trial were martyrs to the cause of liberty. Nehru and Jinnah who had looked with the utmost dismay on Bose's plan for achieving Indian independence under German and then Japanese patronage, feared at this moment for their popularity, and, to the great surprise of many people who respected them, they gave the fullest support to the new myth. Their action increased its circulation and potency a hundredfold; the torturer came to be regarded as an object of veneration while his innocent victim was forgotten. In such extraordinary and not wholly inappropriate circumstances, Bose began to enjoy his lasting second fame.[34]

[34]Philip Mason (Toye), Toye, *Auchinleck* by John Connell, London 1959. Official History of the War against Japan Vols. II and III. F. M. Lord Slim *Defeat into Victory* London. 1955.

Chapter 15

THE LAST PHASE

In 1935, when he was twenty-six, Adam jotted in his notebook: 'If we must now resign ourselves to a time when there is greater and greater likelihood of an early death, let us at least see to it that to die makes sense—and to have lived.' The events of the last phase of Adam's life throw a new and strong light on this little note giving it the gravity of a prophetic utterance.

Whoever studies that life must be perplexed, and at moments even exasperated, by the contradictory forces which influenced Adam and caused him to follow at times so wayward a path; even though he never lost sight of his ideals; even though his actions were never inhibited by the smallest lack of courage. But a change came over him in his last three years. He saw his way clearly. He pursued his goal with a marvellous persistence in the face of every discouragement, and never questioned the rightness of his bold course of action. If the word 'change' is misleading, because Adam was the same man in 1944 as in 1939, it remains the fact that whereas at other times the outlines could be dimmed, in the last stretch of time given to him, they were magnificently clear.

An important and perhaps decisive event was the renewal of friendship between Adam and Helmuth von Moltke. They had first met in England where they had some of the same friends, notably A. L. Rowse and David Astor. They shared a love of Oxford. They had much in common, and their differences, which were also considerable, had the effect of making their relationship complementary.

Moltke was two years older than Adam, and like him had a family connection with the English-speaking world. His mother was the daughter of a certain James Rose-Innes, Chief Justice of the Transvaal in the days of Lord Milner, and later Chief Justice of South Africa. His father was the great-nephew of the famous Field-Marshal von Moltke. The latter died without children so that the family estate of Kreisau in Silesia was inherited by his nephew, Helmuth von Moltke's grandfather. Though born to a great family, to prestige and privilege, the young Moltke's early life was one of some hardship. His father had no notion how to manage his property efficiently and the family trust, founded by the Field-Marshal, was wiped out by the inflation of 1923. The estate ran a rake's progress and in 1930 was taken over by creditors who appointed an inspector in charge. His father 'abdicated' the management of the estate in favour of his eldest son who responded to the opportunity by co-operating with the inspector. By 1935 the debts were paid and the estate reverted to its owners. The inspector remained on in estate employment.

Moltke was a man of immense mental and physical energy and, as his record in estate management shows, one of great efficiency. Like Adam he went to the Law for his profession, though unlike Adam he delighted in it, and in more normal times would have reached the highest positions. By 1935 he had already made his mark. He specialised in international law, and, very much in Adam's spirit, he concentrated on getting what justice he could for Jewish clients, and always by the boldest and most direct methods. The distressing family circumstances of his early manhood in no way embittered him. On the contrary they awoke in him a spirit of compassion and reformist zeal. He attempted bold innovations in land tenure on the Kreisau estate. In the grim years between 1929 and 1933 when the unemployment figures in Germany rose to heights never imagined before, he threw himself into the Social Democrat movement for establishing Labour Camps, and worked as an inmate himself.

Like Adam he had a formidable personality and presence, (he was six foot seven inches in height), which he knew how to use, and like Adam he had boundless courage.

The most striking difference between him and Adam was that whereas the latter delighted in intellectual complexity, Moltke's strength lay in the impressive simplicity and directness of his mind. A friend[1] remembers that he had no taste, indeed a 'loathing' for precious-minded literary

[1] Mrs Edgar Mowrer quoted in *Neuordnung im Widerstand* by Ger Van Roon, Munich 1967. Referred to later as Van Roon.

circles, and for the kind of Hegelianism fashionable at the time. Where Adam would have countered hair-splitting folly by putting forward arguments (with sly parody) of equal elaboration and subtlety, Moltke preferred frankly philistine counter-attack. The same friend remembers a meeting at which a Neo-Hegelian was weighing the arguments as to whether absolute good or evil could be defined. When he came down on the negative side, Moltke came up with a question: 'What's all this you're saying about there being nothing evil? Aren't there such things as intolerable use of language (doubtless a hit at the speaker's style) and bad eggs?'

When the Nazis came into power, Moltke, like Adam, immediately recognised that a terrible thing had happened to Germany and Europe, but unlike Adam he was not a prey to second thoughts, or liable to believe that the guilt of Nazism lay anywhere but with itself. When he met Lord Lothian in July of 1935 he made notes in English on the conversation. On Lothian's views that the harsh terms in the Versailles Treaty and the occupation of the Ruhr made Britain and France answerable for the growth of Nazism, he commented: 'that foreign faults are greatly responsible for German National-Socialism is, I believe, utterly wrong, although it is often used by German people as an excuse.' Lothian asserted his belief that from a phase of disorder Nazism would lead not to further revolution but to a state of stability. Moltke wrote about this: ' . . . it seems to me to be common knowledge, that a dictatorship as every absolute regime has little tendency to change to democratic forms of government by its own free will, and that it tends to invite revolution; I believe it to be impossible that he has thought about that himself.' His final conclusion on Lothian's belief in the need for concession to Hitler shows astonishing perception: 'I fear that his policy will be successful in England: I fear that it will be misleading for Germany; it will induce our Government to believe that we can count on the English neutrality, while in truth, should a European war break out, England would fight on the side of France; this possibility of misleading the others, is what I fear most about the English policy of keeping the balance: England is in reality not an arbiter but a party to the struggle; but its lack of a rigid policy is what induces the Germans to believe that she is an arbiter.'[2]

[2]Van Roon p. 298.

The above may give the idea that Moltke was a very much more de-tached and better judge of politics than Adam. Although he showed a far firmer grasp of the dangers of the British Appeasement policy, this was not altogether so, or is at least very much open to question. Moltke's parents were Christian Scientists, and he himself remained a practising member of that religion until 1931, and it would seem that from the in-fluence of Christian Science he developed a strong vein of pacifism. He would oppose Hitler to the uttermost. He made no compromise at any time, and from first to last regarded Nazism as unredeemable and evil in its essence. But he would not oppose Hitler and Nazism by violent means. In this conviction he remained unalterable, and if his views had prevailed, then that part of the German resistance which he led would have lost all hope of being politically effective. In 1938 and 1939 Adam had been influenced by pacifist ideas, but, as his meeting with Falken-hausen in 1939 shows, he had not been slow to recognise their irrelevance in a world dominated by a madman of genius. Moltke never made this mental and emotional readjustment.

When the war broke out he obtained an appointment through a friend, a lawyer named Professor Viktor Bruns, to the Abwehr, the Counter-espionage organisation of the German armed forces. He was posted to the Auslands-Abwehr section and, as a specialist, to a sub-department dealing with questions of international law. His supreme departmental chief was Admiral Walther Wilhelm Canaris, and among Moltke's senior colleagues was the head of a central section, Major-General Hans Oster. Hitler had no more determined enemies than these two men. Herr Furt-wängler's assertion that many threads of conspiracy passed through Adam's hands may well indicate an early contact involving Canaris, Oster, Adam and Moltke.

Whether that was so or not, Adam did not become what might be called a regular and accredited member of Moltke's resistance group till the spring of 1941. The group itself began at an unlikely moment, in June 1940, from conversations held between Moltke and his contemporary and close friend Peter Count Yorck von Wartenburg.[3] Like Moltke Yorck came of a family honoured as that of a great Prussian hero and

[3]Van Roon. According to Herr Furtwängler the group had an even earlier origin in 1939.

Field-Marshal, one who (unlike von Moltke) was famous not only as a military commander but as a 'resister,' a declared enemy to tyranny in the age of Napoleon. Peter Yorck was stimulated into active anti-Nazism by his horror at the pogrom of November 1938, and he found in Moltke a companion in wrath. From the friendship of these two descendants of famous men the group later began to form. They held their first meeting at Kreisau in mid-August 1940. They took as their motto an aphorism of Goethe, 'A man can only be free where there is natural order, and an order is only natural when it leaves men free.' From the beginning to the bitter end the men around Moltke were sustained by a lofty and intense idealism. At the end of 1940, the *annus mirabilis* of the Nazi regime, Moltke wrote to his wife. 'To-day I have again the feelings that I had in 1930 when I saw the way out of the chaos for Kreisau. Of course it can all go wrong, but that is something different to a situation from which there is no escape.'[4]

Unless, as is very probable, there had been some hidden and now untraceable activity between them, it would seem that Adam and Moltke took up their friendship again on the initiative of a close acquaintance of both, Gottfried von Nostitz. This man saw in Haeften and Adam ideal contacts within the Auswärtige Amt such as the group lacked up to that time. At first Moltke had some slight reservations about Haeften. 'It is a great effort,' he wrote, 'to win such people for "the great solution" because they know [official] Routine too well. Nevertheless if you succeed, then you have a fine companion for the road (einen zuverlässigen Wegbegleiter).'[5] He succeeded in winning Haeften, without any 'great effort,' however, and from this time onward the Moltke resistance group, posthumously known as der Kreisauer Kreis—the Kreisau circle, had Haeften and Adam as their foreign policy representatives. As the senior in official rank Haeften had to observe the greater discretion so that he very rarely attended meetings of group members, Adam acting as his representative.[6] Needless to say Adam was as often inclined to represent himself.

The date of the beginning of this new relationship is interesting and may be held to elucidate or deepen the enigma of Adam's activities. Moltke's letter about Haeften (quoted above) was written on the 5th of

[4]Van Roon pp. 217 and 218.
[5]Van Roon p. 220. [6]Frau Barbara von Haeften. Discussion.

May, 1941 and appears to indicate the result of several earlier meetings. That means that the three men took up a close association during the first days of Adam's collaboration with Bose. Yet, though Moltke undoubtedly knew in detail about Adam's work at the time, there is not the slightest indication that the Bose episode caused him or any of his associates of the Kreisauer Kreis the smallest anxiety concerning Adam's devotion to the cause. This is certainly strong evidence that Herr Melcher's interpretation is the correct one.

For the first two years, counting its foundation from June of 1940, the Kreisau circle were occupied with the organisation of contacts with other groups of resistance. It was the aim of Helmuth von Moltke to bring about a grand coalition, a *union sacrée* of diverse resistance groups, of the civilian and clerical resistance within all the Churches, of the military resistance which he knew personally in the Abwehr, and of the group around Carl Friedrich Goerdeler. There was also an important representation of Social Democrats, notably Julius Leber, a great admirer of Adam, and the circle included prominent members of the former Centre Party. Besides this they sought the collaboration of individuals such as Count Friedrich von der Schulenburg, Oberpräsident of Silesia, his cousin Count Werner von der Schulenburg, the former Ambassador to Russia, and Albrecht Haushofer, professor of political geography in the University of Berlin. A great deal of time was spent in negotiation, in working out compromises between widely differing policies, and, most difficult of all, in deciding on what action was to be taken to rid Germany of Hitler and his rule. The process was inevitably slow and cautious, beset as it was with the utmost danger at every step. For two years activity could not go beyond theorising. It was an intensely frustrating time.[7]

For Adam it was less so than for others. In the strange position to which he had manoeuvred himself as a member of the Informationsabteilung and the Indienreferat he had at least some opportunity for some sort of definite action. The work of the department gave him and Alexander Werth continual excuse for meeting neutral persons in Germany and travelling to neutral countries.

Herr Werth gives some interesting details of this traffic. 'To disguise our contacts,' he has written, 'Trott and I used to apply for permits to

[7]Van Roon p. 262 ff.

visit certain neutral persons on our travels abroad, and then, once we were back in Germany, we would write an account of these visits in order to prove that we had complied with our official orders. Trott was a master in the writing of such things, and when either or both of us laboured at our reports we were torn between laughter and shame.'[8]

The amount of travelling done by Adam from 1940 onwards was considerable. Herr Werth records one journey to Switzerland in 1940, and there were certainly others in 1941. From 1942 to the second half of July 1944, Adam can be shown to have done sixteen journeys abroad for conspiratorial purposes, seven to Switzerland, four to Sweden, four to the Low Countries, one to Turkey. It is possible that he made others of which there is now no record. Little is known of what Adam did on these occasions, though enough to see the direction and the consistency of his main ideas. As in England in 1939, and in the United States, he had one over-riding purpose: to impress on foreign opinion that Nazism and Germany were not interchangeable terms, and that account of this must be taken in the framing of policy. As time went on he saw the urgency of his task. The degradation of war, inseparable even from the justest and most necessary of wars, was clouding the English spirit. The cult of hatred, inseparable from the aggressive spirit needed to animate an effective army, became more and more indiscriminate and, as usually happens, began to influence frustrated civilians more than the troops. The frustrated found a spokesman in Sir Robert Vansittart[9] who preached a form of anti-Germanism which can only be called racist. The spirit of his nonsense was closer to the new spirit of British rule than the generous declarations of Neville Chamberlain in September 1939, and indeed these were now looked on as suspect. Adam learned from study of the British press about this change which had overtaken British feeling, and he was determined to reverse it, if he could.[10]

An opportunity for action appeared in the spring of 1942 when Adam made one of four known journeys to Switzerland belonging to this year.

The background to this episode involved two of Adam's most cherished friendships in England, those with David Astor and Stafford Cripps. No matter what stories were spread these two never had a moment's

[8]Berichte.   [9]In his pamphlet *Black Record* published in 1941.   [10]C.T.

doubt about him. Certain that his friend was working in some clandestine fashion against the Nazis, David Astor had tried, during the first part of 1940, to obtain an appointment for propaganda-work to the enemy, believing that in his own efforts to explore the alienated German world he would somehow meet Adam exploring back; that somehow they would be able to work together again for the cause they both believed in.[11]

He confided these hopes to two people, one was Wilfrid Israel, the other was Sir Stafford Cripps, and both were actively sympathetic. But there was little, indeed there was virtually nothing that either of them could do, unless some definite approach involving Adam were to occur from the German side.

In January of 1942 Cripps, weary of continual Russian insult, resigned his ambassadorship to Russia and returned to England. The British public were ignorant of the way this had happened, and believing nothing but good of their new allies, saw in Cripps the hero of the hour—the man who had come to advise the anti-Communist Churchill to support Russia in her struggle. The Russians were understandably bewildered as the enthusiasm in Britain rose. There was talk on the Left of the desirability of making this supposed friend of the U.S.S.R. Prime Minister.[12]

In these circumstances Winston Churchill, in the course of a Governmental reshuffle, wisely appointed Cripps Lord President of the Council. After the Prime Minister, Cripps was now probably the most powerful and certainly the most popular man in the country. About three and a half months after his appointment as Lord President, Adam approached him secretly from Germany.

He did so through Doctor Willem Visser 't Hooft. At this time, Visser 't Hooft was the secretary of the Provisional Committee which in 1948 officially became the World Council of Churches.[13] Scrupulous in all observance, Visser 't Hooft had no objection at all to helping the enemies of Hitler, and not least when such help was in conflict with the letter of international law. When Adam was in Switzerland in the latter part of

[11]Memorandum to the writer by David Astor.
[12]Winston Churchill. *The Second World War* Volume IV 55-6.
[13]Article in *Time Magazine* (Atlantic Edition) 8.12.61.

April 1942, he had a long exchange of views with Visser 't Hooft, and the latter suggested to him that he should write a memorandum setting out the proposed policy of those he represented. Visser 't Hooft promised to take the paper to England where he was going in the immediate future. It was agreed that he would convey what Adam wrote to Sir Stafford Cripps.[14]

The memorandum is written in English and dated 'end of April 1942.' It is naturally unsigned but Adam's sole authorship is not in doubt. It is written in the first person plural and for that reason, among others, it has been taken as faithfully reflecting the views of Moltke and the Kreisau group.

The paper is in five parts. The first briefly considers three main perils to civilisation from continued war: intensified mass destruction, increasing totalitarian control of life, a trend towards anarchical dissolution. In the next section he appeals for a hearing, and in the third section puts forward the proposition. 'The most urgent and immediate task to stave off catastrophe in Europe is the earliest possible overthrow of the Regime in Germany.' This can either be achieved, he says, as part of a general catastrophe or by 'the establishment of a Government [in Germany] which would return to the standards of civilised Europe.' Perhaps unwisely, Adam then touched on his favourite theme that the ills of Europe should be regarded as European. 'A success of the second possibility,' he writes, 'is only conceivable if it is also linked up outside Germany with the final overcoming of European nationalism particularly in its military expression.' This would seem to indicate that the new civilised German regime demanded in advance a promise of general disarmament and an admission of the guilt of all nationalism. He stresses the Christian essence of the anti-Nazi opposition. He indicates the obstacles to a 'seizure of power by these forces,' enumerating four: the Soviet menace to Germany, Gestapo control of German life, 'the complete uncertainty of the British and American attitude towards a change of government in Germany,' and fear of 'movements of indiscriminate hatred' against Germans of all kinds.

The next section gives the constructive policy favoured by the Kreisau circle: decentralised government in Germany which is associated with

[14]Vierteljahrshefte für Zeitgeschichte. October 1957. 'Memoranden von Schönfeld und Trott' Referred to later as Rothfels 3.

'federalism in Europe [including Britain] and close co-operation with the other Continents,' 'renunciation of economic autarky,' and 'free access to raw materials overseas.' After a general emphasis on social and political security it is stated that 'the New Germany would be willing to co-operate in any international solution of the Jewish problem,' and 'to co-operate with all other nations to overcome the misery existing in the countries now under Nazi rule.'

In this part of the memorandum there is one sentence to which an un-friendly reader might take exception: 'We believe in the necessity to reconstitute a free Polish and a free Czech state within the limits of their ethnographic frontiers.' This could imply the retention of the Sudeten area of Czechoslovakia. It would have been more tactful to have expressed acceptance of the 1933 frontiers, as in the Trott-Scheffer memorandum, while insisting that this did not exclude negotiation on later frontier rectification.

The fifth and last section is a formal plea for serious consideration of the contents of the memorandum. Again one must note an infelicitous ex-pression. 'An exchange of ideas,' he writes in the penultimate paragraph, 'seems to us hopeless only as long as we are faced with a one-sided ten-dency to blame and to judge.' Events in Poland, the Ukraine and else-where made that tendency difficult to resist.

It may seem capriciously ungenerous to point out every phrase or opinion which was best not included in a memorandum which, in its main character, was well thought-out, clearly and pungently expressed, and moving in its sincerity. The reason for doing so is not 'pour chercher la petite bête' but to indicate to the reader how this paper might have been judged by a prejudiced and hostile critic. Its fate depended ulti-mately on such judgment.

Dr Visser 't Hooft arrived in England in May and gave the memoran-dum to Sir Stafford Cripps as promised.[15] He read it with enthusiasm. He showed it to David Astor who gave his opinion on it later: 'It was a brilliant memorandum which will one day be considered a prophetic document showing that Adam Trott had the qualities and calibre of a

[15] *The Church and the Resistance Movement in Germany.* A Lecture given at Göttingen University 15th May, 1957 by George Bell, Bishop of Chichester. Referred to later as Bell.

great European statesman.'[16] Cripps also showed it to Winston Churchill who minuted the document 'Most encouraging.'[17] Cripps sent a verbal message back to Visser 't Hooft, urging further communication though he made it plain that there could be no prospect of negotiating a settlement, no matter what changes occurred, except after the military defeat of Germany.[18] This was a hard condition and forced the conspirators into that dreadful moral dilemma which they had sought to avoid, and which Adam had discussed in 1940 with his friend Helmuth Wilhelm. In order to defeat Hitler these men had to accept the defeat of their country. What debate this message provoked among the Kreisau group is not known. Only one fact is certain, that decision was swift. Conviction was shared that so evil was the mastery of Germany by Hitler that a risk must be taken: even without the assurances regarding defeat, sought from Britain and America, the effort to dethrone Hitler must persist, and hope maintained that public opinion would, in the event of success, force those concessions which secret negotiation had so far not obtained. The task of trying to get a revision of the stern decisions first conveyed to these men by Sir Stafford Cripps, fell chiefly to Adam. It may be said that this work occupied the rest of his life.

The Trott memorandum had however been accepted. This was an advance, and the Kreisau group immediately followed up this partial success.

From a press report it became known that the Bishop of Chichester, George Bell, was going to Sweden in mid-May. The Kreisau group decided to make direct contact with him. George Bell was one of the finest of the leading men in the Church of England of his time, and Moltke and his friends rightly judged that they could have no more effective advocate.

In the event the Bishop was approached by two German clergymen, both of whom were his personal friends. Their appearance in Sweden at the same time may have been a coincidence.[19] Neither knew of the other's journey but both of them were fully conversant with the plans of Kreisau, including the Trott memorandum, and both gave accurate accounts of the growing secret resistance. The first to appear was Pastor

[16]Quoted in Rothfels 3. [17]Rothfels 3. [18]Bell.
[19]Rothfels 3.

Hans Schönfeld who met the Bishop in Stockholm on the 26th of May. Schönfeld told his friend 'about a very important movement inside Germany, in which the Evangelical and the Roman Catholic Churches were playing a leading part.' He seems to have mentioned few names in this description of the Kreisauer Kreis except that of Doctor Eugen Gerstenmaier, the Evangelical Church leader. From Bishop Bell's account of what Schönfeld told him it is possible to see how Moltke's friends saw the shape of things to come. They believed that a palace revolution was imminent within the Nazi party, and that Himmler and the SS would seize power from Hitler. The opposition saw this as a first helpful stage but 'were under no illusion as to the essential preliminary [of the final revolution] being the elimination of Hitler, and Himmler, and the Gestapo, and the SS . . . also the withdrawal of German troops from all occupied territory.' Schönfeld posed the main question which had been asked by Adam in his memorandum: 'Would Britain and the United States be willing to make terms with a Germany freed from Hitler?'

After their second meeting on the 29th of May, in which Schönfeld slightly elaborated what he had told already, the Bishop asked him to give him a memorandum to take to London.

Two days later at Sigtuna the Bishop had yet another surprise. At a small clerical meeting at a friend's house, Dietrich Bonhoeffer arrived. He told Bishop Bell of the circumstances in which he had come from Germany. Determined to reach Sweden in order to meet him, he had obtained a courier's pass through Moltke's friend and colleague General Hans Oster who had arranged the journey in detail. He then confirmed all Schönfeld's information and asked the Bishop to believe in the reality and breadth of the Opposition.

The Bishop was in no doubt as to the difficulty of getting the British Government at that moment to meet any sort of peace overture from Germany with sympathy, and he warned Bonhoeffer and later Schönfeld to that effect. But he realised that the more of concrete fact that he could give, the greater the hope of some result. To follow his own record: 'I said that, while I understood the immense danger in which he stood, it would undoubtedly be a great help if he were willing to give me any names of leaders in the movement. He agreed readily, though I could see that there was a heavy load on his mind about the whole affair. He named Colonel General Beck and Colonel General Hammerstein, former Chiefs

of the General Staff, Herr Goerdeler, former Mayor of Leipzig, Wilhelm
Leuschner, former President of the United Trades Unions, Jakob Kaiser,
a Catholic Trade Union leader. He also mentioned Schacht, as an am-
biguous supporter, a "seismograph of contemporary events." He emphasised the importance of Beck and Goerdeler.'

Later in the day Schönfeld arrived and a curious thing happened. Elated,
perhaps, by so sympathetic a reception by an Englishman of much
influence Schönfeld expressed himself with optimism about the future,
but here, to follow the Bishop's account, 'Bonhoeffer broke in. His
Christian conscience, he said, was not quite at ease with Schönfeld's ideas.
"There must be punishment by God. We should not be worthy of such
a solution. Our action must be such as the world will understand as an
act of repentance. Christians do not wish to escape repentance, or chaos,
if it is God's will to bring it upon us. We must take this judgment as
Christians".'

Before parting they summarised the main purpose of the meeting: to
persuade the British Government to avoid treating the leaders of a resurgent Germany with the harshness they threatened against a Germany under Nazi rule. The two pastors recommended that in further discussion
Adam should represent the German side.

On 18th June, 1942 the Bishop, after seeking advice from the Foreign
Office, wrote to Anthony Eden. He asked for an appointment and ex-
plained that the information he had to impart 'is a sequel to the memor-
andum you have already seen, brought from Geneva by Dr Visser 't
Hooft of the World Council of Churches, and having to do with von
Trott.'

The Bishop met the Foreign Secretary on the 30th of June, and gave
him a full account of his meetings in Sweden. 'Mr Eden,' he recorded later,
'was much interested. He appreciated the fact that I had warned the pastors that the British Government was likely to be very reserved in its
attitude, as opinion in Britain tended to blame all Germans for tolerating
the Nazis for so long. Mr Eden himself seemed more inclined to think it
possible that, in some curious way, the pastors, without their knowledge,
were being used to put out peace-feelers . . . He must be scrupulously
careful not to enter into even the appearance of negotiation with the
enemy, and be able to say truthfully that this was so, both to Russia and
America.'

Before leaving, Bishop Bell gave Mr Eden the names of German leaders and left a copy of Schönfeld's memorandum.[20]

For two weeks after the 30th of June there was no move.[21] Then on the 13th of July the Bishop of Chichester called on Sir Stafford Cripps. To follow Bishop Bell's account again: 'He spoke enthusiastically of Adam von Trott, and he told me of his own talk in May with Dr Visser 't Hooft who had given him a memorandum prepared by von Trott and mentioned in my letter to Mr Eden . . . When I showed Cripps Schönfeld's statement (which had points of agreement with von Trott's memorandum but took a more hopeful attitude about co-operation with Russia), it greatly impressed him. He described it as "far-reaching" and promised to talk it over with Mr Eden. He agreed that encouragement in any case could do no harm, and at best might do much good.'

Here the whole project came to grief. Cripps went to see Anthony Eden and found him unwilling to pursue the matter. He found him furthermore in the belief that the whole of this approach was suspect on account of its association with the name of Adam. According to what Cripps told David Astor, Eden asked advice on the authors of the two memoranda and the answer had come back from the Foreign Office that the record of Adam von Trott indicated a crafty agent of the Nazis most skilfully disguised as an opponent of the regime.[22] There is said on good authority to have been a dossier on the Trott case which contained overwhelming evidence of his clandestine Nazism. One can imagine its contents: suspicions from Czechoslovakia going back to 1936; from America possibly from 1937, with abundant material from 1939 and 1940; from the Far East with a note on his presence in Tokyo at the time of the apparently sinister appointment of Ott, and records of his association with the Astor family and the appeasement party in England in 1939, matters which in the climate of 1942 were liable to be grossly and fantastically misconstrued. But lastly, considering that Bose's radio channel 'Azad Hind' was regularly monitored in Great Britain and India; that his where-

[20]Bell.   [21]Rothfels 3.
[22]David Astor. Discussion and a letter.
The Foreign Secretary may have had the information before meeting the Bishop on the 30th of June. It may explain his reference to Schonfeld and Bonhoeffer being used 'in some curious way'.

abouts must certainly have been known both in Delhi and in Whitehall; that Adam in the company of Bose had been into prisoner-of-war
camps, in Italy moreover from where information flowed to the other
side continually; it is inconceivable that his present position in the Indienreferat and as Bose's advisor was not known. Anthony Eden had never
met Adam and was without prejudice in the matter, except possibly, as
is suggested by the Bishop's record, that he was suspicious of any 'peace-
feelers' at that time. This may be considered secondary. What seems undeniable is that, confronted with the volume of evidence against Adam
which had been collected in the course of five or six years, he could
hardly do otherwise than regard him as a dangerous, deceptive and
treacherous man. He was firm that no negotiation involving Adam was
to be undertaken openly or secretly by the British Government. He had
no way of knowing that what looked like carefully sifted information
was in the main a mass of prejudiced comment and mistaken conclusion,
some of it of the most ridiculous kind.

Mr Eden wrote to the Bishop on the 17th of July. One sentence of his
letter gives the sense of the whole: 'Without casting any reflection on the
bona fides of your informants, I am satisfied that it would not be in the
national interest for any reply whatever to be sent to them.'[23]

The Bishop returned to the attack a week later. While not questioning
Mr Eden's judgment of the national interest he wrote, 'I do greatly hope
that it may be possible for you in the near future to make it plain in an
emphatic and public way that the British Government (and the Allies)
have no desire to enslave a Germany which has rid itself of Hitler and
Himmler and their accomplices.' Towards the end of a long letter he re-
inforced his argument in telling fashion: 'Mr Churchill said in his first
speech as Prime Minister in the House of Commons on the 13th of May,
1940 that our policy was "to wage war against a monstrous tyranny never
surpassed in the dark and lamentable catalogue of human crime," and
that our aim was "victory at all costs." If there are men in Germany also
ready to wage war against the monstrous tyranny of the Nazis from within, is it right to discourage or ignore them?'

Anthony Eden replied on the 4th of August. He referred to a speech
he had made in Edinburgh three months before in which he had said that

[23]Bell.

no one could believe in the reality of a German opposition 'until they have taken active steps to rid themselves of their present regime.' He said nothing about his suspicions of Adam, nor did he particularise the information he had against him to Sir Stafford Cripps who seems never to have known about his connection with Bose and the Indian Legion. The reason, one may conclude, why Cripps was told so little was that he had a weakness which was surprising in a man of such austere character, namely chronic indiscretion.

The Bishop persisted, representing the case of the opposition again to Mr Eden in a further letter, and to the American Ambassador in London, Mr John G. Winant. All this effort was in vain and the story of his intervention really comes to an end with Anthony Eden's letter of the 4th of August. Looking back on these events nearly fifteen years later, George Bell judged the outcome as follows: 'I know that in the summer of 1942 the position of the Allies was critical . . . Nevertheless my own strong conviction is that the negative attitude of the Allies was wrong; that the sound and statesmanlike policy would have been to offer a positive response to approaches made at such terrible risk; and that the failure to do so was tragic.'

There were so many approaches, made by Adam and his friends of Kreisau with such unflagging courage, that it is easy to forget that they were made under a continuous reign of terror, and 'at such terrible risk,' of death, of torture. During 1942 the risk was intensified for Adam through two actions likely to draw disapproving Nazi attention on him. Shortly before his conversations with Visser 't Hooft, he had given Bose some official document which was not intended for his eyes. There was an immense to-do about this, and Adam appears to have been in close danger of losing his post. Had it come to Ribbentrop's personal notice he would almost certainly have done so. The trouble had only just passed when Adam set out for the two visits he made to Switzerland in April.[24]

In the summer after Adam's correspondence with Sir Stafford Cripps, and the affair of the two pastors in which he was closely involved, it was to his interest to lie low or to assume an especially convincing mask of Nazism. He did the opposite, and at this moment chose to challenge the Gestapo itself.

[24]C.T.

He had lately become more familiar with the Gestapo. Through the various questions which the presence of Bose raised, Adam found that he had to discuss Indienreferat matters with many provinces of Himmler's growing empire, and his acquaintance with the whole party hierarchy increased. Once he was bidden to represent his department at a conference presided over by the Führer in person. It was the only time he met him. He was not called on to speak at the meeting and merely attended in a silent junior rôle. He had a distinct impression, nonetheless, that when Hitler turned his baleful blue eyes on him the Führer had the sense of an enemy in the room. Such things may be easily imagined, but many people had an impression of Hitler's abnormal perception and an ability to smell hostility, like some wild animal.[25] Adam met Himmler also in the course of his Indienreferat duties, and seemed to find himself, on this occasion, in a monstrous dream-world, an impression greatly increased by a new security system following which armed black-uniformed figures marched in two circles, each in the opposite direction, round Himmler's central Field Headquarters hut, the result being that, on entering, the walls and the furniture and the neat bespectacled figure of the prim little mass-murderer himself all seemed involved in a seasick whirligig, till the eyes lost the impression of the gyrations without.[26] But of all his meetings the one which most impressed him was with Himmler's ablest lieutenant, Reinhardt Heydrich, the second-in-command under Hitler of the 'Final Solution,' whom Adam visited in Prague in April, 1942, just before his visit to Visser 't Hooft and not long before Heydrich's assassination. 'I remember,' Clarita has recorded, 'that he was fascinated by the phenomenon of Heydrich. It was borne in on him that here was an enemy of the utmost vileness, a man of brilliant talent, a terrifying gambler of genius.'

To consider the second of Adam's acts of incaution.

During the summer of 1942 his friend Franz Josef Furtwängler was informed on to the Sicherheitsdienst. His position was extremely dangerous as the information appeared to come both from without and from inside the Auswärtige Amt. Adam noticed that he was being watched and warned him. To follow Herr Furtwängler's account: 'I said that this was particularly vexing as I was planning to go away on leave. Trott said,

[25]Herr von Kessel. Discussions. [26]Mrs Bielenberg. Discussion.

"Go and take your holiday and don't worry. I'll look after the whole business and your trouble will be my trouble. If you're blown up I'll go up with you." He said this to me at a time when the fear of death oppressed all Germany, when often enough friend denounced friend— it was unbelievable. And indeed he did go into "the whole business." He found that I was on a list of those to be put out of the way. Trott went straight into the lion's den (die Raubtierhöhle), that is to say the Headquarters of the Sicherheitsdienst, and spent an unforgettable Saturday morning lobbying on my behalf. In the evening he came to our agreed rendezvous, and smilingly told me that he had "got round" [literally "bent"] the Gestapo commander, and that my file was disposed of. That is just one example of what it meant to be his friend.'[27]

The Gestapo commander in question was Walter Schellenberg.

The year 1942 was not a fruitful one in the history of the German resistance. In it there occurred an event which inhibited conspiracy for a time. In August a Communist plot run by a secret society, The Red Chapel, was discovered in the Air Ministry.[28] There followed mass executions, though, as with the Röhm purge of 1934, it is impossible to know the extent of these: calculations have ranged from 78 to 400 victims. The Rote Kapelle was a self-contained group and was only lightly affiliated to other components of the resistance,[29] so that the rounding up and extraction of confessions did not (so far as anyone knew) put the Kreisauer Kreis in direct danger. But there was a secondary and deadly danger. The humiliation of Göring at such a conspiracy being discovered in his own Ministry was extreme, and he set himself with all the determination of personal pique to seek out other conspiracies in other Ministries. There was an intensification of Gestapo activity. Clarita remembers an occasion when Adam was on one of his journeys abroad, and Haeften came to their flat in some agitation because an associate of the Red Chapel, a certain Dolf von Scheliha of the Auswärtige Amt, had been arrested with his wife, and Haeften had found out that a letter from him was among the seized

[27]Furtwängler. Letter to Frau Huch.
[28]For details see Wheeler-Bennett p. 538. In his book Herr von Schlabrendorff says that the term Rote Kapelle was invented by the Gestapo. The same may be true of Kreisauer Kreis. Many honoured political titles have originated as terms of contempt.
[29]Details are given by Dr Boveri in Treason in the Twentieth Century.

documents. His close friendship with her husband might thus put Adam also on a list of suspects. 'We never kept dangerous documents at home,' records Clarita, 'and if Adam had to have one in the house to work on, then I always put a box of matches within my reach before going to bed. I supposed that, between a ring of the door bell and opening the door I could burn the papers in a bucket that I had ready for the purpose, and then flush the ashes down the lavatory. All this would have been noticeable enough, but there was no other means of safety in our open, modern flat. But that time I took a whole basketful of papers to the basement and burnt them in the furnace, and that too was an odd and suspect thing to do . . . With the help of Werth, who enlisted the good offices of a distant relative who was an Obergruppenführer in the SS, we managed to get Frau von Scheliha out of prison.'[30] Scheliha himself was executed.

During all this year, in spite of such alarms, there went forward a continuous effort to enlarge the Kreisau circle and Adam played a conspicuous part in this. One point which disturbed the Kreisauer was that they formed something of a generation-group, and they felt the need of closer contact with older men who shared their basic conviction. As early as December 1941 Haeften introduced Adam to Ulrich von Hassell, former German ambassador to Italy, and this was part of a plan to establish contact with the conservative group of older men of whom General Beck, Carl Friedrich Goerdeler, the Prussian finance minister Johannes Popitz, Ambassador von der Schulenburg, Field-Marshal von Witzleben, Admiral Canaris and Hassell were the most prominent. Hassell seems to have taken to Adam immediately, and equally immediately to have disagreed with most of his opinions, as he did with those of almost all 'the Young Turks of Kreisau,' as Goerdeler called them. His diary for the 21st of December, 1941 tells us of an early confrontation. It is also interesting because it shows how Adam's ideas had altered since he talked with Niebuhr in 1939.

' . . . I had a long talk with Trott during which he passionately contended for the avoidance, within as well as without the country, of any semblance of "reaction," "gentlemen's club," "militarism." Therefore, although he too was a monarchist, we should under no circumstances have a monarchy now, for a monarchy would not win support of the people

[30]C.T.

and would not win confidence abroad . . . To these negative points he added the one positive thought that Niemöller should be made Chancellor of the Reich.'[31]

Adam's suggestion that Pastor Niemöller should be the first post-Nazi German Chancellor has been much criticised. Gerhard Ritter describes it as an 'adolescent notion.' For all its eccentricity, and almost comic un-orthodoxy, Adam's suggestion shows a grasp of a great part of this intractable problem. The more obvious candidates for the post, Goerdeler and Beck, were known to politicians and students of Germany, but their names meant nothing to the non-German public anywhere. Hassell himself favoured the Crown Prince, as head of the post-Nazi state. As a monarchist his choice showed logic but an extraordinary unawareness of opinion, both among large sections of the German people and almost all sections of foreign opinion. Martin Niemöller, on the other hand, was the subject of awed admiration throughout the Western world. Adam's proposal was a strange one, nonetheless.

In the first month of 1943 Adam was involved in another attempt to persuade the Western powers to relent on their declared policy only to negotiate with Germany after her defeat. Once more he went to Switzerland.

Not long before this, the United States Government had opened a branch of the Office of Strategic Services (the O.S.S.) in Berne. The official in charge was Mr Allen Welsh Dulles. Adam's purpose was to meet him and explain the intentions of the Kreisau circle to him. Mr Dulles thought it would be indiscreet to see him personally and instead conveyed a message through an intermediary, asking for a statement of what he wanted to say. Adam wrote as follows in English:

'The answer is always given that Germany must suffer military defeat. Hence [anti-Nazis] . . . conclude it is useless to continue the conversation

[31]Martin Niemöller. Pastor and leader of the Confessional Church. Staunch opponent of Nazism, he preached in this sense in St Anne's Church Dahlem. He was arrested in 1937, acquitted by a court and immediately re-arrested and confined in concentration camps until liberated by Allied troops in 1945. No other single case had comparable effect on foreign opinion.

in view of the failure of the Western powers to understand that the Germans are themselves an oppressed people who live in an occupied country and that tremendous risks are taken by the opposition in continuing its activity. As a result, the opposition believes the Anglo-Saxon countries are filled with bourgeois prejudice and pharisaic theorising. There is a strong temptation to turn east. The reason for the eastward orientation is the belief in the possibility of fraternisation between the Russian and German people, although not between the present Governments. Both have broken with bourgeois ideology, both have suffered deeply, both desire a radical solution of social problems which transcends national limits, both are in the process of returning to the spiritual (but not the ecclesiastical) traditions of Christianity. The German soldier has respect, not hatred, for the Russian. The opposition believes that the decisive development in Europe will take place in the social, not in the military, realm. When the campaign in Russia stalls, after the German army has been thrown back, a revolutionary situation may arise on both sides. Fraternisation between Germans and imported foreign workers is also an important element. Hitler has been forced to play up to the labouring classes and has given them an increasingly strong position; the bourgeois and intellectuals and generals are of less and less importance. Hitler will fall and the brotherhood of the oppressed is the basis upon which a completely new Europe will be built.'

This singular document, which does not seem in retrospect to have accurately portrayed internal conditions and ideas in Germany, was not well calculated to please the British or American politicians to whom it was addressed. The uprush of emotion in favour of Russia showed no sign of relaxation in the English-speaking world and was as strong in America as in Britain. Both in British and American factories, an 'arms for Russia' propaganda campaign could always be counted on to produce a large extra output, and criticism of the merciless tyranny of the U.S.S.R., or of its bloodthirsty leader whose achievements in homicide were then well in excess of those of Hitler himself, was regarded as brutally fascist. A paper written by a German warning of the dire effects of a possible spread of Communism was likely to be ill-received as a piece of Nazi chicanery; as 'trying to frighten us' as the English platitude of the day ran, 'with the Russian bogey.' The most highly esteemed of Germans who uttered such warnings then, was likely to be ill-regarded, and in the

Foreign Office whither this paper found its way, Adam was not highly esteemed.

The moment was unpropitious because of a less irrational cause. The year 1942 had been the first year of 'The Final Solution.' The policy had been initiated in January. It got going in the early summer but since, in the interests of German morale, the matter was treated as secret, it was not till the August of 1942 that reliable and accurate information about the policy and its workings reached the West through Gerhard Riegner, the representative of the World Jewish Congress in Geneva. The allied Governments hesitated until December 1942 before issuing a joint condemnation of 'this bestial policy.' They delayed so long because of genuine doubts whether such an incredible story could be true. Adam and Moltke's friends are most unlikely to have had any but the most meagre information on the subject then. The Final Solution was kept secret in Germany as long as it could be, and until the numbers involved in its execution grew to be as immense as the project, more people outside than inside Germany knew anything of the real facts.

This new course in Nazi policy inevitably gave a new impetus to that growing and indiscriminate movement of hatred against Germany and all Germans. It would seem that the next major step in Allied policy was to some extent governed by the conjunction of the battle for Stalingrad and of news of the Final Solution. President Roosevelt and Mr Churchill met in Casablanca in the second half of January 1943. On the 24th they issued a joint statement 'of the firm intention of the United States and the British Empire to continue the war relentlessly until they have brought about the Unconditional Surrender of Germany and Japan.'

Writing nearly three years after the event, Herr von Kessell quoted his diary that, according to his friends among the conspirators, the declaration of the 24th of January jeopardised and possibly destroyed 'six years of oppositional work' in Germany. Winston Churchill devoted his formidable forensic skill to defending the declaration in the fourth volume of his war memoirs, and so eminent an author as Sir John Wheeler-Bennett has reached the conclusion that the Unconditional Surrender Policy prevented another dolchstoss myth and furthermore had no effect on the scale or potential of German resistance to Hitler. The most enthusiastic contemporary apologist for the declaration was Josef Goebbels who asserted that in a dark hour when propaganda stumbled under the weight of defeat, Unconditional Surrender came as a heaven-sent gift. The British defenders of the declaration do sometimes appear to 'protest too much,' and the writer finds it hard not to agree with Herr von Kessel's judgment, and the later opinion of Herr Gerhard Ritter that the whole process whereby Britain and America came to believe that brute force alone was a better solution of the great problem posed by the war than any form of negotiation with anti-Nazi Germans 'was one of the most terrible and fateful errors of militarist thinking which contemporary history knows.'[32] Though the provocation was hideous, one may be reminded of the arrogant political follies of Hindenburg and Ludendorff.

The great problem of the German Resistance was and always had been to obtain the adherence of a respected military chief commanding a large military unit such as an Army Corps, a man whose orders would be unquestioningly obeyed in a coup d'état. They had come near to succeeding since the halting of the German armies before Leningrad, Moscow and Stalingrad, but in the event they never were to succeed, and, contrary to reasonable hope, the German nation continued to fight against the Allied armies long after the defeat of Germany was not only evident, but was no longer open to denial even by the Nazi propaganda machine. The prolongation of the war cost hundreds of thousands of lives. Is it fanciful to see in this extraordinary and ghastly result a consequence of a power-mad policy?

There is no evidence to show that Adam knew that he was under suspicion in Great Britain, and he seems never to have taken into his calculations his experiences in America as the suspected spy pursued by the F.B.I. All that belonged to the past, he seems to have thought, and he had the confidence of a clear conscience. After his memorandum to Mr Dulles, and after the devastating disappointment of the Casablanca declaration, he simply set himself to continue his appointed task on behalf of the Kreisau circle and of his own convictions, to obtain honourable terms for his country in the event of a German rising against Nazism; he pursued that task undismayed by the enormous increase of its difficulties since the

[32]Ritter p. 218.

24th of January, 1943, and the wonder is that in the end he seems almost to have approached success.

The first half of 1943 was a disastrous period in the history of the conspiracy against Hitler. Achievement seemed to come near, eluded them, and finally hope appeared to vanish. In February Goerdeler had a meeting in Berlin with his Swedish friend, Jakob Wallenberg, a member of the celebrated banking family. Through Herr Wallenberg and his elder brother, Marcus Wallenberg, Goerdeler had firm lines of communication, one to London and to Winston Churchill himself, another to the United States Government through Mr Dulles. To the latter Jakob Wallenberg wrote a memorandum in which he thus described what Goerdeler told him:

'He said the decision of the Casablanca Conference for unconditional surrender made his work with the German militarists more difficult, since some of the military insisted that if the German forces had to capitulate, they wanted Hitler to bear the responsibility for it. On the other hand the catastrophe of Stalingrad had occurred and this had made some of the military realise something would have to be done to remove Hitler. Goerdeler told me they had plans for a coup in March of 1943 but he was not sure if it could be carried through because Hitler was taking all precautions and was surrounded by a bodyguard of 3,000 people and hardly dared to appear at the front any more.'[33]

The code name of the proposed attempt in March 1943 was 'Operation Flash.' Little is known about it except that it was on a large scale and included military seizure of power in Berlin, Cologne, Munich and Vienna, and the assumption of command on the Eastern Front by Field-Marshal von Kluge. The whole plot depended on the explosion of a time-fused bomb, disguised in two bottles of brandy which were successfully conveyed into Hitler's aeroplane on the 13th of March as he left Kluge's Smolensk headquarters for East Prussia. The future of Europe was contained in those two brandy bottles which Fabian von Schlabrendorff handed to a member of Hitler's suite. The Fates were against Europe. The fuse was defective. Hitler arrived without mishap at his gloomy home, the Wolfsschanze or Wolf's Lair near Rastenburg.[34]

Another attempt was planned for the 21st of March when Hitler was

[33]Quoted in Dulles p. 149. [34]Wheeler-Bennett p. 562.

due to appear at a military ceremony in Berlin. It failed because of a last-minute change of time-table such as the Führer often resorted to in these days.[35] It was decided not to make a further attempt until the plans had been revised.

Thanks to Oster's thoroughness in destroying incriminating evidence, it cannot be known to what extent the Kreisau Circle was involved in 'Operation Flash.' It is unlikely that Moltke was told of the plan to blow up Hitler's aircraft, for his certain disapproval of such an act of homicide would have added a new and distracting complication. It seems certain from Clarita's memories of the time that Adam was fully informed. In any case the chief conspirators, Oster, Canaris, Olbricht, Tresckow and Schlabrendorff, could count with assurance on the Kreisauer rallying to provisional authority. Beyond that one can say nothing.

Another great reverse came on the Opposition in April. A man who knew something of the secret work of Canaris and Oster in the Abwehr got into trouble with the Gestapo over a currency offence. To save himself he told what he knew, and this was considerable thanks to his friendship with Oster's close collaborator, Hans von Dohnanyi. In the ensuing enquiry by the Gestapo, Dietrich Bonhoeffer's journey to Sweden was discovered. Of the inner core of the conspiracy centring on the Abwehr only Admiral Canaris survived (for a short time) the arrests and forcible retirements which followed. To quote Sir John Wheeler-Bennett:

'At one stroke the conspiracy had been deprived of many of its most valuable treasures: the high integrity of Dietrich Bonhoeffer, the noble character and intellectual ability of Hans von Dohnanyi, . . . and the fearless ingenuity of Hans Oster. It was the end of the original conspiracy against Hitler which had begun at the time of the Fritsch Crisis (March 1938) and had been based entirely on Oster's activities and his co-operation with von Dohnanyi. Their work continued, but in other and different hands.'

The removal of these men at the centre was not the only disaster which befell the conspiracy. At the end of March General Beck was found to be suffering from cancer and had to undergo a severe operation which incapacitated him for several months. It is not to be wondered at, perhaps, that in these circumstances Goerdeler fell into a state of hardly sane des-

[35]For details see Wheeler-Bennett pp. 563-64.

peration, and in a letter to General Olbricht of the 17th of May he proposed that since the military hierarchy seemed incapable of acting to stop the daily atrocities of the regime and the impending disaster to the nation, he was prepared to talk the matter out with Hitler personally. 'I would tell him,' he wrote, 'what he must be told, namely that in the vital interests of the people, his resignation is essential. If such a personal talk can be brought about, there is no reason why it should end badly.' He was eventually persuaded that his hopes of being able to talk Hitler into joining the anti-Nazi movement were illusory.

If faith in their cause had been only a little less, the conspiracy might have faded away under the load of so much misfortune. From the beginning it had always lacked unity, and even those groups which were in fairly close contact, such as the Kreisau circle and the Beck-Goerdeler group, had found themselves in much and sometimes radical disagreement. A representative meeting at Peter Yorck's house on the 22nd of January, 1943 had resulted in a stormy argument and the later attempts of Adam and Haeften and Fritz von der Schulenburg to reach a compromise with Hassell and Popitz had met with fragile success. As happens in bad days, the tenacity of those in opposition could have vanished through fragmentation if the will had been less. But the will was there.

The Kreisau circle held many meetings, usually quite small, in various places, as a rule in the houses of members. There were only three major meetings at Kreisau itself, and Adam is not recorded as attending the first two which were held in May and October of 1942. The third one was held at the Whitsun holiday week-end of 1943, from the 12th to the 14th of June. The subjects for discussion were foreign policy, economic reconstruction, the punishment of war criminals, and the appointment of local administrators in post-Nazi Germany. Adam led the debate on foreign policy. He said that at this stage the policy could only be occupied with certain immediate questions: how would the Allies react to a coup d'état; would they insist on Unconditional Surrender; would they, on the contrary, make concessions to a new regime; would the Russians in the end prove more accommodating than the Western Allies? In replying to these rhetorical questions he made it quite clear that there was no reason for optimism regarding the Western attitude. 'One has the impression from the West,' he said, 'that they will make no concessions.' Regarding the East one could not be so sure. In his study of the Kreisauer Kreis Mr van Roon notes how, in reaction against Nazi propaganda, several of the members had come to take a complacent view of the ethics of Soviet policy and rule, but he points out that at that moment, an approach to Russia did not seem urgent and the debate was concerned with matters of principle.[36] The Kreisauer tended also to believe (in common with most other Germans at that time) that out of fear of Russia, and a sense of European solidarity, the British and the American Governments were willing to conclude an advantageous but not merciless separate peace. They had little idea of the genuine popular Western fervour for Russia, nor of how easily Stalin could frighten Western Governments with hints of a separate peace of his own. In spite of his own abundant optimism Adam saw the matter more clearly, and he undertook the duty of telling his friends the unpleasant truth which he knew only too well from his own experiences, and those of Bonhoeffer and Schönfeld, with which he had been associated.

When the Foreign Affairs discussion was concluded Adam does not seem to have taken a prominent part in the other debates. He wrote in humorous self-disparagement to Clarita who was staying at Imshausen: 'I am thoroughly busy here, but only slightly pleased with myself, and I seem to be at the receiving end; that goes mainly to Freya Moltke's credit, but also to his. One can learn a lot from them, and you must come to see for yourself how they live here, simply yet generously, joyfully and actively.'

A few days after this meeting at Kreisau, Adam went on another journey abroad, this time to Turkey. There was no difficulty in arranging the matter officially, as on the 6th of May the German Ambassador to Turkey, Franz von Papen, had invited Adam to visit him. There were two reasons for this expedition. One was personal, and Clarita remembers that Adam wished the Ambassador to use his influence in favour of a friend of Werner who was held in prison. The second 'Kreisau' reason was to persuade Papen to join the conspiracy. Papen's whole career rested on the fact that great numbers of people of all sorts, good and bad, in the political world could be deluded into believing that his support

[6] Van Roon pp. 254-5.

was valuable. It is surprising to find that the Kreisauer were no exception. The expedition achieved nothing, but it is extremely interesting for the light it throws on Adam at this time, and for this we are indebted to the fact that in Ankara he again met his friend of Californian and China days, Wolfram Eberhard.

Now six years later they took up their friendship again. 'His attitudes had changed,' Professor Eberhard has recorded in a letter written in English to Mr van Roon, 'he was clear about what had to be done, and seemed—perhaps unconsciously as yet—to expect death. He had contacts with several persons in the German Embassy. We participated in some meetings with G. von Walther,[37] and discussed to what degree von Papen could be used. As far as I remember von Trott had a very open discussion with von Papen and asked him to join the group. Later von Walther, as far as I know, followed this up and tried to work on von Papen. Just before von Papen left Ankara to return to Germany (when diplomatic relations with Germany were broken off by the Turkish Government) we tried to convince him that if he would openly break with Germany, the Allies and the Turks would not interfere, and a great number of the German refugees and even others would stay with him.[38] Von Papen admitted this, but left for Germany. As far as I know, von Papen never divulged his complete knowledge of the plans . . .

'During the brief meeting in Turkey, Adam von Trott outlined some of their ideological plans. He discussed the membership of the group (but never mentioned the term "Kreisauer Kreis"), stating that it had Rightists, Social Democrats and Army men. He mentioned that Communists tried to co-operate but that these could not be admitted. He believed that it should be possible at this time to overcome the division of Germans into parties. That party programmes and ideologies were a thing of the past. He also believed that it should be possible to establish a super-national unity, and mentioned that ways should be found to unite with the displaced Europeans at that time in Germany, and with moderate elements in all European countries, to form a real European community based upon equality.

[37]Ambassador Doctor Gebhardt von Walther.
[38]The American diplomat, Mr George Earle, discussed these possibilities with Papen. It is believed that Papen secretly discussed the matter with Weizsäcker who advised against the proposition. Van Roon p. 320.

Ideas of Klassenkampf as well as of old-fashioned nationalism were obsolete, according to him; a new concept of European community could now be created, based upon essential values of the Christian past and community of Europe; based upon social justice; based upon a form of enlightened government by qualified people. We did not discuss how these people would be recruited (elections? a corporate system?) but we did discuss whether Soviet Russia or other Eastern groups could or should be included. Von Trott mentioned discussions which had once taken place in Stockholm with a Soviet diplomat (I think it was the lady who was ambassador) and which had led to nothing. Von Trott seems to have believed that a new community of Europeans would probably include the Western and Central European groups. I remember that I pointed a) to the Soviet threat and the possibility that after the war, all of Central Europe might become Communist; b) to the violent opposition of all occupied European countries against any form of Germany (sic). He thought that the first problem was not the most serious one and that a group in Germany of the type they [the Kreisau circle] had, might be able to reach a compromise and achieve collaboration even with Holland.'

Here, in the briefest outline, was a description of how the Kreisau circle were thinking. To-day their ideas may seem not only familiar but commonplace, but to dismiss them as such is to miss what is important about them. That aptitude to go in for 'spiritual stock-taking' which had become so marked at the beginning of the war in 1939, and had been reflected in the Trott-Scheffer memorandum, persisted throughout the war. In Great Britain, in spite of the ultra-nationalism which is inseparable from war, and in spite of the hate cult which Vansittart made fashionable, indeed partly as a reaction against these things, the stock-taking and dreaming of a peaceful international future went on under many forms. What is interesting about this thumbnail sketch of what was being thought and said in Kreisau is that it bears so close a resemblance to what was being thought and said in London, and, in varying degrees of wit or crudeness, in the many British theatres of war. It is evidence that if the Kreisauer had ever been able to meet Allied representatives in discussion they would have found, among many differences, some common ground.

Adam resumed another friendship of the past in Turkey. His old chief Paul Leverkühn was at this time living in Istanbul as Abwehr representative, and there Adam called on him. His purpose was to prepare Lever-kühn for an intended visit to Turkey by Moltke, a visit which he in fact paid in July, seeking the vanishing goal of a separate peace with the Western powers and a revocation of the Unconditional Surrender policy in the event of an anti-Nazi rising in Germany.

Adam's meeting with Leverkühn seems to have been a very happy one. Since April 1943, Adam enjoyed a more substantial position in the Aus-wärtige Amt, having been accorded from that time the still modest offi-cial rank of Legationssekretär,[39] or, as we might say, Second Secretary. In view of his now more secure position, Herr Leverkühn asked Adam if he would help the son of one of his fellow townsmen in Lübeck, by name Erich Vermehren, who with his wife was employed in the Abwehr Headquarters in Berlin. The young couple wished to obtain an appoint-ment to Leverkühn's office in Istanbul, and to obtain the necessary visas they needed a recommendation from someone of standing in the Aus-wärtige Amt. Unable to resist an appeal to his good nature, Adam agreed and gave the necessary document to Vermehren on his return to Berlin. He was all the more pleased to help Vermehren as he had been nominated for a Rhodes scholarship before the war, and turned down by the selec-tion committee for his 'negative' attitude to Nazism.[40] Six months later the visa transaction was to cause Adam the utmost anxiety and peril. For the moment he thought no more about it.

Adam made four more journeys in 1943, two to Holland, one to Switzerland and one to Sweden. His two visits to Holland were in the nature of confirming agreements with the Dutch resistance which he had made on a first visit from the 5th to the 9th of December in 1942. The contact had an origin in Schönfeld who had recommended him to the Dutch conspirators in the previous summer. Adam's arrival in Decem-ber had puzzled them as it had been reported in the local Nazi press, and it was noticed that he spent time every day with German officials. When he at length met the Dutch resistance leader Professor C. L. Patijn in the latter's house where he and some trusted colleagues were assembled,

---

[39]Auswärtige Amt Archives. Trott was recommended for this promotion as early as July 1942 but it was delayed by Ribbentrop. In November 1943 he was pro-moted Legationsrat or Counsellor 2nd class.
[40]Wheeler-Bennett p. 595.

his reception was distinctly cool. He explained immediately that it was
essential to have a convincing alibi, and on the present occasion he was
officially in Holland to make enquiries about Dutch prisoners-of-war in
Japanese camps. (It is a fair guess that as Dutch prisoners included men
from their Far Eastern colonies, Adam was using the Indienreferat as his
cover.) Surprised by this immediate candour, the Dutchmen asked him
to state what his business in Holland really was. If they were surprised
by his first remarks they were more so by what he now said. Without
any preliminaries or hesitation he replied that he was in Holland to make
contact with reliable Dutchmen belonging to resistance groups; to arouse
a spirit of goodwill in Dutchmen, because the group he represented would
need this in the event of their taking over the Government of Germany,
and he was also there, he said, to obtain a recommendation to the Allies of
certain German personalities who were wholly reliable.

Before such an outspoken affirmation they could only break off relations permanently or take him to their hearts. They did the latter. The
rest of the discussion was occupied with details of maintaining contact between the Patijn group and the Kreisau circle, and of how it were best
to set about obtaining the freedom of certain Dutchmen, valuable to the
Resistance, who were imprisoned in Germany. They also asked, and
were promised, that when the moment for action was at hand they should
be warned by an agreed signal.

From fragmentary records and imperfect memories it is not quite clear
how much was concluded at this first meeting, and how much belongs
to the second and third which occurred respectively on the 18th to the
23rd of August, and the 10th to the 17th of December of 1943. But it is
clear that from the first meeting the mutual trust of these Dutch resisters
and Adam was complete, and when they came to discuss relations with
England the Dutchmen were surprised and distressed to learn of the negative results of the memorandum which Adam had sent to Sir Stafford
Cripps by Visser 't Hooft. Adam told them about this himself, and it
made no difference to the confidence which they themselves had in him.
Adam told them other things about the eventual plans of the Kreisau
circle. They proposed that Goerdeler should be head of the post-Nazi
Government, Hassell the Minister for Foreign Affairs and Adam himself
his Staatssekretär. This news was perhaps more remarkable than appeared to the Dutchmen: it indicated the achievement of union between

the older conspirators and the 'Young Turks,' a union to which Adam had contributed more than most.[41]

At one of these secret meetings in Holland, Adam gave them a copy of the Manifesto which had been drawn up by Moltke and his friends for publication after the coup d'état. They expressed themselves in agreement with all its ideas. He confided it to the keeping of one of Patijn's friends called Van Roijen who was later to be a Foreign Minister of the Netherlands and an ambassador to London.[42]

Adam made a visit to Geneva from the 8th to the 16th of September, but of this nothing of special significance is remembered. Since over a year he had two faithful friends in the German Consulate, Albrecht von Kessel and Gottfried von Nostitz. The visit was possibly a continuation of his conversations in Holland conducted through Schönfeld and Visser 't Hooft. The most remarkable journey he made this year was to Sweden from the 27th of October to the 3rd of November.

He had been to Stockholm once before at the end of September in 1942, but of this visit little seems to be known. It was probably a visit of very tentative exploration and contact-making. Ever since Schönfeld and Bonhoeffer had met the Bishop of Chichester in Sweden, the Kreisau circle had striven to enlarge and draw profit from the contact of Swedish and German anti-Nazis which remained from that bitter failure.

One of the first people Adam saw after arrival in Stockholm on the 27th of October was Ivar Anderson, the editor of the *Svenska Dagbladet*, who kept a record of their conversation. Adam told him that the feeling in Germany was one of growing exasperation and yet, in spite of distrust and hatred of the Nazi leadership, the chance of a change of regime remained very small. He had no doubt that the U.S.S.R. planned to use this state of affairs for its own purposes. He wanted to know Anderson's opinion as to whether a coup d'état which brought about the elimination of the Nazi Government could count on immediate Allied help. Speaking in English he said: 'If we can manage to cause a change of regime in

---

[41]The proposed Government was not in fact settled till June 1944 when Goerdeler was confirmed as Chancellor, but the Ministry for Foreign Affairs left open. Wheeler-Bennett pp. 622-3.
[42]This account of Trott's first three meetings with the Dutch Resistance is taken from Van Roon pp. 329-31. The precise dates are in C.T.

Germany, it would be necessary for us to get help from abroad more or less immediately. We are in no position to wait. The risk of a counter-action, maybe a civil war, is too great. Our own power is so weak that we can hope to carry through our aim only if the course of events is favourable and we get help from abroad. What do you think of our chances of getting help?'

Anderson replied that the likelihood of such help being forthcoming was very small, whereat Adam burst out: 'In that case there is nothing for us to do but wait and see. This is dangerous because it may mean that Russia will win the game.' Then, in a calmer mood, Adam told Anderson that his main purpose in coming to Sweden was to make contact with English or Americans. Anderson promised to help and was as good as his word.[43]

The term 'help from abroad' seems at first sight to indicate the hope of some military action. It is impossible to imagine what Allied military action in Germany was conceivably possible before the landings in France, and, if it was possible, how such action could do other than dis-credit the patriotism of the Kreisau circle and other conspirators. Adam seems in fact to have meant two things only: a renunciation of the policy of Unconditional Surrender, and an immediate cessation of the bombing of Germany.

By clever manoeuvring in the Auswärtige Amt, the opposition had secured the appointment of two sympathisers, Doctor Pfleiderer and Werner Dankwort, as Counsellors in the German Legation at Stockholm. They were able to introduce Adam to many people in Stockholm, but anti-German feeling was rising so much in the country, and was taking on so undiscriminating a character, that their help did not always forward Adam's mission. A meeting with Ambassador Söderblom seems to have been very unsuccessful, but another, with Ambassador Gunnar Hägglöf though not fruitful, seems to have resulted in mutual sympathy. Adam (possibly in some desperation) seems to have charged recklessly at this first encounter into the central question. The Ambassador has written of the occasion: 'I met Adam von Trott zu Solz in Stockholm through one of the counsellors of the German Legation, Dr Pfleiderer . . . in the

[43]This account of the meeting is taken from a translation of Anderson's diary by Mrs Bielenberg quoted in van Roon p. 316.

autumn of 1943 . . . We had luncheon together in a private club in Stockholm. I had returned from a long stay in London for negotiations with the Foreign Office and I was at the time of the luncheon engaged in negotiations with a German delegation. During the luncheon I was asked by Adam von Trott how in my opinion the Allied Governments would react if Hitler was killed and replaced by another regime. We had a long conversation on this subject.'[44]

Werner Dankwort had a Swedish friend who knew his secret and was prepared to give him all the help she could. Her name was Fru Inga Almstrom. She knew one of the attachés in the British Legation, Mr James Knapp-Fisher. He shared a flat in Stockholm with a colleague in the Press Department, Mr Roger Hinks. He has given this brief account of what happened.

'I saw Adam von Trott before he came to the flat . . . I went to a house in, I think, Gärdet, a northern suburb of Stockholm. [Fru Almstrom] had rung me at the Embassy (or Legation as it was then) to ask if I would go for a drink. I knew that she never did this to English people unless there was a good reason and I suspected at once that she wished me to meet a German—something of course strictly forbidden at that time. However I obtained permission from the Minister or from Mr Tennant,[45] and I met one of the most charming, honest and decent men I have ever had the pleasure of meeting. I took to him immediately and we arranged that he should come and outline the details to me alone of a plan he had (he would not at that time say what the plan was about) as our contact was in the room and was a Swede. He asked if he could come later to my own residence. I immediately agreed but begged him to come before 9 o'clock as the outside doors of Stockholm blocks of flats are all closed at that hour and it is difficult to get in without making yourself known. He was, of course, being followed. He was unable to get to the flat until 10.30. I do remember that I had already given up hope that he would turn up and was in my pyjamas when the bell rang making what seemed like a terrifying noise in the flat as I had been waiting for it to ring for nearly two hours.'

[44] A letter to Mrs Bielenberg.
[45] Mr Peter Tennant was head of the Press Department.
[46] A letter to Mrs Bielenberg.

Years later Roger Hinks told a friend about the circumstances under which Adam entered the house. Mr Knapp Fisher had promised Adam that no one besides Mr Hinks would be there, but on that very evening they received an unexpected visit from Harold Nicolson, then on an official visit to Sweden. He was flying back to England that night and was expecting a call from the Legation to warn him of the time of flight. At any other time he would have been abundantly welcome, but on this evening, as he talked on in his polished and delightful way, the two friends exchanged agonised glances. At length, to their infinite relief, the warning message came and he left at ten o'clock. Half an hour later Adam arrived, to their astonishment. He explained that he had darted in as Harold Nicolson (whom he knew slightly) went out, and had then hidden in the building for half an hour to make sure he was not followed to the flat.[47]

He remained and told about the promised plan, not leaving till about four in the morning.

The plan which Adam outlined to the two Englishmen was 'Operation Valkyrie,' the attempt which, but for a table leg which changed history, would have rid the world of Hitler nearly a year before his own chosen time. Adam's knowledge of the plan at this stage would have been rudimentary, but from Peter Yorck and others of the Kreisau circle he had caught the optimism which pervaded the resistance, in spite of so many setbacks, in the later part of 1943. Goerdeler, who was strangely prone to be misinformed,[48] had warned Jakob Wallenberg in August to expect the coup in September.[49] In spite of their many failures to rally against the tyranny, for which no one had blamed them more harshly than Goerdeler, the senior commanders were expected now, by Goerdeler and the Kreisau circle, to make common cause. It only needed the assassination of Hitler and the army would turn on the real enemies of Germany. Plans for Hitler's murder and for the ensuing coup were completed just about the time that Adam had this midnight conference with Knapp-Fisher and Roger Hinks, in November 1943.

As in his previous conversations, Adam's task was to find out whether the British and Americans could withdraw from the Unconditional Sur-

[47]Mrs Bielenberg who heard the story from the late Roger Hinks.
[48]Margaret Boveri. *Treason in the 20th Century*.
[49]Dulles (quoting Wallenberg) pp. 144-5.

render demand, and whether they would, on news of the revolt, call off the increasingly indiscriminate bombing of Germany. Naturally the two Englishmen could give no undertaking about these things, but Adam felt that he had had a friendly hearing, and that what he said would be sympathetically reported.

Through Pfleiderer, Dankwort and Anderson he met many people with immediate experience of England and America. Through Anderson he was introduced to the Foreign Minister, Christian Gunther, who, according to a letter written to Anderson, found in Adam a delightful personality. He could however do nothing for him other than deliver his well-known lecture on Swedish neutrality. A potentially more valuable meeting, also arranged by Anderson, was with Sir Walter Monckton, at that moment Undersecretary to the Ministry of Information. But this meeting also is believed to have had no result.[50] At the end of this visit on 3rd November, Adam was in two minds about it. He could not but be depressed at the news from England and America and how Unconditional Surrender seemed to have become an unalterable article of religious faith; on the other hand his meeting with the two Englishmen of the Legation staff gave him hope that the British Government might possibly be more flexible.[51]

His hope was reasonable, if not justified in the event. One purpose of the thoughtless pronouncement at Casablanca (and the evidence for thoughtlessness comes from the enunciator President Roosevelt)[52] was to please the Russians, and this it had signally failed to do, the Russian hope being to obtain surrender on conditions favourable to Communism.

[50]Van Roon p. 316.
[51]Van Roon and C.T. The authorities are in some conflict at this point, Mr van Roon depicting Trott as almost in despair, and Dr Clarita von Trott indicating, with the documentary support of a letter from Trott to his mother that he felt guarded satisfaction. She also quotes from the Hassell diaries, 27.12.43. 'I spoke with Trott shortly before my departure . . . He judges the situation much as I do. On his official trips he has had the opportunity, as have few others, to look at things from the outside and even to make contact with Englishmen. His English acquaintances were greatly concerned about Russia and deeply interested in developments here. They were, however, suspicious lest a change should turn out to be only a cloak, hiding a continuation of militaristic Nazi methods under another label.'
[52]Churchill. Vol. IV.

That such conditions would have been based on the purge-system, and infinitely worse than what was exacted, is beside the point. The apologies offered by Winston Churchill and the President after Casablanca were not what the Germans heard about it; they heard what Goebbels told them, and for once Goebbels really seemed to be speaking the truth. The British Government realised that a diplomatic and psychological mistake had been made and, again partly to please the Russians, Mr Eden tried to persuade the American Government to correct the blunder. But Mr Roosevelt's obstinacy was prodigious, and indeed this was a mistake which, once made, was almost irreversible. A recantation might have sounded to the Nazis like lack of confidence, and would quite certainly have aroused Russian suspicions once again. However, to return to the particular, Adam's pleading against Unconditional Surrender did not have the ill reception in London in November 1943 that his similar pleas had had earlier. It seems to have had a mixed reception, as appears later.

It has been mentioned that there was a great optimism in the Resistance at this time. It came from a man whom Adam first met soon after his return from Sweden and with whom he immediately made friends. He was Claus Schenck Count von Stauffenberg.

In October this young Colonel had been officially appointed to a senior post under General Friedrich Olbricht, at that time head of what was called the General Army Office (Allgemeine Heeresamt), and was in effect the headquarters of the Reserve Army whose Commander was General Friedrich Fromm. The General Army Office was an important part of the German war machine, being the responsible agency for replacements of military personnel. Stauffenberg became Chief of Staff in the Supply Section. He seems to have first met Adam through Hans-Bernd von Haeften.[53]

Stauffenberg was thirty-six years old, and came of an ancient and aristocratic Swabian family, long connected with the courts of Bavaria and Württemberg. He was a professional soldier and had proved himself an officer of exemplary efficiency. He was out of sympathy with Nazism from the beginning of the regime; stories to the contrary have been proved

[53]Joachim Kramarz. *Stauffenberg*. English edition translated by R. H. Barry. London 1967. Roger Maxwell and Heinrich Fraenkel. *The July Plot* London 1964.

fallacious by his German biographer, Herr Joachim Kramarz.[54] It is true, however, that like Adam and many others he was long perplexed, as a patriotic man, how he should and could oppose Nazism in time of war. But, unlike Adam, he had very limited experience of the world, and for long he deluded himself into believing that the system of Government in Germany was no conceivable concern of any officer in the army. Like many others he allowed himself to be taken in by the fashionable cant about 'German destiny.' In late 1939 his uncle Count Nicolaus von Üxküll and his friend Fritz von der Schulenburg tried in vain to persuade him that the desperate situation of Germany under the Nazis compelled new loyalties. He resisted their arguments and for long remained an escapist.[55] Even when as a staff officer in Russia he saw the full atrocity and folly of Nazi rule over conquered territory, he sought spiritual release, not in opposition, but in service under Rommel in North Africa. There he suffered an experience which changed his life. In the last days of the campaign his car was attacked by low-flying aircraft on the 7th of April, 1943. He was gravely wounded, losing his right hand and forearm, two fingers of his left hand, and his left eye, with severe leg injuries. But for the skill of the great surgeon, Professor Sauerbruch, he might have lost his sight completely and remained inactive for the rest of his life. He was helped by his formidable will and a mystical sense that he had been preserved for some great task. While he was slowly recovering in hospital in Munich he was visited by his uncle von Üxküll who urged him once more to take part in vigorous opposition to Hitler and the regime. Stauffenberg replied that he must think this over. On his uncle's second visit he told him of his decision. He said: 'Since the generals have done nothing so far, the colonels must now go into action.' Üxküll's daughter has left a record of the arguments which her father used.

'In October 1943 [my father] told me of the conspiracy for the first time. He said, "I have been trying for years to convince the younger generation"—in which he included also my other cousins Hofacker, Yorck, and his young friend Schulenburg—"that some move against this regime must be made in Germany by Germans. At last I have got somewhere. Unfortunately I must admit to you that I think it is now too

[54]For details see Kramarz (English edition) p. 44-7.
[55]Kurt Finker. *Stauffenberg und der 20 Juli 1944*. East Berlin 1968

late and the moment is past. Naturally, however, although I think this, I am still heart and soul behind this business, for even though I believe that it has in fact no chance of success, at least it has the advantage that we shall have shown the world that some attempt has been made by Germans to rid themselves of these criminals."[56]

In August Stauffenberg went to Berlin to meet his future chief, General Olbricht, and the latter's friend Major-General Hemming von Tresckow, Chief of Staff to Field-Marshal von Kluge commanding Army Group Centre in Russia. Tresckow was officially on sick leave, but in fact he and Olbricht were working hard on the new major conspiracy 'Operation Valkyrie.' They believed that in Stauffenberg they would find a worthy successor to Hans Oster. It is not clear how much, if anything, Stauffenberg knew about these conspiratorial activities before meeting Olbricht, but it is certain that he entered them immediately. He took over the planning from Tresckow and by November, so the conspirators believed, 'Valkyrie' was ready to go into action.

Stauffenberg was a tall man of magnificent physique and striking good looks. His joyous spirits were irresistible, and everyone who has described him mentions his ringing and infectious laugh. He and Adam were superficially different, but had much in common. Stauffenberg was an extrovert character with little of Adam's brooding introspection and Hamletish tendency to explore the divisions in his mind and feelings, but they shared many ideals. Without Adam's political complexity, his Hegelian side, Stauffenberg was as passionately interested in politics, and his political ideas, even in detail, were very close to Adam's. An outline of guiding principles for post-Nazi Germany, which was drafted by his friend the historian Doctor Rudolf Fahrner after a discussion with him in August 1943, shows again the idea of the conservative revolutionary, and might have been written by Adam. Like him Stauffenberg associated civilisation with religion, using the term in its broadest sense, and fixed his hopes on an egalitarian society dissociated from and owing nothing to class-warfare, a society held together by a devotion to a common purpose. He saw, like Adam, self-centred and warlike nationalism as a decaying force. Insofar as a political programme can be discerned, the draft shows a determination not to go back to the political chaos and chicanery of the Weimar

[56]Quoted in Kramarz.

Republic, an attitude in full accordance with Adam's political belief. The document represents the ideas of a man evidently unfamiliar with the everyday difficulties and antagonisms of political life, and buoyed up by faith and irrepressible hope.

Another characteristic of Stauffenberg, which he shared with Olbricht, Tresckow and others of the conspirators, though rather less with Adam, should be mentioned as it explains much of his character and impulse. This was an intense devotion to the work of Stefan George. He found inspiration in his poem 'Anti-Christ' and on one occasion, when trying to persuade an officer to abandon his scruples and oppose the ruler of Germany he merely quoted the poem, making no comment.[57]

Der Fürst des Geziefers verbreitet sein reich

Kein schatz der ihm mangelt; kein glück das ihm weicht.

Zu grund mit dem rest der empörer!

Ihr jauchzet, entzückt von dem teuflischen schein,

Verprasset was blieb von dem früheren seim

Und fühlt erst die not vor dem ende.

Dann hängt ihr die zunge ám trocknenden trog,

Irrt ratlos wie vieh durch den brennenden hof, . . .

Und schrecklich erschallt die posaune.[58]

In her memoir Clarita has written as follows about her husband and Claus von Stauffenberg: 'It is quite possible that for Adam this friendship was the fulfilment of something which he had been seeking all his life

---

[57]Kramarz p. 156; on page 123 Dr Fahrner's draft is fully quoted.

[58]Wheeler-Bennett 582. The capricious typography in George's full style is likely to confuse the reader. Sir Maurice Bowra supplied the following translation for *The Nemesis of Power*.

The Master of Vermin far stretches his realm:
No treasure that fails him, no luck that forsakes
Destruction take all other rebels!

You clamour, enticed by the devilish show,
Lay waste what remains of the sap from the spring
And feel your need first when the end comes.

Then you hang out your tongues o'er the emptying trough,
Stray like herds without aim through the courtyard in flames . . .
And fearfully rings out the trumpet.

in spite of the fact that he had so many friends to whom he was united by affection, respect, and by tasks and responsibilities shared in common. He said to Mrs Braun-Vogelstein in 1939, "I share only bits of myself and fragments of things with others," but now, after meeting Stauffenberg at a late stage in his life, this was no longer true.'

Clarita knew nothing of the friendship until some months later, and even then Adam never told her the name of this man whom he so much admired and liked and who, he said, by his 'fiery' character had given new impetus and vigour to the opposition. He was careful not to involve her in this particular relationship, and he was wise in this, for in the very month when Adam first met Stauffenberg, an attempt was made to assassinate Hitler and thus set Operation Valkyrie in motion.

It was a most ingenious plan involving the death of the assassin. Some new army overcoats had been designed and Hitler wished to inspect samples personally before the order was put through. A friend of Fritz Schulenburg, a brave officer called Freiherr Axel von dem Bussche, obtained the duty of 'modelling' the overcoats for Hitler, and after exasperating postponements the appointment was at last fixed. Bussche planned to hide bombs in the pockets, ignite them in the Führer's presence and then grapple with him until the explosion tore them both in pieces. Hitler's luck held out thanks to the R.A.F. who, the night before the appointed day, destroyed the store of coats in a bombing attack.[59]

A month or so later another attempt was planned, to be undertaken, according to a warning issued to Goerdeler, sometime between the 25th and 27th of December. It was called off, though the reason for this is not known. The overcoat plan was revived in the next year, but the parade was cancelled again. Shortly after, a certain Captain von Breitenbuch prepared himself to shoot Hitler at a conference which he was due to attend as A.D.C. to Field-Marshal Busch, but at the last moment A.D.C.s were excluded from the meeting.[60] These attempts belong to February, and after them none further was made till the summer.

[59]Wheeler-Bennett pp. 590-1.
[60]Kramarz p. 149. Herr von Schlabrendorff (p. 275) has a different version of the episode. According to him Colonel (not Captain) von Breitenbuch was at the conference at Berchtesgaden but was so closely watched by SS guards that he could not get his hand to his pocket.

This is to take the story into the fateful year 1944. During the winter the strain of living a double life in Berlin, while the city was undergoing remorseless bombing night after night, told on Adam's health. He suffered from high temperatures, disabling attacks of rheumatism, and other disorders consequent on lack of sleep and unremitting nervous tension.[61] Then in February he suddenly and quite unexpectedly came under Gestapo suspicion.

The cause of the trouble was nothing to do with the Kreisau circle (though it suffered grievously from it) nor with Adam's friendship with Stauffenberg, but with the visa granted to the Vermehrens. What had happened was this. On the 10th of September 1943, Frau Anna Solf, the widow of a minister and ambassador of former times, and a firm anti-Nazi, entertained some friends of like mind to tea, according to her frequent custom. Among her guests was a certain Fräulein von Thadden, another courageous opponent of the regime and the head-mistress of a famous girls' school. She brought a friend, a highly agreeable Swiss doctor called Reckse who asserted his anti-Nazism to those whom he met at the tea-party, and arranged to take letters from any of them to their emigré friends in Switzerland. In fact Reckse was a Gestapo agent. In a short time he collected incriminating evidence against all Frau Solf's guests. The Gestapo decided to go slowly. Not till January 1944 did they pounce. They then arrested everyone who had been at the tea-party. Among those who were seized was the former German Consul General in New York, Otto Kiep. This man was a friend of the young Vermehrens, and it was he who had nominated Erich Vermehren for a Rhodes scholarship. The news of his arrest naturally caused them the greatest alarm. Soon afterwards they received orders to return from Istanbul to Berlin. They read this as a death warrant. They made instant contact with British Intelligence agents in Istanbul, and early in February they went over to the British. Their flight would have been looked upon as a very serious matter in any case, but, to aggravate their offence, it coincided, quite fortuitously, with the flight of two other Abwehr staff in Istanbul. Nor was this all. The Vermehrens were flown to England where, either by an indiscretion or an ill-conceived move by the Ministry of Information, their story was given great prominence in the British press.[62] The Gestapo pursued the

[61]C.T. [62]Wheeler Bennett 596.

Solf affair with their extremest virulence, and these aggravating factors spurred them on to further revenge.[63]

The recommendation for a visa was easily traced back to Adam. He was interrogated by the Gestapo several times. As always he kept his nerve throughout the ordeal. By that mixture of presence of mind, will and charm which he understood so well, he convinced the Gestapo of his innocence which, in this case, was in fact quite genuine. Nevertheless his escape, as Clarita recorded, seemed miraculous to his family and friends. It was no moment for rejoicing, however. Having lost their prey, the Gestapo turned on the families of the young husband and wife. They spent the rest of the war in concentration camps and were lucky to survive. There can be no question of blaming the young couple for vile deeds not of their doing, nor for their escape from death at the hands of the most abominable of tyrannies, but those who think badly of Adam's obstinacy in returning to Germany in 1940, or see dubious motives in his action, should remember this episode.

The Solf affair affected the Kreisau circle as a whole in a way that again would probably have been fatal if the will had been less. Helmuth von Moltke knew of the activities of the Gestapo agent and he had warned Otto Kiep against him. The line was tapped, and when the Gestapo went into action in January he also was arrested. As yet the Gestapo knew nothing of a Kreisau circle, and, needless to say, learned nothing of it from Moltke. Another friend of Adam, who had been arrested four months before, was also doomed as an admirer of Frau Solf. He was Albrecht von Bernstorff. Neither of these two men, shining lights in the darkness hanging over Germany, ever knew freedom again.

Gestapo suspicion of Adam arose at the worst imaginable time for his conspiratorial activities in Sweden which now came into some confusion. In February a message came from Roger Hinks, secretly relayed by Fru Almstrom, that the British Legation wished to continue conversations with him. They asked him to come to Stockholm as soon as he could. Of course Adam wanted to go, but having just escaped from the visa affair, he wanted to be quite sure that he was not endangered by an indiscretion. He believed (perhaps from something he had heard on a broad-

---

[63]The facts of the Solf affair are accurately stated in William L. Shirer 1025-6, and those of the Vermehren affair in the above and Wheeler-Bennett p. 594-6.

cast from England) that Roger Hinks had not kept his conversation of November 1943 perfectly secret. As Stockholm carried as large a population of spies and gossips as Switzerland, it is as likely that news of other of Adam's conversations had spread. The matter is obscure; nothing is known except that Adam postponed his visit from February to the middle of March, and then, at his own request, did not see Roger Hinks but another official. The choice on the British side fell on a member of the British Legation who had been consulted throughout.

The conversation, taken up again on English initiative, was disappointing in the result. It only served to show again that the new course in British policy was making for such a degree of inflexibility that the sort of secret negotiations that Adam was attempting were virtually impossible.

The conversations were begun in Fru Almstrom's flat, and on this occasion neither side seems to have had any inhibition about talking in front of her. Long after, she gave an account to Clarita. According to her memory, the British representative made it clear that his Government sought to know whether the German opposition was strong enough to bring about an early end to the war, of course with Allied help. He made no secret of the fact (according to Fru Almstrom) that for obvious economic reasons they wished to be able to cease from heavy bombing of the German industrial centres. Adam replied that he was not authorised to give more information than he had given already, unless he received an assurance that Unconditional Surrender would not be exacted from a German Government which had overthrown the Nazis. He was the spokesman of Kreisau, and if the Kreisauer were to rule in Germany they could not ask less than this. On the other side, The official was now placed in a position of impotence. He could not give a definitive reply to so large a question of policy, which involved the United States Government even more closely than the British Government, and could not be revised without reference to the U.S.S.R., not counting for the moment the Governments in exile. The official, for all that, did not want to let the conversations merely cease. In some hope of compromise he asked Adam to put his opinion in a memorandum. This Adam did and his views were conveyed by telegraph to the British and American Governments. It was Fru Almstrom's impression that when an answer came back it indicated some British willingness, or at least no absolute British refusal to reconsider the question of unconditional surrender, but that the United States Government had a closed mind. [64]

In a diary which he kept at the time Albrecht von Kessel recorded an account of the meeting which he heard from Adam. It differs from that of Fru Almstrom but is not wholly inconsistent with it. It probably represents another stage of the discussion not held in her house, and after a reply had come from England. [65]

'He was greatly discouraged by his latest experiences in Sweden. He had been in touch with influential people who were in sympathy with our movement, and through them he had again sought contact with England. As agreed, he had not asked for declarations or promises apart from one which amounted to no more than a simple gesture, that in the event of the Nazis being overthrown and a broadly based civil Government being established in their place, the British should then cease from further air-attacks on Berlin. Although such an undertaking would have been without military significance because of the geographical restriction, and although, should it have become known through an indiscretion, the English could easily have represented it as a humanitarian not a political gesture, nevertheless von Trott's memorandum had a negative result. From England came a rough refusal.' [65]

This contradictory treatment of Adam, asking him to come to Stockholm urgently and at risk to himself, and then meeting everything he asked for on behalf of the Kreisau circle with a rough refusal, is puzzling. At the time the cruel policy, first put into practice by Göring's air force, of what came to be called 'pattern bombing,' was under much criticism in England, voiced notably by Aneurin Bevan in the House of Commons. Many people, including those in the Government, had an uneasy conscience, and there is nothing more exasperating than to be questioned on a matter of uneasy conscience, especially by your victim and enemy. It is asserted, on good authority, that Adam's protesting plea against the bombing of civilians was very ill received.

---

[64] C.T. Quoting letters from Fru Kempe (formerly Almstrom).
[65] Printed in Rothfels 2. This suggests (probably mistakenly) that Trott had temporarily withdrawn from his request regarding unconditional surrender. His other request was possibly influenced by events in Italy where the removal of Mussolini was followed by intensified bombing.

At the same time this may be only part of the explanation. Roger Hinks and James Knapp-Fisher had certainly broken down the old suspicion of Adam, but it is impossible to believe that they had broken it down entirely. There is interesting evidence of this in a book of memoirs called *Amateur Agent* written by another member of the Legation, Mr Ewan Butler. He belonged to another of its war-time departments, being one of the representatives of S.O.E. He relates that his office had knowledge of Adam's arrival in Stockholm at this time and he continues:'Knowing a very little of what was in the wind, and suspecting a great deal more, we asked London's permission to meet von Trott. It was refused. Roosevelt and Churchill had enunciated the doctrine of unconditional surrender at the Casablanca Conference and any contact with Germans who might seek, as von Trott and his associates did, to get rid of the Nazis and shorten the war, was forbidden . . . The Allies, I am still convinced, missed a great opportunity.'[66]

To anyone knowing Adam's temperament, it would not be surprising to learn that at this moment of raised hopes and shattering disappointment he fell into one of his despondent moods. But the evidence tells a different story. On his way back from this visit to Sweden he wrote to Clarita as follows:

'As I was flying across the sea and through the clouds into a darkly threatened Germany, I was filled again by a sense of deep love and of joy that I have been thrust into the place where I am, and in such difficult times, to fight with others for our homeland. I do not believe that any relationship with any other human being can mean as much to me as this does, and to prove myself in this, and to serve such a cause—this is my first duty. This may sound a bit pompous, and may perhaps even hide a secret and dangerous egotism, but it is true. To recognise one's own unique task, this liberates a man and gives him firmness in life; this allows him a clear choice amid the manifold and conflicting values and principles which confront any citizen of the modern world. In this age we must cast off the burden and the soul-destroying narrowness of the 19th century; we must build a new life through hard work and trials. Now we are only

[66]Ewan Butler. Amateur Agent. London 1963.

at the beginning, but the task stands out black and clear from the outline of ruins.' [67]

Without the key, without knowledge of what he was trying to accomplish, and of the effect on him of his friendship with Stauffenberg, this letter might appear, as in the circumstances it was probably intended to appear to prying eyes, as a piece of fashionable rhetoric. With the key, it is hardly an exaggeration to describe it as inspired.

Franz Josef Furtwängler tells of a revealing incident which happened during this winter of 1943 to 1944. 'Trott had a secretary, a poor, rather drab little creature, "underprivileged," as he said, and to her he always showed special friendliness and consideration. After a bombing attack the girl was buried in the cellar of the house where she lived. Trott mobilised a rescue squad and worked with them himself night and day—but in vain. A month later he was sitting relaxed in my room when he deplored, as a possible symptom of what he used to call "the freezing of the soul," that he had already put off signs of mourning for this faithful fellow-worker—mourning which he remembered in the toil and strife and death and ruin of the Hell which was Berlin at that time!'[68]

The disappointment of his March visit to Sweden did not mean that Adam gave up the attempt to exact a more considerate attitude from the Western Allies, nor did he persist in vain. The details are hidden in secrecy and none of the relevant documentation has been published, but it seems a reasonable guess that, as at other times in Adam's life, there sprang up in England a pro-Adam party while another remained orthodoxly suspicious of him. What is known is that he again received a secret invitation to return to Stockholm, and it has been said (though not proved) that there was even some prospect of his flying to England for a secret meeting. But this time he could not leave Germany. He was prevented not by Gestapo suspicion, which he had temporarily thrown off, but by a farcical indiscretion which forced him into extreme caution.

Adam had always looked on the Press as irresponsible and devoted to mischief for the sake of sensationalism. His dislike was not always reasonable, but on this occasion the Press was true to his worst fears. Among the news-hungry and always news-starved journalists of Stockholm one of them had got on to the Trott story, and, probably innocent of what he

[67]C.T.   [68]*Männer.*

was about, he contributed a chatty paragraph about him to a column. It is remembered as going somewhat as follows: 'A few days or even weeks ago Herr von Trott was to be seen around Stockholm. He has for long been entrusted with important missions abroad on behalf of Germany, even (we believe) before the war. It is not stretching speculation too far therefore to suppose that in this latest trip to colourful and winter-bound Sweden a peace-feeler from the German Government is to be detected.' And more in the same vein. This spicy item was copied by other Stockholm newspapers.[69]

After this there could be no question of any further journeys to Sweden for some time, though contact with the British Legation was still secretly maintained through Fru Almstrom.

By 1944 Werner was back in Germany and the two brothers again took up the long dialogue which, with interruption, they had held together since Adam's young days.

Werner's career in the war was in extreme contrast to Adam's, as was to be expected. In September 1939 he was over thirty-seven and was not called on to join any of the armed services. As usual he made no secret of his anti-Nazism, and made no move of his own to contribute to the German war-effort. In the early summer of 1942, however, he was called up and drafted into the army. He was not considered a suitable candidate for a commission, partly, it is believed, because he was unable to pass the required medical examination, and partly, it may be confidently assumed, because he showed no interest in being commissioned.

He passed through a time of great wretchedness. His duties lay in what we would describe as the Pioneer Corps, and he was occupied in manual labour, including the exacting task of loading heavy ammunition. He was not treated with consideration to his age and health, having (as one would expect) made himself very unpopular with his superiors. One can imagine him driving them to distraction by arguing the rights and wrongs of every single thing he was asked to do.

Adam was worried about his situation and asked Peter Bielenberg for help in getting Werner out of the army and into some more suitable

[69]Berichte. Werth. and C.T.

employment. Peter himself worked now under the Ministry of Economic Affairs and had official charge of certain fish-freezing installations in Norway. He succeeded in getting Werner employment in one of these in the north of the country. He was appointed welfare officer to look after the needs of a thousand Ukrainian workers who (to quote Peter) were 'partly voluntary workers, and partly "volunteered".' Here Werner was less unhappy, with interesting work which laid no burden on his conscience. He proved himself to be very efficient, but his very efficiency brought him into further ill favour with the authorities.

Like Adam he was a deeply religious man, but in a more formal spirit, and in 1942 he became a Roman Catholic. He found that the Ukrainians in his charge, both his Uniat co-religionists and the members of the Orthodox Church, had wholly inadequate facilities for the practice of their faith, and with maddening logic he repeatedly brought this injustice to the notice of the German authorities in Norway. On one occasion in the winter of 1942/1943 he wrote to the Russian Orthodox Patriarch in Berlin, describing the situation to him and asking him to send ikons for use by those within his province. Peter Bielenberg was visiting Werner at the time and he carried the letter to Berlin. Two informers got wind of the affair and Peter was arrested at the Norwegian-Swedish frontier. Fortunately he was able to frighten the Gestapo by means of name-dropping, saying that he hoped he would not have to report them for preventing his attendance at a conference attended by certain leading figures of the Third Reich. They let him go but the informers had done lasting damage. In the first part of 1943 Peter was transferred to other duties and was no longer responsible for this fish-freezing plant in the far north. Without his protection Werner's position grew precarious, and since he never abated a jot of his arrogance towards the Nazis, and never ceased to protest on behalf of the Ukrainians in the name of principle, he also was removed from his post in the course of 1943. He was now over forty and was not liable to conscription, and indeed no one in the army seems to have wished to conscript so disruptive a force. He spent the rest of the war at Imshausen.

For all his profound hatred of Nazism, Werner strongly disapproved of the kind of opposition which his brother was pursuing, and whenever they met, each of them strenuously asserted his point of view: their relationship became once more an argument which could not be brought to a conclusion. Werner believed that it was culpable moral rashness to oppose Nazism while pretending to be its ally. In so doing, he maintained, a man could not avoid infection. He is remembered as saying, 'Do you not believe that you are compromising with the Devil?', and one should remember that for Werner the Devil was no symbol, no abstract idea, but a great, terrible and living force. And Adam would put forward the opposite idea, that there was no other way of fighting Nazism except in disguise, and by practising deceit on the Father of Lies. He is remembered as saying something of this kind: 'Do you think it right merely to be a spectator, watching from the sidelines?' The two brothers explored the argument, delving deep into the philosophical implications with which it confronted them, and neither yielded an inch. They had, however, some matter for agreement when they debated another favourite subject, and their theme here throws an interesting light on Adam's political ideas. He believed that the new Germany must be a Christian state, but for that reason he was convinced (in opposition to many of his friends) that there should be no official mention of Christianity in the constitution. Christianity, so Adam maintained, must become apparent in the spirit and action of the state, but to give it an official Christian designation was to risk degrading an ideal to political and even party use. Werner believed this too.[70]

In April 1944 Adam made his last journey to Switzerland. His purpose was the same as in all his journeys both to Switzerland and Sweden: to persuade the Allies of the folly of the unconditional surrender policy, to warn of its dangers. The difference between what he had to say now and what he had originally conveyed to Mr Dulles lay in renewed emphasis on the danger of Communism and on the fact that 'the democracies may lose the peace, and the present dictatorship in Central Europe be exchanged for a new one.' He emphasised with equal insistence the social dangers incurred by the pattern-bombing policy which was expanding all the time. 'The bombing of large populated areas,' he stated, 'is rapidly completing the proletarianisation of Central Europe. Labour leaders therefore suggest that bombings be concentrated as much as possible on military and industrial targets.'

Adam's message from himself and the Kreisau circle (now without a

[70]Letters to the writer from Mr Peter Bielenberg and Dr Clarita von Trott.

Kreisau) was conveyed to Mr Dulles by a German-American, Mr Gero
von S. Gaevernitz who was his principal adviser on German affairs.[71]

In the course of his visits Adam had made a contact and a friendship
in the British Legation. This was with Miss Elizabeth Wiskemann who
has left a brief record of their relationship. She tells that when she first met
him through a friend of both in Switzerland, she was disturbed by his
habitual indiscretion. She warned him that Adam was a very rare name
outside Germany or Poland and invited him to choose between Tom,
Dick and Harry, but that nevertheless he invariably got in touch by ringing up and saying 'in his nearly perfect English "It's Adam speaking"
[so that] anyone listening could be in no doubt that it was Adam von Trott
zu Solz.' Maybe the indiscretion was not so careless, and one can be reminded of that element in Adam's character which, according to Gustav
Ecke, was resented by underdogs.

She had found him, she tells, 'a bewilderingly brilliant creature, infinitely German in the intellectual complexity in which he loved to indulge: he often talked to me with passionate Hegelian nationalism.'[72]
This element of nationalism she often found antipathetic, especially when
he showed sympathy with the ancient German tradition of the Drang nach
Osten, and the notion that the German mission was to be the master of
the Slav world. Even in so dedicated an anti-Nazi these deeply ingrained
ideas lingered in spite of the hideous abuse of them by Hitler.

On this visit Elizabeth Wiskemann found him changed.

'On the evening of 14th April 1944, I saw Adam Trott for the last time.
He looked a shadow of his former self, grey and haggard. He was obsessed
with the effects of the air-raids on Berlin and the other German towns,
and brought me photographs of rows of corpses, many those of children.
I had to say, "Adam, this human misery is horrible, but there is no message
I could send that would alter the directives given to the R.A.F.; I have
nothing whatever to do with the fighting forces, directly or indirectly.
If I were to say what I think, that this kind of bombing is bad policy as
well as cruel, it would make no difference." In my own mind I was also
saying to myself, as I was often obliged to, "They will say you are squeam-

[71]Dulles pp. 137-8 in which is given the full text of Gaevernitz's report on a conversation with Trott.
[72]Elizabeth Wiskemann. *The Europe I saw*. London 1968. pp. 168-9, and discussion.

ish because you are a woman." He was like a broken man and said he expected to be arrested soon after his return to Germany. The usual exchange followed. "Must you go back?" "Yes, I absolutely must." After he had left, he telephoned once more, of course saying it was Adam. I forget what he had to say but I told him that he had left his gloves behind, a very fine pair. He said "keep them as a gauge," for his safety he meant— I think he had the sense not to say more. In all the discussions that have followed I have felt that people have not allowed enough for the condition of tremendous and mounting nervous strain in which the anti-Nazis had lived for eleven years by then.'[73]

There came a brief, unexpected and idyllic interlude in the last phase of Adam's life. Albrecht von Kessel had obtained a transfer from Switzerland to the German Legation in the Vatican State under Ernst von Weizsäcker. Adam had to go to Italy in the second half of May 1944 and there he met his old friend once more. Kessel suggested that they should spend four days in Venice. He described the episode in a memoir.

'To complete my joy, Adam, who had travelled round the world, did not yet know this city. When I first put my plan to him, when we had discussed the affairs of the moment, he resisted it on the grounds that he was too nervous and depressed to enjoy anything. But after twenty-four hours Venice had him in thrall. The museums and palaces were closed, and the pictures either removed from the churches or boarded up, but what did that matter to us? In these surroundings the war became unreal. One day at noon silver-glistening bombers flew high over the Piazza San Marco. The anti-aircraft batteries opened fire from the surrounding lagoons and soon in the northern sky there was a black cloud of smoke from the burning oil tanks of a machine. Yet still the pigeons rose up in rustling flocks, still the sirocco brought dark clouds to the horizon, . . . undisturbed, the children flew their multicoloured paper dragons over the Piazzetta. Behind them the Doge's palace seemed to float in the air, as full of secrets as an Eastern carpet surrounded with a border of Venetian pinnacles. Even the German sailors, lurching like moving mountains among these graceful people, seemed to fall in childish wonder under the

[73]Wiskemann p. 188.

dangerous magic of the city. Trott's inner resistance to Venice rapidly
disappeared, and never did I see him more relaxed and joyous. There was
something "achieved" (Vollendetes) about him now, and people turned
round to look at him in the streets. He jestingly reproved me as an idler
for whiling away hours and days in this manner, but all the same he
dragged me into a gondola, comfortably stretching himself out, and the
craft glided along the canals like a slender beast of prey, shooting round
corners while the gondolier gave his call. Never in our fifteen years of
friendship were we so much at one.'[74]

During these happy days Albrecht von Kessel once asked Adam to
organise a transfer for himself to Rome. Even if the conspiracy was
successfully accomplished, he said, did not his experiences in Switzerland
and Sweden show that it was too late now to obtain any honourable
terms for Germany? Had not the Nazis gone to such lengths in their
degenerate barbarism that there was now no hope for anything better
than vengeance, whether Hitler was overthrown or not? Was he not
risking his life in a lost cause? Adam replied gravely in the same terms as
Nikolaus von Üxküll had used to Stauffenberg. It probably was too late,
he said, but history demanded the attempt; German honour could never
recover unless it could be said that there were Germans with the resolution
and courage to rise against the worst of their tyrants. So the argument
closed.[75] In spite of his conviction Adam continued energetically in his
task of trying to persuade the Western Allies to deal generously with a
resurgent Germany.

The little holiday in Venice came as a wonderful and beneficial consolation, and in her memoir Clarita notes that when she saw him immediately after, during the Whitsun holiday, she also noticed the effect of an
achieved personality which had struck his friend. This was the last time
that Adam was at Imshausen; the last time he saw his mother and his
sister Vera; the last time he saw his two little girls, Verena and Clarita.
It almost seemed, according to his wife's record, as though he knew that
this was a last time.

'In the glow of a warm and bright early summer's day we went for a
last walk over the hills, and while we were on the hilltops he took in
scene after scene of his beloved homeland. On the way back he told me

[74]Printed in Rothfels 2. [75]Herr von Kessel. Discussion.

that in Berlin, where he was returning, these scenes would remain in his mind's eye and give him strength. He told me also that he thought calmly about his own fate. If he was needed, God would preserve his life, and if not, he accepted his fate with resignation. His simple words, and the way that, quite contrary to his usual custom, he spoke directly of God and the last things, filled me with joy and fear at the same time. His expression was one of complete harmony and its beauty was moving. His mother told me afterwards that she had had the same impression. During the war I sometimes seemed to notice such changes of expression in young soldiers, shortly before they met death.'

After the successful Allied landings in France during the first part of June 1944, the conspirators saw that it was now a matter of the utmost urgency to obtain some sort of undertaking from the Western Allies. Without this, they reckoned, they would never be able to get the support of a senior general commanding a large body of troops. They wanted Adam to go back to Sweden. Yet Adam decided against going himself, calculating that the damage wreaked by the newspaper gossiper still made a personal mission by himself dangerous to everyone concerned. Then he found a way to exploit the activity he had begun.

The Informationsabteilung had a new chief, Dr Franz Six, a convinced Nazi whose faith was weakening under the stress of the disasters. He began to lose faith in the author of these disasters, though he hardly dared to admit as much to others and probably not even to himself. He seemed to be a secret pessimist.[76] He liked Adam, and Adam, though he described him to Furtwängler as 'peasant scepticism crossed with eudemonist belief in the Führer,' liked him.[77] In June Six had some official reason for travelling to Stockholm and the chance seemed too good to miss. By means of secret messages to Fru Almstrom it was planned that a member of the British Legation staff would meet Doctor Six's companion in Sweden, Alexander Werth.

The meeting took place but it was fruitless. The difficulties were enormous, greater than any Adam had had to contend with, for he was never encumbered by the presence of the head of his department on any of his expeditions. The only means by which Werth could be sure of keeping his secret rendezvous was to arrange it for an early hour and to make

[76]*Männer.* [77]Margaret Boveri. *Treason in the 20th Century*.

sure that Six was simultaneously afflicted with a hang-over. This meant staying up to a late hour, plying Six with wine and spirits in which Werth was compelled to join freely to avoid suspicion; he then had to make sure in the morning of completing his business with the British official before Six was sufficiently recovered to go about his official duties.[78] The change of personality on the German side inevitably inhibited the secret conversations, but it did emerge that a British decision in the sense requested by the conspirators could only be given by Winston Churchill, and that it was planned for Adam to be flown to London for an interview with him if he could be in Stockholm for three days. The German negotiator had to be Adam and Adam alone. He who had been so wrongly suspected was now the only man trusted. In his absence the Legation could carry the negotiation no farther.[79] It may be said that now it was neither Adam nor the conspirators who were too late, but the British Government.

When Werth returned with the unsuspecting and no doubt drink-weary Six, he told Adam all that had passed, and Adam determined that he must have a last try.

During this early summer of 1944 Adam wrote an essay which he believed to be his best piece of political writing. He told a friend he had written it with 'the blood of his heart.' It was called *Deutschland zwischen Ost und West*. Fear of this paper being used as evidence against the conspirators caused all but a few copies of it to be destroyed soon after it was written. The remaining and hidden ones were lost in the turmoil of the last days of the Third Reich. It is possible that the Gestapo found a copy and that accounts of Adam's views on German-Russian relations as reported by Kaltenbrunner to Bormann in August 1944 [80] may reflect its contents. These reports contain nothing of outstanding interest in this respect, so if the reflection is real it is a weak and pale one. A more interesting document is one called *Europe between East and West*, and it has been conjectured that this is in fact Adam's *Germany between East and West* in a second version, or edited by another hand.[81] The paper reproduces the arguments which Adam had used to Dulles and goes on to foresee a post-war state of affairs in which British foreign policy could find

---

[78]C.T. [79]Dr Alexander Werth. Discussion.
[80]*Spiegelbild einer Verschwörung* Stuttgart 1961. Referred to later as Spiegelbild.
[81]Herr Kramarz accepts the paper as by Trott. p. 165.

its interest in playing Germany off against Russia. This would be to Germany's advantage, the paper goes on, if it were not that there had grown up a British obsessive opinion that the Germans were incorrigibly aggressive. From that opinion, so the author (or Adam) speculated, a belief had grown that it was folly to conclude any peace except one of the most merciless kind. The paper ends with a question mark.

In the middle of June Adam went with Clarita to meet friends in Stuttgart. Eugen Gerstenmaier and Hans Schönfeld were there among other friends, and a Swiss couple of the name of Mottu whom Adam had helped with introductions to Americans on a former occasion. Clarita tells of this occasion in her memoir:

'In the evening in the hotel Adam took Philippe Mottu aside and (unter vier Augen) gave him messages to be delivered to certain people in the United States as soon as news of the rising in Germany broke. So Mottu told me years afterwards . . . Late on a Thursday afternoon we all went together to the Service of Instruction (Katachetenumterricht) which was led by Hauptpastor Thielicke, and our Swiss friends were astonished when they saw how the largest church of Stuttgart was crowded with people, most of them young. That was the last time Adam and I were together. Somehow he seemed to be more distant, difficult to reach, deeply absorbed in that which he had to do.'

He contrived to organise an official reason for another visit to Sweden. He went to Stockholm on the 23rd of June and stayed for ten days till the 3rd of July.

Less is known of this journey to Stockholm than of the preceding two, and it has been a natural subject of speculation. It is known with a fair degree of certainty, however that the offer to fly Adam to England for consultation remained open, but on a condition he could not accept, namely that he should not return to Germany.[82] It is fairly clear, too, that this last contact of Adam with the Allies was also his last failure to obtain the measure of support that the resistance regarded as essential if they were to overcome the patriotic scruples of army commanders. This is not to say that he met with total failure. From what has been pieced together by German researchers, the last message which he was able to bring from the British was to the effect that once the resistance had rid

[82]Professor Winckelmann. Discussion.

the world of Hitler and set up a provisional non-Nazi German Government, there was a hope, but only a hope, that the Allies would enter into negotiation in a more sympathetic spirit than that of the Casablanca declaration. This was an advance from the studied unfriendliness with which Adam's earlier advances from Switzerland had been met, but it was nonetheless a very long way from the constructive policy of encouragement which the conspirators were seeking.

Several authoritative accounts of the conspiracy of 1944 state categorically that during this visit to Stockholm Adam met the Russian envoy to Sweden, Madame Kollontay. Such a meeting is described as 'reported' to him by Mr Dulles in his book, and it appears that this guarded reference has been taken by later writers to be a statement of fact. None of Adam's surviving friends, nor his widow, have any recollection of his referring to such a meeting, and there is a suspicious lack of evidence from those who knew him in Sweden. It is not absolutely impossible that he met Madame Kollontay, but in the writer's opinion the supposition is probably a confusion with another episode with which Adam had some but very little connection. This was the extraordinary Kleist affair which belongs to 1943. The story is involved and remains something of a mystery. Here it is only necessary to remember that a certain Dr Peter Kleist, an employee of Alfred Rosenberg, was approached in Sweden by a mysterious man called Edgar Clauss with what appeared to be suggestions from Soviet authorities for a separate peace between Germany and Russia. Whether the approach was genuine, and what, if so, was the Russian intention, remain unanswered questions. After being told about it, Ribbentrop encouraged Kleist who pursued the matter further with full ministerial approval. Adam's connection is merely that while the intrigue was still going on, Kleist consulted him and Ambassador von der Schulenburg, both of whom showed a natural interest in this extraordinary development. Otherwise they took no part. Adam's remarks to Wolfram Eberhard about unsuccessful approaches to Soviet authorities clearly refer to the Kleist affair. The latter was brought to an end partly by circumstances and partly by Hitler's initiative in which he seems to have been influenced by his probably unfounded suspicion that Clauss was a Jew! To have reopened the intrigue in Stockholm would have been extraordinarily foolhardy and, given Adam's distrust of the 'Free German Movement'[83] in Moscow, aimlessly so. Without definite evidence to the contrary it is safe to assume that the meeting is a fiction.[84]

Evidence varies regarding Adam's personality during this last phase of his life. Clarita's beautifully felt and expressed description of him under the sway of a mystical sense of inevitable fate undoubtedly holds the key to the essential man at this time when the integration of his character was manifest as never before in his life. Nevertheless, just as in his first days in Berlin, according to the memory of his friend Kessel, he was a man of many different moods, so now he still showed the variety of his character. Inevitably the appalling fate threatening his country, and the terrible sense of utter loneliness from which a conspirator against even the most atrocious rule can never be free, sometimes weighed on his mind and tempted him to despair. Yet there is no lack of testimony to show how his high spirits and sense of fun would suddenly rise and cheer his colleagues in his office. Mrs Bielenberg has written a remarkable description of her last meeting with him in Berlin in March 1944, and their last talk in which the grave and the gay were mixed in the old way that entranced his friends throughout his life. She tells of their last moment together and how as he rode away on his bicycle he 'gave me a cheery wave and cocked a discreet snook in the direction of the Nazi professor across the road.'[85] At the end of his last visit to Sweden he was once again overtaken by that dark mood which Elizabeth Wiskemann had witnessed on his April visit to Switzerland. In a letter written in English to Clarita, and telling of her meetings with Adam, Fru Almstrom gave a memorable account of his state of mind on the eve of the last attempt of the conspirators.

'I will try to give a few glimpses, which are incredibly vivid in my memory and which have meant much to me personally. He was a dedicated man—the last time I met him a few weeks before he was imprisoned . . . very much so. I remember one evening, when he was exhausted men-

[83]C.T.
[84]The Kleist affair is told autobiographically in *Zwischen Hitler und Stalin* Bonn 1950, and the outlines of the story has been given in English by Mr James Graham-Murray in *The Sword and The Umbrella*. London 1964.
[85] *The Past is Myself* by Christabel Bielenberg. London 1968.

tally and physically and I asked him to go back to the hotel and sleep. He looked at me and said: why should I sleep, when there is so much to do ... and besides, old people do not need so much sleep. Whereupon I logically answered: but you are only 35. No, Adam said, I am at least 60 and I will never be younger—I think I have done what I was supposed to do in my life, whatever was asked of me to do—and I am ready to die, but still there are a few things to do. The day before he left, he told me that he had been asked by the British and the Americans not to go back to Germany, because he could at that moment do more good outside his country than inside. Then he shook his head and said: perhaps I could—but that is no more the question for me, I have done what I could for my country, but I also have a duty towards those who are dedicated to the same thing as I. I must share with them, whatever comes. And—there is Clarita and the children——'

He returned to Berlin on the 3rd of July.

In July of 1944 Stauffenberg described the moral responsibility of the conspirators concisely and perfectly: 'It is now time that something was done, but he who has the courage to do it must do it in the knowledge that he will go down to German history as a traitor. If he does not do it, then he will be a traitor to his own conscience.' By different ways, not without mutual help, in all probability, Stauffenberg and Adam had reached the same grim and inescapable conclusion.

The desolating story of the 20th July, 1944 has been told many times already. It is not the intention to repeat the story now but to tell what happened to Adam during those days with only necessary reference to the main events in which he took part.

The attempt of the 20th of July was the third of that month. The first was planned for the 11th of July. About six weeks before this, Stauffenberg had been promoted to be Chief of Staff and deputy to Colonel-General Fromm. This gave him access to certain conferences attended by the Führer, and he decided in June that he must make the attempt himself. The conference of the 11th was held in the Berghof at Berchtesgaden and according to the original arrangements Himmler and Göring were to attend also. Here was a splendid opportunity of ridding Germany at one blow of her three worst and most powerful men. In the event neither

Himmler nor Göring attended, so Stauffenberg, who had a bomb hidden in his briefcase, decided to postpone the attempt. This was a perfectionist impulse and most people will agree with the judgment that it 'proved to be an extravagance the resistance could ill afford.'[86]

It is easier to see now than then that Nazism without Hitler was nothing.

The second attempt was fixed for a conference held at the Wolfsschanze in East Prussia, four days later. All was set to bring 'Operation Valkyrie' into action, but again Stauffenberg did not ignite the bomb in the briefcase. This was because at the last moment he was called on to 'make the presentation,' or give the main address in person. This threw out his plans for igniting the bomb which always presented special difficulties to him as a result of the loss of one hand and the injury of the other. It also made it impossible for him to leave the room.[87]

On the evening of the next day, the 16th of July, a meeting was held in Stauffenberg's apartment in Wannsee near Berlin. Those who came were, apart from the two Stauffenberg brothers, Colonel Ritter Mertz von Quirnheim who was Stauffenberg's successor as Olbricht's Chief of Staff, Ulrich von Schwerin-Schwanenfeld, who was Field-Marshal von Witzleben's adjutant, Fritz von der Schulenburg, Peter Yorck, Colonel Georg Hausen who was Canaris's successor in the now very much reduced Abwehr, Colonel Caesar von Hofacker who was Stauffenberg's cousin, and Adam. Records of what was said by these men, everyone of whom was to die cruelly within a few weeks, are not precise and come largely from a suspect source, the records of the Gestapo. But, with knowledge of the inclinations of the personalities, German researchers, notably Herr Kramarz, have been able to reconstruct a fairly reliable outline.

Colonel von Hofacker seems to have led the first part of the conversation. He had much to tell and was surely listened to with great and perhaps appalled interest. He was on the staff of General von Stülpnagel, the military Governor of France, and he brought news of the hopeless military situation on the Western Front. The thought of military defeat was repulsive to them all, but nonetheless the Western Front held their greatest

---

[86]Roger Manvell and Heinrich Fraenkel *The July Plot* London 1964.
[87]Kramarz p. 182. He differs from Manvell and Fraenkel and others in his account which he bases on *Spiegelbild* p. 21 quoting a deposition by Berthold von Stauffenberg.

hope. After much persuasion, and doubting, and self-question, Field-Marshal Erwin Rommel, the darling of the German army, and the only German General to have captured the imagination of Germany's enemies, had given qualified support to the conspirators. He commanded Army Group B under von Kluge, Commander-in-Chief in the West. He was averse to assassination, but he was not averse to support of a new regime after an assassination. He believed, to his credit, that he could not abandon the master who had given him the opportunity of fame, without giving that master a warning and a chance to save himself. He believed that it was his duty to appeal to the reason of that madman. He was as good as his word. His message to Hitler, sent the day before on the 15th, concluded thus: 'The troops are fighting heroically everywhere, but the unequal struggle is nearing its end. I must beg you to draw the political conclusions without delay. I feel it my duty as Commander-in-Chief of the Army Group to state this clearly.' Hitler's reply had not been received. It was unlikely to be acquiescent. If it was not, then the Field-Marshal was with the conspiracy on the terms he had indicated.

Rommel's very late conversion to anti-Nazism has been described by Sir John Wheeler-Bennett as 'meretricious.' His meaning is not obscure, but the judgment shows some historical ingratitude for with only one difference in the course of events, Rommel's conversion could have been decisive. To the men in Stauffenberg's rooms in Wannsee, Hofacker's news could only appear as news of a great deliverance, for here, in spite of the follies of the unconditional surrender policy, and the refusal of allied politicians to enter into useful negotiations with the German resistance—here, at last, was their need, a respected Army Commander with great numbers of men at his disposal, who was ready to declare on their side. Such was the news, long hoped for, which Hofacker could confirm.

Adam was the spokesman for foreign affairs, as he had been in the days of Kreisau. After Hofacker he must have sounded like a prophet of doom. So far as appears, from what can be pieced together, he seems to have spoken in some conflict with Stauffenberg. The latter saw immense hopes now, since the news about Rommel, of negotiations in the West on a 'soldier-to-soldier' basis—a very frequent soldier's dream. In this Adam supported him, with all the more confidence since he knew from his reading of the British press in the Informationsabteilung of Rommel's popularity in Britain. But Adam had to disillusion him and others at that meeting, of any hopes of a separate peace. He had had recent and unique experience of the mentality then dominant in the British official world. He knew of the statesmanlike policy in the West which asserted and insisted that the alliance must persist, in spite of difficulties, till the end of the war; he knew, also at first hand, of the dark side of that policy. Stauffenberg seems still to have hoped that it would be possible, after the overthrow of Hitler and Nazism, to conclude some kind of military alliance with the British and American armies to safeguard the Eastern frontiers of the German Reich against Russian seizure. Adam insisted that such an idea was a wish-fulfilling dream and no more: overtures for peace or an armistice could have no effect in the West unless they were synchronised with similar overtures to the East, and the terms demanded by the Western allies, he warned, would be severe in the extreme. He urged that he should be included in the delegation to the West, while Ambassador von der Schulenburg, supported by his former military attaché in Moscow, General Ernst Köstring, should be charged with negotiations in the East.[88]

Such was the discussion in the main. It concluded with a unanimous agreement that the next opportunity of assassination must be seized and the deed carried out. Any further delay was not only politically undesirable but might finally and fatally compromise the whole design. Operation Valkyrie depended on a cover plan in the form of a large-scale internal security exercise. The alert for this supposed exercise had now gone out twice, and every time involved people of doubtful adherence and even hostility to the anti-Nazi cause. A third alert might easily uncover the secret intention. It was agreed therefore that Stauffenberg would explode a bomb at the next Führer conference to which he was bidden.[89]

On the day following this meeting the conspiracy suffered a new and terrible set-back, perhaps the worst since the removal of Canaris and Oster. On the 17th of July Field-Marshal Rommel's car was successfully attacked by British aircraft. His driver was killed, and he himself barely escaped. He was severely wounded, his skull having been fractured in two places. There was no question of him returning to active service before a considerable time. The hopes of the conspirators in France now lay

[88]*Spiegelbild*. Kramarz. [89]Kramarz.

with the Military Governor General von Stülpnagel, and the overall Commander-in-Chief, Field-Marshal von Kluge. The former was a brave and reliable ally, but he commanded an insignificant number of troops; von Kluge commanded all the troops, but he was a fair-weather friend. With the elimination of Rommel hopes for sustained and decisive anti-Nazi action in the West sank low.

On the next day, the 18th of July, Stauffenberg received orders to attend a Führer conference at the Wolfsschanze on Thursday the 20th. On this occasion he was given warning that he would be expected to address the meeting. His subject was the reconstitution of fresh divisions for the defence of East Prussia.[90] He made his plans accordingly.

Adam and Stauffenberg met for the last time on the day before the attempt. To quote Herr Kramarz: 'The day of 19th July passed like any other day. Stauffenberg was just as radiantly enthusiastic, just as calm, and working at just the same pace as before. He gave not a sign of the tension under which he must have been living. But as so often before, on 19th July he wanted to be with friends, and this time went to Trott zu Solz.' Adam's apartment was in Dahlem, and it is Clarita's deduction that Stauffenberg called on him on his way to Wannsee where he spent the rest of the night with his brother Berthold. It is known that when Stauffenberg was in Dahlem that evening, he went into Niemöller's Church, St Anne's, and prayed.

On the same day Adam sent Clarita a letter which she kept after destroying some parts of it (given in brackets) which she memorised, '[The reason I have written to you so little in the last days is not that I have too little but too much to tell you. During the next weeks and perhaps for longer, you may not hear from me at all.] But what remains is deep confidence in our life *together* which we live at two poles, far from each other, but as part of a unity and under the same sign. I think *very* often and with great longing of you and the sweet children, and also of the valleys and hills, their peace, and our walks together on the high ground. Never despair [in all the troubles that must certainly come]. They give us opportunity to recognise in fulness the gravity, the breadth and the strength of life and the Creator of life, in a way that has been denied to many generations.'

[90]Kramarz p. 184.

How much of Adam is in that brief note to his wife! At a moment of supreme crisis he turned in affection, as most men do, to those near him; but he turns also to philosophic reflection, to a sense of man's place in the cosmos, to ethical considerations, and, inevitably in his case, to the gentle, hauntingly lovely landscape of his homeland. He expresses the serene mood which he never lost in his last troubled days.

On the morning of the 20th of July Clarita telephoned to Adam in his office. 'In the four years of our marriage,' she relates in her memoir, 'I had never telephoned to Adam without a definite reason. On this occasion I had none. I did it simply because I had a constant wish to be in touch with him, and also because I thought that if there should be a state of emergency this means of communication might soon be lost. He was overjoyed by my call because in it he found evidence of a close sympathy between us that went beyond words; so I heard from Waltraud von Goetz [his cousin].'

The reader should remember in brief the sequence of events on that fatal day. Early in the morning of the 20th Stauffenberg and his A.D.C. Lieutenant Werner von Haeften, the brother of Hans-Bernd, flew from Berlin to Rastenburg in East Prussia and from there motored to the Wolfsschanze. He entered the Führer conference soon after 12.30. General Heusinger, Director of Operations, was standing next to Hitler indicating the military situation on a map spread out on a large oaken table. Stauffenberg thrust forward towards the table and placed his briefcase on the floor by the table leg on the inner side to Hitler. He murmured to Colonel Brandt, Heusinger's Chief-of-Staff, that he must make a telephone call and left the room. A few moments later Brandt found the briefcase in his way and moved it a few inches to the right, to the far side from Hitler of the table leg. At 12.45 the bomb exploded, killing, among others, the unlucky Colonel Brandt who the year before had carried Schlabrendorff's brandy bottles in Hitler's aeroplane. Stauffenberg and Werner von Haeften left the Wolfsschanze before the alarm was effective. They flew back from Rastenburg to Berlin where they arrived shortly before 4 o'clock in the afternoon. They believed that the attempt on Hitler's life had been successful. But already news of Hitler's escape had reached Berlin. Fromm, who had flirted with the idea of a coup d'état, hastily changed sides. From then on the great conspiracy to save Germany from Hitler rapidly began to collapse in elaborate confusion.

Wilhelm Melchers wrote an account of his experiences on the 20th, many of which he shared with Adam. 'It must have been at about three in the afternoon when Trott rang me up in my office and asked me to come to his room (that of State Secretary Keppler in the Auswärtige Amt). Trott was unusually pale. He was standing in the middle of the room and as soon as I had shut the door leading to the next door room where his secretary was working he came towards me. "It's done," he said in a low voice. While I stared at him speechless he lifted his hand and moved his forefinger as though pulling a trigger. I asked "And you have the news—really and for certain?" He answered that he had had a telephone call from the officers with the agreed message "The room is free." He said he had wanted to tell me this quickly. Then he pointed to his writing table where there was a letter ready for signature. It ended with the prescribed greeting "Heil Hitler." Suddenly he laughed and said to me in a whisper: "I won't have to sign under that horrible greeting any more".'

While Melchers was on his way back to his own office he heard strange news: that Hitler had escaped death and that there was to be a special communiqué broadcast from his Headquarters. He continues the story: 'I rang Trott from my office and asked him for an interview urgently "on official business." When I arrived I did not find him alone. On a chair in a corner of the room sat Dr Werth, his colleague and friend. I saw at once that he had the news, and I told him about the special broadcast which he seemed to have just heard about from Werth. We were puzzled as to where this news had originated and Trott said he hoped that this was only a tactical manoeuvre. We agreed that events would soon show what was the truth about this business. Werth said that all now depended on whether the military group would go forward with their part of the programme, regardless of whether Hitler was dead or not.'

It looked at first as though Werth's hope was to be fulfilled. One of the first of the planned moves in 'Operation Valkyrie' was for military units to seal off the central area of Berlin in which the Chancellory and the main Governmental buildings are situated. Melchers's narrative continues:

'We moved to the window and looked down the Wilhelmstrasse. It was true—the street was almost empty and had clearly been sealed off. Cars and pedestrians were allowed to leave, but after a few minutes the street was quite empty and military patrols in steel helmets turned back people who wanted to leave their houses.

' "Thank God!" said Trott. "It's working after all—dann klappt die Sache also doch!" It no longer mattered now whether the assassination attempt had succeeded or not. The coup d'état was going forward. There was no doubt about it. We had to act with energy and risk our heads as the soldiers were doing. There could be no turning back.

'Our dismal mood gave way to one of relief and exultation. All over the Wilhelmstrasse windows were being opened and everyone was waiting excitedly for what would happen next. We no longer hesitated to appear at our window. "I hope Haeften comes soon," said Trott, and he asked me to go out and look round the building to find out what was happening, especially in the corridor of the personnel department.

'... Gesandter Bergmann, the head of this department and a close friend, dragged me into his room and gazed at me in silence for a long time. Then he said: "Melchers, what's coming won't be funny. Have another look at your notebook and your desk, and be careful when you telephone." I asked him if he thought that the Government quarter had been sealed off on Himmler's orders. He asked me in return whether I had reason to believe otherwise. We were interrupted and parted.

'In the meantime Haeften had arrived in Trott's room. Werth returned shortly afterwards. Trott and Haeften talked together in low voices. Haeften seemed to have heard nothing about the special broadcast. They said over and over again that everything had been prepared in so much detail that failure now was impossible, even if Hitler was still alive, and they still seemed to believe that he was not. Haeften expected at any moment to receive orders from the military group to take over the Auswärtige Amt and hold it till a new chief was appointed. It appears that he had a document in his pocket authorising him to take certain steps immediately, and to arrest certain people ... Haeften asked me whether I had seen Bergmann and what he had said. I told him briefly. We then decided that Bergmann must be told all immediately, as his co-operation was urgently needed. But Haeften hesitated. He thought that though Bergmann's attitude was beyond doubt, he was too much of a civil servant to take part immediately in an enterprise of such uncertain outcome.

'[In his absence] Trott, Werth and I again looked down the street. It was still empty. Guards stood at the door of every house. Then Trott tried to ring up Haeften's brother, Stauffenberg's A.D.C., but he could get no answer. He tried a second time without success.

'Haeften returned. He was disappointed. What he feared had happened. Bergmann had replied that he preferred not to have heard what Haeften had said.'

Three fatal events occurred as the day wore on, while the four friends waited impatiently for the next stage. The troops sealing off the Government quarter of Berlin were commanded by Major Ernst Remer who was in no sense a conspirator or an anti-Nazi, and was in ignorance of the purpose of 'Operation Valkyrie.' During that afternoon he was summoned to the office of Goebbels who was at large. Goebbels informed Remer of the real situation and, in case he had doubts about rumours of Hitler's death, he put him in telephonic communication with the Führer in person, and thereupon the Führer in person gave Remer orders to take full military authority in Berlin and crush the revolt. Remer accepted his new orders with enthusiasm. That was the first disaster. Then the Berlin radio station had been captured but no orders had been sent to the puzzled occupying troops. Goebbels was able to persuade their commander that he had acted under a misunderstanding, and so he retired.[91] The radio returned to Nazi hands. From this a third disaster inevitably followed. At 6.45 the promised special communiqué from the Führer's Headquarters was broadcast, announcing to the German people that in the attempt on his life 'the Führer was unhurt except for minor burns and contusions.' Strangely enough, Adam, Werth, Haeften and Melchers seem not to have heard the broadcast. To go back to the personal record, taking it up again at about 7 p.m. of this day.

'We all clung to the thought that the coup d'état was evidently still going forward, since the Government quarter still remained sealed off as before. We looked out of the window over and over again. Then the terrible thing happened—the street was opened to traffic again; people and cars again streamed past . . . Again Haeften went to the telephone to ring up his brother. When he came back he was deathly pale. In his eyes was the dawning realisation of what danger we were in. Why did his brother not answer?'

They decided to break up their meeting. Adam said he would remain

[91]Wheeler-Bennett 654-7.

in the office till eight but in fact, as he told Melchers the next day, he remained there till eleven, in the hope of hearing from Stauffenberg, but his telephone remained silent. Clarita writes in her memoir: 'Can one find the courage to imagine what he went through in those four lonely hours in that room?'

When Adam left he joined Alexander Werth at the Foreign Press Club and there, at 12.30, they heard together the broadcast voice, shaky, and raucous with anger, of Adolf Hitler.[92]

Now that he knew the worst Adam sought out Hans-Bernd von Haeften again, unless it was that they had already arranged a rendezvous. At all events they went out together in the middle of the night to the Grune-wald. There they decided what each would say if either or both of them were arrested.[93]

By the morning of the 21st the turncoat Fromm had seen to it that five of the conspirators, including three of the principal military leaders, were dead. Ludwig Beck had committed suicide. Claus von Stauffenberg, Friedrich Olbricht, Albrecht Mertz von Quirnheim, and Werner von Haeften had all been shot on Fromm's orders in the courtyard of the War Ministry in the Bendlerstrasse. If Fromm had had his way others would have followed, including Peter Yorck, but the Gestapo intervened. They wanted interrogations. It seems to have been Fromm's purpose to remove all those who knew of his earlier flirtations with the enemies of his Führer whose favour he now sought at the last minute with a fierce display of devotion. His endeavours were unsuccessful. 'This wretched man,' as Sir John Wheeler-Bennett rightly describes him, was arrested on the 21st and executed eight months later, 'but not before,' to quote the same authority, 'he had experienced in his own person the worst cruelties and indignities of which the system which he had helped to create, had served, and had helped to save, was capable.'

Haeften felt sure that he would be arrested, if only as the brother of Stauffenberg's close accomplice. He went to his family home in Mecklen-burg to say goodbye. He returned to Berlin on the 22nd, and on the 23rd he was arrested as he had foretold.

[92]C.T.
[93]Frau Barbara von Haeften. Discussion. Van Roon p. 159, gives the date as the night of the 20/21st.

Adam was in much doubt as to what would be his fate. It depended on how much the Gestapo knew about his activities, and in fact they knew very little, a thing he could suspect but not know for certain. He still had some days of freedom and during that time he received tempting offers of escape. On the 21st a military friend, Count von Berg, visited him and found him 'very calm but in despair.' He offered to fly him to Madrid in a courier aircraft, dressed in a uniform of his regiment and with the necessary papers. Adam said he would give his answer the next day. On the 22nd he turned the offer down. He said that his flight could endanger his wife and children, and later events show that his fears were well grounded. He added that since he had not been arrested already, there was a chance that the Gestapo might overlook him.[94]

On the 21st he was again visited by Melchers who flew into a rage at the thought of how the conspiracy had been bungled. To quote his narrative: 'Trott suddenly grew very gentle. "Are you angry?" he said, "Remember these people must pay for this thing with their lives?" There was a depressed silence between us. I asked Trott if there was still some form of Resistance group in the army. I asked if he had any hope for the future. "No," he answered, "there is no hope left now, or for the future. This is the end. The disaster must take its course—till there shall be left no stone upon another. Hitler will carry on this madman's war till everything is destroyed. And yet," he added, "it is good all the same that there were people ready to break this reign of terror. It remains a historical fact, and more than that, a symptom".'

That evening Adam walked in the Grunewald with Waltraud von Goetz. She was always known then as 'Teddy.' In her memoir Clarita recalls 'Teddy's' account of this last talk together. 'Adam said that he felt like a tree that had been deprived of its branches, and by that he seemed to refer to the friends whom he had lost already. He went on to defend the military group, and in the course of doing so said that he regarded the frustrated conspiracy not as a military but as a moral failure. He thought the ultimate reason for failure was England's refusal to co-operate. Deep down, he did not believe in his own survival.' He told her that he intended to write a 'political testament,' and this he seems to have done

[94]A letter from Count von Berg to Dr Clarita von Trott quoted in C.T.

and to have hidden it somewhere near Peter Bielenberg's house in Berlin, but it has never been discovered.[95]

The week-end passed and still Adam was free. On Monday the 24th Franz Josef Furtwängler visited him in his office to urge another escape plan, to go to Furtwängler's native village near the Swiss frontier, Stühlingen, from where he knew of a safe way to the Swiss village of Schleitheim. Adam faced his hard duty again and turned the offer down.[96] He said: 'If you are arrested, disown any document involving us both, or any record there may be of a telephone conversation. I've warned Werth already: he won't mention your name. I am taking everything on myself.' He then warned Furtwängler to leave quickly as to be seen in his company was probably dangerous. His faithful friend ended his account of him in his book with the simple words: 'Das war ein Mann.'

In the early afternoon of the next day, Tuesday the 25th of July, Adam was arrested.

Ernst Kaltenbrunner was put in charge of the investigations into the attempt of July 20th. What methods his agents resorted to in the interrogation of Adam are mercifully unknown. The record is written with the genteel euphemism of Gestapo practice. The Gestapo assumed that Adam's connection with the plot was much less than it was; it is extraordinary, in fact, how little they knew about his activities: nothing about his dealings in America, Switzerland, Belgium or Holland, and nothing about the most compromising of his meetings in Sweden. Their main evidence was of his friendship with Stauffenberg, and the frequency of their meetings was unhappily clear from the fact that Stauffenberg's chauffeur, in accordance with correct procedure, noted down all his master's journeys in an official log-book. From this friendship, and the fact that Adam did not conceal his opinion that the war was lost, they deduced knowledge of and acquiescence in the plans for the assassination. The deduction of course was correct, but it was never proved.

Adam's own Nazi superiors in the Informationsabteilung, Six and Keppler, withdrew into shocked reserve, but there were friends both inside and outside the official world who dared to try to help Adam, both in

[95]C.T. [96]*Männer.*

orthodox fashion and the reverse. Two men went directly to Kaltenbrunner. One was Herr Rudolf Rahn who at that time held the weird
and not enviable post of German Ambassador to Mussolini's ramshackle
republic in Northern Italy. He was of course quite unsuccessful. So was
the other, A.C.N. Nambiar who, very touchingly, went to see Kaltenbrunner on behalf of the Indienreferat of which, he said, Adam 'was the
very soul.' Its continuation, he said, was imperilled if Adam was no longer
there to guide it. Kaltenbrunner replied that he had no intention of inter-
ceding for traitors, and by a glance made it plain that further pleadings
could be dangerous for the petitioner.[97]

Peter Bielenberg and Alexander Werth decided that only the boldest
and most direct action could save Adam now. They learned that Adam
was imprisoned at Oranienburg near Berlin and that, with the shortage
of police vans, he was being brought every morning to the Prinz Al-
brechtstrasse in an ordinary four-seater car. They planned to ambush the
car, liberate Adam, smuggle him to Poland, and into an area of swamp
and forest near Graudenz (or Grudziadz in Polish) where Polish partisans
were still holding out, incredible as it may seem. Peter was at this time a
director of an aircraft factory at Graudenz which was supplied with an
arms depot. To accomplish the plan Peter first went to Graudenz to collect
arms, and there the attempt came to grief. He was arrested as a known
friend of Adam. He acted with presence of mind and courage, and as a
loyal friend. When questioned he in no way minimised the closeness of
his relationship with Adam; on the contrary he insisted that he was a
devoted friend and had been such for nearly ten years. He believed that
this would delay proceedings by leading to further interrogations and
that, since he was unconnected with the conspiracy, the association of his
name with Adam might help the latter. His main intention was to draw
the case out by obstructive argument in the hope that before Adam
was tried the war might come to an end. To help his friend he thrust
himself as far as he could into the power of the Gestapo. But this ingenious design was without result.[98]

Clarita, with great courage, had come to Berlin in the hope of seeing
her husband. In her absence a further calamity came upon the family.
The effect of the attempt on Hitler was like that of a wound on some

[97]Berichte. Nambiar. C.T.   [98]C.T.

savage creature at bay. He gave orders on the 20th of July for a policy of Sippenhaft or 'kindred seizure.' It was intended that all the near relatives of the conspirators should be arrested and executed as a sacrifice to the wrath of the insulted divinity of the Wolfsschanze. Only circumstances prevented this act of barbarism being carried out in full, but many wholly innocent victims fell. Their number is not known. If Hitler had had his way he would have soothed his outraged dignity with a purge comparable in size to one of Stalin's.[99]

At Imshausen Frau von Trott presided over the household which for more than a year had included Adam's own family who had a small separate establishment in the main house which also sheltered many refugees. She watched the hastening ruin of her country with grief and active indignation. Living in Hesse, with its large Jewish population, she saw rather more than was common of the worst of Nazi crimes, the genocidal policy of the 'Final Solution.' At one time there appeared to be a slight and inadequate relaxation of the policy, when orphaned Jewish children (orphaned for the most part by an obvious process) were gathered into what appeared to be a normally run institutional home in Kassel. It was an illusion. An order came for their removal and it was reliably reported that they were to be sent to an extermination camp. Frau von Trott rallied all the influential people she knew, appealing to Churchmen and Bishops and to the hereditary Prince of Hesse, and writing to the Gauleiter in a desperate endeavour to get the order rescinded. She is believed to have asked for an audience with the Führer. She strove in vain and the order was carried out.

This was in 1943. Now a year or so later the heaviest of all her afflictions had fallen on her, and with the arrest of her son, her favourite child for whom she held no hope of deliverance, it seemed that the cup of her sorrow was full. But there was more to come. Following the Führer's policy of Sippenhaft two Nazi officials called at Imshausen early on Sunday the 13th of August with orders to remove Adam's two children, Verena aged two and a half, and Clarita who was nine months old. Frau von Trott and Adam's sister Vera protested, but protest was useless. Yet

99Wheeler-Bennett p. 685.

though they were helpless they demanded to know from the officials precisely what their orders were, and what was to be the fate of the two little girls. In the presence of those two formidable women and under Frau von Trott's stern eye the officials told them something of what was intended. The children would be taken to a Nazi orphânage where they would be brought up with other children in similar circumstances, and they added that if the family kept quiet about the matter, no harm would come to the two girls. The officials agreed that Vera and Adam's old housekeeper (whom he had sent to Imshausen for safety before the 20th) might accompany them as far as Kassel. There was nothing they could do, more. They had to obey these horrible orders.[100]

It was late in the day when the two women returned with heavy hearts from their mission. Vera went to her mother expecting to find her distraught. She found her in her accustomed place for the time of day, and in her accustomed attitude, sitting in the big chair in her room with a book, queenly and severe. She asked Vera for all details of the journey. She listened attentively, asked questions, and showed no emotion. Then, when she had heard all, she said to her daughter: 'You expected to find me weeping, didn't you, and perhaps you are thinking now that I have become a hard-hearted old woman. I am not that, but all the tears that I have, I have shed already for the Jewish children who were taken away from Kassel.'[101]

Adam never knew about the removal of his children.

After Fromm's drum-head court martial of Stauffenberg and the three who died with him, all the trials of the conspirators were conducted by the Volksgerichthof or People's Court of Law, and, until his death in an air-raid on the 3rd of February 1945, the presiding judge was a man called Roland Freisler. It is possible that Adam had met this repulsive character in his lawyer days in Kassel, for he disgraced that good city by his origins and had practised there as an 'assessor' till his promotion to Under-Secretaryship in the Prussian legal Ministry. He is said to have been riled by his further promotion to presidency of the People's Court as his ambition was to be appointed Reich Minister of Justice. The circumstance is

[100]C.T. [101]Frau Vera von Trott zu Solz. Discussion.

said to have made him peculiarly zealous to behave as a Nazi of the extremist school in his conduct of the political cases with which the People's Court dealt.[102] Whatever the facts, Freisler showed himself in the ensuing trials to be all that can be alleged against Nazi notions of justice. He screamed obscene abuse at prisoners in the witness box; he interrupted any line of defence that showed signs of favouring the prisoner's cause; he never listened to an impartial word unless by some accident it favoured the prosecution. These 'attentat-trials' were the gravest over which he had been called on to preside, and he excelled himself, so much so that the Nazi Minister of Justice, Otto Thierack, was moved to protest to Hitler, by way of the Party Chief Martin Bormann, that since the judge's conduct . . . 'created an unfortunate effect . . . the seriousness and dignity of the court suffered . . .'[103] Freisler has been compared to Judge Jeffreys, unfairly in the writer's opinion. Loathsome as Jeffreys probably was, some doubt remains as most contemporary accounts of him are from his victims and enemies. The most reliable account of Freisler is from himself. Shortsightedly he and Goebbels arranged for a film to be made of the trials. The surviving copies have been subjected to drastic cuttings for purposes of public showing, and what remains is a fragment of a fragment. It is quite enough however to show the sort of stuff that Freisler was made of.[104]

Two days after the removal of his children from Imshausen, Adam came up for trial, on the 15th of August. This session of the court was devoted to a trial of the prisoners from the Auswärtige Amt, and among the accused were Ambassador von der Schulenburg and Hans-Bernd von Haeften. When Adam confronted Freisler the furious little judge was at an unusual disadvantage because apart from the friendship with Stauffenberg he had no concrete evidence with which to give conviction to his tirades, and furthermore Adam, with his experience of law courts, knew how to base his defence on strictly legal grounds. He knew the law court manner too. He was scrupulously polite and answered slowly. Freisler was thrown back on insinuation and found it impossible to advance the case. He made what he could of the fact that Adam had been a Rhodes scholar and had not done active political work as a Nazi at any time. 'Well,' he said in his rambling way, 'four years of English education, and

---

[102]Manvell and Fraenkel 181-2. [103]Manvell and Fraenkel and *Spiegelbild*.
[104]A copy which the writer has seen is in the Imperial War Museum, London.

not interested in our movement or active in it—surely that places you
under certain auspices. With that sort of background one doesn't enter
the Foreign Ministry and the Foreign Service of the Reich, does one?
For surely it is questionable whether four years of English education are
just exactly the right preparation for it.' He added, 'Were you ever a
soldier?' 'No,' said Adam. 'Why not?' rapped Freisler in his harshest
manner. Adam answered quietly: 'I volunteered at the outbreak of the
war and was at first exempted. Then I was sent to America by the Foreign
Ministry and this was regarded as tantamount to the risks of military
service. I went through the English blockade——' Here Freisler interrupted him with a stream of sarcasms about the risks he might have run
in neutral America, and then turned to his friendship with Stauffenberg.
As this was the most unfavourable evidence against Adam, Freisler thought
to make the best of it by hardly allowing the prisoner a word while
keeping up a wild and rambling invective about café politicians who pretended ignorance of military affairs. Asked what his opinion of the situation was, Adam, in spite of frequent interruption managed to assert that
if Germany could hold out till the next spring there might be a chance
of a tolerable end of the war so far as foreign policy was concerned, but
that 'if the pace of military events in the West were to leave no time for
discussion with the enemy through a central solution——' Freisler interrupted again, perhaps because in saying such things the prisoner might
be provoking dangerous thoughts in the listening public. 'To put it
plainly,' the judge shouted, 'if—in your defeatist view—the pace of events
in the West were to make it impossible to murder the Führer in time—
well, to put it in straightforward language, what was to happen then?'
'Then,' replied Adam, 'this separate operation in the West was to be
supplemented by the so-called Berlin Solution.'[105] Freisler said: 'You
mean that one of the commanders in the West could negotiate with the
commanders of the plutocracies and say: I capitulate!' Adam boldly answered: 'Yes.' That was his last word in court. It may have indicated that
he had been told that since the attempt of the 20th of July the policy of
unconditional surrender had been reaffirmed by the British Government
in the House of Commons. Freisler concluded this part of the trial with a
barely coherent tirade ending 'Well, four years of English education is

[105]The meaning is not clear at this point.

not a bad qualification! Yes, there were two characters together that afternoon, you and von Haeften, two characters from the same office. I have
no further questions.'[106]

Hans-Bernd von Haeften was called next. Unlike Adam, he had no
reason to play for an acquittal; the mere fact that he was a brother of
Werner von Haeften was guilt enough in Freisler's eyes and he assumed
his death sentence. His purpose was to speak his mind and he reduced his
judge to angry spluttering impotence. Hoping, one may suppose, to cow
the prisoner into nervous excuses, Freisler was rash enough at one moment
to ask him, 'And what, pray, is your opinion of our Führer?' To which
Haeften replied in a voice as loud as the judge's: 'I regard him as the in-
carnation of evil!'

All the prisoners were condemned to death by hanging. Freisler, according to his wont, loading them with obscene and stupid insult. He
described Adam as 'a dishonest and ambitious climber . . . one who came
from the sewers and must be thrown back into the sewers.' There is a
remarkable photograph of Adam taken at the moment when sentence
of death was being passed on him. He looks much older than his thirty-
five years, and without knowing his identity it would be easy to guess
that here is a man who has been through much suffering. Yet the expression on his face shows an extraordinary serenity, and there is almost the
suspicion of a smile. His loyalty was no longer troubled.

Hans-Bernd von Haeften was executed the same day. Adam was
allowed to live for eleven days more.

Clarita was still in Berlin. She wanted to go to the trial in the hope that
Adam would see her and receive some assurance from her presence.
Werner came to her home and warned her that she also was in the utmost
danger. He told her that after leaving she must not on any account return
to the flat in Dahlem. At an arranged place in the street they met Alexander Werth, and he took her to the Volksgericht. On the way he told her
the dreadful news about the two children. Undeterred, she insisted on

[106]A transcript taken from the aforementioned film by the office of Chief Counsel
for War Crimes (Document MG. 1019.) and further notes taken from the film by
Mr Harold Kurtz and the writer. The text may be inaccurate at the mention of
the Berlin Solution. The recording of prisoners is very faint compared to that of
Freisler and sometimes virtually inaudible.

going to the court. Arrived there, she showed the presence of mind and
ready wit of great danger. It was a miracle, she records in her memoir,
that 'I was not arrested there and then as an office girl pointed me out to
one of the SS men who demanded to see my identity card. By three little
sentences which truly came to me by inspiration, I persuaded the man to
take me to the court and he even found me a seat from where I might
have succeeded in my plan of seeing Adam. "We understand these things,"
murmured the man. But the office girl objected again and so I had to
leave.'

Clarita returned to the court on the 16th and the 17th to apply for
official leave to see her husband. 'After the children had been taken away,'
she writes, 'and the death sentence had been passed, I had nothing to
lose.' Permission was refused on the 18th, and on the evening of that day
she was arrested. Werner was with her and he accompanied her to the
police station of Schmargendorf where, says Clarita, 'the Gestapo were
waiting for me.'

Werner's action, at a moment when Sippenhaft was the order of the
day, was wholly typical of him and the fearlessness he shared with his
brother. Equally typical was his strange reaction to the conspiracy. He
was greatly offended that he had not been told anything about it by Adam.
He regarded this as unworthy of the trust that a man should repose in
his brother, and as contemptuous of his judgment. No argument to the
effect that it would have been a betrayal of trust to spread knowledge
of the conspiracy for family reasons had any effect on him. Greatly as
he cherished Adam's memory, heartbroken as he was at the tragedy in
which his brother's life ended, he found this hard to forgive.

There could be no hope, and yet hope was maintained that somehow
Adam would be reprieved. Those who knew him best remembered his
extraordinary skill in extricating himself from apparently fatal situations,
and they took comfort from the fact that no case had been made out
against him in the People's Court. These were optimistic illusions, but
it does appear that before the trial there had been some solid grounds for
hope, known only to a very few, and to none of Adam's friends or family.
They were concerned with the enigmatical conduct of Himmler at this
time.

There is evidence that the SS were as divided as the army or the Foreign
Service regarding what should be done to rescue Germany from total

defeat. According to Doctor Horst Mahnke who was adviser to Adam's chief, Professor Six, the latter was not as indifferent to the fate of Adam and Haeften as appeared from his behaviour after the 20th of July. Six belonged to the faction in the SS which favoured negotiations with the Allies. At the very end of the war this was undoubtedly the attitude of Himmler also, but it is easy to suspect that he was thinking along such lines as early as the first part of 1944, and it even appears to be a plausible theory that he knew more than anyone guessed about the conspiracy, planning in the event of its success to gain greatly from it. None of this can be proved,[107] but Doctor Mahnke's recollections suggest further reasons for believing in its possibility at least.

He recalls that Six asked him and a high-ranking SS officer called Doctor Schmitz, to draft a letter to Himmler in which it was stated that though the arrested persons from the Auswärtige Amt (including Adam and Haeften) could be assumed to be guilty, the expected death sentences could with advantage be replaced by sentences of imprisonment 'because in the negotiations certainly to be expected there would be need of personalities who were known abroad.' This letter was conveyed to Himmler, and he expressed himself in agreement. He in turn put the proposition before Hitler. The reaction of Hitler was the characteristic one. He was reported to have received Himmler's recommendation with raging delirium—a *Tobsuchtanfall*—screaming that these Foreign Service men were the worst of the lot and that they were to be hanged to a man as soon as possible. Himmler did not pursue the argument.[108]

Adam was forbidden to communicate with anyone outside, but a warder (possibly acting as an *agent provocateur*) promised to smuggle out a letter to Clarita on the day of his trial. It was a long letter written in haste, and in it for the last time he describes all that 'Imshausen, the valleys and hills, the woods and fields where we wandered together, the deer, the noises and smells of nature' meant to him, and how the memory of them brings him peace even then.

At the very end he was allowed to send two letters, one to his wife, one to his mother. The text of the first is as follows:

[107]In his biography of Hitler Mr Alan Bullock emphatically rejects any such proposition.
[108]Berichte. Two interviews with Dr Mahnke.

'Beloved Claritchen,

'This is, almost certainly, the very last of my letters. I hope that you got my previous longer one.

'Before all else, forgive me for the deep sorrow that I have had to cause you.

'Rest assured that I am still with you in thought and that I die in profound trust and faith.

'To-day there is a clear "Peking sky" and the trees are rustling. Teach our dear sweet little ones to be grateful for these signs from God, and for the deeper ones, but in an active and valiant spirit.

'I love you very much. There is still so much to write to you—but there is no more time.

'May God keep you—I know that you will not let yourself be defeated and will struggle through to a life where I shall be standing by your side in spirit, even when you seem to be all alone. I pray for strength for you—and do the same for me, I beg. In these last days I have read the *Purgatorio*, *Maria Stuart*, and *Jürg Jenatsch* which strangely moved me. Otherwise I have had few things of this kind, but much within me which I have been able to think about quietly and make clear to myself. So do not grieve too much on my account—essentially all is clear to me even if deeply painful. I wish I could know what the practical effects of all this are for you. Whether you want to go to Reinbek or stay [at Imshausen]. They will surely surround you with love, my dearest little wife. In my former letter I asked you to give my greetings to all our many friends; I have this at heart. You know just who they are and will give the messages correctly without my help.

'I embrace you with all my soul and know that you are with me.

'God bless you and the little ones.

'In steadfast love

Your Adam.

'Give Werner and Heini the same trust that they gave me in love and loyalty. Greet Imshausen and its hills from me.

Your Adam.'

He wrote to his mother:

'Dearest Mother,

'Thank God I have the opportunity to write you a short note: You have always been very near to me, and you are now. In gratitude I cling hard to that bond which has bound us together for ever. God has been merciful to me in these weeks and has sent me joyous, clear strength for everything, or almost everything—and He has taught me where and how I failed. I ask your forgiveness above all for imposing on you this great sorrow, and that I must not be there to support you in your old age.

'Tell Werner that he too has become very close to me in these last weeks and that had we seen each other again I would have gone back on every step that led to our estrangement and would have had a deep fruitful reconciliation with him. To him and to his chivalrous care I commend my beloved Clarita and the sweet little ones, of whom I saw so little, and I ask him to extend his protection to their individuality and their freedom to find their own way of life. Stand by them in all their need!

'I ask this of Heini too—in love and gratitude.

'To you last a grateful kiss from the heart until we meet again.

'A greeting to all who can remember me without rancour.

'Your son who loves you very much
                    Adam.'

None of the three letters was delivered till six months later, in February 1945.

On the same day as they were written Adam was executed, on the 26th August 1944. By Hitler's personal orders, the act of hanging in all these executions was to be performed in the most brutal and agonising fashion. The revolting details need not be recalled, but it should be said that the executioners, coarsened men as they were, could not bring themselves to descend to the level of bestiality decreed by their Führer, and the vilest of the prescribed cruelties were enacted in token fashion. Hitler's purpose was to obliterate the memory of those who had dared to conspire against him by subjecting them to the uttermost degradation in death. He was not the first to attempt and to fail in such a policy.

The fact that Roland Freisler had not been able to make out a case against Adam was compensated by the authorities in the announcement of the execution. It was declared that Adam had been condemned because he had betrayed military secrets to the enemy. This was obviously a fabrication to allay public opinion. No mention of such a thing occurs in the transcript of Freisler's examination of Adam, and it was privately denied, at the time of the announcement, both by Adam's official defence counsel, and Dr Mahnke who attended the trial as official observer for the Auswärtige Amt. In the light of everything known about Adam the allegation is not worth a moment's serious thought.

On the 26th of August Clarita was visited in her cell by Dr Harold Poelchau, a Protestant clergyman in the prison service whom she knew slightly. He had a long and valiant record as an opponent of Nazism. He had been a member of the Kreisau circle. Even at that moment he was hiding Countess von Moltke in his house [109] and acting as message bearer between her and her husband in the Tegel prison of which he was chaplain. It is a remarkable fact that his indefatigable work for the anti-Nazi cause was never suspected by the Gestapo, in spite of its extent. Clarita has related that as soon as he entered her cell she knew that he had come to tell her that Adam was dead. No conventional word of sympathy, however sincere, could be of avail in the presence of this tragedy, but before he left Dr Poelchau had a word of comfort nonetheless. He said to Clarita: 'If this blow of fate had only struck old and tired men, then the sacrifice would not be one from which strong seed can grow.'

[109]Schlabrendorff p. 194.

Chapter 16

EPILOGUE

In the late summer of 1944, Adam's younger brother Heinrich was an officer in a unit of the Indian Legion, stationed not far from Bordeaux. The Legion was in a sorry state, still torn by internal divisions. Many of the Indian officers and men objected to fighting against British troops, and the great majority felt that they had been grossly swindled. An added misfortune came to them when something of a rôle was found for them: certain units of the Legion were used in punitive expeditions against the French Resistance. Tnis raised French hatred against them so that, ignored for the most part by their German allies and the subject of rancour and vengeance by the population, they were a dejected, friendless band.

After the death of Adam, Heinrich determined that he could no longer continue an officer in the service of Hitler. He found some of his German fellow-officers and some Indian troops of like mind. With the officers and a group of about thirty Indians he set out and made contact with a Resistance group under Communist leadership. Heinrich told them who he was, the brother of the conspirator against Hitler, supposing in his innocence that this would make him and his companions welcome. It did nothing of the sort. The name of Trott zu Solz was meaningless to these Frenchmen, and they had heard nothing to make them think well of the men of July the 20th. What they saw was a detachment of the hated Indian Legion. They put the German officers under arrest and shot all the Indians. It seemed clear that their intention was to do the same to the German officers after some useful interrogation. The officers were taken as prisoners-of-war to various Resistance headquarters and finally to a barracks held by non-Communist resisters. They were probably saved by the fact that a quarrel broke out between the Communists and the others as to whom these prisoners belonged. A British officer acting as liaison between the Army and the Resistance arrived by a fortunate chance, and he was able to insist that these prisoners must be made over to the American authorities. Heinrich and his fellow-officers were removed to an American prisoner-of-war camp. Heinrich had no more success in making a favourable impression on the Americans than he had had with the French. His name meant nothing and connection with the July conspiracy did not seem a good recommendation. Before taking them into the prison camp the escorting American sergeant gave them a friendly warning to say nothing about their anti-Nazism as there had been some cases of anti-Nazi prisoners being killed by their fellow-inmates. There was no suggestion that anti-Nazis were owed some protection. In the end Heinrich was transported to England where friends of Adam, David Astor among them, were able to obtain preferential treatment for him, but not without difficulty and not till the end of the war was he given his freedom.[1]

This farcical and macabre drama illustrates at a humble level how the spirit of the new course in Allied policy worked in practice.

Policy towards Germany was a subject of debate in the House of Commons on the 2nd of August 1944. It was on this occasion that, at the end of a long speech describing the state of the war, Winston Churchill referred, in terms which were untypical of him in their lack of generosity, to the events of the 20th of July. He said: 'Not only are those once proud German armies being beaten back on every front and by every one of the many nations who are in fighting contact with them, every single one, but in their homeland in Germany tremendous events have occurred which must shake to their foundations the confidence of the people and the loyalty of the troops. The highest personalities in the German Reich are murdering one another, or trying to, while the avenging armies of the Allies close upon the doomed and ever-narrowing circle of their power.' A little later he said: 'Important as may be these manifestations of internal disease, decisive as they may be one of these days, it is not in them that we should put our trust, but in our own strong arms and the justice of our cause.'

He was followed by Arthur Greenwood who spoke with less eloquence in a similar strain. 'I am arguing,' he said, 'that there is a situation between

[1]Herr von Trott zu Solz. Discussion.

two partners who have now parted company. Neither of them can be trusted by this country. It would be a fatal mistake if having broken the Nazi party . . . we were to present any better terms to the militarists of Germany than we have done to the discredited Nazis. I think the House is more or less agreed about that.' Both the Prime Minister and Greenwood seemed to be speaking from a conviction that Stauffenberg was a second Ludendorff.

These harsh judgments on men who had risen courageously against the Nazi tyranny did not pass unchallenged in the House of Commons. Mr George Strauss spoke in a different strain. He reminded the House of the ideals for which the country had gone to war, in which connection he asserted that the then fashionable notion that the Germans were an evil people without exception had now been 'blown sky high.' 'I suggest,' he went on, 'that now we know that there is an element in the German army which is probably strong, and which thinks that the continuation of the war is foolish and suicidal, we should change our whole policy and tell the German people what is the alternative to continuing the war, so that they will know what they are risking if they do not take steps to bring it to an end. It is difficult for them at present. How can one expect a movement of that sort to be widespread and broadly based if the Germans have nothing to go on except the repeated cry of unconditional surrender?' Referring, it would seem, to the Morgenthau plan,[2] he urged the Foreign Secretary Mr Eden to issue a statement of terms making it clear that the Allies had no intention of uprooting populations. He was heard by the House with irritation and frequent interruption.

The Ministerial speeches showed an extraordinary degree of unawareness of the information about the conspiracy available to the Government from the Legations in Sweden and Switzerland and from Mr Dulles's office. Mr Eden seems to have forgotten or to have rejected as misguided all that he had heard from the Bishop of Chichester the year before. He made the last speech of the debate and it contained a categorical assertion that the demand for unconditional surrender remained the basic policy of

---

[2]In 1943 Henry Morgenthau Jr put forward a plan for a monetary policy in which he suggested that after the war Germany should be deprived of all modern heavy industry, reducing the population to a primitive pastoral existence. As the plan was not disowned it was widely mistaken for an official pronouncement.

His Majesty's Government. He made the announcement in appropriately unimaginative language.

It is probably true that at this late date in the war the Government could not get out of the commitment to unconditional surrender, and the reception of George Strauss's speech in the House of Commons indicates that it had become popular in the country. All the same it seems doubtful whether Winston Churchill and Arthur Greenwood would have spoken in such contemptuous terms of the conspirators, if Rommel had been in a position to declare for them and to lead an Army Group out of the battle in France. In such circumstances the conspirators, for all their failure in Rastenburg and Berlin, might have been able to show an immediate gain.

It seemed at the time and for long after that the failure of the July conspiracy was total and ignominious. The honour which is accorded to martyrdom in a great cause, and sometimes all the more when the great cause fails, was for long denied to these men, both abroad and in their own country. That they acted late in the war seemed a proof of mere opportunism; that many of them were officers in the German army suggested that they aimed to substitute tyrannous Prussian militarism for tyrannous Nazism; that many of them belonged to the aristocracy offended 'the century of the common man.' In England the malign influence of Vansittartism lingered on. In Germany honour was hesitantly accorded to men who had acted against their oath to the head of the State. The immense sanctity attaching to such an oath is not readily understood outside Germany where, more than elsewhere, it is looked upon as sacramental in a religious sense. It is not looked on as a solemn agreement which dissolves when one of the contracting parties plays the other false, as in the case of Adolf Hitler and the German people; it is seen, regardless of the immorality or deceit of a head of the State, much more as the bond without which the nation cannot exist as such. It is safe to say that none of the conspirators entered the plot without grave self-question on this matter, but it was a long time before a majority of their compatriots, deeply ashamed of the Nazi episode as most of them were, grasped the fact that these men had given the right answer. The process took most of twenty years. To-day there is a general opinion in Germany that though they failed in their attempt, though they failed to leave a political heritage of great account, they did not fail in their last and greatest purpose, to retrieve the honour of Germany. The formation of such opinion was facilitated

by the fact that the attempt was made without the smallest help or even
encouragement from foreign powers. The latter intended no such result,
but, so it seems to the writer, in that respect alone the ungenerous attitude
of the British and American Governments can be defended.

The story of Adam von Trott's life is not that of a saint of anti-Nazism;
it is something more human. To see it in hagiographic terms is to miss
its significance, as though one were to see *Hamlet* solely as an edifying
play on the subject of stainless filial duty. His story is of a man who met
temptation and resisted it, sometimes with difficulty, and sometimes without perfect success; of a man whose perception could be clouded, and
who sought for moral truth with the stumbles of our human weakness.
All the more wonderful his ultimate moral triumph. There are two keys
to his story. One is to be found in the force of his intellect which showed
to its greatest advantage and in its greatest strength at the very moment
when counsels of withdrawal from the contest of his life were not only
tempting but far more reasonable and intellectually defensible than at any
other time. His restless intellectual curiosity led him into many adventures of the mind, and it led him finally to the attainment of vision. The
other key is closely related to the first. It has been wisely said that ideas are
the source of courage. The wonder of the courage that was in Adam is
surely to be found in the fact that it gave him the spiritual energy to be
true to the vision to which he had attained, in the certain knowledge
that on his chosen path there lay no consolation other than the conviction
that he was serving a high ideal. Of all the conspirators none acted so
completely without illusion as to earthly reward. Courage of that
kind can only spring from great ideas.

In the winter of 1944 to 1945 Adam's children were returned to the care
of their mother when she was liberated from prison. In this instance, perhaps influenced by the fact that no case had been made in court against
Adam, and in the increasing chaos of German administration, the persecution of relatives was not maintained.[3]

Adam's mother lived till 1948 when she died on the 11th of March at

---

[3]What happened to the children was not discovered by the family till two years
later. They were taken to an orphanage in Bad Harzburg and maintained
there under the names of Gretel and Bertha Steinke. Dr Clarita von Trott. A
letter.

the age of seventy-three. To the end she guarded the memory of her second son with love, pride and resignation.

Imshausen was involved in many changes as the confusion of war overwhelmed Germany, though by good fortune that part of Hesse was never a scene of battle. It became in the end a very different place from the sedate home of Adam's day, but the transformation was one which would have gladdened his heart. By a process of many stages Imshausen evolved into a children's home run by a religious institution presided over to-day by Adam's eldest sister Vera. As of old, it radiates a great and unique spirit.

In September of 1958 Adam's name was given public commemoration in the naming of a settlement erected on the Warteberg just outside Kassel.[4] The settlement is a housing estate built for the reception of German peasant farmers and agricultural workers rendered homeless by the mass-expulsions from the East after the war. Within the settlement a small commemorative edifice bears his profile in bas-relief and the words 'Er starb für die Freiheit.' He died for Freedom.

Nearly ten years before this, in 1949, a more personal memorial had been inaugurated near Imshausen and Solz. A cross stands on a pedestal on which is written Adam's name and the dates of his birth and death. The rest of the inscription reads 'Executed with friends in the struggle against the destroyers of our homeland. Pray for them. Heed their example.' The cross itself is of unusual height and the uttermost simplicity. It bears no figure and consists only of a vertical and a horizontal beam of perfectly conceived proportions. Because the beams are slender, and the cross stands alone on a hill, the memorial is of daunting austerity, and it conveys, as great religious works of art sometimes do not, a sense of the cross as a symbol of pain nobly endured. All around it, visible to a great distance, lies the Hessian landscape which he loved.

---

[4]The origin of the memorial is curious. Certain Hessian deputies met Mr R. H. Crossman on a visit to England. In the course of conversation Mr Crossman remarked that he was surprised that members of the German resistance, for example his Hessian friend Adam von Trott, were so little commemorated in their own country. The remark was not lost on one of the visitors. Dr Clarita von Trott. A letter.

INDEX

The name Adam von Trott is abbreviated to T throughout

Thomas, General Georg, 277-8

Thomsen, Hans, 295

Tiefenbacher, Clarita; *see* Trott zu Solz, Clarita von

Tillich, Paul, 85

Tocqueville, Alexis de (1805-59), 85

Tokyo—T's stay in, 201-2, 216-8;
—Mentioned: 366, 383

Toronto, 190

Toye, Hugh, 351*n*

Treitschke, Heinrich von (1834-96), 295

Tresckow, Major-General Henning von (1901-44), 394, 408

Trollope, Anthony (1805-82), 29

Trott zu Solz, Adam von (1909-44)

1909-33, *Early Life*

birth and ancestry, 9-14; childhood, 15-16; education in schools at Berlin, 17, Kassel, 17-9, Hannoversch-Munden, 20-3; at Universities of Munich, 24-5, Göttingen, 27 *et seq.*, 43 *et seq.*; goes to Y.M.C.A. meeting in Switzerland, 29-30; goes to Mansfield College, 34-7; to University of Berlin, 41-3; takes first law examination, 49, and acts as Referendar at Nentershausen, 52; returns to Oxford as Rhodes scholar, 53-61; makes study of Hegel for doctorate at Göttingen, 62-75; final days at Oxford, 74-9, 88-97

1933-7, *Legal Career in Germany*

T as Wehrsportslager at Marburg, 98-9; assistant magistrate at Rotenburg, 99-102; appointed to Hanau, 102; writes to *Manchester Guardian* about Jews, 103-11; attached to Public Prosecutor's office, Kassel, 115-32; Magistrate at Kassel, 132-42, where produces essay on Kleist (133-9); works at firm of Leverkühn in Berlin, 142-51; revisits England, 151-

3; returns to Kassel, 153-4; works in Hamburg, 155-66; attends labour camp at Jüterbog, 166-9; lives at Kassel and takes final exam for Assessorship, 169-76; turns down offer to join I.·G. Farben, 176; decides to visit China despite family opposition, 177-8, 180-2; pays two visits to England to get support from Rhodes Trust, 179-80, 183-4

1937-8, *First Visit to U.S.A. and Far East*

visits U.S.A. (New York, Virginia, Washington and Boston), 185-90; goes to Canada, Chicago, Kansas City and California, 190-93; visit to China, 193-8; spends year in Peking and visits Japan (201-2) and Manchuria, (202-3); his impressions of Far East, 203-4, 215-8; returns to Germany, 218-20

1939 *Peace Efforts in England*

decides to try and achieve agreement between England and Germany, 221-6; visits Oxford friends and makes contact with the Astors, 227-9; adopts Weizsäcker's appeasement plan, 233-9; returns to England, goes to Cliveden and there meets Lothian, Halifax etc., 229-36; has interview with Chamberlain, 248-9; failure of his mission, 250-5; reports to Berlin and returns to England, 256-8; renews contacts in London and Oxford, 259-67; failure of his mission, 268-70; invites David Astor to Berlin, 270-1; final visit to Cliveden and last efforts for peace, 271-85

1939 *Second Visit to U.S.A.*

goes to U.S.A. to secure her neutrality, 287; produces Trott-Scheffer Memorandum, 297-300; has secret interview with Lothian, 300-1 and

B
Trott zu Solz
Sykes
Tormented loyalty